Anti-Communism in Twentieth-Century America

Anti-Communism in Twentieth-Century America

A Critical History

Larry Ceplair

 PRAEGER

AN IMPRINT OF ABC-CLIO, LLC
Santa Barbara, California • Denver, Colorado • Oxford, England

Library of Congress Cataloging-in-Publication Data

Ceplair, Larry.
  Anti-communism in twentieth-century America / Larry Ceplair.
    p. cm.
  Includes bibliographical references and index.
  ISBN 978–1–4408–0047–4 (hardcopy : alk. paper) — ISBN 978–1–4408–0048–1
(ebook)
1. Anti-communist movements—United States—History—20th century.
2. Political culture—United States—History—20th century. 3. Political activists—
United States—Biography. 4. United States—Politics and government—1919–1933.
5. United States—Politics and government—1933–1945. 6. United States—Politics
and government—1945–1989. I. Title.
E743.5.C37 2011
973.91—dc23   2011029101

ISBN: 978–1–4408–0047–4
EISBN: 978–1–4408–0048–1

15 14 13 12 11   1 2 3 4 5

This book is also available on the World Wide Web as an eBook.
Visit www.abc-clio.com for details.

Praeger
An Imprint of ABC-CLIO, LLC

ABC-CLIO, LLC
130 Cremona Drive, P.O. Box 1911
Santa Barbara, California 93116-1911

This book is printed on acid-free paper ∞

Manufactured in the United States of America

To Christine, the love of my life and the source of my happiness.

Contents

Introduction   1

1   Official Anti-Communism, 1919–1939   19

2   Unofficial Anti-Communism, 1919–1939   33

3   The Second "Red Scare," 1939–1941   53

4   World War II   65

5   Official Anti-Communism, 1945–1948   75

6   Official Anti-Communism, 1949–1957   91

7   Institutional Anti-Communism, 1945–1957   113

8   Ex-Communist and Conservative Anti-Communism, 1945–1957   131

9   Liberal and Left-of-Liberal Anti-Communism, 1945–1957   153

10   Civil-Libertarian Anti-Communism, 1945–1957   171

11   The Decline and Periodic Revivals of Domestic Anti-Communism   191

Conclusion   215

Afterword: Can It Happen Again? Or, Is Anti-Terrorism the New Anti-Communism?   221

Abbreviations 227
Notes 229
Bibliography 315
Index 353

Introduction

Anti-communism was one of the strongest political forces affecting the United States during the twentieth century. Loudly and repeatedly heralded as an indispensable component of national security, it provoked three "red scares," all of which had deleterious effects on significant numbers of people, organizations, institutions, and national values. These "red scares" amplified and institutionalized two fears: fear of what the Soviet Union might do if not contained and fear of what the members, ex-members, and sympathizers of the Communist Party of the United States (CPUSA) might do if not exposed and their actions proscribed. These fears were then magnified into threats and effectively wielded by political elites, making communism and Communists appear to be larger-than-life bogies, requiring extreme measures to counteract.* But why? Why did a significant number of people and organizations feel so threatened by communism and Communists that they worked so assiduously, for so many years, to embed anti-communism into the political culture of the United States? An adequate answer to that question requires a more systematic and objective analysis than the topic of anti-communism has heretofore received. A full, critical treatment of anti-communism is necessary if

---

*In this book, the convention is to capitalize "Communist" (an adherent to a political party) but not "communism" (a political doctrine).

one is to comprehend the political and cultural history of the twentieth-century United States.[†]

This critical treatment involves the classification of anti-Communists into types, to demonstrate that anti-communism was not a monolithic entity, that it served to promote a variety of different agendas, and that it is best understood by illuminating the diversity and plurality of its practitioners. Although I employ somewhat of an encyclopedic motif, providing examples to fit each type or style I identify, I do not list all of the prominent practitioners of each particular type or style. In effect, then, this book should be read as a guide to the most significant varieties of anti-communism, and not as an exhaustive or inclusive roster of anti-Communists.[‡]

SOME CONCLUSIONS ABOUT ANTI-COMMUNISM

First, anti-communism did not derive its power from any doctrinal or ideological qualities. Indeed, it lacked the substance and coherence necessary to be classified as a doctrine or an ideology. It was an *idée fixe* which simplified and reduced the complex issues facing the United States, and became, as a result, an agenda item for adherents of a wide variety of other political doctrines.[1] Thus it became a symbiotic *idée fixe* that did not necessarily benefit the host.

Second, the "Communist threat" on which anti-communism was based could not be measured or, in some cases, even substantiated. As a result, many of those who feared this "threat," as well as all of those who stood to benefit from proclaiming the "threat," trumpeted their warnings in a highly emotional, attention-getting manner.[2] Monsignor

---

[†]Full disclosure: I am not now nor have I ever been a member of any Communist Party, Communist-front group, or New Left organization. Nor am I a "red-diaper baby." I have, however, been accused of being a "revisionist on the left" (Philip Dunne, *Take Two* [New York: McGraw-Hill, 1980], 196–97). During the course of my research into the motion picture blacklist, and during my membership in the New American Movement, a socialist-feminist organization (circa 1975–1980), I became friendly with many former members of the Communist Party.

[‡]I will not include a parallel narrative of the activities of Communists in the United States, but I will stipulate that the Communist Party, USA's lock-step relationship with the Soviet Union and the resulting tergiversations of Party lines provided anti-Communists with much of the evidence they needed to brand the CPUSA as the agent of a foreign power and to refuse to work with it or its members. Nor will I chronicle the behavior of the world's Communist regimes, because it was not a significant component of anti-communism in the United States, and it is very well chronicled by others. See, for example, Stéphane Courtois et al., *The Black Book of Communism: Crimes, Terror, Repression*, trans. Jonathan Murphy and Mark Kramer (Cambridge, MA/London: Harvard University Press, 1999).

Charles Rice (see Chapter 7), who had been a fierce anti-Communist during the height of the Cold War, later admitted: "We exaggerated the danger, we went overboard, we were un-American and uncharitable, we lost our perspective."[3] Paul Jacobs, an equally fierce, Jewish anti-Communist, later wrote about the campaign to identify and purge Communists from the American Jewish Committee: "We honest believed that the Communists were a threat, although we never really discussed what it was they were threatening."[4] During the first postwar decade, however, their own and others' cries of peril were loud and pervasive, and they touched on or provoked deep-seated anxieties in many people.

Third, anti-Communists did not base their campaign on the actual beliefs of individual Communists, which were rarely examined in an empirical and objective manner, or their actions, which were, for the most part, legal. Rather, the anti-Communists' case rested mainly on what they alleged that Communists, as an entity, believed and what Communists, as an entity, would do, in some undetermined future, to advance those beliefs.

Finally, anti-Communists based their alarms on a bundle of beliefs, most of which were based on a fact, but none of which were factually (or logically) developed. For example, it is factually correct to say that near the end of World War II U.S. President Franklin D. Roosevelt and U.K. Prime Minister Winston Churchill made concessions to Soviet Marshal Josef Stalin at Yalta (February 1945). It is not factually correct to state that Roosevelt and Churchill "surrendered" eastern and central Europe to the Soviet Union. It is a fact that the Chinese Communist Party conquered China. It is also factually correct to say that the United States did not massively intervene to save the government of Chiang Kai-shek. It is not factually correct to say that the United States "lost" or "surrendered" China to the Communists. Finally, it is factually correct to say that some Communists and fellow travelers who were employed by the U.S. government provided data and information to the Soviet Union. It is not factually correct to say that the U.S. government was "riddled" with Communists; that Communists in the government seriously undermined the national security of the United States; or that the Truman administration engaged in a "conspiracy" to cover up the leaks and espionage. In a calm political atmosphere, all of the preceding conclusions would have required verification, but, during the fear-laden Cold War atmosphere, in which anti-communism flourished, the standards of evidence and logic were regularly disregarded.[5]

The failure to submit the "threat" of communism to rational analysis or empirical verification made anti-communism in the United

States distinctive. If, for example, one compares domestic anti-communism in the United States with that in the United Kingdom and Canada (the homes of relatively small, not very intrusive Communist parties) and that in France and Italy (the homes of large, militant Communist parties), one will find missing in these other countries "un-British," "un-Canadian," "un-French," and "un-Italian" crusades. What are the reasons for this significant difference?

A CROSS-CULTURAL ANALYSIS OF POST–WORLD WAR II ANTI-COMMUNISM

At the height of the third "red scare" (the domestic Cold War), Albert Einstein asked: "Why should America be so much more endangered than England by English Communists? Or is one to believe that the English are politically more naïve than the Americans so that they do not realize the danger they are in?"[6] In fact, the Cold War mentality in the United Kingdom never reached the heights it did in the United States, despite the fact that the United Kingdom was a society arguably under greater strain than the United States. After all, it was a declining power, on the verge of losing most of its important colonies, and suffering severe economic deprivations. It also had in place some potentially suppressive statutes. Even so, the government of the United Kingdom did not feel pressured to throw anywhere near its full weight behind anti-communism.[7] According to Richard Thurlow, there was a two-year "red-scare atmosphere" in the United Kingdom (1949–1950), but it was "strictly limited to manipulable proportions."[8] As Steve Parsons points out, "comparatively few people were dismissed and none went to prison on political grounds." In addition, Communists were not automatically discharged from academic, professional, or trade union positions. Furthermore, apparently only one known Communist was dismissed from a media company.[9]

Eleanor Bontecou—one of the first people in the United States to examine the discrepant treatment of Communists by the United States and the United Kingdom—concluded that the approach of the latter was "based on faith in the strength of the institutions of democracy rather than on the fear of the threat of Communism." Thus, instead of using "the bludgeon techniques of suppression," the British preferred to do battle with communism in "the intellectual and moral arenas," thereby maintaining their traditional values.[10] H. H. Wilson and Harvey Glickman attributed the difference to the good or common sense (or political tolerance) of the British people, the nature of the parliamentary system, and "the social responsibility displayed by British conservatism." They credit the administrators of the British loyalty program with acting far more responsibly than their counterparts in the United States, showing "mature judgment, good sense, and a sense of moral propriety." These authors also note that the question of Communists in the education system and the media industries "proved to be noninflammable" and that professional organizations hardly addressed the issue of loyalty. Finally, the British did not glorify ex-Communists nor employ them as professional witnesses. In sum, Wilson and Glickman conclude:

> Leaders of all major parties and government officials have insisted upon looking at the reality of the Communist challenge. They have not completely identified the domestic Communist party and its aims with the international position and foreign policies of the Soviet Union. They have distinguished Communism as a political movement from Communists who serve the Soviet Union by engaging in espionage. This distinction has enabled the application of techniques adapted to counter-espionage without creating an atmosphere of generalized doubt, suspicion, or fear.[11]

For his part, Herbert H. Hyman contrasted the wide, highly publicized sweep of the U.S. loyalty program to the British government's policy of quietly focusing on known Communist employees in sensitive posts. Instead of mass proscription and forced resignation, the British government transferred personnel deemed to be security risks to less sensitive positions. Hyman suspects that the British population was much more tolerant in this regard than the U.S. population, but he acknowledges that he lacks the empirical evidence to demonstrate that fact.[12]

Canada, like the United States, was a large country, with a western frontier, a large number of immigrants, and an even smaller Communist Party (estimates of its membership range from 10,000 to 20,000). The Party had been kept in close check by government policies similar to those in effect in the United States. Following the German–Soviet Nonaggression Treaty (1939), 110 Party leaders were interned as traitors, and the Party itself was outlawed in Canada in1940.[13] During World War II, the Canadian government enacted far stricter security measures than the United States, banning hundreds of newspapers and periodicals and outlawing more than 30 organizations.[14] Nevertheless, Canadians evinced a measurable degree of sympathy for their Soviet ally.

That sympathy evaporated in February 1946, when it was revealed that Igor Gouzenko, an agent of Soviet military intelligence, stationed in Ottawa, had defected and revealed to authorities the existence of a spy ring. His revelations led to the appointment of a Royal Commission, the arrest and trial of 22 people (10 of whom were convicted of violating the Official Secrets Act), and the establishment of an advisory Security Panel.[15] Although a 1950 public opinion survey indicated that the magnitude of public intolerance of Communists in Canada was comparable to that in the United States,[16] a Canadian "red scare" along the dimensions of that in the United States did not occur, although several authors suggest that Canada was second in intensity only to the United States in its anti-communism zeal.[17] During the Canadian version of the Cold War, several trade unions were officially decertified and left-wingers were purged from the National Film Board. Nevertheless, there was no "un-Canadian" investigating committee, Alien Registration Act, Taft-Hartley Act, or Internal Security Act; the loyalty investigations and lists of subversive organizations were not publicized; and no Canadian counterparts to J. Edgar Hoover and Joseph McCarthy emerged.[18]

Probably the most significant factor explaining the differences between Canada and the United States was that the Canadian Liberal Party enjoyed an unshakable hold on political power. Its leaders were, therefore, better able to make the case for an anti-Communist program that did not undercut basic liberties.[19] Another factor limiting Canada's reluctance to follow the lead of the United States in its domestic anti-communism might have been that the Canadians feared the hegemonic influence of the United States more than it did the Canadian Communist Party.

In France and Italy, the two countries with the largest Communist parties in the West, anti-communism represented only one strand—albeit a broad one—in these nations' respective postwar histories. Although both France and Italy lacked a stable governing majority, neither adopted inquisitorial institutions or fomented a McCarthyist type of anti-communism. France and Italy handled their "Communist problem" via the political process, with the behind-the-scenes assistance of representatives of the American Federation of Labor (see Chapter 7).

THE EXCEPTIONAL NATURE OF ANTI-COMMUNISM IN THE UNITED STATES

Contemporary observers, who were not anti-Communist, regularly remarked on the phenomenon of such a small, powerless party provoking so much worry. Carey McWilliams stated: "The paradox is so strange, indeed, as to suggest that we might feel much easier if the Communists had succeeded here as well as they have in France and Italy. For we would then be forced to deal with Communism as a political reality and not as a 'menace.' "[20] The French philosopher, Jean-Paul Sartre, speaking to people in the United States, wrote:

> [Y]our anti-communism is much more dangerous than ours—for a strange reason: that you have no Communists. Frenchmen who hate Communists or fervently condemn Soviet policy meet Communists every day and everywhere. Thus, however violent their antipathy, they have to recognize that their opponents are men and not devils. . . .
>
> And because the enemy is unseen and unknown, he is the devil and must be fought to the death. Moreover, he appears to be everywhere, just because he cannot be pinned down in a definite place; suspicion grows, infects everybody. . . . And since communism is evil, all that is evil is Communist.[21]

In a similar vein, Claude Bourdet, the editor of the Paris *Observateur*, noted: "Communists are so scarce that practically nobody in the United States has ever met one; thus any amount of fear and horror can be aroused against them."[22]

A second group of contemporary commentators based their explanations on various types of cultural clashes or contradictions peculiar to the United States. Gordon W. Allport concluded that the targeting of Communists as scapegoats "must . . . be explained as a double phenomenon, involving first and foremost a realistic clash of values," which provokes "autistic thinking, stereotyping and diffusion of emotion—primarily of fear." During those periods when values are threatened, "differential thinking is at a low ebb" and "there is a magnification of two-valued logic. Things are perceived as either inside or outside a moral order." Whoever or whatever is "outside" faces moral obloquy.[23]

Reinhold Niebuhr, however, focused on what he identified as the contradiction, which was, in his estimation, more heightened in the United States than elsewhere between the hopes that people harbored before 1945 and the realities of the postwar era. Niebuhr suggests that, prior to World War II, the people of the United States had suffered from a "collective schizophrenia," as a result of which they enjoyed domestic security and well-being while blithely ignoring the hellish international situation that was developing. During the war, the alliance with the Soviet Union "generated many illusions which obscured the menace of communism." As a result of these contradictions, the people of the United States suffered a "collective psychosis" between

1945 and 1954, which led them to take "a position of apoplectic rigidity" to the Soviet Union and to sink into "a mood of despair."[24]

Twelve years later, Niebuhr offered a different explanation, based on the clash of national myths. According to this analysis, the two sides in the Cold War subscribed to two completely different myths of world redemption. The U.S. myth (it is a country altruistically pursuing the cause of human rights in the world) was challenged by the Soviet myth (the United States is a crass imperialist country). Given that the United States and the Soviet Union, like all other nations, construct their myths from "imaginative elaborations of actual history" and justify their behavior by such myths, it is natural that each country's citizens must protect its myth against competing myths, and cast the believers of competing myths in the role of devils.[25]

In the mid-1950s, a small group of liberal academics (Daniel Bell, Nathan Glazer, David Riesman, Seymour Martin Lipset, and Richard Hofstadter) wrote a series of explanations for the strength of the U.S. anti-communism movement, which, in the words of Bell, "showed a remarkable convergence in point of view." It centered on the role that status groups and status anxieties played in the third "red scare." According to Hofstadter those people who evidenced the strongest anti-communism were those who lacked both "a clear, consistent and recognizable system of status" and a "sense of belonging."[26]

A parallel approach, focusing on social strains, was developed by the sociologist Talcott Parsons, who diagnosed McCarthyism as "a relatively acute symptom" of two superimposed strains that emerged in the postwar United States. The newness and scope of the country's international power and the pace of economic change provoked "high levels of anxiety and aggression focused on what rightly or wrongly are felt to be the sources of strain and difficulty." According to Parsons, communism served as the primary symbol to connect "the objective external problem and its dangers with the internal strain and its structure."[27]

Another sociologist, Edward A. Shils, offered a more extended, complex, and historically based version of the "strain" model, which he called "populism [or the populist culture of the United States] under strain." He identified three long-term strains—antagonism between intellectuals and bureaucrats, antagonism between politicians and businessmen, and a hyperpatriotic, xenophobic fear of conspiracy—and three short-term ones—a conspiracy theory about intellectuals, the bipolarized international situation, and an embittered Republican opposition, passionate to take office and ready to seize "any stick with which to beat the administrative dog." In other words, the combination of a populist-inclined minority under severe strain and political opportunism created a disequilibrating social crisis, in which a genuine national security problem became distorted and inflated.[28]

Finally, there is the consensus theory, most ably explicated by Louis Hartz. Basing his thesis on some of the conclusions reached by Alexis de Tocqueville in his master-work *Democracy in America*, Hartz attributes the "unusual response" of the people of the United States to communism to "an absolute 'Americanism' as old as the country itself."[29] The roots of this Americanism grew not from feudal, socialist, or "genuine revolutionary" traditions, but rather from an "absolute and irrational attachment" to the principles of John Locke and "a submerged faith" in the "self-evident" truths of the ideals based on those principles. Whenever this faith is confronted by an opposing ideology of significant power, the outcome is a powerful negative judgment of all believers in that ideology, inside and outside the United States, who are dismissed "with a fine and crushing ease."[30]

Murray B. Levin, basing his analysis on the work of de Tocqueville and Hartz, posits, as the result of what he calls the "Lockean general will," a fragile American identity characterized by anxiety, restlessness, and rootlessness, and embedded in an egalitarian culture that is uniform and increasingly one-dimensional. This identity, he states, "is built on a bedrock of changeless principle. The American principle—selected bits and pieces of John Locke and Adam Smith—rigidified through two centuries of unchallenged dominance and steeled in the crucible of Horatio Alger, has become the American absolute," an absolute "manifested as the will of the majority." This majoritarian will, during times of rapid or dislocating change, cannot tolerate deviance or difference.[31]

None of the preceding explanations is entirely satisfactory, however. The theses of McWilliams, Sartre, and Bourdet are unprovable. Niebuhr's contradictions explanation is undercut by his misreading of the prewar decades: People in the United States were very much aware that they were living through a domestic hell (the Depression) and a rapidly darkening international arena. Moreover, his "social myth" explanation is merely an interesting notion. The status-politics group is too dependent on newly minted abstractions: "pseudo-conservatives," "former" or "ex-masses," "suddenly enthroned lower classes," "the intolerant," and the "radical right." And, as Hofstadter later acknowledged, "status politics" was too narrow a concept.[32]

Shils's strained-populist thesis fails in several ways.[33] His populism is an abstract, ahistorical one, which unsuccessfully tries to weave together every conceivable strand of discontent, while his secrecy/conspiracy notion fails to account for the scope of social disequilibrium of the postwar United States. Finally, it is simplistic to posit, as Shils does, the existence of a single "crucial dividing line in politics . . . between pluralistic moderation and monomaniac extremism."[34]

The models offered by Hartz and Levin are based on an oversimplified and reductionist reading of Locke and de Tocqueville; in addition, they are static and hypermetaphorical. Although terms such as "irrational Lockianism," "will of the majority," "national will," "American soul," and "American psyche" do point to something important, they explain virtually nothing about the behavior of a large group of people at any given period of time. In addition, the values and institutions of the United States change constantly.

Allport's contribution is useful not because of the cause he assigns (clash of values), but because of its effect (the inside–outside perception). Once the secrecy/conspiracy mantle is removed from Shils's exposition, one finds a useful status-anxiety argument. That is, there is no primordial, certain standard for defining an American; as a result, the United States is a country of people "uncertain of their own conformity with a given standard" who are primed, during times of stress, "to abuse others for inadequate conformity with it." In sum, the "looseness of American loyalties" leads to hypersensitivity about loyalty, and the high mobility of people in the United States and the lack of powerful traditions leads to hyperpatriotism and vocal Americanism.[35]

If we combine the insights of Allport and Shils with an aspect of Richard Hofstadter's "paranoid style," we reach a more persuasive approach. According to Hofstadter "the paranoid style" is "an old and recurrent mode of expression" in the public life of the United States, which becomes significant during periods when there is "a confrontation of opposed interests which are (or are felt to be) totally irreconcilable, and thus by nature not susceptible to the normal political processes of bargain and compromise."[36] As a consequence, the endemic "inside–outside perception" and "paranoid style" (negativity toward the "other") can, under exceptional circumstances, produce the type of hyperpatriotic, vocal Americanism of the type that prevailed during the three "red scares" of the twentieth century.

Indeed, negativity toward the "other," in the forms of anti-radicalism and nativism, long predates the "red scares." Anti-radicalism first appeared in the late 1790s, when the Federalist majority in the Congress passed the Alien and Sedition Acts, aimed against the "radical" Jeffersonian critics of the federal government. It resurfaced, in the form of attacks on Garrisonian abolitionists, in the pre–Civil War decades. For our purposes here, the most significant outburst of nineteenth-century anti-radicalism can be considered to have occurred in 1886, following a bomb explosion at a demonstration of workers against police violence at Haymarket Square in Chicago, which killed several policemen. According to Henry David, a public outcry for "the immediate suppression of radical groups arose." It represented, he wrote, the "first major 'red scare' in American history" and "produced a campaign of 'red-baiting' which has rarely been equaled."[37] But despite the equating of labor militancy and "foreign agitators" that resulted, this radical scare did not become institutionalized. The process of a permanent institutionalization of anti-radicalism commenced with the Immigration Acts of 1903 and 1918, which prohibited, first, the entry of anarchists and, second, any person who had advocated the overthrow of any government.

Nativism is an organized, fear-driven response to the conjuncture of a severe social or economic crisis and the presence of some distinctive group of people, usually newly arrived foreigners, who stand out from the resident population, because of skin color, costume, language, work habits, or customs. Nativists blame the newest arrivals or "unassimilated" older arrivals for the country's (and their own) travails and demand their exclusion. In the United States, the first three major outbursts of nativism were directed against Irish Catholics, in the 1830s, 1840s, and 1850s. Then, when immigration increased after the Civil War, nativists issued dire warnings about the dilution of the Anglo-Saxon racial strain among U.S. residents. The Chinese on the U.S. west coast were the first target, and the attacks on them were both legal (discriminatory and exclusionary legislation and court decisions) and extralegal (mob attacks). During the debate on the bill to bar further Chinese immigration, Representative Benjamin Butterworth (Republican-Ohio) stated, in terms that could be used in any future nativist or anti-radical speech, "I oppose the immigration of a class whose presence is inimical to the healthful growth of our institutions, whose presence wars against our system of Christianity, whose manners, customs, beliefs, and practices war against our system of government."[38] Meanwhile, in the eastern portion of the country, the influx of eastern and southern Europeans spurred another phase of racial nativism. Congress responded to this enmity by passing a law, in 1891, excluding persons with certain diseases, polygamists, idiots, the insane, paupers, and other "undesirable" types from entry into the United States. President Grover Cleveland vetoed this bill.

During the first two decades of the twentieth century, however, Congress did succeed in passing a series of restrictive immigration laws. The insane, impoverished, prostitutes, and anarchists were barred in 1903. Four years later, further bars on the poor were imposed, anyone who was considered a threat to labor standards in the United States was prohibited entry, and citizenship was to be stripped from any U.S.-born woman who married an alien. The standards for naturalization were raised and the Bureau of Immigration's powers extended. Finally, in 1917, overriding President Woodrow Wilson's veto, Congress barred all immigration from Asia and imposed a literacy test on all other immigrants.

Anti-radicalism and nativism began to cohere in the concept of Americanization, which had been one of the main components of the prewar progressive era and formed one of the strongest pillars of Wilson's national security apparatus. Wilson told a group of newly naturalized citizens, on May 10, 1915:

> You cannot dedicate yourself to America unless you become in every respect and with every purpose of your will thorough Americans. You cannot become thorough Americans if you think of yourselves in groups. America does not consist of groups. A man who thinks of himself as belonging to a particular national group in America has not yet become an American.[39]

Seven months later, in his Annual Message, Wilson warned Congress: "There are citizens of the United States ... born under other flags but welcomed under out generous naturalization laws to the full freedom and opportunity of America, who have poured the poison of disloyalty into the very arteries of our national life." He urged Congress to pass legislation to "save the honor and self-respect of the nation. Such creatures of passion, disloyalty, and anarchy must be crushed out."[40]

When World War I began, Wilson equated advocacy of peace and pacifism with treason and promised that he would repress any "disloyalty." He labeled the peace movement "a new intrigue," and he warned its proponents: "Woe be to the man or group of men that seeks to stand in our way in this day of high resolution, when every principle we hold dearest is to be vindicated and made secure for the salvation of the nations."[41] The Department of Justice drafted 17 bills to increase the government's control over thought and speech, and Congress passed several of them—most notably the Espionage Act, the Trading with the Enemies Act, the Sedition Act, and the Alien Act.

A network of government agencies was created to conduct wartime counterespionage, including the Military Intelligence Division, the Office of Naval Intelligence, the Censorship Office, and the passport office. The agents of this network launched dozens of raids on radical organizations, threatened newspapers and magazine editors, arrested more than 2,000 antiwar sympathizers, and barred distribution of more than 100 publications. In February 1917, U.S. Attorney General Thomas Gregory authorized the founding of the American Protective League, a national volunteer surveillance organization whose membership peaked at 250,000. The American Protective League conducted surveillance of, and aided in raids against, antiwar types, and was accused of violating the civil liberties of leftists, especially members of the Industrial Workers of the World.

Anti-communism in the United States grew out of and became the institutionalized version of the anti-radicalism, nativism, and Americanization movements. This transformation occurred as the result of several factors: Communism was a foreign doctrine, headquartered in a foreign country; its proponents in the United States had foreign-sounding names; they trumpeted an ideology that was antithetical to capitalism, religion, and the traditional principles of Western democracy; they were "conspiratorial"; and their goal was to install a "red" (Russian-type) regime. As a result of these factors, the first official "red scare" became the national response to the domestic unrest following the end of World War I.[42] The second "red scare" (1939–1941) aided the growth and institutionalization of anti-communism. The third "red scare" (1945–1957) embedded it in the culture of the United States.

In effect, "red scares" were, to a large degree, resentment driven—the direct outgrowth of periods when a large number of people in the United States felt insecure and frightened, their expectations and hopes seemingly thwarted. Unable to locate the exact cause of or cure for these feelings, they did what past, equally insecure masses of the people had done in similar situations: they listened to their elected officials, the leaders of their civic organizations, and the media, and focused on nearby unfamiliar or strange entities—foreigners, radicals, or foreign radicals—against whom they could vent their frustration and rage. It was during these conjunctures of heightened anxiety and a highly publicized symbolic "cause" that people made the leap from a belief—that Communists and fellow travelers, the carriers of a foreign ideology, might constitute a threat to the national security, values, and democratic processes of the United States—to certain "knowledge"—that Communists posed an immediate, dire threat. This "knowledge" allowed for no counter-examples or contradictions, not even the fact that relatively few revolutionaries or spies existed during any of the "red scares."

Anti-communism resembled anti-radicalism in several respects. Although both were driven mainly by elites (government officials, business leaders, and labor union leaders), they both mobilized mass-membership organizations (American Legion, American Federation of Labor, and various Catholic groups). As a result, only a few organizations dedicated to anti-communism had to be created during the Cold War. Among them were the elitist-led (Dwight D. Eisenhower, Allen Dulles, Lucius Clay), CIA-funded National Committee for a Free Europe, established in 1949 at the peak of the Cold War, and the John Birch Society, founded in 1958 when the Cold War at home and abroad was abating.

Anti-Communists developed a far more effective array of political and public relations skills than anti-radicals did, though they used many of the same devices. Perhaps their best weapon was the blurred distinction (or the "one size fits all" rhetoric). They summarily branded all atheists, anarchists, dissenters, foreign-born radicals, socialists, labor militants, and Communists (along with those who defended them) as "godless Reds."[43] In addition, anti-Communists expertly utilized the tactic of exposure, wielding inflated lists of "subversive" individuals and organizations. (Once a person or organization is "outed," he, she, or it remains "out." Legal remedies are expensive and time consuming, and retractions are never given the same coverage as the original accusation.)

A significant number of anti-Communists obsessively compiled lists of names of "subversive" people, organizations, and activities, and publicized them far and wide. During the first "red scare," for example, New York State Senator Clayton R. Lusk, chairman of the Joint Legislative Committee to Investigate Seditious Activities, was asked the purpose of the raids he had authorized against radicals. "Names," he replied. When J. Edgar Hoover was appointed to head the newly created General Intelligence Division of the Department of Justice, his first project was to amass a card file containing the names of more than 200,000 "subversives."[44] One decade later, J. B. Matthews, a disillusioned member of several dozen Popular Front groups, after confessing his heresies in *Odyssey of a Fellow Traveler* (1938), was appointed the chief investigator for the Un-American Activities Committee of the House of Representatives. He was an "indefatigable collector" of letterheads, mastheads, dinner programs, flyers, and announcements. As a result of the voluminous file of names and organizations he amassed, he became known as "the unofficial 'dean' of the counter-subversive community."[45] Because all these lists were indiscriminately gathered and no objective filter was used, the "garbage in, garbage out" syndrome was the unfortunate consequence. Totals (i.e., the number of alleged "card-carrying Communists" and of Party fellow-travelers) were arrived at in an equally arbitrary manner. In 1958, Ralph S. Brown, Jr. asserted that the estimated number of close Party sympathizers "is one of the shakiest statistics in American politics." [46]

Anti-communism flourished in the post–World War II era, because the label (of communism), its symbol (redness), and the thing feared (Communists) had become much better defined. As Allport noted, it was "not that people knew precisely what they meant when they said 'Communist,' but with the aid of the term they were at least able to point consistently to *something* that inspired fear." In essence, the term had developed the power to signify a clear menace.[47] Those responsible for fusing label, symbol, and thing did so by combining a series of unexamined, but fiercely advocated assumptions, few of which were provable, but all of which were, if true, sufficiently scary. Thus they made anti-communism a sort of religion, whose disciples advocated a set of doctrines taken completely on faith:

1. Soviet leaders were evil people, relentlessly driven by an evil ideology, and bent on world domination.[48]
2. There was no such thing as a "local" conflict, and virtually every attack on a sitting government represented a calculated element of the Soviet drive toward global supremacy.
3. Soviet behavior irrevocably divided the postwar world into two irreconcilable sides or camps.
4. One of those camps was monolithic and evil, the other multiplinthed and good, motivated by a God-given, light-upon-a-hill moral responsibility for universal welfare.
5. If one was not unreservedly on the side of the good, one was, ipso facto, on the side of evil.[49]
6. The domestic "thems" were as threatening as the foreign "thems."
7. Whereas liberals and conservatives join organizations or seek employment in government bureaus, Communists "infiltrate" them.
8. The magnitude of the "threat" was vast and its end unforeseeable.

This sort-of-religion was energized by the religious fervor of many Catholics and Protestants. Frank Gibney, a conservative Catholic, noted the Catholic type of fervor in his commentary on a dinner to honor Roy Cohn, the former Chief Counsel of the Senate Permanent Investigations Subcommittee, which was chaired by Senator Joseph

McCarthy (Republican-Wisconsin). Cohn had been forced to resign, in July 1954, at the end of the "Army-McCarthy" hearings. The 2,500 paying (mainly Irish Catholic) guests represented, according to Gibney, "a most comprehensive assembly of 'McCarthyites,' . . . an assortment of zealots comparable in their intensity only to the personnel of meetings organized in past years by groups like the old Communist-sponsored League Against War and Fascism." They were, according to Gibney, every bit the "dupes" that they proclaimed their opponents to be: "They were . . . particularly honest, God-fearing, and, above all, decent 'dupes,' but people convinced that every premise has to have an immediately visible conclusion, and that political conviction and moral certitude are indistinguishable." Gibney was most bothered by what he perceived as the "indomitable godliness, the constantly repeated thought that Heaven had put a blanket security clearance on the activities of Joe [McCarthy] and Roy [Cohn] (God bless them) and personally endorsed their crusade."[50]

In effect, the anti-Communists constructed a nearly impregnable belief system, capable of deflecting any facts or evidence challenging it. An example of this type of deflection was provided by the anti-Communist writer Irving Kristol, when he finally accepted as true that the CIA had secretly funded the periodicals and organizations he supported as bastions of cultural freedom in the 1950s. In defense of his failure to acknowledge that information earlier, Kristol said: "Rumors there were, but they were not particularly credible. Most of these rumors issued from sources—Left-wing, anti-American, or both—that would have been happy to circulate them, true or not, and one discounted them in advance."[51]

Thus, in some ways, Communists and anti-Communists were mirror images of each other. Both were zealous believers in an inerrant dogma, and, as Alan Barth noted, "believers in the suppression and punishment of dissent."[52] For example, Monsignor Rice acknowledged that he was equally as merciless as the Communists,[53] and Roy Brewer, in his fight against Communists in the motion picture industry, used the Communists' *"own tactics"* against them.[54] Both Communists and anti-Communists confused loyalty (to the Party and to the nation, respectively) with orthodoxy, and both believed that conformity of opinion was superior to diversity of opinion. Finally, both were convinced that orthodoxy and conformity (to the Party and to the nation, respectively), however accomplished, would make the Communist Party invincible and the United States secure.

CATEGORIZING ANTI-COMMUNISM: A NEW APPROACH

The amalgamation of all opponents of communism into "anti-Communists" obscures the variegated essence of this group. Although previous authors have realized the necessity of some form of categorization, none of their efforts seem to me to be sufficiently precise or enlightening. The most extensive effort to categorize anti-Communists was made by Richard Gid Powers. In his effort to rescue anti-communism from the many criticisms it has drawn, he acknowledged that there were "many American anticommunisms," but he decided to divide them into two very broad types, "responsible" or "irresponsible". According to this author, both types actually pursued the same goal: "to expose the grim reality behind the glorious ideals professed by Communists," Nevertheless, "responsible" anti-Communists demonstrated a genuine moral conviction, a "real knowledge" of communism, and possessed authentic "wisdom" regarding the "the ways of man." The "irresponsible" anti-Communists, in contrast, promoted "fantastic conspiracy theories" and "Red web" scenarios." (On occasion, Powers refers to the "irresponsible" types as "vengeful" or conspiratorial "countersubversives," deluded "crackpots," and denizens of "the lunatic right.") When discussing anti-communism in the 1920s, he contrasts "old-stock countersubversives," waving their conspiracy theories, with a "new breed," who gave the country "witheringly accurate assessments of what Communists were doing in an America and a world that was unknown to the countersubversives."[55]

The problem is that Powers does not inform his readers which instruments he has used to measure the moral convictions, real knowledge, and wisdom of "responsible" anti-Communists. In addition, according to his own evidence, some exemplars of "responsible" anti-communism—the American Legion, the Catholic Church, and the American Federation of Labor (AFL)—have behaved, on many occasions, "irresponsibly." (Powers cites examples of American Legion thuggery, and two prominent anti-Communist Catholics he identifies, Patrick Scanlan and Charles E. Coughlin, intermixed their anti-communism with rabid anti-Semitism.) Further, AFL leaders espoused reckless conspiracy theories and AFL members acted like thugs on many occasions. Finally, many anti-Communist Congressmen and executive branch officials could be safely located on the "irresponsible" side. In fact, Powers implies that during the first "red scare," several people with "a real knowledge of communism"—including Attorney General A. Mitchell Palmer, his employee J. Edgar

Hoover, some members of the U.S. Congress, and the New York legislature's Lusk Committee—were "countersubversives."[56]

Powers's terminology is ultimately too broad and too subjective and agenda laden to be useful in formulating a clear assessment of the origins and nature of anti-communism. A more neutral taxonomy is needed—one that distinguishes between official (i.e., governmental) and unofficial (i.e., nongovernmental) forms of anti-communism.[57] To be sure, official anti-communism was by far the more powerful component of the anti-communism apparatus. It possessed the power to spy, subpoena, indict, and prosecute. Unofficial anti-communism, however, possessed complementary powers: to inform, to publicize, to boycott, and to blacklist. In all varieties of official and unofficial anti-communism, there is a range of types: the true believer, the pragmatist, the opportunist, and the palpably dishonest. (There is a very thin line separating the last two.) The following diagram serves as the template for the discussion that follows.[58]

Official anti-communism

Legislative   Executive   Judicial

Unofficial anti-communism

Institutional   Ex-Communist   Conservative   Liberal   Left-of-liberal

Civil-Libertarian anti-communism

1

Official Anti-Communism, 1919–1939

John Reed aptly titled his book on the November 1917 revolution in Russia, *Ten Days That Shook the World*. But the earlier revolution there, in March 1917, which overthrew the tsarist autocracy, did not shake the people of the United States. In fact, it was greeted with enthusiasm by public opinion and U.S. government officials, especially after Paul Miliukov, the new Minister of Foreign Affairs, announced that the provisional government would continue to fight on the side of the Allies.[1] Those attitudes began to shift when the Bolsheviks ousted the provisional government in November, and they worsened when the new regime announced its intention to propose an armistice to the Central Powers and began to confiscate and nationalize property.

At the top level of the U.S. government, Secretary of State Robert Lansing expressed his antipathy toward the Bolshevik regime from its outset, but President Woodrow Wilson wrote, on November 13, 1917, "I have not lost faith in the Russian outcome by any means."[2] Later, in his Fourteen Points speech delivered to Congress on January 8, 1918, Wilson devoted Point VI to Russia. He called on the nations of the world to evacuate all Russian territory and to allow the new regime "an unhampered and unembarrassed opportunity for the independent determination of her own political development and national policy and assure her of a sincere welcome into the society of free nations under institutions of her own choosing."[3]

When the Bolsheviks signed the Treaty of Brest-Litovsk, ending hostilities with Germany, on March 5, 1918, however, the President turned against the regime. Wilson approved the sending of U.S. troops to Archangel and Murmansk; in August, he classified Russia as a "belligerent."[4] In September, Lansing denounced the Communist doctrine of "internationalism" and called it "an actual menace to the present social order." He warned the people of the United States that they had to choose between two conceptions of world order: traditional nationalism or Russian internationalism.[5] Moreover, Wilson, at the Versailles peace conference, pursued a policy of quarantine, limiting and indirectly coercing the Bolshevik state and blocking the spread of Bolshevism to other countries in Europe. The victors should, he said, "leave Russia to the Bolsheviks—they will stir in their own juice until circumstances make the Russians wiser."[6]

Public opinion regarded the treaty of Brest-Litovsk as an act of betrayal and the Bolsheviks as German agents, who had achieved power as the result of German intrigue.[7] As a result, the public shifted the intolerance it had generated against the Germans during World War I to the Bolsheviks, and the anxiety provoked by postwar price inflation, unemployment, demobilization, reconversion, and massive labor unrest was now vented against Bolsheviks-*cum*-German agents. Aided by sensational newspaper headlines and comments by super-patriotic groups and individuals, the public made a series of associations: Russian revolutionaries with German war-mongers; antiwar activists in the United States with the signers of the Brest-Litovsk treaty; and those who welcomed the Bolshevik revolution with the Bolsheviks who announced an imminent world revolution to overthrow capitalism. According to Robert K. Murray, "Horror stories of every kind filled the columns of American newspapers" and 1919 became a year of "turbulence and chaos."[8] Supreme Court Justice Louis D. Brandeis remarked on "the intensity of the frenzy" and the "disgraceful exhibition—of hysterical, unintelligent fear."[9]

Three labor strikes—in Seattle, Boston, and the steel industry—are worth noting for the manner in which conventional labor demands were transmuted by the atmosphere of 1919 into examples of "Bolshevik" activity in the United States. The Seattle strike began on January 21, 1919, when 35,000 shipyard workers struck for higher wages and shorter hours. The Seattle Central Labor Council decided to support them by means of a generalized strike. The decision was supported by American Federation of Labor (AFL) locals, but Seattle-area newspapers called it a "revolution," members of the U.S. Congress and national newspapers labeled it a "Red strike" and "a stepping stone to a bolshevik America," and Seattle Mayor Ole Hansen announced it was a plan by the Industrial Workers of the World (IWW)[10] to establish a soviet in his city. Hansen called in federal troops, and, in the face of the forces he mustered against the strike, it was called off on February 10.[11]

In August 1919, members of the Boston police force, rankled by their low salaries, long hours, and poor working conditions, voted to organize a union, and they quickly received a charter from the AFL. When 19 union leaders were first suspended and then fired, approximately four-fifths of the police force went on strike. All of the Boston newspapers labeled the strike decision "Bolshevistic"; business leaders and organizations branded the strikers "agents of Lenin" and "bolshevists." In the face of this onslaught, the Central Labor Union voted not to generalize the strike, and the police canceled it. When the city police commissioner refused to rehire the strikers, he was backed by the governor of Massachusetts, Calvin Coolidge, who stated: "There is no right to strike against the public safety, by anybody, anywhere, any time." Coolidge received national acclaim as a symbol of anti-radicalism and a staunch upholder of "Americanism." One year later, he was nominated as the vice-presidential candidate on the Republican ticket.[12]

Finally, the strike launched by the National Committee for Organizing Iron and Steel Workers against United States Steel, on September 22, 1919, provoked sensational newspaper headlines about a pending revolution and the "bolshevizing" of the United States. Violence on the picket lines increased the hyperbole. The governor of Indiana asked for federal troops to help quell the labor unrest. General Leonard Wood placed the city of Gary under martial law and launched a series of raids against radicals, arresting them and seizing their literature. In its investigation of the strike, the U.S. Senate Committee on Education and Labor concluded: "Behind this strike there is massed a considerable element of IWWs, anarchists, revolutionists, and Russian Soviets." Given this publicity the strike failed utterly, ending in early January 1920, without a single gain by the strikers. Although the workers had been supported by the AFL and had made traditional demands, their strike enormously increased public hatred for "Bolshevism" and intolerance for unions as carriers of the radical germ.[13]

For all the publicity garnered by these three putative strikes, this "red scare" was not as universally intimidating as the post-1945 one would be. For example, the movement to secure amnesty for Socialist leader Eugene V. Debs, who was convicted of violating the Espionage Act, engaged millions "in a broad national debate about the government's wartime speech policies." In addition, in the 1920 presidential

U.S. Attorney General A. Mitchell Palmer, director of the first "red scare." (Library of Congress)

election campaign, the two candidates who attempted to exploit the "red scare" fared poorly: Palmer's "undiluted Americanism" did not win him the Democrats' nomination and General Leonard Wood's promise to kill Communists like "rattlesnakes" failed to entice Republicans. The winner, the Republic candidate Warren G. Harding, said, during the campaign: "Too much has been said about Bolshevism in America."[14]

Nevertheless, this "red scare" had sharply reduced the membership of left-wing parties in the United States, and anti-communism had carved out a secure bureaucratic niche in the government of the United States

THE LEGISLATIVE BRANCH

In February 1919, in the wake of the Seattle strike and the formation of the Communist Party of America and the Communist Labor Party,[15] a subcommittee of the Senate Judiciary Committee held hearings to investigate "Bolshevik propaganda." One of the witnesses, Archibald E. Stevenson, who had been head of the propaganda section of the

New York City branch of the Military Intelligence Division, insisted on providing the subcommittee with a list of people whom he labeled as "dangerous," because they were either, in his words, "pacifists" or "radicals."[16] Following its hearings, the subcommittee recommended that legislation be enacted to prohibit all types of anti-American propaganda. In November, several peacetime sedition bills were introduced into both houses of Congress. One passed the Senate, but it died in the House of Representatives the following year.[17] Congress did, however, amend the immigration law to allow for the deportation of any alien who joined or was affiliated with any organization that wrote, circulated, or had in its possession any literature "advising, advocating or teaching opposition to all organized government, or the overthrow by force or violence of the Government of the United States or of all forms of law."[18]

In fact, during the 1920s, the bulk of anti-Communist legislation was enacted by the states: 32 states and Alaska passed red flag laws which made it a felony to use or display a red flag in a public place, and 34 states and the Alaska and Hawaii territories passed either a sedition, criminal syndicalist, or criminal anarchy law. [19]

In 1930, the U.S. Congress returned to the field of battle against communism, when Congressman Hamilton Fish (Republican–New York) proposed that the House of Representatives establish a Special Committee on Communist Activities in the United States, to investigate the Communist Party (CPUSA) and all affiliated organizations, the Communist International and all its appendages, Communist propaganda, and any person or group advocating the overthrow of the government by force or violence. His resolution was approved overwhelmingly, by a vote of 210-18. After 6 months of hearings, the Committee reported that the Communist Party had a dues-paying membership of 12,000 people, but noted that it exercised little noticeable influence. Nevertheless, the Committee recommended banning Communist literature from the U.S. postal system and interstate commerce, canceling the naturalization certificates of Communists, deporting alien Communists, and declaring the CPUSA illegal. However, public support for the committee's work was low, few major publications praised the committee or its reports, and no legislation resulted.[20]

As the Depression deepened, and radicalism on the right and left grew, some Congressmen became concerned about what they called "subversion." One of them, Congressman Samuel Dickstein (Democrat–New York) proposed, in January 1934, a resolution to investigate Nazi activities in the United States. This resolution was adopted, along with a "basket clause," authorizing the investigation of "the diffusion within the United States of subversive propaganda that is instigated from foreign countries and attacks the principles of the form of government as guaranteed by our Constitution." John McCormack (Democrat–Massachusetts), who was appointed as chairman of this Special Committee on Un-American Activities, was urged by Ralph Easley, head of the National Civic Federation, to use the committee to "smash" communism in the United States.[21]

Although most of the committee's 24 executive and 7 public sessions were devoted to Nazi propaganda, 2 executive sessions and 3 public sessions focused on or included Communist activities. The mode of questioning of Communist witnesses contrasted markedly with what was to come: the questions were pointed and deliberate, aiming at demonstrating that the CPUSA was closely tied to the

Representative Samuel Dickstein (second from right), whose resolution created the Special Committee on Un-American Activities, meeting with musician Paul Whiteman and Representatives Caroline O'Day and James H. Gildea, March 1937. (Library of Congress)

Communist International (founded in Moscow, March 1919) and that the Communist-run fur dyers and needle workers unions were engaged in extortionate practices. The Communist witnesses, including Party leader Earl Browder, answered, without protest, the questions put to them. By comparison, the anti-Communist witnesses were then (as they were later) given full license to expound at length. On November 15, 1934, Walter S. Steele, the editor of *National Republic Magazine* and a representative of the American Coalition (of 109 "patriotic" organizations), was allowed to introduce into the record a lengthy report of 600 "national Communist organizations and closely cooperating movements in the United States."[22]

One month later, two sessions were devoted to an attempt, in the words of committee counsel Thomas W. Hardwick, "to give a brief outline of the picture throughout this country, with communism boring in on various departments and in various economic and labor practices." Each witness slated to testify, he continued, would represent "an important and reputable organization that has definite and well-formed views on the question."[23] Representatives from three veterans' groups, the National Civic Federation, the AFL, the Chamber of Commerce of the United States, and the Departments of War, Navy, and Labor, among others, held forth against communism in the United States.

Ten of the 19 pages of the Special Committee on Un-American Activities' final report were devoted to communism. The report concluded that Communist agitation was widespread, but noted that the Communist movement was not sufficiently strong numerically "to constitute a danger to American institutions" at this time. The report nevertheless urged Congress to enact stringent legislation to prevent the spread of un-American propaganda by requiring all organizations with a foreign connection to register with the Department of State; to make unlawful any effort by word or deed to change any government in the United States by force or violence; and to empower federal attorneys to proceed against witnesses who refused to appear, testify, or produce records before any lawful committee of Congress. In the face of strong opposition from, among others, the American Civil Liberties Union, the American League Against War and Fascism, prominent law professors, and the print media, none of the proposed bills became law, and this version of the Special Committee went out of existence.[24]

In 1937, anti-Communists in Congress, spurred by a new alliance of congressional Republicans and southern Democrats opposed to the

Representative Martin Dies, chairman of the Special Committee on Un-American Activities (1938–1944). (Library of Congress)

passage of New Deal reform legislation, renewed their investigations of "subversive activities." In the ensuing years, this alliance was further strengthened by support from the AFL, the Catholic Church, fundamentalist Protestants, and national business organizations.[25] This bloc strongly supported Congressman Martin Dies (Democrat–Texas), when, on May 26, 1938, he introduced House Resolution 282, which urged the Speaker of the House of Representatives

> to appoint a special committee to be composed of seven members for the purpose of conducting an investigation of (1) the extent, character, and objects of un-American propaganda activities in the United States, (2) the diffusion within the United States of subversive and un-American propaganda that is instigated from foreign countries or of a domestic origin and attacks the principle of the form of government as guaranteed by our Constitution, and (3) all other questions in relation thereto that would aid Congress in any necessary remedial legislation.

In his speech supporting the resolution, Dies characterized communism, Nazism, and fascism as dictatorial political systems.

Moreover, he forthrightly asserted that his proposed resolution had a fourth, indeed predominant, purpose—namely, the exposure of subversive activities. Dies admitted that it might be difficult to enact legislation to eliminate such activities, but he asserted that "exposure in a democracy of subversive activities is the most effective weapon we have in our possession."[26] The House approved the resolution, by a vote of 191-41, and appropriated $25,000 to fund the newly formed committee's investigations. Dies and five of the other appointees to this Special Committee were militantly anti–New Deal and strongly opposed to the newly formed Congress of Industrial Organizations (CIO), which had launched a series of mass strikes in the automobile, steel, rubber, and electrical industries.

On August 4, 1938, Dies became front-page news for the first time, when he announced that he was going to Hollywood to investigate charges that the Hollywood Anti-Nazi League was a Communist-dominated group. He announced that he would afford its members, whom he labeled "dupes, . . . the opportunity to reply to charges that they were participating in communistic activities." Dies, who had shown no previous interest in the motion picture industry, had received information from one of the Special Committee's investigators that there was "evidence of subversive activities in Hollywood" and that "all phases of radical and Communistic activities are rampant among the studios."[27] The Anti-Nazi League responded with a barrage of telegrams to the President and Congress, a mass rally, and a national radio broadcast. Finding no significant group in Hollywood willing to cooperate with him, Dies first postponed and then canceled the planned hearings, citing as his reason that his committee lacked funds and time. Nevertheless, he labeled Hollywood "a hotbed of Communists and radicals."[28]

Ignoring Hollywood for the time being, the Special Committee opened its first public hearings, on August 12, 1938, with an inquiry into the German-American Bund. The following sessions were devoted to communism, however, and four of the witnesses provided a cornucopia of names of individuals and organizations involved in this political movement. John P. Frey, president of the AFL Metal Trades Department, charged that communism, via the CIO, "[had] secured an official foothold" in the labor movement, and that Communists were using sit-down strikes and mass-picketing to familiarize workers "with the tactics they are to apply when their revolutionary program is to be put into action."[29] He then proceeded to provide several lists of names: 204 "known Communist Party members" of the

National Maritime Union; 288 Communists in the CIO; 60 top Communist leaders; 59 Communist delegates to the last Steel Workers Organizing Committee convention; and 9 United Automobile Workers' executives who were Communist or Communist influenced. Frey was followed by Walter Steele, who provided a list of Communist organizations, state Party leaders, 640 organizations affiliated or allied with the CPUSA, 483 Communist publications, Communist schools and camps, signers of petitions, and members of Popular Front organizations. H. L. Chaillaux, the director of the American Legion's National Americanism Commission provided the names of Communist members of a large number of Popular Front Organizations. Finally, J. B. Matthews provided extensive lists of names and organizations.[30] The Special Committee then called a series of witnesses to testify about the subversive nature of the Federal Theater Project (a component of the New Deal's Works Project Administration [WPA]) and the Workers Alliance, a union representing WPA workers.

Under Dies's leadership, the Special Committee originated many of the techniques that were to be used more effectively after World War II by the permanent Committee on Un-American Activities and also by Senator Joseph McCarthy. Dies regularly accused the U.S. government of employing Communists, showcased ex-Communist and anti-Communist witnesses brandishing their long lists of names, practiced guilt by association, and attempted to intimidate and bully unfriendly witnesses.[31] A Gallup Poll, taken in early December 1938, reported that 74 percent of those who knew about the Special Committee's existence approved of it. The respondents explained that their approval was based on their belief that it was necessary "to keep our eyes open in the midst of all this world trouble" and to "weed out those who want to overthrow the American system."[32]

When the time came, in early 1939 to renew the Special Committee's mandate for another year, several liberal congressmen attacked its methods and questioned its purpose. Dies replied:

[C]an it be said that we have erred in exposing men prominent in this Government who by their own admissions subscribe to communism? Can it be said we erred in going into certain labor unions and showing by uncontradicted evidence, by the testimony of officials and members of the union itself, that here were Communists who had infiltrated legitimate labor unions, had seized strategic positions, and were converting those labor unions into instrumentalities of class warfare?[33]

After the House renewed the Special Committee (by a vote of 344-45 and with an appropriation of $100,000), Dies introduced three anticommunist bills: a bill to provide for the exclusion and expulsion from the United States of alien Fascists and Communists; a bill to require the registration of certain organizations with the U.S. government; and a bill to make Communists and Fascists ineligible for employment by the U.S. government.[34] None of these bills became law, but Dies promised to continue to use "pitiless publicity" to expose Communists.[35]

THE EXECUTIVE BRANCH

Executive branch anti-radicalism had begun to lessen in the early months of 1919. Thomas Gregory, the outgoing U.S. Attorney General, and his successor, A. Mitchell Palmer, reviewed the cases of those convicted of espionage, to ascertain which were eligible for clemency, and Palmer released from parole 10,000 enemy aliens. On May 1, 1919, however, it was discovered that 36 package bombs had been mailed from New York City to a variety of government personages. Newspaper headlines called the scheme a May Day Bolshevik plot, and mobs broke up radical meetings and parades in many cities. An editorial in *The New York Times* warned Palmer to drop "the policy of tolerance" and replace it with "one of vigorous prosecution [of] the Bolshevist movement." Four weeks later, a bomb exploded on Palmer's front doorstep, and the Department of Justice decided to initiate a mass roundup and deportation of alien radicals.

In August 1919, Palmer established the General Intelligence Division and appointed J. Edgar Hoover to head it. Hoover immediately began to collect a card-index file with the names of more than 200,000 "radical" individuals, organizations, and publications. The roundup did not actually begin until November 7, when Hoover launched a series of raids, jailing of radicals, and deportations.[36] By the spring, however, public fear of radicals had dissipated and Hoover's tactics had provoked a wave of criticism regarding the lack of due process. Assistant Secretary of Labor Louis F. Post began a careful review of the deportation cases, rejecting those with procedural violations, and Congress ended the funding for Palmer's crusade. Nevertheless, the Bureau of Investigation, the General Intelligence Division, and the Immigration Bureau[37] maintained their vigorous anti-Communist efforts.

In 1921, Hoover became assistant director of the Bureau of Investigation, and its director in 1924. (In 1935, the Bureau

J. Edgar Hoover, the most relentless and dedicated official anti-Communist, 1924.
(Library of Congress)

became an independent agency within the Department of Justice and
was renamed the Federal Bureau of Investigation [FBI].) Following
the suppression of the spring 1932 Bonus Army march on Washington,
D.C., he urged the executive branch to heighten its anti-radical operations. Hoover was convinced that the Bonus Army march—an attempt
by veterans of World War I to shame the U.S. government into paying
them a promised bonus—heralded a new strain of subversion, which
threatened the national security of the United States.[38] His efforts were
supported by the new President, Franklin D. Roosevelt, who believed
that his duties as commander-in-chief of the armed forces required
him to investigate all organizations that might be disseminating any
information or teachings contrary to the democratic ideals of the
United States. In 1934, Roosevelt authorized Hoover to investigate
the activities of Nazi sympathizers; two years later, he broadened
Hoover's power to investigate any "subversive" activities, particularly those of Communists and fascists. In response, Hoover immediately ordered all FBI field offices to "obtain from all possible sources

information concerning subversive activities." In November 1938, Roosevelt approved the widened scope of activities of the FBI's General Intelligence Section.[39]

THE JUDICIAL BRANCH

The U.S. judiciary cannot accurately be labeled anti-Communist, although on several occasions, notably during and after World Wars I and II, it proved itself a less-than-staunch defender of the First Amendment rights of radicals. During World War I, according to Paul L. Murphy, U.S. Supreme Court justices were "generally insensitive to the issue" of civil liberties and consistently looked for ways to uphold government treatment of radical people and groups.[40]

After the war, the federal courts dealt regularly with cases of political free speech, and, during the 1920s, they usually deferred to the judgments of Congress, state legislatures, and prosecutors in cases involving radical free speech, by upholding convictions under federal espionage statutes and state syndicalist laws.[41] But in *Fiske v. Kansas*, 274 U.S. 380 (1927), the Supreme Court did reverse a conviction under the Kansas criminal syndicalist act, though it did not declare the act unconstitutional. Four years later, the Court declared unconstitutional California's Red Flag Law, because it was too vague and could be used to interfere with constitutionally protected speech.[42] Six years later, in its first case involving a Communist, the Court continued this trend of reversing decisions barring radical speech. The appellant, Angelo Herndon, a black man and a member of the Communist Party, had been indicted and convicted under a nineteenth-century Georgia statute for plotting insurrection. The Court, in a 5-4 decision, reversed the conviction.[43]

Perhaps the Supreme Court's most interesting decision occurred four months before the signing of the German-Soviet Nonaggression Treaty of August 1939, which provoked the second "red scare." In *Kessler v. Strecker* (307 U.S. 22, 1939), the Court provided a very strained reading of Section 2 of the Immigration Act of 1918, which, on its face, seemed to allow the government to deport an alien who, after entering the United States, joined an organization that taught, advised, or advocated the overthrow of the U.S. government. The appellant had entered the United States in 1932 and joined the Communist Party, but left the Party before applying for naturalization.

Justice Owen Roberts did not find the statute clear on its face, and he stated, in his majority opinion:

> In the absence of a clear and definite expression [by the Congress], we are not at liberty to conclude that Congress intended that any alien, no matter how long a resident of this country or however well disposed toward our Government, must be deported if, at any time in the past, no matter when or under what circumstances or for what time he was a member of the described organization. In the absence of such expression, we conclude that it is the present membership or present affiliation—a fact to be determined on evidence—which bars admission, bars naturalization, and requires deportation.[44]

Despite this trend, Paul L. Murphy concluded that "very few clear rules" regarding protected speech had emerged from the Court's rulings.[45]

2

Unofficial Anti-Communism, 1919–1939

Unofficial (or nongovernmental) anti-communism may be categorized into several types: institutional, ex-Communist, conservative, liberal, and left-of-liberal. Although none of these labels—especially "liberal" and "conservative"—are precise, and although there is an overlap between the institutional, ex-Communist, and conservative categories, these types have acquired a conventional meaning that allows a reasonable basis for making distinctions among them.

INSTITUTIONAL ANTI-COMMUNISM

Institutional anti-communism was the best organized and most effective nongovernmental type of anti-communism. It consisted of civic organizations whose members deemed it their patriotic duty to act unilaterally, when necessary, as well as to cooperate with local, state, and federal governments and other civic organizations to expose Communists and Communist organizations. The leaders of many of these institutions—notably, the American Legion, the Catholic Church, and the American Federation of Labor (AFL)—developed close ties with the Committee on Un-American Activities and the FBI.

Religious

Anti-radicalism had been Catholic Church doctrine since the publication of the *Manifesto of the Communist Party* (1848), and socialism and communism had been branded as atheistic by several papal

encyclicals. In 1910, church officials in the United States established the
Militia of Christ for Social Service to combat socialism within the AFL.
The Bolshevik revolution and the ensuing persecution of the Russian
Orthodox Church exacerbated Catholic hostility toward communism.

During the 1930s, Catholic Church leaders in the United States
strongly opposed recognition of the Soviet Union, and sharply challenged those (i.e., almost the entire left) who supported the Loyalist
(government) position in the Spanish civil war.[1] In 1937, Pope Pius
XI issued the Holy See's strongest condemnation of communism,
Divini Redemptoris. That same year, the Knights of Columbus inaugu-
rated a Crusade Program, with "Communism the Destroyer" as one
of its components. Supreme Knight Martin Carmody proclaimed it
the duty of Knights to "Combat Communism—Our Common foe.
Feel, think, speak and live against it. . . . To the allies of Communism,
grant no peace." He hired an anti-Communist lecturer to travel
around the United States exposing the danger.[2] The following
year, the Church hierarchy expressed its concern over the spread of
"subversive" teachings and activities and founded the Crusade
for Christian Democracy to contain it. The Crusade advocated the

Father Edmund Walsh, S.J., the leading Catholic authority on the Soviet Union,
1922. (Library of Congress)

teaching of civic and social virtues in the young and the pursuit of social reform.[3]

Perhaps the leading advocate of Catholic anti-communism was Edmund A. Walsh, Society of Jesus, who had founded the foreign service school at Georgetown University and directed the Vatican's famine relief program in the Soviet Union (1922–1923). After his return to the United States, Walsh commenced a three-decade-long educational mission to warn the public of the Soviet threat to spiritual ideals. He delivered hundreds of lectures, wrote dozens of articles, and authored four books on the subject. In December 1934, while testifying to a session of the Special Committee on Un-American Activities, Walsh warned that Communists sought to overthrow by force and violence the government of the United States and to replace it with a Soviet system. The Communist Party, he continued, "[was] not a National political party," but an organic component of the Communist International. Its menace lay in the "quality" and not the quantity of its membership. Communists were "skilled propagandists," Walsh said, who "[might] well become formidable social dynamite in the present unsettled times."[4] He told the National Catholic Educational Association, in April 1936, that international communism was waiting for the nations of the world to engage in another war, to give it the opportunity "to strike a telling blow at democracy."[5]

Another well-educated Catholic, Monsignor Fulton J. Sheen, a professor at Catholic University, used his "Catholic Hour" broadcasts to criticize communism as a threat to spiritual values. He urged one of his doctoral students to research and write a dissertation on the philosophy of communism, and later wrote the preface to the published version. Both Sheen and his student, Charles J. McFadden, believed that communism was based on a "complete philosophical system," and "the failure to appreciate this fact has, in many ways, rendered our [country's] defense against the onslaught of Communism extremely ineffective." McFadden devoted half of the book to what he called "an orderly textual presentation of the fundamental philosophical principles of the Marxian theory" and the other half to "a critical evaluation of these principles in the light of a Catholic philosophy."[6]

The educated voices of Walsh and Sheen were regularly drowned out by the demagogic rants of Father Charles Coughlin, who had begun his radio broadcasts on a local station in 1926. Shortly after he began his national broadcasts in 1930, Coughlin declared himself to be the champion of Christ against communism, or, as he referred to it, "the red serpent." In July 1930, he appeared as a friendly witness before the Special Committee to Investigate Communist Activities in the United States.[7] Four years later, Coughlin founded the National Union for Social Justice to combat communism, capitalism, and the New Deal; in 1936 he co-founded the National Union Party, to challenge Roosevelt's reelection. Coughlin warned that the presidential election of 1936 pitted "Christ against chaos and Christianity against communism." When his popularity as a "radio priest" began to decline, Coughlin announced the formation of a Million League, composed of "Social Justice Platoons," which he suggested could be merged "into a great thinking army." One month later, his newspaper printed an appeal for the creation of a Christian Front of Social Justice Platoons, who would not be afraid to be labeled as fascist or anti-Semitic—according to Coughlin, Communists used those epithets to attack their opponents.[8]

Perhaps no aspect of the Communist issue divided Catholics more than the developments in organized labor. The debate began in 1935, when a Committee for Industrial Organization was established within the AFL, to organize the millions of workers previously ignored by the AFL. In 1938, this group was expelled from the AFL and renamed the Congress of Industrial Organizations (CIO). Walsh condemned the sit-down strikes used by the new industrial unions as "an alien importation," borrowed from the Communists.[9] Many others in the Catholic hierarchy joined the anti-CIO chorus, but numerous priests and lay members defended it. Foremost among them was Father John Ryan, who organized and picketed alongside Communists, defended the CIO against charges that it was controlled by Communists, and criticized the red-baiting of Coughlin, Patrick Scanlan, and the *Brooklyn Tablet*.[10]

The most prominent Catholic labor-oriented organizations of the 1930s also took divergent positions on the issue of Communists in labor unions. In the spring of 1933, Peter Maurin and Dorothy Day created the Catholic Worker Movement, a nonviolent, social justice organization, which was regularly attacked by Church leaders for being insufficiently anti-Communist. In 1936, Day responded that even though communism was wrong, Communists frequently supported good causes: "The Communist often more truly loves his brother, the poor and oppressed, than many so-called Christians." Moreover, the *Catholic Worker* rejected the linkage of anti-communism with patriotism and Christianity.[11] The following year, when the movement was attacked for taking a neutral position in the Spanish Civil War and supporting the CIO, the editors of the *Catholic Worker* responded: "Christian love, being addressed to all men, is the worst adversary of Communism." They urged Catholics to "forget the negative ideal of fighting Communism and concentrate on building up the mystical body of Christ."[12] Dorothy Day also publicly criticized Coughlin for his anti-Semitic statements and Scanlan for defending him.[13]

Other church groups, however, were deeply concerned that Communists were helping to organize the new industrial unions. In late 1935, the Jesuits opened a School of Social Sciences at St. Joseph's College (Philadelphia) to train Catholics for anti-Communist labor activity. Two years later, the Catholic Trade Union Association was founded in New York City, to promote sound, Christian-based (i.e., non-Marxist) trade unionism. (This organization later changed its name to the Association of Catholic Trade Unionists [ACTU], to avoid the impression it was practicing dual unionism.) At its peak, the ACTU had 24 chapters and 10,000 members. With the full support (and close control) of the church hierarchy, the ACTU became a virtual mirror image of the CPUSA: It established a Catholic Union of Unemployed, a Catholic Labor Defense League, workers' schools, a newspaper, and a speakers' bureau. During the ACTU's first few months of existence, a small group in New Jersey tried to limit red-baiting, arguing that anti-communism was a poor organizing tactic. The majority, however, believed that the struggle against communism had to take priority over every other issue. In fact, the first issue of the *Labor Leader*, the ACTU's official newspaper, stated that "no Catholic can remain in a union that is run along Marxist or unChristian lines."[14] Nevertheless, before the Nonaggression Treaty, the ACTU remained a strong defender of the CIO, and Father Charles Rice, who would become the ACTU's leading anti-Communist, regularly denied that the Communists had any positions of influence within the CIO.[15]

Many Protestants were also actively anti-Communist. The Methodist League Against Communism, Fascism, and Unpatriotic Pacifism formed in 1936, and, two years later, the Southern Baptist Convention proclaimed that there was "no room" for "radical Socialism" or "atheistic Communism" in the United States.[16]

American Legion

Close behind the Catholic Church in institutional effectiveness relative to anti-communism was the American Legion, which was founded in

May 1919. That November, at its first national convention, the delegates condemned "all forms of anarchy and Bolshevism," urged the deportation of all individuals who defamed the American way of life, and pledged to "attack the red flag wherever it may be raised." They swore "to foster and perpetuate one hundred percent Americanism." The first edition of the *American Legion Weekly* promised to drive "the Reds out from the land whose flag they sully," and the Los Angeles post declared "a war of extermination against members of the IWW and against Bolshevism."[17] By 1919, the American Legion's membership exceeded 800,000. As part of its message, the group called for the deportation of alien Bolsheviks and IWW members, and it pledged its support to the suppression of "un-Americans."[18]

During the 1920s, American Legion posts regularly tried to persuade local officials to deny public fora to "un-Americans," sponsored state criminal syndicalism laws, and provided material for prosecution under those laws. Between 1919 and 1921, according to a report by the American Civil Liberties Union (ACLU), Legionnaires engaged in 50 illegal acts of violence. Even though the attendant bad publicity led the American Legion to curtail such acts, the ACLU reported, in1927, that the Legion had "replaced the [Ku Klux] Klan as the most active agency of intolerance and repression in the country."[19] In 1923, the American Legion invited Benito Mussolini to speak at its national convention, and National Commander Alvin Owsley said, "the American Legion stands ready to protect our country's institutions and ideals as the Fascisti dealt with the destructionists who menaced Italy! . . . [T]he Fascisti are to Italy what the American Legion is to the United States."[20]

When Homer Chaillaux became head of the American Legion's National Americanism Commission, in 1934, he transformed it into "a reinvigorated center for information on 'un-Americanism,' " wrote patriotic tracts, drafted legislation, and collaborated with the FBI and the Committee on Un-American Activities. Two years later, in response to a mandate from the Legion's annual convention, to eliminate un-American propaganda activity and drive from the country all destructive "isms," Chaillaux published *ISMS: A Review of Alien Isms, Revolutionary Communism and Their Active Sympathizers in the United States*. The second edition of this book devoted 255 of its 283 pages to communism, and stated in the preface: "the greatest need at this particular time is the enlightenment of all our people to the menace of Communism."[21]

Labor

Officials of the AFL, led by Samuel Gompers (the organization's president until 1926), regularly attacked the Bolshevik seizure of power in Russia, the ensuing dictatorship, and the various Communist-created labor organizations that emerged during the 1920s. Gompers proclaimed the AFL to be a bulwark against "Bolshevism" and labeled as "Bolshevist" those who criticized his organization. In 1920, he convinced the AFL to end its affiliation with the International Federation of Trade Unions, because the latter had issued a report about the Polish invasion of the Soviet Union, which, in Gompers's view, strengthened the Soviet government.[22] In 1921, Gompers co-authored *Out of Their Own Mouths: A Revelation and an Indictment of Sovietism*, and he convinced the delegates at the AFL convention to oppose recognition of and trade with the Soviet state.[23] In the following years, state and municipal central labor unions were expressly warned that they would lose their charters if they did not strictly follow AFL principles and policies.[24]

For 10 years, between 1925 and 1935, AFL leaders waged a no-holds-barred war against "left-wing" (by which they meant Communist, not Socialist) elements in the needle-trades unions, notably the International Fur Workers. As part of this campaign, the AFL leaders formed alliances with manufacturers and the New York City police department. In December 1934, AFL president William Green testified before the Special Committee on Un-American Activities, stating that "So direct and so fundamental is the opposition and philosophies of Communism to American ideals of democracy that they cannot exist together." The movement, he said, although not sufficiently strong to constitute a danger to the United States, aims to undermine the trade-union movement by taking control of organized labor, and to create "a revolutionary organization to overthrow American economic and political institutions."[25] That same year, Green announced that the most important task facing labor in the United States was "to make war" on communism.[26] In 1935, the AFL's national convention amended its constitution to read as follows: "no organization offered or controlled by Communists or advocating the violent overthrow of our institutions, shall be allowed recognition in any Central Labor Body or State Federation of Labor."[27]

A few years later, some CIO founders—notably David Dubinsky, head of the International Ladies Garment Workers Union—fearing the growth of Communist influence in the new federation, reaffiliated their organization with the AFL. The *New Leader*, which Dubinsky's union subsidized, then became one of the AFL's most powerful anti-Communist voices.[28] In Los Angeles, the local branches of the garment, auto, rubber, and shoe workers withdrew from the city's Communist-controlled Industrial Council and formed the Los Angeles Trade Union Conference.[29]

EX-COMMUNIST ANTI-COMMUNISM

It is important, in introducing this category, to differentiate ex-Communists from ex-Soviet sympathizers. The first type comprises those persons who were members of the Communist Party and were either expelled or left the Party of their own accord. The second type identifies persons who were enamored with the 1917 revolution and the prospect of building a workers' state, but did not join the Communist Party and, at some later point, became disillusioned. Examples of ex-Soviet sympathizers include Emma Goldman and Alexander Berkman, who changed their positions as a result of the Bolshevik crushing of the Kronstadt uprising (1921); Max Eastman, who became disillusioned after attending the Thirteenth Party Congress (1924); Edmund Wilson, who abandoned his flirtation with communism after reading about the purge trials (1935–1937); and Louis Fischer, who lost faith in the movement after the signing of the German-Soviet Nonaggression Treaty (1939).

It is also important to distinguish ex-Communists from former Communists. The latter far dwarfed the former in number; nevertheless, ex-Communists, though relatively small in number, had their power multiplied by the "open-house invitation" extended to them by virtually every legislative investigating committee and administrative tribunal in the United States, especially after 1945, and what Alan Barth called "the eager credence" accorded their every allegation or accusation.[30] These ex-Communist witnesses, however, believed they were the bearers of "truth." For example, former *Daily Worker* editor Louis Budenz, who became the most ubiquitous professional witness, stated that "the most truthful people in the world are the ex-Communists."[31] Arthur Koestler, perhaps the most famous ex-Communist, wrote that "only those who have worked inside the hermetically closed regime know its true character and are in a position to convey a comprehensive picture of it."[32]

Several anti-Communists have demurred from those statements by Budenz and Koestler and have subjected ex-Communist witnesses to harsh criticism. Moving from left to right, the discussion here begins with Isaac Deutscher, who was expelled from the Communist Party of Poland and later joined a Trotskyist party in the United Kingdom. In his review of *The God That Failed*, the best-known collection of ex-Communist testimonies, Deutscher wrote that ex-Communists know least what communism is all about: Many of them were not deeply involved with the Party apparatus; most were incapable of detachment or transcendence; and they knew well only their "own sickness," not its cause or cure. Deutscher also perceived "an irrational emotionalism" in these individuals' testimony, and accused them of bringing with them to the witness stand "the lack of scruple, the narrow-mindedness, the disregard for truth, and the intense hatred with which Stalinism has imbued [them]." According to this author, ex-Communists were locked into an "inverted" Stalinism, rendering them as incapable of distinguishing Nazism from communism as they had once been incapable of differentiating fascists and social democrats.[33]

Sidney Hook, a different type of anti-Stalinist anti-Communist, in his generally favorable review of the most famous ex-Communist testament, Whittaker Chambers's *Witness*, noted that Chambers utilized the same type of logic to lump together liberals and Communists as he once used to classify liberals with fascists. In addition, Hook wrote, Chambers possessed "an intellectual impatience, a hunger for absolutes, a failure of intelligence concealed in a surge of rapture or in a total commitment to action which requires a basis in irrational belief to sustain and renew itself." Although Hook concluded that the book was very instructive about "the mortal threat of the Communist movement," he noted that Chambers's work lacked "an intelligent guide to victory or even survival."[34] (Chambers is discussed in chapter 3 and 8.)

Reinhold Niebuhr, a liberal anti-Communist, essentially concurred with Hooks's analysis. According to Nieburhr, some of those who had renounced their Communist faith "[had], in the violence of their reaction, embraced the dogmas of the extreme Right, thus exchanging creeds but not varying the spirit and temper of their approach to life's problems."[35] Richard Rovere, another liberal, bemoaned, in private, the influence of ex-Communists, whom he blamed for the "extreme and irrational positions" being taken on McCarthyism. Rovere referred to the ex-Communists as "aggrieved and unhappy people."[36]

Hannah Arendt, a moderate liberal, wrote that ex-Communists, by advising the use of totalitarian methods to fight a totalitarian enemy, had sowed mistrust and strengthened "the dangerous elements which are present in all free societies today," and which were liable to crystallize into a totalitarian form of domination.[37]

The moderately conservative President Dwight D. Eisenhower stated, in 1953:

> The Communists are a class set apart by themselves. Indeed, I think they are such liars and cheats that even when they apparently recant and later testify against someone else for his Communist convictions, my first reaction is to believe that the accused person must be a patriot or he wouldn't have incurred the enmity of such people. So even when the "reformed" Communists have proved useful in tracking down some of their old associates, I certainly look for corroborating evidence before I feel too easy in my mind about it.[38]

Finally, the staunchly conservative William S. Schlamm stated: "It is his pompous insistence on tragedy that defeats many an ex-Communist," as well as "the tacit, and sometimes not so tacit, innuendo that he alone has been chosen to save the world."[39]

As in all the unofficial anti-Communist categories, stratifications among ex-Communists can be discerned. Indeed, as Deutscher noted, this legion "[did] not march in close formation."[40] Some ex-Communists became reluctant witnesses in congressional, administrative, and judicial processes. Others became professional witnesses. Still others wrote books and articles about their experiences. A few did all three.

The first two prominent ex-Communists were Benjamin Gitlow, twice the Party's vice-presidential candidate, who had left the Party in 1929, and Walter G. Krivitsky, a high-ranking Soviet intelligence officer who defected in 1937 and came to the United States in 1938. Both Gitlow and Krivitsky testified before the Committee on Un-American Activities in 1939. That same year, Krivitsky wrote *In Stalin's Secret Service*; Gitlow's *I Confess: The Truth About American Communism* was published in 1940. Nevertheless, the heyday of the ex-Communist was still several years away.

CONSERVATIVE ANTI-COMMUNISM

Conservatism in the United States is very difficult to define precisely. In fact, Richard Hofstadter has written that the United States did not provide "a receptive home for formal conservative thought or classically conservative modes of behavior."[41] What did take root, instead, was a "practical conservatism," which was, according to Michael Paul Rogin, a "complicated" set of doctrines combining "moralism and pragmatism, moderation and extremism, 'populism' and pluralism."[42] Before 1945, Russell G. Fryer noted, in his account of modern conservatism, "an individual author or book occasionally surfaced to create interest in conservative ideas within a limited circle of disciples; but no discernible intellectual movement could be identified." Ex-President Herbert Hoover had probably been the shining example of conservative thought and action, but his response to the Great Depression discredited him and his way of thinking. The only two writers Fryer considers worth mentioning are the libertarian Albert Jay Nock and the classical liberal John Chamberlain.[43] The current idols of conservatism—Friedrich Hayek, Leo Strauss, and Willmoore Kendall—did not have extensive influence until the 1950s.

Although Fryer does not discuss anti-communism per se, it is clear that the roots of conservative (or right-wing) anti-Communism can be traced to the Bolshevik Revolution of November 1917. Nevertheless, as Patrick Allitt recently noted, the conservative critique of communism developed slowly and did not become "an obsessive concern" until after World War II.[44] Prior to that time, conservative intellectuals focused on what they perceived as the decline of culture in the United States, and conservative politicians concentrated their fire on the centralizing tendencies of the New Deal state. The Liberty League, the only significant interwar conservative organization, did not adopt an anti-Communist plank.[45]

The most prominent and effective conservative anti-Communists were the publishers of newspapers and magazines and a small group of journalists. William Randolph Hearst, in late 1934, turned his newspaper chain against the New Deal. Four years later, when J. B. Matthews testified before Dies's committee, the Hearst newspapers gave his testimony full front-page coverage. According to Louis Pizzitola, "Hearst reporters and newsreel men were immediately dispatched to cover Matthews, and they followed him with almost religious devotion for years to come."[46] Three other conservative publishers also enlisted in the anti-Communist ranks: Henry Luce (*Time, Life*), Robert McCormick (*Chicago Tribune*), and DeWitt Wallace (*Reader's Digest*).

Two of the most prominent anti-Communist journalists—Isaac Don Levine and Eugene Lyons—had evolved from leftist sympathizers of the Russian Revolution to severe conservative critics of the Soviet Union. Levine, a Russian-born journalist, covered the revolution from 1919 to 1924, and departed a foe of the Soviet Union. In 1925, he compiled an anthology, *Letters from Russian Prisons*; later, in 1932, he wrote *Red Smoke*, a critique of the first five-year plan and Stalin's dictatorship. In his memoir, Levine wrote, "During the entire Stalin era, I fought his cult with unflagging zeal in the public prints and from the lecture platform."[47] Lyons had lost his faith in the revolution after spending several years in the Soviet Union, where he contributed to *Soviet Russia Pictorial* (the magazine of the Friends of Soviet Russia, Tass (the official Soviet news agency), and United Press International. On his return, he wrote two critical accounts of Stalinist Russia: *Moscow Carrousel* (1935) and *Assignment in Utopia* (1937). The latter was one of the longest (600-plus pages) and most detailed critiques of the Soviet Union to be printed in the United States during the 1930s. Four years later, Lyons wrote *The Red Decade*. He moved steadily to the right thereafter, becoming an editor of *American Mercury* and *Reader's Digest*.[48]

Alongside these conservative anti-Communist publishers and writers, there existed, during the interwar period, an ultra-right, anti-radical, and nativist presence, whose impact and influence are difficult to measure. Regin Schmidt calculated that there some three dozen ultra-right organizations in 1919, enrolling approximately 25,000 members, and Paul Murphy stated that the number had swelled to more than 100 by the mid-1920s. Although most of these groups were very small, they enjoyed, according to Norman Hapgood, very close ties to William J. Burns, who headed the Bureau of Intelligence in the Department of Justice. In 1927, one of the largest patriotic organizations, the Daughters of the American Revolution, issued a pamphlet titled *The Common Enemy*, which linked communism, Bolshevism, socialism, liberalism, and ultra-pacifism. The same group also compiled a blacklist of 60 organizations and 200 individuals.[49] It is likely that many of these ultra-rightists supported, in the autumn of 1936, the National Union Party—a coalition of the followers of Charles Coughlin, Francis Townsend, and Gerald L. K. Smith. William Lemke, its nominee for President, stated: "I do not charge that the President of this nation is a Communist but I do charge that [Communist Party Secretary Earl] Browder, [International Ladies Garment Workers president David] Dubinsky and other Communist leaders have laid their cuckoo eggs in his Democratic nest and that he is hatching them."[50]

In addition, two individuals published materials that advanced the ultra-right cause. Between May 1920 and October 1922, Henry Ford's *Dearborn Independent* devoted 91 issues to the *Protocols of the Elders of Zion*, using them, among other purposes, to demonstrate that international communism was a "Jewish-inspired evil."[51] Ten years later, Elizabeth Dilling, following a visit to the Soviet Union, began lecturing on the evils of communism and co-founded the Paul Reveres to promote Americanism and combat communism. Her 1932 pamphlet, *Red Revolution: Do We Want It Here?*, was distributed by the Daughters of the American Revolution. Dilling then self-published two books, *Red Network* (1934) and *The Roosevelt Red Record and Its Background* (1936), in which she compiled extensive lists of "Communist" organizations and "Communists."[52]

The positions advocated by these ultra-right individuals and groups were disquieting to many. For example, Henry Steele Commager, professor of history at Columbia University, issued a warning about the "pernicious doctrines of suppression and oppression, censorship and regimentation assiduously preached by pseudo-patriotic groups" and the "treasonable activities of Red-baiters and witch-hunters, of Ku-Kluxers and Blackshirts, of vigilantes and company police." According to Commager, these groups used communism as "a bugaboo" to frighten "old ladies, timid business men and Congressional committees."[53]

LIBERAL ANTI-COMMUNISM

Liberal anti-communism, prior to 1941, was incoherent. (Indeed, liberalism per se was incoherent.) As a result, liberals did not create their own organizations, and they were divided in their responses to the Soviet purge trials and reports of Communist atrocities in Spain. Scattered liberals harbored anti-Communist feelings during the interwar decades, and left-of-liberal radical intellectuals, such as Sidney Hook and V. F. Calverton,[54] gravitated toward liberalism during the late 1930s, but none could provide liberal anti-communism with a discernible shape or theme. Insofar as one can assign a date to the starting point for an organized liberal anti-communism, it might be the Communist attack on a Socialist meeting that occurred in February 1934. The movement gathered force through the trickle of books and articles critical of the Soviet Union,[55] the Soviet purge trials, and the Spanish Civil War, and it became a significant force in late 1939, following the announcement of the German-Soviet Nonaggression Treaty.

As liberals moved toward anti-communism, they were followed by cries of betrayal from the Popular Front adherents they had left behind, who believed that fascism represented a much greater evil than Soviet communism, and who remained steadfast in their belief that the Soviet Union alone served as a bastion against the political movements then occurring in Germany and Italy. Those liberals who hesitated—such as Roger Baldwin of the American Civil Liberties Union—admitted to being confused. In his narrative of his political views during the 1930s, Baldwin used the terms "grave doubts," "naive optimism," "misplaced faith," "illusions," and "contradictions" to describe his situation. Nevertheless, he refused to be persuaded by what he called "mere political prejudice" and demanded "a lot of evidence" proving that the Soviet Union's professed goals of liberty and the conquest of poverty "had been betrayed by unyielding police power."[56] As a result of this type of thinking, many liberals refused to join the anti-Communist Committee for Cultural Freedom, because, they said, its attacks on communism and the Soviet Union divided and weakened the anti-fascist left. In fact, a significant number of liberals were among the 400 "supporters of democracy and action," who, in mid-August 1939, ridiculed the notion that the Soviet Union would sign a nonaggression treaty with Germany, and proclaimed the Soviet Union as a "bulwark against war and aggression."[57]

It is interesting to note that the two thinkers who probably had the greatest influence on the development of liberal anti-communism did not, during the 1930s, consider themselves to be liberals. John Dewey, a sharp critic of the liberal tradition, capitalist society, and the New Deal, considered himself a sort-of-socialist. He advocated a "radical" liberalism, which could, he hoped, become a "vital and courageous democratic liberalism," offering a means of avoiding "a disastrous narrowing of the issue" to the struggle between fascism and communism and a vehicle to undertake thoroughgoing changes in U.S. institutions.[58]

The Moscow trials brought Dewey wholly into the anti-Communist ranks, via the efforts of Hook, who had organized the American Defense Committee for Leon Trotsky. The Committee's Declaration of Purposes, written by Dewey, stated that the Committee was "indifferent to the political program of Trotsky" and that its goal was to establish a committee of inquiry into the charges leveled against Trotsky as "a practical [scientific] way of settling a controversy [about the credibility of the trials] which threatens the unity of the forces opposed to threatening political and social reaction."[59] Following the "investigation," Dewey, in a series of public statements made in December 1937, clearly linked the methods of the Soviet Union and those of Nazi Germany.[60] Further, Dewey stated that those liberals

who criticized the Commission's findings were engaging in "intellectual dishonesty" and "treachery to the very cause of liberalism." For
if liberalism means anything, he stated, "it means complete and courageous devotion to freedom of inquiry."[61] Dewey became the honorary
chairman of the Committee for Cultural Freedom, but resigned after
the revelation of the German-Soviet Nonaggression Treaty because
he feared that the Committee's furious attacks on the Communist
Party and its allies might lead liberals into the ranks of the equally
repugnant right-wing critics of the treaty.[62]

The other "liberal" thinker, Reinhold Niebuhr, until the mid-1930s
considered himself a Christian socialist, one who used Marxist ideas
to help explain the difficulties of social reform. In *Moral Man and
Immoral Society*, Niebuhr wrote that Marxists, for all their moral
cynicism, are "not cynical but only realistic in maintaining that

Reinhold Niebuhr, considered by many to be the intellectual progenitor of Cold
War liberalism, 1961. (Library of Congress)

disproportion of power in society is the real root of social injustice."[63] Two years later, he stated, "the liberal culture of modernity is quite unable to give guidance and direction to a confused generation which faces the disintegration of a social system and the task of building a new one," whereas a Marxist is correct "in setting the absolute demands of justice against the inequalities of the present social order [and] in believing that the destruction of economic power through collective ownership will make for a more equal justice."[64] As part of his ongoing critique of liberalism, Niebuhr regularly targeted John Dewey. In *Moral Man*, for example, he criticized Dewey's educational and moral theories for failing to do justice to "the complexities of human behavior."[65] Three years later, in his review of Dewey's *Liberalism and Social Action*, Niebuhr again criticized what he called Dewey's naive and sentimental views about human nature.[66] In sum, Niebuhr, during the 1930s, believed that liberal theory, with its reliance on rationality, weakened its adherents' ability to comprehend or confront the irrational force of fascism. Only those ideologies based on the need for power and coercive methods would suffice, he suggested.[67]

In 1935, Niebuhr contemplated the possibility of a united democratic front against international fascism, including the Communists, and he expressed his belief that, in terms of international politics, the Soviet Union was behaving in a realistic, nationalist manner. Even so, he became increasingly concerned that the Western world was becoming frozen into a fascism-versus- communism bipolarity, and he was unable to conceive of a political alternative. Fascism was the more demonic, of course, but he was concerned that neither the Socialists, liberals, nor Communists understood its essence. Thus, for the next four years, Niebuhr absented himself from secular political organizations, devoting himself to theological work and religious activity.[68]

Just as many radicals moved toward anti-Communist liberalism during the late 1930s, so a significant number of liberals gravitated toward a more conservative-based anti-communism. Two prominent way stations were available to assist them in their journeys: the magazine *Common Sense* was a refuge and haven for antiwar and non-interventionist liberals, while the magazine *New Leader* was a depot for what Ralph de Toledano called "migratory souls" departing the Communist Party and liberalism.[69]

LEFT-OF-LIBERAL ANTI-COMMUNISM

Left-of-liberal (or anti-Stalinist) anti-communism can be subdivided into four types: anarchist, sectarian, schismatic, and radical intellectual. All held in common the belief that the Soviet form of communism had debased the October 1917 revolution, distorted Marxist communism, and degraded Marx's vision of a socialist future. Richard H. Rovere estimated that the organized non-Communist left "added up to less than 10,000, . . . split into sects and factions within sects, fighting the Communists and each other like so many fraternities on a Midwestern campus."[70]

Anarchist anti-communism was most forcefully promoted by Emma Goldman and Alexander Berkman, who had become disenchanted with the Soviet Union after having been deported there from the United States. After the pair left the Soviet Union in 1921, they wrote a series of anti-Soviet books, pamphlets, and articles. (Goldman's output included *My Disillusionment in Russia* [1923], *My Further Disillusionment in Russia* [1924], and *Living My Life* [1931]; Berkman's main effort was *The Bolshevik Myth* [1925].) In her first book, Goldman wrote that she had found "reality in Russia grotesque" and living there a "ghastly experience." She described the regime as "formidable, crushing every constructive revolutionary effort, suppressing, debasing and disintegrating everything."[71] When she briefly returned to the United States in the spring of 1934, Goldman wrote an article accusing the Soviet Union of being the "most unpardonable offender" among those who "are at each other's throats" instead of the throats of their common enemies, exterminating all political opposition and engaging in wholesale character assassination. She acknowledged that Italy and Germany are equally guilty of those crimes, but noted that on the left, "the barbarity of fascism and Nazism is being condemned and fought by persons who have remained indifferent to the Golgotha of the Russian politicals . . . All these good people are under the spell of the Soviet myth."[72] Carlo Tresca, in contrast, had regarded the Communists as useful allies in the fight against fascism—at least until the Communists in Spain instituted their murderous campaigns against anarchists and syndicalists during the Spanish Civil War, at which point Tresca became a fervent anti-Communist.[73]

Sectarian anti-communism was mainly the domain of the Socialist Party of America. It had expelled its left-wing members in 1919 and, after they became the core of the new Communist Party of America, the two parties commenced bitter polemical and occasionally physical battles. John Spargo, a Socialist, wrote one of the first (and most popular) anti-Bolshevik books. On the Communist side, according to Irving Howe and Lewis Coser, "From 1928 to early 1932, the *Daily Worker*, in attacking the American Socialists, printed some of the most fantastic vituperation that can be found in any political newspaper." During those years, Communists systematically raided and broke up Socialist meetings as well.[74] In 1934, Communists worked to defeat Upton Sinclair's campaign for governor of California. Communist leader Earl Browder called the Party's assault on Sinclair "an essential feature of our struggle against social[ist]-fascism."[75] Thus it is not surprising that in the following years, when the Communists had tempered their anti-socialist polemics in the hope of building people's or popular fronts against fascism, Socialists kept their distance and criticized the methods the Communists used to control the front groups.[76]

Schismatic anti-communism consisted of those persons who had broken with, or been expelled from, the official Communist Party, but still considered themselves Communists—mainly the Lovestonites and the various Trotskyist parties. After the Comintern expelled Jay Lovestone from the CPUSA in 1929, he and his tiny group of followers founded the Communist (Opposition) Party, which they renamed the Independent Labor League of America in 1936. The Moscow trials and the Spanish Civil War transformed Lovestone from an anti-Stalinist to a full-fledged anti-Communist. He aided the United Automobile Workers' president, Homer Martin, in purging the union of Communists and then went to work for the International Ladies Garment Workers Union.[77]

The Trotskyists, who were expelled from the Communist movement for criticizing the degeneration of the Soviet Union into a centralized bureaucracy, named themselves the Communist League of America and depicted themselves as the upholders of a true road to socialism in the Soviet Union. Even though the Soviet Union was not, in their eyes, a true socialist state, they defended the October 1917 revolution and the first Bolshevik government, led by Lenin. Although it attracted a significant number of intellectuals, Trotskyism remained a small movement, regularly splitting into even smaller sects. The Communist League of America was renamed the Workers Party of the United States in 1934 and the Socialist Workers Party (SWP) in 1938.[78]

Trotskyism overlapped with the anti-communism of a small group of radical intellectuals, and the two types began to coalesce in 1933.

Several dozen radical intellectuals had become fellow travelers of the CPUSA during the early days of the Great Depression, and they joined the National Committee for the Defense of Political Prisoners (formed in 1931, as an adjunct to the Party's International Labor Defense) and the League of Professional Groups, which had been formed to support the 1932 presidential campaign of the Communists William Z. Foster and James Ford.

Following the election of 1932, many radical intellectuals became dissatisfied with the CPUSA's manipulation of these groups. Sidney Hook, perhaps the foremost U.S. scholar of Marxism at that time, said that his change of attitude was reinforced by his reading, in 1933, of Foster's *Toward Soviet America*. Hook remembered that he came to believe "that the American Communist Party, even when led by an indigenous American like Foster, was incapable of reorienting its thinking to the historic conditions and traditions of the country it inhabited."[79] Following a CPUSA-led assault on a Socialist Party rally in Madison Square Garden in February 1934, Hook and other radical intellectuals wrote an "Open Letter to American Intellectuals." In it, they urged a wholesale resignation of members from the CPUSA, claiming that the recent acts of Party leaders had provided "a lurid and unforgettable picture of the degeneration which has taken place in the Communist movement."[80] The following year, these dissidents formed the Non-Partisan Legal Defense. Many of them also joined the American Workers Party, which had been formed in late 1933 by A. J. Muste, another anti-Stalinist radical intellectual. In 1934, the American Workers Party merged with the Trotskyist Communist League of America, and the newly expanded group was renamed the Workers Party of the United States.

Two years later, another stream of anti-Stalinist intellectuals appeared, when the editors of *Partisan Review* (which had begun life as a publication of the Communist Party's New York John Reed Club) became increasingly disenchanted with the literary policy of the CPUSA and the newly created League of American Writers. A few years later, *Partisan Review* reappeared as an independent publication with a new goal: to create an independent radical cultural opposition to the CPUSA and the Popular Front. It drew its supporters and contributors mainly from the anti-Stalinist left. Although the editors and many of the contributors were sympathetic toward Trotsky, Trotsky and his followers remained critical of the publication.[81]

The Soviet purge trials (of the "Trotskyite-Zinovievite" left opposition, in August 1936, and of the "Anti-Soviet Trotskyite" right opposition, in January 1937) brought more radical intellectuals (and some liberals) to anti-Stalinism. These intellectuals formed the American Committee for the Defense of Leon Trotsky, which shortly thereafter established the Commission of Inquiry into the Charges Made Against Leon Trotsky in the Moscow Trials.[82] A few years later, Hook attempted to organize a League Against Totalitarianism, which ultimately became the Committee for Cultural Freedom. According to Hook, its function was to challenge the cultural organizations and values of the Popular Front, which were "corrupting the springs of liberal opinion" and "making a mockery of common sense."[83]

Eventually, those anti-Stalinist intellectual radicals who were associated with *Partisan Review* founded their own anti-Stalinist cultural organization, the League for Cultural Freedom and Socialism. In their inaugural statement, they proclaimed that its purpose was to meet the challenge posed to culture by "advancing reaction" and to fight for a "revolutionary reconstruction of society."

> It goes without saying that we do not subscribe to that currently fashionable catchword: "Neither communism nor fascism." On the contrary, we recognize that the liberation of culture is inseparable from the liberation of the working classes and of all humanity. Shall we abandon the ideals of revolutionary socialism because one political group, while clinging to its name, has so miserably betrayed its principles? Shall we revert to a program of middle-class democracy because the Kremlin government, in obedience to its own interests—which are no longer the interests of the Soviet people or of the masses anywhere—directs us to do so?[84]

Although the between-the-wars opposition to Stalin and Stalinists did not unite the parties or groupings of the non-Communist left, separately their members churned out a vast amount of anti-Communist material and oratory, as did the other types of unofficial anti-communism during these years. Despite the fact that anti-Communists seldom worked in tandem and regularly criticized one another, their writings and pronouncements, as a totality, helped lay a solid foundation for the two "red scares" that followed.

3

The Second "Red Scare," 1939–1941

All varieties of interwar anti-communism were strengthened by the second "red scare,"[1] which was catalyzed by the signing of the German-Soviet Nonaggression Treaty in August 1939, and which continued until German armed forces invaded the Soviet Union in June 1941. During these 22 months, the foundations were laid for the much longer and deeper third "red scare" (also known as the domestic Cold War). And yet, this second "red scare" was, to some degree, an anomaly. On the one hand, like the other two anti-Communist waves, it signaled that anti-radicalism remained a hot-button issue in U.S. politics; it occurred during a period in which anxiety prevailed about the state of the world; and it was associated with a series of unsettling strikes in major industries. On the other hand, this particular episode occurred during a time when neither the Soviet Union nor the CPUSA posed an obvious internal or external threat to the United States. No world war preceded it, nor was any armed conflict involving the United States seemingly pending. The U.S. government had declared the country's neutrality; the Soviet Union was not threatening to invade the United States or any of its allies; and the CPUSA, although critical of the Roosevelt administration's aid to Great Britain, was not speaking or acting in a disorderly fashion.

Nevertheless, official and unofficial anti-Communists utilized two acts by the Soviet Union and the CPUSA's sharp about-face in response to those acts to advance their agenda and become much better organized. The first act, the signing of the Nonaggression Treaty, which summarily repudiated the collective security policy Soviet leaders had been advocating since 1935, displayed to many a scary naked *realpolitik* (or opportunism). Then, the series of invasions Soviet leaders launched against their western neighbors, one month after the Nonaggression Treaty was signed, made the Soviet Union seem every much the aggressor that Germany, Italy, and Japan were.

When the world's Communist parties switched from an anti-fascist policy to a policy of non-intervention following the signing of the Nonaggression Treaty, virtually no one outside the ranks of the Communist Party and its orbit of fellow travelers accepted the rationale offered by Party spokespeople: Soviet leaders were forced into the treaty because the United States and the United Kingdom were trying to foment a war between Germany and the Soviet Union. Rather, the treaty was viewed as an alliance between aggressors. The subsequent acts of the Soviet Union—especially its war against Finland, which seemed to parallel the unprovoked attacks of Germany on its neighbors—merely strengthened public opinion that peace was not the goal of either signatory.

OFFICIAL ANTI-COMMUNISM

The anti-Communists in the U.S. government took particular advantage of the Nonaggression Treaty. The Special Committee on Un-American Activities subpoenaed CPUSA leaders Earl Browder and William Z. Foster, as well as the ex-Communist Benjamin Gitlow and the Soviet defector Walter Krivitsky. During his questioning of Gitlow, Dies stated: "Now that Russia and Germany are allies, 100,000 Communist party members might combine with Nazis to perform sabotage and espionage if we went to war with Russia and Germany were on the same side."[2] In October 1939, Dies released the names of 563 U.S. government employees who were members of the American League for Peace and Democracy and demanded that they be prosecuted as Comintern agents. His committee's second annual report (released in January 1940) identified the CPUSA as a branch of the Soviet Union, declaring that the group operated in the United States as "a foreign conspiracy marked as a political party." A significant portion of the committee's third report (released in January 1941) alleged that the Soviet Union was masterminding a plan for Communist control of the labor movement as a means to undertake a violent overthrow of the government.[3]

A few months later, in April 1941, the Dies committee issued 90 subpoenas for production of evidence (*duces tecum*)—50 for leaders of the CPUSA and 40 for leaders of Nazi and fascist groups. "We want," he said, "to get all the facts concerning these organizations" as a means of constructing "a comprehensive picture of what these groups are doing."[4] Committee member J. Parnell Thomas (Republican–New Jersey), during his questioning of Party leader Earl Browder, put matters bluntly: "It seems to me that the New Deal has been working hand in glove with the Communist Party." Two months later, Thomas accused the Roosevelt administration of hampering the committee's work, because it has "so often made itself the official or unofficial sponsor of the very Communist groups which the Committee is trying to investigate."[5]

Other members of Congress used the German-Soviet treaty as a motive for attacking the National Labor Relations Board (NLRB), which had played a major role in the establishment and survival of industrial unions, and was widely rumored to employ a significant number of Communists. It had come under attack from a host of anti-Communists (e. g., Father Charles Coughlin, the American Federation of Labor (AFL), every major business organization, conservative Democrats and Republicans). In 1939, one of those conservative Democrats, Representative Howard Smith of Virginia, launched an investigation of the NLRB. Although some reputed "Reds" resigned from the NLRB later the next year, members of the House Appropriations Committee promised a thorough investigation of "left-wing influences" on the organization. Several NLRB lawyers either left on their own accord or were pushed out, but some remained in place.[6]

In late 1939, Congress passed the Hatch Act, barring federal government employees from belonging to organizations advocating the overthrow of "our constitutional form of government in the United States." Congress also included a clause in an appropriation bill, which precluded the awarding of any relief funds to persons who advocated, or who were members of, an organization that advocated, the overthrow of the government of the United States through force or violence. In early 1940, Congress restored the Espionage Act of 1917. The Department of Justice launched a prosecution against Earl Browder and two other Communist Party officials for passport violations. (Browder was convicted and sentenced to a four-year prison term, but President Roosevelt commuted his sentence in May 1942.)[7] The U.S. Attorney General also approved the prosecution of California CPUSA leader William Schneiderman for allegedly lying on his citizenship application, and several Communist labor union officials were arrested.

In reality, all of the aforementioned acts were mere pinpricks compared to the Alien Registration Act (commonly referred to as the Smith Act), an omnibus anti-Communist bill that became law (and the keystone in the arch of official anti-communism in the United States) in May 1940. As a result of the low public opinion of the CPUSA, the bill's debate and enactment generated no significant opposition inside or outside of Congress. This act required the mandatory registration and fingerprinting of all resident aliens; it facilitated the deportation of anyone who challenged the armed forces; and it made it unlawful for any person:

> (1) to knowingly or willfully advocate, abet, advise, or teach the duty, necessity, desirability, or propriety of overthrowing or destroying any government in the United States by force or violence . . . ;
> (2) with the intent to cause the overthrow or destruction of any government in the United States to print, publish, edit, issue, circulate, sell, distribute, or publicly display any printed or written matter advocating [said overthrow . . . ;
> (3) to organize or help to organize any society, group, or assembly of persons who teach, advocate, or encourage [said overthrow]; or to be or become a member of, or affiliate with, any such society, group, or assembly of persons, knowing the purposes thereof.[8]

Although the Alien Registration Act included most of the provisions of the failed anti-Communist bills of the 1930s, it did not fully satisfy a significant number of Congressional members who wanted to impose additional penalties on Communists. The Selective Service Act, passed in September 1940, contained the express wish of Congress that employers not hire Communists or German-American Bundists to fill job vacancies caused by conscription. In October of that same year, Congress passed the Voorhis Act, requiring all organizations with international ties to register with the Department of Justice and provide information on their meeting places, activities, propaganda, officers, and contributors. It also passed a Nationality Act empowering the executive branch to denaturalize any former alien who was a Communist and disallowing the naturalization applications of anyone who had, within the previous 10 years, belonged to an organization advocating the violent overthrow of any government in the United States. Congress also gave the U.S. Attorney General the authority to order the dissolution of any of those organizations he considered to be national security threats.

The executive branch contributed to the anti-Communist sentiment as well. According to former U.S. Attorney General Robert Jackson, following the Nonaggression Treaty, President Roosevelt became "very anti-Communist—militantly so."[9] In February 1940, Roosevelt issued an executive order giving the FBI full control over all espionage matters. Later that year, the president authorized the U.S. Attorney General to order wiretaps for agencies investigating subversives.[10] FBI Director Hoover took full advantage of these presidential directives. He informed Roosevelt that FBI agents had collected "identifying data relating to more than ten million persons," and that in the event of a national security emergency, if it became necessary to detain or intern any person deemed to be a national security threat, this information would "make such action readily doable."[11] Hoover also regularly claimed that every slowdown or strike at a defense plant was instigated by Communists.[12] As Hoover's agency ramped up to fight the perceived Communist threat, between 1936 and 1945, the number of FBI agents increased from 609 to 4,730, and its support staff increased from 971 to 7,442.[13]

At the same time, the Department of Justice was responding vigorously to suspected Communist activity in the labor movement. Attorney General Jackson accused Communists of provoking two defense-industry strikes: against Vultee Aircraft in late 1940 and against Allis-Chalmers in January 1941. His successor, Francis Biddle, ordered the deportation of the West Coast longshoremen union's leader, Harry Bridges,[14] and accused Communists of provoking a strike against North American Aviation in June 1941. In early June 1941, after Congress appropriated $100,000 to be used "exclusively" for the investigation of federal employees who were members of "subversive" organizations or groups advocating the overthrow of any government, the U.S. Attorney General created its first list of subversive organizations. Eight organizations were so named. One year later, 12 Communist groups, 14 native and foreign fascist groups, and 21 Japanese groups were listed. Although it was supposed to be kept secret, a copy of this list was leaked to the Dies committee.[15]

In June 1941, the Department of Justice employed, for the first time, the Alien Registration Act—albeit not against the act's intended target. The occasion for its use was an internal union dispute. Members of Minneapolis Local 544 of the International Brotherhood of Teamsters (AFL), who were dissatisfied with the leadership of International Teamsters' President Daniel Tobin, had voted to affiliate with the CIO. In an effort to support Tobin, who was a backer of President Roosevelt, federal agents raided the headquarters of the Socialist

Workers Party (SWP) in Minneapolis and St. Paul, on the pretext that the local's leaders were members of the SWP. The agents seized all the printed material in the party's offices. The next day, July 1, a federal grand jury indicted 26 of the union's members, alleging that they were in violation of an 1861 seditious conspiracy statute as well as the Alien Registration Act. Eighteen of those indicted were convicted of violating the Alien Registration Act and were given prison sentences ranging from 1 year to 16 months.[16] The Supreme Court chose not to review the convictions.

Perhaps the most massive anti-Communist effort undertaken by the federal government in the run-up to World War II was the broad surveillance of refugees from Nazi-occupied countries, all of whom were regarded as enemy aliens, Communists, or fellow travelers. Dossiers were compiled by the FBI, Immigration and Naturalization Service, Office of Censorship, Department of State, Office of Naval Intelligence, Military Intelligence Division, Un-American Activities Committee, and, once the United States joined the war effort, the Foreign Nationalities Branch of the Office of Strategic Services.[17]

Official anti-communism also received strong boosts from state governments. One state (New York) excluded from state employment any person advocating the forceful overthrow of the government. Another state (Oklahoma) used its criminal syndicalist law to arrest 14 CPUSA leaders. Four state legislatures (in New York, California, Oklahoma, and Colorado) created un-American or subversive activities investigating committees. The New York Board of Higher Education declared members of Communist, Nazi, and fascist organizations unfit for employment, and the University of California Board of Regents declared that Communist Party membership was incompatible with faculty status.[18] Many state legislatures (25, according to William Z. Foster; 15, according to Robert Justin Goldstein) barred Communist Party candidates from the 1940 ballot.[19]

UNOFFICIAL ANTI-COMMUNISM

During the two months before the German-Soviet Nonaggression Treaty was signed, it was business as usual for the traditional institutional anti-Communists. Henry Monsky, president of B'nai B'rith, stated that Communism is "equally as hateful and dangerous" as Nazism and fascism. Two weeks later, Los Angeles Archbishop John J. Cantwell appealed to a group of Catholic women to devote all their possible time and energy to fighting communism and the other evils threatening religion and democracy. (He did not mention Nazism or fascism.) Also, on August 15, 1939, at the 21st Annual Departmental Convention of the American Legion, Major-General David P. Barrows (U.S. Army, retired) announced: "To all Communists . . . If you start any rough stuff, such as you did in Europe, we shall kill you first."[20]

These and other anti-Communist institutions simply intensified their assaults after the Nonaggression Treaty was announced. For example, the Association of Catholic Trade Unionists (ACTU), which had not previously pursued a policy of militant factionalism or schism within the unions to which its members belonged, increased that activity. In November 1939, it supported an anti-Communist slate for election to leadership positions in the Transport Workers Union; in 1941, it did likewise in the United Electrical, Radio and Machine Workers of America. Its main tactic, however, the Association of Catholic Trade Unionists was the creation of "conferences" within Communist-controlled unions. This method had first been proposed, in late 1938, as a means of better organizing the struggle against Communists, to "fight fire [Communist fractions] with fire [ACTU conferences]."[21]

Non- and anti-Communists in the CIO, in response to the Communists' attacks on the Roosevelt administration's foreign policy, openly began to distance themselves and their organizations from the Communists in their organization. Sidney Hillman, head of the Amalgamated Clothing Workers of America, criticized the CPUSA's role in the CIO, and he hinted that his union might leave if Communist influence was not curtailed.[22] In late August 1940, the United Automobile Workers (UAW) union approved a resolution that condemned "the brutal dictatorships and wars of aggression of the totalitarian governments of Germany, Italy, Russia and Japan." UAW executive Walter Reuther declared the Popular Front dead—"put in the ash can once and for all"—as a result of the deal between Stalin and Hitler. A few months later, at a CIO executive board meeting, John L. Lewis made anti-Communist remarks. He then abolished the position of West Coast Director, held by the longshoremen's leader Harry Bridges; replaced, as CIO organizational director, the moderate anti-Communist John Brophy with the more aggressive Allan Haywood; and authorized an effort to end Communist control of the International Woodworkers of America. At the CIO's 1940 national convention, a resolution was passed condemning Nazism, fascism, and communism, characterizing them "as inimical to the welfare of labor, and destructive of our form of government."[23] The American Federation of Teachers expelled four Communist-led locals in New York and Philadelphia, and left-wingers lost their positions in the American Newspaper Guild. In addition, New York's American Labor Party voted to remove from office all known Communists and their sympathizers.

The situation might have been even worse, except that Communists in the CIO decided to avoid open breaks by not strongly advocating the new Communist Party position.[24] Len De Caux, the public relations director of the CIO (and member of the CPUSA), likened the atmosphere in the CIO at this time to the mood that prevailed during "the later Cold War hysteria."[25]

The Nonaggression Treaty also catalyzed the transformation of Whittaker Chambers from former Communist to ex-Communist. Chambers had become a writer for *Time* in 1939, where he was, according to Alan Brinkley, "savagely" and "harshly" anti-Communist in everything he wrote, and he was "particularly vicious in writing about the work of left-leaning intellectuals."[26] After reading about the treaty, however, Chambers decided to inform someone in the U.S. government about Communists or fellow travelers in the government who had been (and still were), according to Chambers, serving the interests of the Soviet Union. He spoke to Isaac Don Levine, who tried to get Chambers an appointment with President Roosevelt. Marvin McIntyre, the White House Appointments Secretary, told them to see Assistant Secretary of State Adolf Berle, Jr., who oversaw intelligence affairs. At that September 1939 meeting, Chambers claimed that he named 18 past and present "agents."[27]

Berle, however, in a journal entry following the publication of Chambers's book *Witness*, noted that Chambers's account of what had transpired on the night of September 2, 1939, "is not in detail inaccurate, but the whole impression is wrong." According to Berle's account, Chambers was a very poor "witness" that night: "he did not state anything he told me as personal knowledge," but only as hearsay.

> He did not even remotely indicate that he personally had been engaged in the operation. He did not charge individuals with espionage—they were merely "sympathizers" who would be hauled out later when the great day came. . . . Further, under cross-examination, he qualified everything to the point of substantial withdrawal.[28]

Although no new conservative anti-Communist groups formed in the aftermath of the Nonaggression Treaty, conservative

anti-communism was in the process of being fortified by two important writers, on their way from Trotskyism to the *National Review*.
Max Eastman, in his 1938 comments on the CPUSA's new
constitution, noted that it sealed "the victory of Stalinism over the Bolshevik program and prepared the way for "an American totalitarianism." Therefore, he concluded, "liberals who give support or
tolerance to the Communist Party . . . are aiding in propagation of
the Totalitarian State of Mind, which should be the chief enemy."[29]
James Burnham joined the totalitarian camp in 1941, writing that the
world was undergoing a "managerial revolution," and suggesting that
those nations (Russia, Germany, and Italy) "which have advanced fur-
thest toward the managerial social structure are all of them, at present,
totalitarian dictatorships."[30]

Liberal anti-Communists organized in a fitful manner after the
announcement of the Nonaggression Treaty. Many of the liberals
who streamed out of the Popular Front groups joined the William
Allen White Committee to Defend America by Aiding the Allies.
However, this organization was not pro-labor enough for some of its
members, and, in May 1941, they defected and joined with other leftists to form the Union for Democratic Action (UDA). According to
James Loeb, Jr., one of its founders, UDA was established because of
dissatisfaction with the White Committee's conservatism and
its narrow focus on intervention. The UDA founders wanted an
organization that would fight for democracy at home as well as
abroad.[31]

The UDA's main energizing force was Reinhold Niebuhr, whose
thinking had been completely altered by the Nonaggression Treaty
and the German offensive against Western Europe. Disgusted with
the isolationism of the Socialist Party, he resigned from it and became
an outspoken advocate for all aid to the Allies short of war. Because
the founders of UDA all had experience of the disruptive tactics Communist fractions used to control organizations and the lock-step manner in which the CPUSA followed the Moscow line, they specifically
excluded Communists from UDA membership. Niebuhr wrote, in
May 1940: "I have myself worked in dozens of organizations with
Communists, but their present orientation is so completely under the
control of Russian policy that I will not again knowingly have
anything to do with any organization in which they function."
Niebuhr was elected UDA's first chairman, and he worked tirelessly
on its behalf.[32] In fact, according to Arthur Schlesinger, Jr., it was the

combination of Niebuhr's personality and writing that "helped accomplish in a single generation a revolution in the basis of American liberal thought."[33]

That same year, another liberal group, the American Civil Liberties Union, banned from its governing committee or staff any person "who is a member of any political organization which supports totalitarian dictatorship in any country, or who by his public declarations indicates his support of such a principle." The board immediately put this policy into effect by expelling Elizabeth Gurley Flynn, one of the ACLU founders, who was a member of the CPUSA.[34]

For the most part, anti-Stalinist anti-Communists condemned the German-Soviet Nonaggression Treaty and the subsequent Soviet invasions of Poland, Estonia, Latvia, Lithuania, and Finland. The only significant defections were those members of the Socialist Workers Party who accepted Leon Trotsky's pronouncement that these invasions were the revolutionary acts of a workers' state, which every genuine Marxist-Leninist must support. Ultimately, approximately half of the membership refused to defend the Soviet Union, condemned it as a bureaucratic collectivist state, and left to form the Workers Party.[35] Jay Lovestone dissolved his oppositional Communist organization at the end of 1940, and publicly stated the following year that the CPUSA is "nothing more than a foreign agency of the Stalin dictatorship in Russia."[36] Socialist Party leader Norman Thomas challenged Browder to repudiate the Soviet invasion of Finland or "stand branded as Stalin's stooge," and Thomas also joined in the effort to purge the board of the American Civil Liberties Union of Communists and fellow travelers.[37]

The two left-wing anti-Communist groups formed prior to the announcement of the Nonaggression Treaty—Sidney Hook's League for Cultural Freedom and the *Partisan Review*'s Committee for Cultural Freedom—did not unite. The members of the latter group, although they condemned Popular Front anti-fascism, insisted that only an international "militant struggle for socialism" could defeat fascism.[38] Hook claimed that this organization housed "radical intellectuals disillusioned with Stalin but still in the Leninist orbit."[39]

An assorted group of leftists, whom James Wechsler referred to as "popular-front intellectuals," had a difficult time finding a resting place after the Nonaggression Treaty. According to Wechsler, they were pushed less by the pact than "by the utterances of the American Communist Party, the succession of ambiguous, frequently conflicting, but no less dogmatic statements which streamed out of party headquarters in the days after the signing of the pact." They were, he recalled, "almost unanimous in feeling that the party had been reduced to the role of a social secretary for Moscow, sending out apologies for its employer's antics without any comprehension of what they meant." The result, Wechsler, noted, was the appearance of "a new kind of refugee—the homeless radical." He noted that several of these orphans were "tentatively groping toward a new alignment, a loose, flexible body comparable to the 'New Beginnings' group which emerged in post-Hitler Germany, socialist in ultimate objective but committed to no orthodox doctrine or to any International."[40] Wechsler and several other "homeless radicals" met in October and November 1939 , but they failed in their goal to organize an independent left.[41] According to Richard Rovere, they could not overcome their "heritage of bitterness and distrust."[42]

The Nonaggression Treaty also provided an impetus to academic anti-Communism, in the form of a collective, totalitarian condemnation of it, fascism, and Nazism.[43] In late 1939, the American Philosophical Society sponsored a symposium on totalitarianism. The Soviet Union, fascist Italy, and Nazi Germany were all labeled as totalitarian states by one of the contributors.[44] That same year, Peter F. Drucker remarked, in *The End of Economic Man*, that the Soviet Union, in the preceding few years, had adopted "one purely totalitarian and fascist principle after the other."[45]

CONCLUSION

Although the second "red scare" damaged the reputation of the Communist Party, it did not wreck it, mainly because the scare lasted less than two years. In addition, the Soviet Union, though it had left itself open to anathematizing, was not perceived as a threat to U.S. national security, and there were too many other domestic "subversives" who seemed to be more immediate threats than the CPUSA. In addition, for most of that period, the FBI and the Dies committee were rivals in a contest to expose espionage. In fact, the Roosevelt administration publicly rebuked Dies's efforts to raise the Special Committee's investigative status to that of the FBI. It was only at the end of 1940 that U.S. Attorney General Robert Jackson arranged a deal between the Special Committee and the FBI to exchange information.[46] Nevertheless, Dies's targeting of the motion picture industry, the Alien Registration Act, and Hoover's enlarged FBI and lists of "subversives" provided a secure foundation for the much more effective official anti-Communist effort to come.

Unofficial anti-communism was strengthened as conservatives and nongovernment organizations became more determined critics of the Soviet Union and opponents of the CPUSA, and liberals began forming their own non- (and usually anti-) Communist organizations. On the surface, at least, this "red scare" declined in force during the second half of 1941, following the German invasion of the Soviet Union. In July 1941, the leaders of the Soviet Union and the United Kingdom signed a mutual assistance pact; in September of the same year, President Roosevelt extended lend-lease aid to the Soviet Union. Five months later, following the Japanese attack on Pearl Harbor, the three countries joined together in a Grand Alliance against the Axis. The CPUSA line changed dramatically, and Communists became among the strongest supporters of the war effort.

4

World War II

OFFICIAL ANTI-COMMUNISM

Despite the Grand Alliance (the United States, the United Kingdom, and the Soviet Union) and the hyperpatriotic stance of the CPUSA, congressional and legislative investigating committees—the engines of previous "red scares"—did not go into hibernation during World War II.

Although he scheduled few public hearings and did not appear at any of them, Martin Dies, the chairman of the Special Committee on Un-American Activities, produced and issued annual reports on communism.[1] In its published annual report for 1944, the Special Committee provided an appendix listing 245 "Communist-Front Organizations" and 344 pages of the names of people (more than 20,000) who had signed petitions, sponsored organizations, or appeared on letterheads. (Eleanor Roosevelt, President Franklin Roosevelt's wife, appeared on the list 20 times.[2]) The committee also compiled a 30-volume report on the subject of communism in Hollywood, which it did not make public.[3] Dies's particular targets were the CIO, CIO Political Action Committee (CIO-PAC), Union for Democratic Action, and "Communist sympathizers" in the Roosevelt administration. He targeted the Office of Price Administration, Federal Communications Commission, Office of Civilian Defense, and Board of Economic Warfare. Following one of his public disclosures that security risks were employed in these agencies and departments, conservatives in the House of Representatives mounted a campaign to deny salaries to those people named by Dies. In response, Roosevelt issued an Executive Order setting up an interdepartmental committee to handle complaints of subversive activity, and Democrats in the House moved to establish a subcommittee of the Appropriations Committee to do likewise.[4]

In 1944, when Dies decided not to run for reelection, his staff director, J. B. Matthews, prevailed upon him to authorize the publication of all the files Matthews had collected. Seven thousand sets of Matthews's 7-volume work, containing some 22,000 names of individuals and organizations, was published. Because of the raw, undifferentiated nature of this list, the Special Committee later formally withdrew it from circulation and tried to curtail its distribution.[5]

Dies's mantle as Congress's leading anti-Communist was quickly assumed by others. That autumn, Senator Pat McCarran (Democrat–Nevada), who would subsequently sponsor or usher through more anti-Communist legislation than any other member of Congress, used dramatic language to emphasize his anti-Communist stance: "Communism is not just knocking at the door of our democracy—it is using a battering ram on the portal of our democratic house."[6] In the other chamber, Congressman John Rankin (Democrat–Mississippi) would push through a resolution making the Un-American Activities Committee permanent.[7]

Although the executive branch relaxed its strident anti-communism, the Department of Justice and the FBI remained on the alert. The U.S. Attorney General's list of Communist-front or Communist-controlled organizations, which became a potent weapon of the third "red scare," was distributed to the heads of executive branch departments in May 1942. At the same time, the Special War Policies Unit, which had been created to investigate suspect groups, had finished its examination of nearly 300 such groups. At the end of 1942, it recommended that any applicant for citizenship who admitted to membership in any of 180 "leftist" or 75 "rightist" groups named by the Special War Policies Unit should be carefully scrutinized.[8] Nevertheless, the Attorney General did not wield the Alien Registration Act against the CPUSA. For its part, the FBI continued to compile its own lists of known or suspected Communists. In late 1942, Hoover authorized a massive investigation of the motion picture industry, titled "Communist Infiltration—Motion Picture Industry" (COMPIC), and a few months later, he ordered the Los Angeles office to compile a list of all employees of the industry who were members of the Communist Party or front groups.[9]

The Supreme Court, just before the war ended, delivered an opinion that seemed to promise it would continue to pay strict attention to procedural defects in deportation cases. In *Bridges v. Wixon*, the

Court, by a 5-3 majority, overturned the Attorney General's order to deport Harry Bridges for being affiliated with and a member of the Communist Party. Justice William O. Douglas wrote that the Attorney General had given to the term "affiliation" "a looser and more expansive meaning than the statute permits." Regarding the finding of "membership," Douglas found errors in the admission of evidence to that effect. Eleven years would pass before another justice would note and discount, as Douglas did, a record showing "little more than a course of conduct which reveals cooperation with Communist groups for the attainment of wholly lawful objectives."[10]

Midway through the war, the Court decided another deportation case of potentially greater scope. It is worth discussing at length, because of what Justice Frank Murphy said in his majority opinion. William Schneiderman, the leader of the California state unit of the CPUSA, had become a citizen in 1927, while he was a member of two Communist organizations. In 1939, the Department of Justice sought to cancel his citizenship, charging him with violating the 1906 Naturalization Act. Schneiderman was accused of fraudulently swearing his belief in the principles of the Constitution of the United States, because when he took the oath he was a member of an organization advocating and teaching disbelief in or opposition to organized government.

Justice Murphy began his majority opinion by noting the "possible relation of this case to freedom of thought" and dismissing the materiality of "our relations with Russia, as well as our views regarding its government and the merits of communism." The Court, he continued, should have "a jealous regard" for Schneiderman's rights and should let its judgment "be guided so far as the law permits by the spirit of freedom and tolerance in which our nation was founded, and by a desire to secure the blessings of liberty in thought and action to all those upon whom the right of American citizenship has been conferred by statute."[11]

Murphy then stated that the 1906 law "should be construed as far as is reasonably possible in favor of the citizen," especially when the charge of fraud was made long after the certificate of citizenship was granted and the citizen had, in the interim, violated no laws. Thus, Murphy continued, the government bears a "heavy burden": it must prove lack of attachment to the principles of the Constitution by "clear, unequivocal, and convincing" evidence.

Murphy next made several key points, which would be disregarded two years later: "Under our traditions, beliefs are personal, and not a matter of mere association, and that men, in adhering to a political party or other organization, notoriously do not subscribe unqualifiedly to all of its platforms or asserted principles." The difficulty of the government's attempt at "proof by imputation" is "increased by the fact that there is, unfortunately, no absolutely accurate test of what a political party's principles are." Murphy held that the Communist Party is not so different in this respect than other parties, and that there is "a material difference between agitation and exhortation calling for present violent action which creates a clear and present danger of public disorder or other substantive evil and mere doctrinal justification or prediction of the use of force under hypothetical conditions at some indefinite future time."[12]

UNOFFICIAL ANTI-COMMUNISM

The ranks of ex-Communists were enhanced when two significant Soviet defectors went public during World War II: Jan Valtin [Richard Julius Herman Krebs], a Soviet secret police operative who had defected in 1938, and wrote *Out of the Night* (1941), and Victor Kravchenko, a CPUSSR Commissar and member of the Soviet Purchasing Committee, who defected in 1944, and wrote several newspaper articles about the Soviet Union. (Two years later, he also wrote the memoir *I Chose Freedom: The Personal and Political Life of a Soviet Official*.) The FBI interviewed Whittaker Chambers twice during the war (May 1942 and June 1945), but it did not make his accusations against supposed Communists public, and Chambers also remained silent on the subject.[13]

Conservative anti-Communists were divided. Some, like Herbert Hoover, continued to oppose U.S. involvement in the European war because of their belief that the alliance between the United States and the Soviet Union had transformed the war from one defending democracy to one aiding a totalitarian country. Hoover, in September 1945, criticized his fellow conservatives for being "unorganized and impotent."[14] Conservatives in Congress did not offer much opposition to the extension of lend-lease funding to the Soviet Union in 1941, nor again in the spring and summer of 1943, but they sharply criticized the Roosevelt administration's "wasteful and inefficient" handling of this program, which some of them linked to the administration's grandiose plans for the role of the United States in the postwar world. They also announced their opposition to the use of lend-lease money for postwar reconstruction. Some conservative newspapers called on the

Roosevelt administration to cease underwriting Soviet imperialism.[15] Although many Republicans voiced their suspicions about the intentions of the Soviet Union, the 1944 Republican platform made no mention of it, and Thomas Dewey, the party's presidential candidate, spoke little about foreign policy during his campaign. However, John Bricker, his running mate, named seven U.S. government employees, whose "subversive records . . . conclusively prove that Franklin Roosevelt and the New Deal are in the hands of radicals and the Communists."[16]

Conservative intellectuals, as usual, spoke in diverse ways. William Henry Chamberlin softened his usual criticism in *The Russian Enigma* (1943), while Friedrich A. Hayek's *The Road to Serfdom*, which became one of the fundamental texts of postwar conservatism, did not single out the Soviet Union as a particular threat. In fact, Hayek's greatest fear was that the United States, by unconsciously abandoning the classical liberal world of economic freedom and respect for the individual in favor of a planned economy, was blindly following the example of Germany and marching toward totalitarianism.[17]

In contrast, two conservative intellectuals, Max Eastman and William C. Bullitt, regularly sounded alarms about the Communist threat. Eastman, now writing for the conservative *Reader's Digest*, had warned, in the week following the Japanese attack on Pearl Harbor, that the Soviet Union remained a totalitarian state and support for its struggle against Nazi Germany should not be allowed to obscure its totalitarian essence. He repeated this warning in 1943. Moreover, in an article he co-wrote in June 1945, Eastman proclaimed that China had become the site of a coming showdown between a democratic United States and a "totalitarian Russia."[18]

Bullitt, a former U.S. Ambassador to the Soviet Union, sent Roosevelt a series of messages during the war warning the administration not to trust the CPUSA or Soviet leaders. Shortly after the German invasion, Bullitt wrote the following words: "Communists in the United States are just as dangerous enemies as ever, and should not be allowed to crawl into our productive mechanism." Eighteen months later, he issued another warning: "Stalin places first the welfare of the Soviet State and treads softly, therefore, in extending Communism to other countries; but there is no evidence that he has abandoned either the policy of extending Communism or the policy of controlling all foreign Communist parties."[19]

In 1944, in an article he wrote for *Life* magazine, Bullitt warned about Soviet designs on Europe. In a subtle piece, in which he used the expectations and hopes of "Italians" and "Romans" as his vehicle, Bullitt warned about the impending Soviet domination of Eastern Europe and its designs on Western countries. "There are many signs in Italy," Bullitt wrote, "that if the British and ourselves pull out prematurely the Soviet government will step in." One of those signs was the activities of the well-funded and -organized Italian Communist Party. Bullitt was also one of the first to sound the apocalyptic warning that became a mantra of conservative anti-Communists: the fight in Italy, he claimed, was actually a struggle over "the deepest moral issue of the modern world—the issue of man as a son of God with an immortal soul, an end in himself, against man as a chemical compound, the tool of an omnipotent state, an end in itself."[20] Finally, in 1945, in *The Great Globe Itself*, Bullitt publicly attacked Roosevelt's foreign policy.

The editors of *Life* magazine took a less-apocalyptic stance. They acknowledged that the Soviet Union represented "the no. 1 problem" for the United States, but they also noted that most Americans did not wish to resolve that problem by going to war. The editors recommended that the United States meet this challenge by a policy of good deeds internationally and "our economic power of persuasion." They did not mention domestic communism.[21]

Institutional anti-communism was bolstered by the FBI's "contact programs" with the American Legion, Knights of Columbus, Veterans of Foreign Wars, Boy Scouts of America, American Bar Association, and B'nai B'rith. These organizations agreed to collect information and submit reports.[22] The Association of Catholic Trade Unionists (ACTU), although it had largely abandoned its organizing and educating activities, increased its attacks against the left and drew closer to the American Federation of Labor.[23] Father Charles Rice, the leader of the ACTU in Pittsburgh, wrote, shortly after the German invasion of the Soviet Union:

> We may expect the Communists to execute another brazen about-face. They will be super-patriots. . . . I solemnly warn the workers of the Pittsburgh district to have nothing to do with Communists or their stooges. . . . We must, for the good of America and the trade union movement, absolutely refuse to co-operate with them or their stooge organizations.[24]

Rice then unsuccessfully attempted to help "some of the old-timers" at Westinghouse Local 601 (of the United Electrical Workers) prevent the "Stalinites" from taking control. Rice later said, "During the war few would listen to me."[25]

In Baltimore, Father John F. Cronin, another active labor priest who had, before the war, lectured on economics and established Schools of Social Action in Baltimore and Washington, D.C., wrote an article telling Catholics how to identify Communists in the labor movement and how to deal with them once they were identified. In 1942, he was drawn, by both anti-Communists and the FBI, into a faction fight in a Baltimore local of the Industrial Union of Marine and Shipbuilding Workers. Although Cronin's efforts were unsuccessful there, later that year he won the support of a conference of Catholic clergy for his plan to combat communism in the labor movement.[26] In 1943, he wrote an article calling domestic Communists a "Second Front menace"; the next year, he authored an article identifying specific shipyards and defense factories as having Communist employees. At the end of 1944, Cronin was asked by the Social Action Department of the Church's National Catholic Welfare Conference to undertake a study of the spread of communism in the United States. He sent questionnaires to every diocese in the United States, consulted the seven volumes compiled by Matthews for the Dies committee, and received information from the FBI. In his "Tentative Confidential Report," Cronin stated that communism, both at home and abroad, "is a serious threat to the Catholic Church and to the welfare of the United States."[27]

Two of the most prominent Catholic Church spokesmen, Monsignors Sheen and Walsh, had decided, for the sake of the war effort, to substantially lessen their anti-Soviet remarks. Nevertheless, Sheen, in a series of "Catholic Hour" broadcasts approving the wartime alliance, continued to criticize the Soviet form of government and its ideology.[28] Walsh, at a December 1944 conference on United States Soviet Union relations, stated that the ideology of the Bolshevik revolution had not been modified by the war, but rather was "only now entering its most important external phase." One month later, he predicted that the leaders of the Soviet Union would be embarking on an expansionist agenda, absorbing territory, widening their sphere of influence, and coordinating a worldwide campaign via "instructed national groups."[29]

On its own, without the goading of the ACTU, an anti-communism wave in the labor movement was gaining ground. CIO president Philip Murray made several behind-the-scenes moves to weaken Communist influence, and Sidney Hillman tried to convince the Roosevelt administration to pass a law barring Communists from employment in the defense industries.[30] A growing number of union members, especially in CIO unions, resented the Communist Party's "no-strike" pledge and its support of wage scales based on piece-work.

For their part, AFL leaders began to position the federation to play an expanded role in fighting communism overseas. In 1943, the Executive Council created an International Labor Relations Commission; the following year, it established a Free Trade Union Committee. The latter group was directed to provide funds to the workers in the liberated countries of Europe who were organizing "free democratic trade unions." Former Communist Jay Lovestone headed both of these groups. One of Lovestone's associates from his United Auto Workers days, Irving Brown, was authorized to open AFL offices in Paris and Brussels.[31]

Liberals, like conservatives, were divided in their responses to the war. A liberal anti-Communist group, the Union for Democratic Action (UDA), had been established in the spring of 1941 as an antifascist, non-Communist group to support the lend-lease program and the British war effort. After the German invasion of the Soviet Union, however, most UDA members supported the new alliance between the Soviet Union and the United States and hoped that it would continue after victory over the Axis. Even so, they refused to build a political alliance with the CPUSA, and Reinhold Niebuhr urged members not to abandon "the process of eliminating Communism from union leadership and from all organizations which stand on the left wing of democracy."[32]

Another group of liberals, who had been advocating direct military participation by the United States, established Freedom House in October 1941. After the United States entered World War II, this organization became a center of information and assistance for those who believed that the Communists were, under the cloak of patriotism, infiltrating a wide variety of organizations. At the war's end, Freedom House strongly advocated taking a very firm stance against Soviet demands and established itself as a symbol and center for the fight against totalitarianism abroad and for freedom and democracy at home.[33]

Finally, in 1944, a group of New York City liberals, led by labor leaders David Dubinsky and Alex Rose, along with Reinhold Niebuhr, left the American Labor Party (ALP), to found the Liberal Party of New York. They took this step because they believed that the ALP was being pushed sharply leftward by pro-Communist labor leaders. The new party was envisioned as "a genuinely independent outlet for political action, free of the two major parties, and of the Communists as well."[34]

Those standing to the left of the liberals struggled to find a unified position. Some of those who had been active in the Trotsky Defense Committee—namely, Dewey, Tresca, and James T. Farrell—formed a Civil Rights Defense Committee to aid the appeal of the Socialist Workers Party members convicted for violating the Alien Registration Act.[35] Although the Committee for Cultural Freedom had become moribund, some of its former members mobilized to protest against the pro-Soviet film *Mission to Moscow* (Warner Bros., 1943). They wrote and distributed a manifesto condemning the movie for depicting "the kind of historical falsifications which have hitherto been characteristic of totalitarian propaganda." Dewey and Suzanne La Follette wrote their own denunciation of the film, charging the movie makers with engaging in "crass historical distortions."[36] They could not build a full-fledged movement around that issue, however. For his part, Dwight Macdonald, in the late summer of 1943, started a new magazine, *politics*, that he hoped would become a unifying forum for the wide variety of anti-Stalinist, pacifistic, and anti-statist writers. While Hannah Arendt recalled that the new magazine was "a focal point for many who could no longer fit into any party or group,"[37] it did not unify them.

Academic anti-communism was strengthened by the efforts of the former Menshevik David Dallin, an expert on Soviet international behavior, who wrote a series of books warning of the problems in the Grand Alliance. Using an objective, non-ideological analysis, he presented a case suggesting that Soviet leaders lacked faith in the durability of pacts, alliances, or assurances of friendship. According to him, their belief that capitalist countries were permanent enemies would lead them, once the war ended, to protect their own interests by widening the Soviet Union's sphere of interest in Europe. Expansion, he warned, was a necessary element of Soviet communism. If it was allowed to occur, he stated, it would mean the transplantation to those countries of the Soviet "type of mechanical, disciplined social apparatus."[38]

CONCLUSION

During World War II, the CPUSA regained much of its political strength, and some of its allies. A slight majority of the American people believed that the Soviet Union could be trusted to cooperate with the United States after the war, and most published commentaries on the subject expressed an optimistic tone.[39] President Roosevelt's foreign policy advisers favored cooperation with the Soviet Union, though they divided over whether to do so in a "hard" or "soft" manner. Many unofficial anti-Communists, despite their hope that the alliance would continue after the war, nevertheless had become better organized against, and more determined to contest, the CPUSA and its fellow travelers.

Barrington Moore, Jr., a sociologist who had worked for the Office of Strategic Services during the war, expressed his surprise, in late 1944, that "certain sections of the daily press" (the Hearst, McCormick, and Patterson chains, specifically) were expressing fears that "the United States faces a period of class struggle and revolutionary violence in which the Communist Party will play a prominent part." In Moore's estimation, "most of the foreseeable conditions of the postwar years do not favor a growth of the Communist Party."[40] He was correct about the CPUSA, but he failed to foresee that the postwar Soviet Union would be perceived by many to be an expansionist power determined to impose its system on neighboring countries. Nor did he foresee that the CPUSA would make itself prominent by accusing the government of the United States, in its responses to the Soviet Union, of deliberately provoking war. In those circumstances, both official and unofficial anti-communism closed ranks.

5

Official Anti-Communism, 1945–1948

Even though the post–World War II era in the United States was a time of growing wealth and well-being, it was also one of the most insecure and anxious. The U.S. involvement in the second world war had followed a decade-long economic depression and ended with the death of the only president whom most adults had known, two atomic bomb detonations, labor unrest at home, a series of independence struggles abroad, and rapidly deteriorating relations with a wartime ally, the Soviet Union. A series of fears and panics occurred. Doris Kearns Goodwin, when she decided to write her memoir about growing up in the early 1950s, "when our lives seemed free from worry," quickly recalled "the sweeping fears of polio, communist subversion, and the atomic bomb that hung over our childhood days like low flying clouds."[1]

As a result, the hope that followed the battlefield victory was paralleled, and sometimes obliterated, by pessimism. The editors of *Time* magazine wrote: "What the world would best remember of 1945 was the deadly mushroom clouds over Hiroshima and Nagasaki." It was the year that civilization discovered "the means to commit suicide at will. . . . The war was over, but peace was only the absence of war."[2] James A. Wechsler remembered that, by 1946, "there seemed solid reason for pessimism."[3] Movie producer John Houseman described the early postwar period as one of "general anxiety and low cultural energy"; he concluded that the spate of "tough-guy" films being made during this era present "a fairly accurate reflection of the neurotic personality of the United States of America in the year 1947."[4]

John M. Fenton of the Gallup Poll wrote that the postwar period was "a period faced with great uncertainty, an era that the typical American entered cautiously."[5] Most historians echo these sentiments. Eric F. Goldman wrote that alongside a "tonic sense of new possibilities," a "sense of a scarifying future" existed.[6] William H. Chafe remarked on how rapidly people's optimism disappeared.[7] Seymour Martin Lipset and Earl Raab noted that "beneath the dazzling prosperity there existed some deep social strains and nagging doubts." They cite, specifically, the "rise of status insecurity" and "fear of dispossession."[8]

Perhaps the deepest social strain was caused by the conflict between labor and management. Organized labor—notably the CIO unions—emerged from the war determined to advance a program of full employment, higher wages, and price controls. Workers, already restive over the widening gap between wages and prices and the unemployment caused by the drastic reduction in war production, became mutinous when Congress ended price controls in November 1945. Nearly 2 million workers lost their jobs, and workers' real income fell sharply. As a result, between August 1945 and August 1946, more than 5 million strikers engaged in 4,630 work stoppages nationwide. It was the largest strike wave in U.S. history, and it involved the biggest industries: coal, auto, electrical, steel, and railroads. In addition, based on their war experiences, women and blacks were demanding better opportunities, and these demands were provoking fear and hostility from white males. This combination of anxiety and anger proved to be fertile ground for the "red scare" that ensued. As discussed in Chapter 4, the seeds had already been planted, and they were fertilized and watered by the sensational media accounts of Soviet activities in Europe and the Middle East, the alarmist warnings about those activities coming from Republicans and the Truman administration, and the enactment of a series of anti-Soviet doctrines, plans, and treaty organizations.

This book is not the proper forum to examine the causes of, or assign blame for, the Cold War. (Nor does it discuss, in any detail, international events.) Suffice it to say that cracks in the alliance appeared immediately after the Yalta Conference (February 1945) and widened steadily after the death of President Roosevelt (April 1945). According to John Lewis Gaddis, the members of the victorious coalition were, during the war, engaged in ideological and geopolitical conflict; after the war, there was "a growing sense of insecurity at the highest levels in Washington, London, and Moscow, generated by the efforts the wartime allies were making to ensure their own postwar security."[9] By the autumn of 1947, the cracks had become, rhetorically at least, a chasm.

In effect, a new form of superpower rivalry had emerged between the United States and the Soviet Union, reflecting a traditional clash of the competing national security interests of great powers, but complicated by deeply embedded ideological differences. Each country was seeking a wider sphere of influence: the United States in a global aspect, the Soviet Union on its periphery. More specifically, the United States was pursuing a global policy of military security and free trade,[10] whereas the Soviet Union was focusing its attention on rebuilding at home and installing, via military pressure, friendly governments in the countries bordering it. Ultimately, differences of policy and style became transformed by the rhetoric of each country's spokespeople into threatening postures. Mutual misunderstanding and a competing set of mutually false assumptions impelled the Cold War forward. Although neither country faced a serious threat to its national security from the other, the leaders of both countries, motivated by their respective domestic considerations, acted as though a threat existed and deliberately instilled a climate of fear and a culture of insecurity.[11]

This climate profoundly transformed anti-communism in the United States from the slow-moving river of unease it had resembled during the 1930s into a raging torrent of panic. This torrent was constantly fed by revelations about spying,[12] accusations about Communist infiltration of the U.S. government, and the news reports regarding the establishment of the Soviet bloc in Eastern Europe, the victory of the Chinese Communists, the detonation of an atomic device by the Soviet Union, and the Korean War. By tying all these events together, official and unofficial anti-Communists succeeded in convincing a large majority of U.S. citizens (more than 70% in early 1948) that the Soviet Union was determined to rule the world; that the United States would be in a war, presumably with the Soviet Union, within the next 25 years[13]; and that the internal security of the United States needed immediate and thorough attention.

Institutional and legislative anti-Communists paved the path leading to the enhancement of internal security known as the domestic Cold War. From the institutional ranks, the National Association of Manufacturers and the U.S. Chamber of Commerce led the way, becoming the core of a revitalized business lobby that was determined to regain control of the workplace and reduce the political influence of organized labor. To do so, the business lobby formed an alliance with the Southern Democrat/Republican bloc in Congress,[14] launched costly advertising campaigns against the workers' strikes, red-baited the strikers, and accused them of fomenting disorder.

The National Association of Manufacturers began its campaign with its 1944 pamphlet, *Freedom from Victory*. Eric Johnston, then-president of the Chamber of Commerce and soon to be head of the associations of motion picture producers, appointed a committee to report on "the menace of socialism in Europe and its effect upon this country." This committee, which was chaired by Francis P. Matthews, a former head of the Catholic Knights of Columbus, issued five reports on communism between 1946 and 1952, demanding the creation of government loyalty tribunals, investigations of Communist influence in Hollywood, a public list of subversive organizations, purges of Communists from educational and opinion-making professions, and restraints on labor unions.[15] Father John F. Cronin wrote two of these pamphlets: *Communist Infiltration in the United States* and *Communists Within the Labor Movement*. Cronin had access to FBI and Un-American Activities Committee reports for both, and he was assisted by John Frey of the American Federation of Labor. It is estimated that 300,000 copies of the first pamphlet were distributed in the months leading up to the Congressional election of 1946.[16]

In early 1947, at the behest of U.S. Attorney General Tom Clark, the Advertising Council—a vast umbrella organization of U.S. businesses—helped organize the American Heritage Foundation, which launched a massive "indoctrination in democracy" campaign. A few years later, it sponsored a very well-funded campaign to promote the "American Economic System."[17]

These business campaigns coalesced with the efforts of a growing bloc of Republicans and conservative Democrats determined to roll back New Deal legislation—in particular, the National Labor Relations Act.[18] This bloc also supported Congressman Rankin's January 1945 motion to give permanent status to the Un-American Activities Committee. His proposal passed by a narrow margin, 208–186, despite former chairman McCormack's warning that this event would be the first time in the history of the House of Representatives that an investigating committee had been given permanent status and that "there is a big difference between establishing a standing committee to investigate and establishing a special committee for a particular Congress."[19] The standing committee began its life with a hearing into the Office of Price Administration. After that point, virtually every investigation and report issued by the committee involved Communists, notably its investigation of communism in the motion picture industry.[20]

ANTI-COMMUNISTS TARGET THE MOTION PICTURE INDUSTRY, 1946–1947

The motion picture industry was an alluring target for anti-Communists. Attacks on it guaranteed a steady stream of media attention, as Dies had discovered when he went after members of the industry during the late 1930s. This time, however, the forces of resistance in Hollywood were much weaker, and industry leaders were facing major problems: Box-office receipts had begun to decline; the Department of Justice was pursuing an antitrust suit, seeking divestment of the theater chains operated by five of the major studios; and the assistance of the Department of State was needed to reopen many foreign markets.

Industry leaders, feeling vulnerable, tried to use the FBI as a buffer against Rankin. A representative of Will Hays, head of the producers' associations, met with Director J. Edgar Hoover, to inquire whether the FBI would be collaborating with Rankin's committee. If that were the case, Hays assured Hoover, the Motion Picture Producers Association would provide whatever information was desired. Hoover informed Hays that the Bureau had no connection whatsoever with the investigation. Hoover then sent a memo to the Los Angeles office ordering it to keep completely away from the investigation and to refuse Un-American Activities Committee investigators the use of FBI offices and records. Independently of Hays's inquiry, producer Walter Wanger contacted an FBI official asking if Hoover would issue a statement asserting that no plot existed in Hollywood to overthrow the U.S. government.[21]

Rankin, however, pushed ahead, telling the House of Representatives, on July 9:

> [A]ppeals for an investigation are coming to us from the best people in California, some of the best producers in California are very much disturbed because they are having to take responsibility for some of the most loathsome, filthy, insinuating, un-American undercurrents that are running through various pictures sent throughout the country to be shown to the children of the Nation. . . . They also have Communist schools for the purpose of indoctrinating or teaching the script writers to write those insidious subversive lines into the scripts . . . So we are

going to get to the bottom of it, we are going to use every resource at our command: all the government agencies—the FBI, Military Intelligence, Naval Intelligence, and the Un-American Activities committees of the State of California.[22]

At a news conference a few days later, Rankin repeated Dies's old charge that Hollywood was a "hotbed of Communism."[23] In August, Rankin sent Louis Russell, a former FBI agent, to California to begin the investigation. Russell prepared a preliminary report, which was titled "First Confidential Report," but he made only four copies of it.

At that point, ex-Communist Louis Budenz unexpectedly provided the Un-American Activities Committee with the "smoking gun" it needed. In a radio speech given in October 1946, Budenz disclosed that the CPUSA took its orders from a secret Moscow agent (subsequently identified as Gerhart Eisler, by newspaper reporter Frederick Woltman). When Budenz appeared before the standing committee on November 22, he asserted that the leadership of the CPUSA was completely subservient to the "will, whim and wish of Moscow," that every Communist was "a member of the Russian fifth column," and that Communists "try though all sorts of fellow-traveling organizations and groups to enter into every phase of American life—I mean from Hollywood to Hell's Gate."[24]

Chairman John Wood (Democrat–Georgia) and chief counsel Ernie Adamson traveled to Los Angeles in early December 1946 to hear the testimony of two witnesses, and Wood promised he would return in January or February 1947 to "hold a real hearing."[25] Two months later, immigration authorities arrested Gerhart Eisler, and he was brought before the Committee on Un-American Activities on February 6. When he refused to be sworn, he was cited for contempt and removed. His sister and political enemy, Ruth Fischer (née Elfriede Eisler), then took the witness stand and was asked, by Karl Mundt (Republican–South Dakota), Is your (other) brother, Hanns, in Hollywood a Communist? She replied: "He is a composer of films and he is a Communist in a philosophical sense." She also testified that Hanns was close with Gerhart.[26]

While the Committee was planning its investigation of Hanns Eisler (and the movie industry), the 1946 congressional election occurred, marking a decisive political turn rightward of the electorate. In April, newly appointed Republican national chairman B. Carroll Reece had accused the CIO-PAC of being the "spearhead of Red reactionism in the United States."[27] One month later, he announced that the upcoming election was "a fight basically between Communism and

Republicanism." He charged that "a group of alien-minded radicals," the creatures of political action committees, had seized control of the Democratic Party.[28] A number of Republicans, seeking seats for the first time, red-baited their Democratic opponents. Other Republican candidates, such as Richard Nixon, stressed the socialist and left-wing character of their opponents' program and the support they were receiving from the "Communistic" CIO-PAC and NCPAC. One of Nixon's campaign advertisements read: "A vote for Nixon is a vote against Socialization of free American institutions, ... the [National Citizens] Political Action Committee ... and its Communist principles."[29]

The exact impact of this red-baiting and guilt-by-left-association cannot be measured, but polls taken during the course of the months leading up to the 1946 election indicated that voters were mainly concerned about the high cost of living, inflation, and strikes. In addition, a poll taken a few weeks before the election, querying which party was best able to handle the nation's labor problems, indicated that Americans favored Republicans by a two-to-one margin (46% to 23%).[30] In any event, for the first time since 1928, Republicans won control of both houses of Congress. The Democratic vote count dropped by 10 million, and the Party lost 54 seats in the House of Representatives and 5 seats in the Senate. Candidates supported by the CIO-PAC lost 243 of the 318 contests they entered.[31] In sum, according to Jonathan Bell, the election "represented a massive defeat for liberalism in the Democratic Party."[32]

Early in the new year of 1947, the new chairman of the Un-American Activities Committee, J. Parnell Thomas (Republican–New Jersey), made public a letter he had sent to Attorney General Tom Clark, demanding that the Department of Justice take "long overdue" action to crack down on "the Moscow-directed fifth column" in the United States. Clark pledged that his department would "cooperate fully" with the committee.[33] Thomas began his own crackdown at the end of March, when he scheduled five days of hearings. Most of those persons who testified represented anti-Communist organizations, including the American Legion, Veterans of Foreign Wars, Daughters of the American Revolution, the American Federation of Labor, and the U.S. Chamber of Commerce. California Senator Jack Tenney and FBI Director Hoover also testified.

Hoover told the Committee that "Communist activity in Hollywood is effective and is furthered by Communists and sympathizers using the prestige of prominent persons to serve, often unwittingly,

Members of the House Committee on Un-American Activities, 1948. From left to right: Richard B. Vail, J. Parnell Thomas, John McDowell, Robert Stripling (chief counsel), and Richard M. Nixon. (Library of Congress)

the Communist cause." He urged the committee to investigate "those fields which mold public opinion and in which Communists have been successful in effecting infiltration, such as the radio, the motion pictures." Hoover also stated that the small size of CPUSA membership was "relatively unimportant" because of the members' "enthusiasm," the Party's "iron-clad discipline," and its deceit and trickery. It was, he concluded, "a fifth column if ever there was one. It is far better organized than were the Nazis in occupied countries prior to their capitulation."According to Hoover, the Communist Party's "allegiance is to Russia, not the United States," and its goal "is the overthrow of our Government." He implied, on two occasions, that the FBI and the Un-American Activities Committee were doing a better job of exposing Communist infiltration of the government than the Department of Justice was doing in removing those infiltrators.[34]

The last witness was Eric Johnston, who had replaced Will Hays as president of the Motion Picture Producers Association and the Motion Picture Producers and Distributors of America. "If," he stated, "the

Communists set out to capture Hollywood, they have suffered an overwhelming defeat." Johnston did not deny that there were Communists in the industry, but asserted that Communist propaganda never reached the screen. When Nixon asked if the industry was doing anything to stop the infiltration of Communists or to root out those already there, Johnston replied that there was no legal means available to him to do so. When pressed by other members of the committee, Johnson stated that it was up to the unions or the Department of Justice to police Communist employment. Rankin lectured him in return: "I am surprised at your attitude. I think you are going to have to change your position and join us in this crusade to save America from its enemies within our gates. And you can't wink at them in the moving picture industry . . . You need a house cleaning, and you need it very badly." In a later exchange, Rankin used the word "fumigate" to describe the steps needed in Hollywood.[35]

Both Nixon and Mundt asked Johnston why no anti-Communist movies had been made. Johnston told Nixon that he was sure they would be. Whether the transformation was caused by, or merely followed by, Johnston's assuring words, the studio heads soon began their careers as de facto anti-Communists. Two days after the hearings ended, *Variety* featured the following headline: "Studios Speed Anti-Red Pix."[36] Ten days later, Darryl F. Zanuck, the head of Twentieth Century-Fox, sent a secret memorandum to company executives conveying his idea for an anti-Communist movie, to be titled *Iron Curtain*. This film would depict, Zanuck wrote, "the activities of recent foreign agents in the United States and Canada and the subversive activities of the Communists." Zanuck hoped footage of Hoover's March testimony to the Un-American Activities Committee could be used, but when Hoover refused to grant permission, the studio decided to focus on the exposure of the Canadian spy ring exposed by Igor Gouzenko.[37] *Iron Curtain* was released a year later, in 1948. Even though the Special Agent in Charge, Los Angeles (SACLA) reported that *Iron Curtain* had fared poorly at the box office,[38] virtually every studio produced at least one anti-Communist movie. In 1949, Republic released *The Red Menace*, RKO released *I Married a Communist*, and M-G-M released *Conspirator*. Three more anti-Communist movies would be released in 1951, and six more in 1952.[39] Although only a few of the studio heads were ideological anti-Communists, they made these movies for two practical reasons: to satisfy the Committee and, it was hoped, to ride a popular wave of public anti-communism to box-office success.

On May 8, 1947, a subcommittee composed of three members of the Committee on Un-American Activities (Thomas, Wood, and John McDowell [Republican–Pennsylvania]) and two staff people (Robert Stripling and Louis Russell) came to Los Angeles to hold a 10-day inquiry. According to Stripling, their "primary task was to uncover and subpena [sic] Hanns Eisler."[40] Thomas, however, had a larger agenda, telling the press, "We know where to go and we know whom to see." He was referring to information the Committee had received from members of the Motion Picture Alliance for the Preservation of American Ideals, which had been formed by Hollywood anti-Communists in 1944. Eisler was subpoenaed, but 12 witnesses appeared voluntarily, among them 2 studio executives, Jack Warner and Henry Ginsberg (Paramount). The other 10 witnesses—Roy Brewer, Lela Rogers, 4 writers, 3 actors, and 1 director—were members of (or sympathetic) to the Motion Picture Alliance. According to Thomas, hundreds of "Communists" were named by these "friendly witnesses." Thomas advised Hollywood to "clean its own house of insidious Communist propaganda and not wait for Congress to spotlight the sorry spectacle." He announced that he would hold public hearings in Washington, D.C., starting June 16.[41]

On his return to Washington, D.C., Thomas spoke before the House of Representatives and reported that "In the opinion of the subcommittee, there is no question as to the serious inroads that the Communists have made in the motion picture industry, and it presents a problem which can only be corrected by complete exposure on the part of the Committee on Un-American Activities and prompt action by the studio heads." He stated that his committee intended to intensify its investigation of the movie industry; serve subpoenas on "Communist actors, writers, directors, and producers; confront them in public session with the testimony and evidence against them"; and investigate "the responsibility and extent of the influence on the part of Government agencies or officials in the production of flagrant Communist propaganda films."[42] Although the hearings would be postponed until October 1947, a subpoena was served on Hanns Eisler, ordering him to appear in late September for a separate hearing.[43]

Shortly after the March 1947 hearings, a new form of institutional anti-communism—the indiscriminate-listing industry—took shape. These groups gathered and published lists of media "subversives" and then offered their services as "researchers" to companies that employed people on the list. Two of the most prominent, American

Business Consultants and Aware, Inc., were founded by three former FBI agents and a former Naval intelligence agent, respectively.[44]

THE EXECUTIVE BRANCH, 1946–1948

Although there was a powerful coterie of dedicated anti-Communists in Congress, the anti-Communists in the executive branch were mainly concentrated in the Department of Justice, particularly in the FBI, and the CIA's Office of Policy Coordination.[45] While Truman's advisors moved slowly, generally in response to events, FBI Director Hoover maintained a laser-like focus on domestic anti-communism. Soon after Truman became president, Hoover inundated him with memoranda regarding the internal security threats facing the United States. In addition, in January 1946, the FBI adopted Assistant Director D. Milton Ladd's recommendations regarding the establishment of a Security Index for all known Communists and initiation of a campaign to strengthen laws against Communists.[46] In the summer of 1947, Hoover decided to make FBI files on Communists in Hollywood available to investigators from the Committee on Un-American Activities, and he convened FBI executives to discuss the agency's anti-Communist strategy. When they found that significant gaps existed in the brief they had written to convince Congress to outlaw the Communist Party, agents were dispatched to gather more information from "discreetly trusted representatives" of the AFL and the Daughters of the American Revolution, as well as Monsignor Fulton J. Sheen, Walter Steele, Benjamin Mandel, Karl Baarslag, and Father Edmond Walsh.[47] Within the next few years, the FBI established links with a significant number of anti-Communists, official and unofficial, all of whom provided it with information about "subversives" and defended the agency against its critics. By 1954, the FBI had compiled some 430,000 files on "subversive" groups and individuals, and placed more than 26,000 (mainly Communist) names on its Security Index. Its legion of informants and infiltrators surpassed 100,000.[48] In addition, Hoover or his designated aides, to keep the domestic anti-Communist fires burning, regularly leaked information to favored newspaper columnists and members of Congress, and Hoover allowed some favored journalists (Ralph de Toledano, Walter Trohan, Ed Montgomery, Karl Hess, and George Sokolsky, among others) access to FBI files.[49] Former FBI executive William Sullivan stated that the agency, during the Eisenhower administration, "kept Joseph McCarthy in business," giving him all that it had.[50]

Other members of the executive branch, taking their cue from President Truman, did not move with equal dispatch. Truman did not appear eager to launch a domestic cold war, but political pressures forced him to act as if the Communist "threat" were real. Presidential aide Clark Clifford stated, in his memoir, that the outcome of the 1946 elections "not only weakened President Truman, it emboldened [J. Edgar] Hoover and his allies." Pressured by Hoover and Attorney General Tom Clark, Truman accepted a recommendation from the House Committee on Un-American Activities to establish a Temporary Commission on Employee Loyalty.[51] Although the Commission reported in November 1946 that it had not been able to discover how extensive the security threat was, Clark stated, in a memo to the chairman of the commission:, "I do not believe that the gravity of the problem should be weighed in terms of numbers, but rather from the viewpoint of the serious threat which even one disloyal person constituted to the security of the Government of the United States." Truman, however, was less certain. In February 1947, he wrote, in a letter to Pennsylvania Governor George H. Earle, "People are very much wrought up about the Communist 'bugaboo,' but I am of the opinion that the country is perfectly safe so far as Communism is concerned."[52]

Nevertheless, in March 1947, Truman issued Executive Order 9835, which established procedures for "a loyalty investigation of every person entering the civilian employment of any department or agency of the Executive Branch of the Federal Government." The head of every department and agency was mandated to create a loyalty board. In addition, the Department of Justice was required to furnish the loyalty review boards with extensive information:

> the name of each foreign and domestic organization, association, movement, group, or combination of persons which the Attorney General, after appropriate investigation and determination, designates as totalitarian, Fascist, Communist or subversive, or as having adopted a policy of advocating or approving the commission of acts of force or violence to deny others their rights under the Constitution of the United States, or of seeking to alter the form of Government of the United States by unconstitutional means.[53]

The following month, Clark commenced a series of speeches proclaiming the Truman administration's concern with domestic communism, and in September he launched a series of deportation proceedings against alien, allegedly Communist, labor union officials. More than one dozen individuals were arrested and held without bail.[54] Clark's department was also hard at work preparing a new and vastly extended Attorney General's List of Subversive Organizations, which was made public in December 1947.[55] The following year, the National Security Council recommended that the Truman administration "urgently develop and execute a firm and coordinated program (to include legislation if necessary) designed to suppress the Communist menace in the United States in order to safeguard the United States against the disruptive and dangerous subversive activities of Communists."[56]

Despite these moves, it is interesting to note that the President's Committee on Civil Rights, which issued its report at the end of October 1947, expressed its concern that "public excitement about 'Communists' has gone far beyond the dictates of the 'good judgment' and 'calmness' " recommended by Justice Louis Brandeis in his dissent in *Schaefer v. United States* (251 U. S. 466, 1920), and noted that "a state of near-hysteria now threatens to inhibit the freedom of genuine democrats." The committee sought a middle ground, somewhere between relying on "hysteria and repression as our weapons against totalitarians" and legitimately exposing "real Communists and Fascists." It recommended that federal and state governments enact systematic registration procedures for all groups that might attempt to influence public opinion, and that the federal government clarify the loyalty obligations of federal employees and establish more rigorous standards and procedures to protect the civil rights of public workers.[57]

Although Truman made no public reference to this section of the report, he would have preferred to find a middle ground on which he could consistently stand, but the exigencies of electoral politics and the urging of his advisers forced him, in the election campaign of 1948, to tack between Henry Wallace on his left and congressional Republicans on his right. Wallace had been forced to resign as Secretary of Commerce (in September 1946) because of his public opposition to Truman's increasingly anti-Soviet foreign policy; as a result, he had become the left's only realistic alternative to Truman. His support mechanism, the Independent Progressive Party (IPP), represented the last significant united effort of left-liberals and Communists.[58] In November 1947, Clark Clifford, one of Truman's advisers, counseled the president to make every effort "to identify him [Wallace] in the public mind with Communists" and to point out that the core of the Wallace backing was made up of "Communists and fellow-travelers."[59]

During the campaign, the Truman administration and the Republican-led Congress competed with each other in playing the "red card." In June 1948, former Communist Elizabeth Bentley revealed to a federal grand jury that she had participated in a Soviet spy ring and named the members of it. When she failed to produce any evidence supporting her charges, the Department of Justice, to cover its embarrassment (and to avoid weakening Truman's reelection chances), decided to seek indictments of the top leadership of the CPUSA. On July 20, 1948, 12 leaders of the CPUSA were charged with violating the conspiracy provisions of the Alien Registration Act.

Eleven days later, anti-Communists in Congress, determined to keep the pressure on Truman, brought Bentley to Washington, D.C., to tell her story about Communist infiltration of the U.S. government to a Senate investigating subcommittee and the Committee on Un-American Activities. When she again failed to provide corroborating evidence, the Committee on Un-American Activities decided to call Whittaker Chambers.[60] Chambers, among his other revelations, accused a former State Department official, Alger Hiss, of being a Communist and of passing secret documents to the Soviet Union. (Hiss denied the charges. He was indicted for perjury in December 1948, convicted in January 1950, and served 4 years in prison. For the impact of this event on conservative and liberal anti-Communists, see Chapters 8 and 9.)

These events forced Truman to separate himself from Republicans in Congress as decisively as he had separated himself from Wallace. At a press conference on August 5, 1948, Truman agreed with a reporter that the congressional spy scare was a "red herring."[61] Eight weeks later, in Oklahoma City, Truman went on the attack. He explicitly stated, "Our Government is not endangered by Communist infiltration," and he accused the Republicans of using that charge as a "smoke screen." In fact, Truman countercharged the Republicans with having "impeded and made more difficult our efforts to cope with communism in this country." Rather than hurting the Communist Party, he said, they had helped it and become, as a result, the "unwittingly the ally of the Communists in this country."[62] Moreover, the Democratic platform of 1948 congratulated the Democrats for being the party "under which were conceived the instruments for resisting Communist aggression."[63]

Truman's Republican opponent, Thomas E. Dewey, chose neither to exploit the spy issue nor to red-bait the president. The Republican platform simply pledged that Dewey, if elected, would root out communism "wherever found," vigorously enforce the existing laws against Communists, and enact such new legislation "as may be necessary to expose the treasonable activities of Communists."[64] Dewey directly addressed the issue in a speech he made in Cheyenne, Wyoming, one month before the end of the campaign. He stated that, if elected, he would "no longer regard Communist activity as a 'red herring,' " and he promised that after his inauguration "there will be no Communists in the government."[65]

Although Truman won a narrow victory and the Democrats regained control of both houses of Congress, a conservative anti-Communist majority (in the form of a Republican/southern Democratic bloc) continued to control both the Senate and the House of Representatives. In the wake of their defeat, the Republicans adopted a much more polemical anti-communism. Truman chose not to attempt to outshout the Republicans on this issue, nor did his administration outflank them by constructing a comprehensive strategy for dealing with the issue of domestic anti-communism. In fact, in his four main speeches, between 1949 and 1951—his inaugural address and three State of the Union messages—Truman did not say a word about domestic communism.

6

Official Anti-Communism, 1949–1957

Between 1949 and 1952, the domestic Cold War intensified, and the executive and legislative branches remained sharply divided over how to deal with anti-communism. The capture of Beijing by the Chinese Communists (in January 1949), the explosion of a Soviet nuclear device (in March 1949), and the arrest of Judith Coplon, a Department of Justice employee, who had been passing documents to a Soviet agent (also in March 1949), provided congressional, institutional, and conservative anti-Communists with ammunition for their double-barreled conspiracy weapon. They accused the Roosevelt and Truman administrations of tolerating Communists and fellow travelers in the U.S. government, thereby allowing the Soviet Union to get hold of "atomic secrets," seize control of Eastern Europe, and pave the way for the Communists to seize control in China. They also accused the Truman administration of covering up this negligence. In October 1949, after a long and contentious trial, 11 leaders of the CPUSA were convicted of violating the conspiracy provisions of the Alien Registration Act, and all their lawyers were cited for contempt of court.

The events of 1950 sharply heightened the anti-Communist barrage. In January, Alger Hiss was convicted of perjury, and President Truman announced that, to protect the country from "any possible aggressor, he had directed the Atomic Energy Commission to continue its work "on all forms of atomic weapons, including the so-called hydrogen or super-bomb."[1] In early February, Klaus Fuchs, who had worked on the atomic bomb at the Los Alamos, New Mexico, facility was arrested in the United Kingdom on charges of espionage.

Also in that month, the Republican Party issued its Statement of Principles and Objectives for that year's congressional elections. It denounced "the soft attitude of [the Truman] Administration toward Government employees and officials who hold or support Communist attitudes," and pledged the "complete overhaul of the so-called loyalty and security checks of Federal personnel."[2] FBI Director J. Edgar Hoover reportedly told the Senate Appropriations Committee that there were approximately 540,000 Communists and fellow travelers in the United States, and he requested funding for 300 new FBI agents to deal with them.[3] Less than one week later, Senator Joseph McCarthy (Republican–Wisconsin), while delivering a speech in Wheeling, West Virginia, and perhaps taking his cues from the Republicans' Statement, attributed the nation's current "position of impotency" to "the traitorous actions" of the Department of State, which he described as "thoroughly infested with Communists." Claimed McCarthy, "I have in my hand 57 cases of individuals who would appear to be either card carrying members or certainly loyal to the Communist Party, but who nevertheless are still helping to shape our foreign policy."[4] That same month, the Soviet Union and the People's Republic of China signed a mutual-aid treaty.

In March 1950, Victor Kravchenko told the Committee on Un-American Activities that the Fuchs case was "only a prelude" and warned that much more "is still to come regarding the scope of Soviet espionage in America and other western countries."[5] In a radio address, Hoover told the nation that there existed "few walks in American life where [Communists] do not traverse. . . . Wherever they may be, they have in common one diabolic ambition: to weaken and eventually destroy American democracy by stealth and cunning."[6]

That summer, the Korean War began (in June), and Harry Gold, the Rosenbergs, and Morton Sobell were arrested and charged with providing atomic secrets to the Soviet Union.

Nevertheless, in the midst of these unsettling occurrences, Truman endeavored to erect a barrier against a more radical anti-communism. At a dinner held by the Federal Bar Association at the end of April 1950, he told attendees: "The fact of the matter is—because of measures we are taking—the internal security of the United States is not seriously threatened by Communists in this country. . . . They are noisy and they are troublesome, but they are not a major threat. . . . There is a right way and a wrong way to fight Communism. This administration is doing it the right way, the sensible way."[7]

For their part, Senate Democrats tried to find a middle-ground anti-communism, which required that they defend the Truman

Senator Joseph McCarthy, at the height of his anti-Communist career, speaking on a CBS television program, 1953. (Library of Congress)

administration and undermine McCarthy. Thus, when Republicans demanded an investigation of McCarthy's charges by the conservative-dominated Appropriations Committee, the Democratic leadership secured the passage of a resolution authorizing a subcommittee of the more liberal Foreign Relations Committee "to conduct a full and complete study and investigation as to whether persons who are disloyal to the United States are or have ever been employed by the State Department." Ultimately, this plan backfired, and the chosen subcommittee provided McCarthy with an unexpected forum from which he could further broadcast his accusations. The chairman of the subcommittee, Millard Tydings (Democrat–Maryland), failed in his effort to force McCarthy to produce evidence substantiating his charges, but also failed in his effort to discredit McCarthy. Rather, the highly publicized charges and countercharges that were bandied about during the July hearing kept McCarthy's name in the headlines, and Senate Republicans began to accuse Tydings of hounding McCarthy instead of finding Communists in the executive branch.[8] In fact, the Republican accusations of a cover-up became intense enough to convince Truman to release the loyalty files of those accused by McCarthy, after initially refusing to do so.[9]

The subcommittee's majority report concluded that only 40 of the people on McCarthy's list of 81 "loyalty risks" were currently employed and none was a "card-carrying Communist." The report accused McCarthy of making "groundless," "wild and baseless charges," using the "Big Lie" technique, "adopting the vile methods of the Communist themselves," and perpetrating a "fraud" on the Senate. The report ended with the following statement: "The result [of McCarthy's charges] has been to confuse and divide the American people, at a time when they should be strong in their unity, to a degree far beyond the hopes of the Communists themselves whose stock in trade is confusion and division."[10] (This type of statement was used over and over by Truman administration spokespeople and liberal anti-Communists, to little avail. It gained no traction among other anti-Communists, nor did it seem to influence public opinion.) In any event, only 12 Senate Democrats openly criticized McCarthy, while a few criticized the subcommittee's report.

This effort to occupy an anti-Communist middle ground was also undertaken by seven Republican senators who, three weeks before the subcommittee's report was published, signed a "Declaration of Conscience," authored by Margaret Chase Smith (Republican–Maine). Originally friendly with and sympathetic to McCarthy, and a person who believed that one of the main objectives of the federal government should be the exposure and eradication of communism in the United States, Smith had begun to question "the validity, accuracy, credibility, and fairness" of McCarthy's charges. She was urged by radio commentator Ed Hart and newspaper columnist Doris Fleeson to challenge McCarthy publicly, but she hesitated to do so, because she was a first-term senator and because she thought it was up to Democratic senators to respond to attacks on a Democratic administration. Finally, Smith decided to act. She composed her statement, showed it George Aiken (Republican–Vermont), and they decided to ask five other liberal Republican senators to join them. Although McCarthy was not specifically cited, the "Declaration" clearly referred to his tactics. It stated: "Certain elements of the Republican party have materially added to the confusion [that threatens the security and stability of the United States] in the hopes of riding the Republican party to victory through the selfish political exploitation of fear, bigotry, ignorance, and intolerance." It went on to accuse those "elements" and the ineffective leadership of the Truman administration of "unwittingly, but undeniably, played directly into the Communist design of 'confuse, divide, and conquer.' " It concluded with the following statement: "It is high time that we all stopped being tools and victims of totalitarian techniques."[11] Nevertheless, this attempt at establishing a trend toward Republican middle-ground anti-communism also made little impact.

During the summer of 1950, in direct response to the Korean War, the Secretaries of Labor and Commerce invited executives of the major ship-owning companies and maritime unions (with the exception of the International Longshoremen's and Warehousemen's Union—still led by Harry Bridges—and the Marine Cooks and Stewards—which had been expelled from the CIO)[12] to a conference on "questions of national security." The attendees agreed on a plan that would block Communists from serving on merchant marine vessels during the war. The Coast Guard was authorized to seek information from the FBI and the Office of Naval Intelligence as a means of determining "bad security risks." "Risks" were defined as "Communist Party card carriers, subversives, or [those] who are notorious as consistently carrying out policies of the Communist Party." All such people would be summarily denied the right to sail. In August 1950, Congress passed a law giving the president full power over foreign-flag vessels in U.S. waters. In October, the president issued an Executive Order superseding the July agreement and extending security screening to waterfront employees. By May 1953, 915 waterfront employees and 1,833 seamen had been denied clearance, 352 appeals were pending, and 1,165 people had been cleared after appealing their initial denial.[13]

Meanwhile, President Truman, to block the possibility that the Mundt-Nixon internal security bill might become law, sent a special message to Congress. He stated that the CPUSA, as a political party, did not represent a threat to the United States; according to Truman, it was being adequately checked by the vigilance and good sense of the citizenry. What is needed, he said, was a bill "accurately devised to meet the real dangers" of espionage and sabotage, not the pending "broad and vague" bill, which, he stated, endangered First Amendment freedoms. Truman recommended remedying certain defects in the present espionage laws and giving the U.S. Attorney General enhanced authority to keep track of aliens subject to deportation. He urged the members of Congress not to be "swept away by a wave of hysteria."[14] Pat McCarran, who had, a few years earlier, sponsored a rider to an appropriations bill giving the Department of State full authority to dismiss any employee suspected of disloyalty and who had been a sharp critic of the Tydings subcommittee's report, used

Senator Pat McCarran, the most effective congressional anti-Communist. (Library of Congress)

the occasion of Truman's message to get behind the Mundt-Nixon bill and add to it other anti-Communist provisions that had been floating around the Congress for years. He then maneuvered to turn this omnibus anti-Communist bill into the Internal Security Act.

McCarran's bill passed the Senate by a vote of 70-7 and the House by a margin of 354-20. It opened with a congressional finding:

> There exists a world Communist movement which, in its origins, its development, and its present practice, is a world-wide revolutionary movement whose purpose is, by treachery, deceit, infiltration into other groups (governmental and otherwise), espionage, sabotage, terrorism, and any other means deemed necessary, to establish a Communist totalitarian dictatorship in the countries throughout the world through the medium of a world-wide Communist organization.

The finding also stated that the CPUSA was a "rigidly and ruthlessly disciplined" organization, seeking to overthrow the U.S. government "by force and violence." Therefore, to preserve and protect national security, the act required every "Communist-action" and "Communist-front" organization to register with the Attorney General. It also established a Subversive Activities Control Board, authorized to determine which organizations were "Communist-Action" or "Communist-Front" groups. Moreover, it denied entry to the United States to seven types of aliens, from those who sought to enter the country to engage in activities that were prejudicial to the public interest or that might endanger the country's welfare or safety, to those who had written anything even remotely radical.[15] President Truman vetoed the bill, because, he wrote, it would "actually weaken our existing security measures," liberties, and rights. He concluded: "At a time when our young men are fighting for freedom in Korea, it would be tragic to advance the objectives of Communism in this country, as this bill would do."[16] His veto was over-ridden by votes of 57-10 in the Senate and 286-48 in the House.[17]

Anti-communism was exploited by Republicans at every level in the elections of 1950, but a Gallup Poll taken at the end of September indicated that money issues (45%) dominated the worries of those asked, with war (21%) in second place.[18] Although the Democrats lost seats in both houses of Congress, they retained control of both bodies. Richard Fried has argued that the Republicans' guilt-by-association strategy played a key role only in California, Utah, and Maryland; in most of the other states, he concluded, local factors played the key role in Republicans' election gains.[19]

In 1951, McCarran took control of official anti-communism. First, he blocked Truman's attempt to establish a Commission on Internal Security and Individual Rights, which would have the power to examine thoroughly all the laws, practices, and procedures regarding treason, espionage, sabotage, and all other subversive activities, and to recommend changes. McCarran, however, preferred to keep the loyalty spotlight on congressional committees.[20] Indeed, a few months later, the Senate, under McCarran's aegis, created the Special Subcommittee to Investigate the Administration of the Internal Security Act and Other Internal Security Laws (also known as the Senate Internal Security Subcommittee) to investigate "the extent, nature and effects of subversive activities." McCarran chaired the subcommittee, and he appointed as staff, according to Michael Ybarra, "something of an all-star team of anti-subversives" with experience working for the Un-American Activities Committee and Senator McCarthy.[21] This subcommittee quickly became the main channel connecting the FBI with Congress. McCarran used it to launch a full-scale investigation of the "Communists" in the Department of State who had, he believed, turned the U.S. government against Chiang Kai-shek. (After the hearings had ended, McCarran pressured the Department of Justice to indict one of the witnesses, Owen Lattimore, for perjury, as discussed later in this chapter.)

That same year, the Un-American Activities Committee reopened its investigation of "Communist Infiltration of the Motion Picture Industry," which resulted in a greatly expanded blacklist (more than 300 names). In the next five years, this committee vastly widened the scope of hearings it held and witnesses it heard. Virtually no profession escaped its scrutiny. The number of contempt citations also escalated, but only a small number were ultimately upheld by the courts.[22]

In 1952, McCarran initiated a successful campaign to enact into law an immigration and nationality bill (the McCarran-Walter Act).[23] Among its many provisions, this law barred "subversives" from entering the United States and gave the executive branch sweeping powers to summarily deport any alien who engaged in activities prohibited by laws relating to espionage, sabotage, or public order; subverted national security; or acted in a manner prejudicial to the public interest. It also authorized the deportation of immigrants and naturalized citizens who joined the Communist Party or Communist-front organizations. President Truman vetoed the bill, stating, "Seldom has a bill exhibited the distrust evidenced here for citizens and aliens alike—at a time when we need unity at home and the confidence of our friends abroad." Truman also objected to the "sweeping," undefined powers given to the Attorney General to deport any alien who had engaged in activities " 'prejudicial to the public interest' or 'subversive to the national security.' "[24] The Senate overrode the veto by a vote of 57-26 and the House by a vote of 278-133, and hundreds of people, many of whom were trade unionists, were arrested and ordered to be deported by the Immigration and Naturalization Service.[25]

THE NEW ADMINISTRATION HEIGHTENS
THE DOMESTIC COLD WAR, 1952–1956

The Republican Party's 1952 platform contained much stronger and more extensive anti-Communist language than any prior platform had demonstrated.[26] It forthrightly stated that both the loyalty program and the containment policy of the Truman administration had failed. In a four-paragraph section on communism, the Truman administration was accused of "appeasement of Communism at home and abroad," and it was proclaimed that "There are no Communists in the Republican Party. We have always recognized Communism to be a world conspiracy against freedom and religion. We never compromised with Communism and we have fought to expose it and to eliminate it in government and American life." In comparison, the Democratic platform contained only a few sentences on anti-communism, defending the loyalty program and proclaiming how well the Truman administration had strengthened the nation's defenses "against the menace of Soviet aggression."[27]

In an ironic twist, the Republicans nominated a presidential candidate, Dwight D. Eisenhower, who did not have strong anti-Communist credentials. Most supporters of Senator Robert A. Taft, his opponent for the nomination, considered Eisenhower to be the candidate of "international liberals," who was unqualified "to lead the United States in its life-and-death struggle with the [Soviet] Empire he and his superiors helped to make so powerful."[28] Right-wing Republicans considered Eisenhower to be an appeaser who had supported some of the targets of the anti-Communists (e.g., George Marshall) and opposed the Internal Security Act and the Subversive Activities Control Board. Probably in an attempt to placate this vocal branch of the party, Eisenhower, in his first campaign speech, promised to uproot from responsible places in the U.S. government, "any kind of Communistic, subversive or pinkish influence." Moreover, during the campaign, even though public opinion polls indicated that the Communist-in-government issue was not a major issue for voters, Eisenhower repeatedly stated that it was.[29] Shortly before the election, George Sokolsky summarized the dilemma for many conservatives: stay home and watch Adlai Stevenson be elected or vote "without much enthusiasm" for a candidate about whose ideas and principles "they know too little."[30]

In the end, Eisenhower won the presidential election, and Republicans gained a small majority of eight in the House of Representatives and a tiny majority of one in the Senate. Public opinion polls, however, indicated that government corruption and the Korean War—not concern with communism or spying—motivated people to vote Republican.[31]

In any event, as a result of the Republican majority in the Senate, Joseph McCarthy was appointed as chairman of the Committee on Government Operations, and in turn he appointed himself chairman of its Permanent Subcommittee on Investigations.[32] From that position, he launched investigations of the Voice of America, U.S. Information Service, Post Office Department, Army Signal Corps, and the leadership of the U.S. Army.

McCarthy was a unique figure in twentieth-century politics. Usually one-issue politicians are quickly marginalized, but McCarthy's outsized personality, his refusal to abide by the rules of the political game, his tenacity, and his tone-deafness fueled his nearly five-year, comet-like path across the United States. No contemporary seemed to know how to confront or comfortably ride this comet, probably because he placed himself at the center of the most sensational issue of his time and further sensationalized it. He developed into an art form what Muhammad Ali later dubbed the "rope-a-dope" tactic in the boxing ring.[33] No other politician bobbed and weaved as effectively as McCarthy when it came to meeting demands that he present direct evidence to substantiate his charges. Few could pin him to the ropes or corner him. Although McCarthy was far from alone in practicing guilt-by-association, he flamboyantly raised this tactic to heretofore unknown heights. As Edward R. Murrow said, in the coda to his *See It Now* critique of McCarthy, on March 9, 1954, "He didn't create the situation of fear; he merely exploited it, and rather successfully."[34]

There is little agreement among analysts as to what McCarthy or McCarthyism actually represented. Nevertheless, it is a mistake to conflate the man with the ism. McCarthy was a disruptive force, because his style of politics brought to the surface the seething discontent of a significant percentage of the people of the United States during the early 1950s.[35] McCarthy was all style, and it was his particular style of anti-communism and anti-liberalism that won him support from virtually every point on the conservative and right-wing spectrum, from rabid anti-Semites to Republican office holders.[36] His former aide, Roy Cohn, called McCarthy "a salesman, . . . selling the story of America's peril."[37] On the other hand, "McCarthyism" was and remains an elastic label, stretchable enough to serve almost any political purpose. Though the Senator did not define McCarthyism in his book on that subject,[38] he told two journalists that it meant "Americanism that is ready to stand up and fight communism."[39] In fact, the arch-conservative anti-Communist commentator, Fulton Lewis, Jr., stated: "To many Americans, McCarthyism is Americanism."[40] However, to the senator's opponents, then and now, "McCarthyism" is synonymous with unfair, unsubstantiated accusations.

The man's popularity rose and fell over a period of five years, peaking with an approval rating of 50 percent in January 1954. The ism has remained a part of the political vocabulary of the United States, regularly revived as a smear technique, by both the left and the right.

In the House, the new speaker, Joseph Martin (Republican–Massachusetts), declared, "We in this Congress would make a tragic error if we did not fully comprehend that Marxism is the greatest enemy of representative government that the world has known." Martin defined this phenomenon as a "political malady...which has spawned those twin evils, socialism and communism."[41]

On the other side of the Senate aisle, soon after the new Congress opened, Pat McCarran introduced three anti-Communist measures: a bill to prevent employment in or under the United Nations of any person of "questionable loyalty"; a bill to amend the 1857 contempt of Congress law, to allow the granting of immunity to witnesses who otherwise refused to testify before a congressional investigating committee; and a bill to make it unlawful for a member of a Communist organization to hold an executive position in or be employed by any labor organization, and to permit employers to discharge any employee who was a member of any organization listed by the U.S. Attorney General as "subversive."[42]

Dan Gillmor called the 83rd Congress the "investigating Congress," and he noted that it set a record "in the amount of time, money and attention lavished on investigations of communism, subversion, espionage and other menaces to the Republic, real or imaginary." According to Gillmor, 105 probes were begun during the first month of its first session, and one-fourth of the appropriations for investigations were used for inquiries into subversion. Senators McCarthy and William E. Jenner (Republican-Indiana) held a series of " 'interlocking subversion' hearings,...shuffling and reshuffling the witnesses like so many cards."[43]

As for the new Eisenhower administration, its tone and its behavior were emphatically more anti-Communist than those of its predecessor. For example, whereas Truman had publicly criticized McCarthy, McCarthyism, and congressional investigating committees on numerous occasions, Eisenhower regularly refused to answer direct questions about the senator and exhibited deference to congressional investigating committees.[44] Whereas Truman downplayed the "threat" of domestic Communists, Eisenhower, during the first two years of his presidency, gave it his full attention. Given that the CPUSA had been seriously wounded by the trial and conviction of its top leaders, the flight into hiding of several other leaders to avoid prosecution, and the mass exodus from the ranks, it is a distinct possibility that the anti-communism of the Eisenhower administration was a device deployed to hold the Republican Party together.

In his first State of the Union address to Congress, Eisenhower declared that the heads of all executive departments and agencies had been "instructed to initiate at once effective programs of security with respect to their personnel."[45] Two months later, he issued Executive Order 10450, extending the loyalty system to all agencies of the federal government and substituting "security risk" for "disloyalty" as the basis for dismissal.[46] Attorney General Herbert Brownell, Jr., who had been designated by the president to oversee the campaign against domestic subversion, reported in March 1953 that approximately 10,000 naturalized citizens were under investigation for "subversive" activities, and some 300 had already been deported.[47] He also filed 14 petitions with the Subversive Activities Control Board asking that the named organizations be designated "Communist-Action" groups and ordered to register.[48] In June 1953, he told a television audience, "We believe that without fanfare and steadily over the next few months, we will be able to weed out from the Federal payroll every security risk."[49] Four months later, the White House announced that, between June and September 1953, 1,456 government employees had been dismissed (863) or forced to resign (593) "for security reasons."[50]

1954 was probably the peak year of the domestic Cold War, despite the fact that membership in the CPUSA had declined by more than two-thirds since 1944 (from 79,000 to around 23,000).[51] In a series of polls sponsored by the Fund for the Republic, taken that summer, 66 percent of the respondents favored removing from U.S. public libraries any book written by a Communist; 91 percent favored firing any Communist who was a teacher; 90 percent favored firing any Communist working in a defense plant; 68 percent favored the prohibition of any Communist speaking in public; 77 percent favored taking away the citizenship of any Communist; 73 percent stated that they would report to the FBI any neighbor or acquaintance suspected of being a Communist; 78 percent believed that a Communist could not be a loyal American; and 72 percent of Republicans and 62 percent of Democrats had a favorable opinion of congressional committees investigating communism.[52]

Perhaps in response to its reading of these polls, or for other reasons it did not make clear, the Eisenhower administration decided to expand its campaign against domestic Communists.[53] In his January 1954 State of the Union address, the president reported that "more than 2,200 employees have been separated from the Federal government," and he asked Congress for additional funding for the loyalty program. Eisenhower also asked Congress to enact a law that would strip the citizenship from anyone convicted of "conspiring to advocate the overthrow of this government by force or violence."[54]

A few months later, in a national radio and television address titled "The Fight Against Communism," U.S. Attorney General Brownell stated that the U.S. government intended to use, in a constitutional manner, "new and powerful weapons" to destroy the CPUSA. Among those "weapons" were legislation to remove the citizenship of any person found guilty of advocating the forceful overthrow of the government; to allow employers, during a time of national emergency, to discharge any person deemed likely to engage in espionage or sabotage; to give the Subversive Activities Control Board the power to eliminate Communist control of any industrial organization or labor union involved in "vital sectors" of the economy; to allow the death penalty for anyone convicted of peacetime espionage; and to widen the wiretapping authority of the Department of Justice and allow it to use wiretap evidence in court cases. This legislation was necessary, Brownell said, because "the threat of communism is a very real one. Communists are scheming, practical and devious men and women dedicated to the destruction of our Government and way of life." And yet, in the next breath, he seemed to indicate that the Eisenhower administration's policies had already eliminated that threat. Brownell bragged about the extensive FBI infiltration of the Communist Party, thereby making "their conspiracy a very hazardous occupation," and he touted his own department's indictments and convictions of Communist Party leaders, which, he said, had dealt "a serious blow to the Communist Party."[55]

Meanwhile, in Congress, Martin Dies, who had returned to the House of Representatives the previous year, introduced a series of bills that sought to declare the Communist Party and similar "revolutionary" organizations illegal and to make membership or participation in them a criminal offense. Hubert Humphrey (Democrat–Minnesota) introduced a similar bill in the Senate. In August 1954, after much maneuvering, Congress enacted the Communist Control Act, which effectively stripped members of the Communist Party of most of their due process rights. When the act reached his desk in August, Eisenhower signed it and stated: "The new law which I am signing today includes one of the many recommendations made by this Administration to support existing statutes in defeating the Communist conspiracy in this country." The president noted that his administration had already stepped up enforcement of the laws against subversives, having convicted 41 Communist Party leaders, indicted 35 others, and deported 105 "subversive aliens." Eisenhower further noted that he had signed the witness immunity bill and a bill requiring "Communist-Action" and "Communist-Front" organizations to register with the Subversive Activities Control Board, and had created a Division of Internal Security in the Department of Justice. All of this activity had been accomplished, he concluded, while preserving "the rights of the accused in accordance with our traditions and the Bill of Rights."[56]

As the Communist Control Act was making its way through Congress, Senator McCarthy was escalating his attacks on the U.S. Army. Once again, a Senate subcommittee—this time his own—scheduled hearings into these charges. But, in the mind of one senator at least, McCarthy had gone too far. One week prior to the start of the hearings, Senator Ralph Flanders (Republican–Vermont) accused McCarthy of being "a one-man party, and that its name is McCarthyist," and of concealing, by his words and deeds, the "mortal danger in which our country finds itself from the external enemies of mankind." Flanders was congratulated by only two Senators: Herbert Lehman (Democrat–New York) and John Sherman Cooper (Republican–Kentucky).[57] Although the hearings opened on March 16, 1954, the public sessions did not commence until April 22. The 36 public sessions were televised, a factor that directly contributed to McCarthy's loss of reputation. On June 1, a few weeks before the hearings ended, Flanders denounced McCarthy as someone who had divided his country, his church, and his party. Were he, Flanders concluded, "in the pay of the Communists, he could not have done a better job for them."[58] Ten days later, Flanders introduced a resolution charging McCarthy with "unbecoming conduct" and calling for him to be removed from the Government Operations Committee. No senator congratulated Flanders, nor did any join with him as a co-sponsor of the resolution, but the motion was agreed to and referred to the Committee on Rules and Administration. As it made its slow way through Senate channels, it gained increasing support from both sides of the aisle.

Meanwhile, the Republicans, in the congressional election campaign, again used the Communists-in-government charge as their main issue against their Democratic challengers. But this time the tactic did not work: the Democrats won control of both houses of Congress.[59] One month later, the Senate condemned McCarthy. To keep their anti-communism credentials intact, however, those same senators, in January 1955, unanimously approved the following resolution:

That the Communist Party of the United States is recognized to be a part of the international Communist conspiracy against the United States and all the democratic forms of government. It is the sense of the Senate that its appropriate committees should continue diligently and vigorously to investigate, expose, and combat this conspiracy and all subversive elements and persons connected therewith.[60]

In his next two State of the Union addresses, Eisenhower briefly noted that his administration would "continue to ferret out and destroy Communist subversion" and would not "relax its efforts to deal forthrightly and vigorously in protection of this government and its citizens against subversion."[61] His public remarks on the topic decreased significantly, however. The party platforms of 1956 only briefly mentioned domestic anti-communism. The Democrats condemned "the Republican Administration's violation of the rights of Government employees by a heartless and unjustified confusing of 'security' and 'loyalty,' " while the Republicans credited themselves with having "left no stone unturned to remove from Government the irresponsible and those whose employment was not clearly consistent with national security."[62] Eisenhower, in his 1957 inauguration speech and subsequent State of the Union address, did not mention the subject of anti-communism at all.

Nevertheless, the Senate Subcommittee on Internal Security (SISS), now chaired by James Eastland (Democrat–Mississippi), remained on the job. In late 1955, it issued an 844-page Cumulative Index to its previous hearings and reports. In addition, following the voluntary appearance of CBS News broadcaster Winston Burdett before the subcommittee, it launched an investigation of communism in press, radio, and television. The Eastland-led Subcommittee issued subpoenas to the people named by Burdett and to thirty-eight others, including 16 to employees of *The New York Times*. Those witnesses who invoked the Fifth Amendment were fired, and their union, the American Newspaper Guild, refused to back them. The *New York Times* publisher, Arthur Ochs Sulzberger, condemned them for failing to "meet the obligations" that "every member of our news or editorial staff must assume." Four were cited for contempt for challenging the relevancy of the subcommittee's questions, but after an extensive legal process, none was convicted of the charge.[63]

Over at the FBI, J. Edgar Hoover also soldiered on. He continued to provide information to the SISS and the Committee on Un-American Activities. On his own authority, without the approval of the president or the U.S. Attorney General, he launched COINTELPRO-Communist Party as an attempt to harass, disrupt, and discredit, by any means, the Communist Party. Hoover then traveled around the country collecting honorary degrees and delivering anti-Communist speeches.

His influence and power were at their peak: Republicans deferred to him, and Democrats dared not call for his removal.

THE ROLE OF THE JUDICIARY

The relative objectivity about radical speech that federal judges had displayed during the late 1930s and World War II years waned rapidly after 1945, partly because of the Cold War and partly because four more conservative justices were appointed to the U.S. Supreme Court (Harold Burton, Fred Vinson, Tom Clark, and Sherman Minton).[64] The federal judiciary's much more restrictive approach to radical free speech was heralded by two decisions at the appellate level, both upholding contempt of Congress charges against witnesses who used the First Amendment as their reason for refusing to answer questions posed to them by members of the Committee on Un-American Activities. In the first case, *Barsky et al. v. United States*, Judge E. Barrett Prettyman stated: "Congress has the power to make an inquiry of an individual which may elicit the answers that the witness is a believer in Communism or a member of the Communist Party."[65] One year later, in the Hollywood Ten cases (*Lawson v. United States* and *Trumbo v. United States*), Judge Bennet C. Clark wrote that a properly appointed congressional committee "has the *power* to inquire whether a witness subpoenaed by it is or is not a member of the Communist Party or a believer in communism." In his *obiter dicta*, Clark stated: "No one can doubt in these chaotic times that the destiny of all nations hangs in the balance in the current ideological struggle, between communistic-thinking and democratic-thinking peoples of the world. Neither Congress nor any court is required to disregard the impact of world events, however impartially or dispassionately they view them."[66]

The first major case involving Communist free speech was decided in 1950. It concerned section 9(h) of the Taft-Hartley Act, which required labor union officials to sign non-Communist affidavits. Appellants argued that this clause violated their First Amendment rights. Chief Justice Vinson, who wrote the majority opinion, agreed that the clause did have a chilling effect on speech, but indicated that it did not violate the First Amendment because its purpose was to protect the public from political strikes that might block interstate commerce, not from hearing the political ideas of appellants. "Political strikes" were "evil," Vinson wrote, and Congress has the power to attempt to prevent them and to protect the public from that evil, "even though First Amendment rights of persons or groups are thereby in some manner infringed."[67]

In April of the following year, a U.S. District Court judge delivered what was perhaps the strongest statement about the evil effects of Communist activity in the United States. In his sentencing statement about Julius and Ethel Rosenberg, Judge Irving R. Kaufman accused them of murder, betraying their fellow countrymen, abetting "Russian terror," "putting into the hands of the Russians the A-bomb years before our best scientists predicted Russia would perfect the bomb," and altering "the course of history to the disadvantage of our country." He also blamed the Rosenbergs for "the Communist aggression in Korea."[68]

Two months later, in June 1951, the U.S. Supreme Court upheld the conviction of 11 of the top leaders of the CPUSA for violating the Alien Registration Act. According to Harry Kalven, Jr., the petitioners were "charged with talking but convicted of action"; it was their identity as speakers for the Communist Party—not their Communist speech—that was deemed dangerous.[69] Nevertheless, Chief Justice Vinson, basing his majority opinion on a set of questionable assumptions, stated:

> The formation by petitioners of such a highly organized conspiracy, with rigidly disciplined members subject to call when the leaders, these petitioners, felt that the time had come for action, coupled with the inflammable nature of world conditions, similar uprisings in other countries, and the touch-and-go nature of our relations with countries with whom petitioners were in the very least ideologically attuned, convince us that their convictions were justified on this score.[70]

In addition, the Court consistently rejected cases challenging state and city loyalty programs, congressional investigating committees, and deportation of aliens.[71]

There were, to be sure, some cracks in this dike. At the end of 1950, Federal District Court Judge Sylvester J. Ryan ordered the release of 16 aliens who had been detained at Ellis Island under a provision of the Internal Security Act. The denial of bail, Ryan ruled, was "arbitrary and an abuse of discretion on the part of the Attorney General." The government had not, Ryan added, presented any factual evidence to substantiate the claim that the detainees represented a threat to national security nor a "scintilla" of evidence that proved they were agents of a foreign power.[72] In 1951, the U.S. Supreme Court reversed a lower court's dismissal of a complaint against the Attorney General of the United States for placing three organizations on his list of sub-versive organizations.[73] The following year, the Court ruled that a state cannot require its employees to establish their loyalty by extracting from them an oath denying past affiliation to the Commu-nist Party.[74]

In a 1953 case involving conscientious objector status, Supreme Court Justice Felix Frankfurter (joined by Justices William O. Douglas and Hugo Black) dissented against the majority ruling that the appli-cant did not have to be shown the negative FBI report and names of those interviewed. Frankfurter wrote: "The enemy is not so yet near the gate that we should allow respect for traditions of fairness, which has heretofore prevailed in this country, to be overborne by military exigencies." Douglas, in his dissent, stated: "The use of statements by informers who need not confront the person under investigation or accusation has such an infamous history that it should be rooted out from our procedure."[75] Also that year, in a case that did not involve a Communist, the Court affirmed a Circuit Court of Appeals ruling overturning the conviction of a man who had refused to reveal to a House subcommittee the names of the purchasers of books dis-tributed by his organization. Justice Frankfurter ruled that the resolu-tion enabling the subcommittee to act was given too broad an interpretation and too great a scope, thereby interfering with the respondent's First Amendment rights.[76]

Perhaps the most significant set of rulings challenging the domestic Cold War came from Luther W. Youngdahl, a U.S. District Court Judge in the District of Columbia circuit. His rulings came in perhaps the most extraordinary case of the third "red scare": the persecution and prosecution of Owen Lattimore. Virtually the entire anti-Communist apparatus had mobilized against this professor of Asian studies, who had served as an advisor to Chiang Kai-shek during World War II. Lattimore was the target of McCarthy, McCarran, J. Edgar Hoover, the Department of Justice, the right-wing press, the "China Lobby," and several ex-Communists. Following his testimony before McCarran's subcommittee, the senator publicly pressured Attorney General James P. McGranery to indict Lattimore for perjury, even though several Department of Justice officials and the FBI questioned the basis of such an indictment.

Lattimore was indicted in December 1952, on seven counts of per-jury stemming from his testimony to the Senate Internal Security Sub-committee. In May 1953, however, Youngdahl dismissed four of the seven perjury counts and declared the other three of doubtful materiality. He noted "the necessity of weighing the balance between the broad powers of Congress to investigate and the protections offered by individuals by the Bill of Rights." He concluded his opinion with the following statement: "Communism's fallacy and viciousness can be demonstrated without striking down the protection of the 1st Amendment of discourse, discussion, and debate. When public excitement runs high as to alien ideologies, it is the time when we must be particularly alert not to impair the ancient landmarks set up by the Bill of Rights." By a vote of 8-1, the Circuit Court of Appeals upheld this ruling. The prosecutors revised the indictment, but in January 1955 Youngdahl threw out every count because, he wrote, "To require defendant to go to trial for perjury under charges so formless and obscure as those before the Court would be unprecedented and would make a sham of the Sixth Amendment and the Federal Rule [7(c)] requiring specificity of charges." Five months later, when the Circuit Court of Appeals failed to achieve a majority for overruling this decision, the Attorney General decided to drop the case against Lattimore.[77]

By 1956, nearly 40 percent of the Supreme Court's cases involved communism or subversive activities.[78] A new set of Eisenhower appointees (Earl Warren, John M. Harlan II, and William Brennan), who turned out to be much more moderate than those appointed by Truman, soon changed the direction of the Court, however. This new direction became evident in 1955, when the Court, in *Quinn v. United States* (349 U. S. 155), liberally construed the Fifth Amendment's privilege against self-incrimination. The following year, in *Slochower v. Board of Education of New York City* (350 U. S. 351), the Court overturned the firing of a Brooklyn College professor who had invoked the Fifth Amendment at an investigatory hearing, ruling that the college's charter provision allowing summary dismissals was unconstitutional. That same day, the Court handed down its decision in *Pennsylvania v. Nelson* (350 U. S. 497), which overturned a conviction under the state's sedition law, ruling that it had been superseded by the Alien Registration Act. This decision had the effect of invalidating sedition statutes in more than 40 states and territories. In addition, in *Cole v. Young* (351 U. S. 356), the Court overturned a firing under the Internal Security Act because no determination had been made that the petitioner was in a position to adversely affect "national security" as the term was used in that act.

Six decisions, in June 1957, completed the Supreme Court's effort to place procedural safeguards around anti-Communist legislation and investigative processes. In the first case, the Court held that it was a denial of due process to refuse to admit to a state bar an otherwise qualified candidate with a real or alleged Communist background.[79] The conviction of Clinton Jencks, for lying on his Taft-Hartley affidavit, was reversed on the grounds that the government had refused to allow the defense to see the reports written by the two paid FBI undercover agents whose testimony had been the basis of Jencks's conviction. Justice William Brennan wrote: "We hold that the criminal action must be dismissed when the Government, on the ground of privilege, elects not to comply with an order to produce, for the accused's inspection and for admission in evidence, relevant statements or reports in its possession of government witnesses touching the subject matter of their testimony at the trial."[80]

The decision in *Yates v. United States*, without specifically saying so, contradicted the *Dennis* decision. In the *Yates* ruling, the conviction of 14 leaders of the California Communist Party, under the organizing clause of the Alien Registration Act, was overturned, and a much more concrete set of facts was henceforth required for conviction under the advocacy clause. Justice Harlan wrote: "We need scarcely to say that however much one may abhor even the abstract preaching of forcible overthrow of government, or believe that forcible overthrow is the ultimate purpose to which the Communist Party is dedicated, it is upon the evidence in this record that petitioners must be judged in this case."[81]

In *Watkins v. United States* (354 U.S. 178), the Court held that the power of a congressional investigating committee is broad but not unlimited, and it lacks the power to expose for the sake of exposure.[82] The ruling in *Sweezy v. New Hampshire* (354 U.S. 234) limited the inquiry power of a state legislative investigating committee. Finally, the *Service v. Dulles* decision (354 U.S. 363) overturned the discharge of a Department of State employee, on the basis that the Department had not complied with its own regulations regarding administrative hearings on alleged security threats.

These cases unleashed a storm of protest from conservatives and congressional Republicans, but brought a chorus of praise from liberals. Several members of Congress proposed bills to weaken the power of the federal courts in the area of subversion. Nevertheless, after June 1, 1957, the U.S. government did not file any further cases alleging violation of the Alien Registration Act. At the same time, the government continued to apply pressure to the Communist Party via the registration provisions of the Internal Security Act, the deportation clauses of the McCarran-Walter Act, and the rejection of passport applications. However, the passport power was revoked in June 1958, when the Supreme Court ruled that Congress had not given the Department of State the authority to withhold passports from citizens because of their beliefs or associations.[83] Later, following seven more years of litigation, the Supreme Court decided (by a vote of 8-0) that the registration provisions of the Internal Security Act amounted to self-incrimination in violation of the Fifth Amendment.[84]

CONCLUSION

Clearly, between 1947 and 1954, a bipartisan domestic Cold War consensus had been forged in the Congress, but its anti-communism was not mirrored in the executive branch, even though the Eisenhower administration was markedly more anti-Communist than its predecessor. These disagreements between the two branches, however, did not derail or even slow the official anti-Communist juggernaut, which swept up in its jaws tens of thousands of people and disrupted hundreds of organizations, several departments of the U.S. government, and many vocations and industries. It also provoked and sustained a great deal of anxiety among the citizenry. The momentum finally slowed and came to a halt because few credible "subversives" remained to be investigated or prosecuted, and the federal courts began to limit what investigators and prosecutors could do. Nevertheless, anti-communism as an attitude and ideology of government officials remained strong, and critics of the Cold War did not get appointed or elected to public office.

Institutional Anti-Communism, 1945–1957

Institutional anti-Communists were second only to official anti-Communists in their determination to expose Communists and exclude them from nongovernment organizations as well as from the movie and broadcast industries. Starting with a guilt-by-association premise (if one's ideas or methods are comparable those of the CPUSA or if one is an apologist of the Soviet Union, one is, ipso facto, a Communist or a Communist sympathizer) and utilizing the transcripts of congressional hearings, the publications of the various state and federal investigating committees and those of the indiscriminate listers, institutional anti-Communists proved very effective in calling attention to the "Communist threat," provoking expulsions and schisms, and policing blacklists.

RELIGIOUS AND RELIGION-BASED GROUPS

Catholics

The leaders of the Catholic Church had only slightly tempered their hostility toward the CPUSA and the Soviet Union during World War II. Their concern for the fate of Catholic churches in Eastern and Central Europe kept them from supporting the United States–Soviet Union alliance, and when Catholics in the Soviet-occupied countries came under severe duress, the Church's antagonism toward the Soviet state skyrocketed. From 1945 onward, every Soviet act received pronounced scrutiny in the Catholic press (circulation = 9 million). The

Knights of Columbus were particularly active in this regard: they established a Crusade for the Preservation and Promotion of American Ideals, took out newspaper advertisements; made radio broadcasts, distributed free copies of Monsignor Sheen's *Communism and the Conscience of the West* (discussed later in this section), and organized discussion groups and town meetings in all parts of the United States.[1] The news service of the National Catholic Welfare Conference and the Catholic Information Society of New York distributed numerous circulars, pamphlets, and announcements.[2] The Catholic War Veterans boycotted "subversive" enterprises, particularly suspect movies, and established anti-Communist educational programs; a number of small Jozef Cardinal Mindszenty Circles and Freedom Foundations blossomed; and the Polish American Congress, which had been established in 1944 to promote a free and independent Poland, evolved after the Yalta and Potsdam conferences into a staunch anti-Communist organization.[3]

In November 1945, Father John F. Cronin completed his report, *The Problem of American Communism in 1945: Facts and Recommendations*. Cronin urged that the church proceed by preaching "social justice," providing "Catholic social teaching to the workers," and widely distributing information on communism to the public. In a separate memorandum, he recommended that the church hire ex-FBI agents to organize anti-Communist lay groups, "completely independent of the church." Although Cronin failed to establish a permanent connection with the FBI, Bureau employees provided him with material for the pamphlets he wrote for the U.S. Chamber of Commerce. Cronin later assisted Richard Nixon with his contributions to the Mundt-Nixon bill and the prosecution of Alger Hiss, and he helped establish two anti-Communist publications (*Counterattack* and *Plain Talk*).[4]

Monsignor Fulton J. Sheen, although he labeled communism "an *active* barbarism outside Western civilization," rejected the use of "vituperation, name-calling and personal hate" as well as the notion that Catholics "are called on to be God's agents to execute vindictive judgment on the Communists."[5] One of his biographers wrote: "His [Sheen's] thesis was that Communism is to be hated as a doctor hates pneumonia in a sick child. But the Communist, the potential child of god, must be loved as a sick child is loved."[6] Sheen, who recommended five moral, educational, and spiritual ways to counter the Communist message, did not agree with Senator Joseph McCarthy's approach, and he never met the senator. He did, however, meet regularly with FBI agents.[7] Moreover, in 1957, he was one of three religious representatives to meet with Richard Arens, staff director of the

Committee on Un-American Activities, to discuss "the ideological fallacies of communism." Sheen told Arens that communism could best be met by informing people about its philosophy and tightening the treason laws.[8]

For his part, Father Edmund A. Walsh continued to lecture on Soviet power, but he rarely spoke in public about domestic anti-communism.[9] In his speeches and writings about the Soviet Union, Walsh approved the use of any measure necessary to defend Christian civilization, including atomic bombs. In his 1951 book *Total Empire*, Walsh argued that those who used the term "Cold War" to describe the current international situation had failed to understand what was actually occurring. Soviet communism, he stated, "never relaxes," and he insisted that the threat it posed must be met by a permanently enhanced military power and "a renaissance of spiritual power in the souls of men through recognition of the strength religion supplies to the stability of mind." In terms of the domestic Communist threat, he warned of an elaborate underground apparatus constructed by the CPUSA, wherein "every reliable Communist is the focal point of a small group of secret sympathizers on whom he can count and to whom he transmits the Party line." In Walsh's opinion, this threat had to be met by strong anti-Communist legislation such as the Internal Security Act.[10]

The most active and perhaps most effective Catholic anti-Communists were the church officials who worked with the Association of Catholic Trade Unionists (ACTU). After the war, the ACTU pursued a one-plank program: "dump the Communists," by any means necessary. Its main target was the Communist-led unions in the CIO. To ensure their removal, the ACTU's chapters began contesting elections at the local and national levels; joining hands with the AFL, the Committee on Un-American Activities, and employers to promote dual unionism; supporting the curtailment of the democratic rights of left-led unions; and pushing CIO president Philip Murray, a Catholic, to expel those leftists who could not be won over. As a result of their efforts, many left-led unions were weakened and isolated. The Detroit chapter aided the Reuther brothers' campaign to take control of the United Auto Workers, and the Pittsburgh and Schenectady chapters aided the Carey faction in gaining power in the United Electrical, Radio and Machine Workers of America (UE).[11]

Perhaps the most effective ACTU leader was Father Charles Rice. Although he had remained antagonistic toward the Soviet Union during the war, he did not have much of an impact on the workers in

Pittsburgh, who had adopted a friendly attitude toward the alliance. After the war ended and Eastern and Central European countries were occupied by the Red Army, however, the attitude of Slavic and Catholic workers in the area changed. Rice moved immediately to build on that altered outlook. In addition to writing a series of anti-Soviet columns in the *Pittsburgh Catholic*, he produced *How to Decontrol Your Union of Communists*, a handbook that contained a list of Communist-controlled unions. According to those who opposed him, Rice also engaged in ferocious red-baiting.[12] One member of the Carey group later testified that Rice taught the insurgents to imitate "Communist strategy" and schooled them in the art of name-calling, red-baiting, rabble-rousing, and the disruption of meetings in which they were in the minority. "Rice taught us 'anything' went."[13]

One month prior to the UE national convention scheduled for September 1949, Rice and some of the people supporting Carey went to Washington, D.C., and met with Congressman Francis Walter and some of the staff of the Committee on Un-American Activities. The committee scheduled hearings to investigate Communist infiltration of the local a few days before the election of delegates to the UE convention, and subpoenaed three people (Tom Quinn, Thomas J. Fitzpatrick, and Frank Panzino) who were prominent in Local 601 and who were candidates for office in the upcoming election. All three invoked the First and Fifth Amendments as their basis for refusing to answer the committee's questions, and all were cited for contempt of Congress.[14] Despite this interference, the resolutions and slates of the incumbent UE leaders won easily. The following day, Carey announced the formation of a new union, the International Union of Electrical, Radio and Machine Workers, "to wrest the UE from Communist control."[15] UE leaders, incensed at the support the CIO leaders were giving to Carey, left the CIO. In November 1949, the CIO convention formally expelled the UE.

The following year, in the days leading up to representation elections at the Sylvania and Westinghouse plants in Pennsylvania, which pitted the UE against Carey's new union, the ACTU and the Carey faction put tremendous pressure on the Catholic workers. According to one Catholic worker, "Father Rice would have the parish priest call in the wife of a UE leader or an active supporter and tell her that her children might not be able to continue in parochial school." Rice labeled the UE as an antireligious organization that was trying to destroy the church. One of the ACTU's circulars stated: "The UE International Union and many of its followers are on the side of

Communism. They are Communist weapons for the overthrow of Government and Religion."[16] Again, the Committee on Un-American Activities subpoenaed UE leaders and cited several for contempt. This time, the effort was successful: at the Westinghouse plants, the UE lost representation rights for 73 percent of the workers to IUE.[17]

Ironically, two lawyers for the ACTU were red-baited by Catholic Church officials during a strike for higher wages and shorter hours by the grave diggers at Calvary Cemetery in New York. As employees of the New York diocese, they were confronting Francis Cardinal Spellman, perhaps the most zealous anti-Communist in the Catholic Church. He and Monsignor George C. Ehardt accused the union— Local 293 of the United Cemetery Workers—of being Communist controlled, fired the negotiating committee, and threatened to dismiss the strikers if they did not return to work. When the workers asked two Catholic Labor Defense lawyers to intervene with the diocese, diocese officials accused the lawyers of being Communists.[18]

Although most Catholic Church officials approved of Senator McCarthy, a few opposed his methods. For example, Father John F. Cronin had, in spring 1950, tried to steer McCarthy toward a more cautious, less erratic approach and, failing to do so, quietly pulled away. Public critics included Robert Hartnett, the editor of *America*, the Jesuit publication; Bishop Bernard J. Shiel (of Chicago); Congressman Eugene McCarthy (Democrat–Minnesota); and the editors of *Commonweal*. In addition, during the 1954 campaign to block Senate condemnation of McCarthy, the Knights of Columbus remained silent on the issue.[19]

Protestants

The front of religious anti-Communism was widened by a new generation of fundamentalist Protestants, who proclaimed "godless" communism to be the main enemy of a Christian America.[20] The publications of the National Association of Evangelicals (founded in 1943) and the Church League of America (founded in 1937) regularly denounced the presence of Communists in churches and the U.S. government, while the preachers associated with the American Council of Christian Churches (formed by Carl McIntire), the Christian Crusade and Anti-Communist Leadership School (formed by Billy James Hargis), and Youth for Christ (Billy Graham's organization) constantly issued pronouncements on the satanic nature of communism. Graham, in a 1949 speech, stated: "Communism is a religion that is inspired, directed, and motivated by the Devil himself, who has declared war against almighty God." All of these Protestant leaders were staunch supporters of McCarthy. Hargis and McIntire supplied him with research material and helped him write some of his speeches. In addition, McIntire was particularly close to J. B. Matthews and the Committee on Un-American Activities.[21]

Jews

A strain of organized anti-communism among Jewish people in the United States can be traced back to 1906, when the American Jewish Committee (AJC) was founded, but it was always one of many agenda items, frequently overshadowed by others, notably anti-Nazism. In the early years, the main concern of the AJC was to disavow any connections between Jews and Bolshevism, but to word those pronouncements very carefully, so as not to provoke anti-Semitism in the Soviet Union.[22] In addition, a number of Jewish socialists, notably Abraham Cahan, who had at first welcomed the Russian Revolution, became fervent anti-Communists as the result of their bitter struggles with the nascent Communist parties.[23]

During the 1930s, Jewish groups with less nuanced positions were organized. The Jewish Labor Committee was formed in February 1934 by Jewish members of the garment workers' unions to fight Nazism in Europe, defend Jewish interests, and battle against anti-democratic forces in the United States. From the beginning, this organization refused to join forces with any Communist-led groups, and it resolved, in 1938, to join "only with those Jewish and non-Jewish bodies who adhered to the viewpoint of broad state liberty and democracy in all countries."[24] After 1941, the Jewish Labor Committee became increasingly concerned about the fate of Soviet Jews and even more strongly anti-Communist.

At about the same time, a student Zionist organization, Avukah, was founded to fight against anti-Semitism, defend civil liberties, participate in anti-fascist action, and aid the migration of Jews to Palestine. According to an article about the group published in the *Harvard Crimson*, it had charters at every important college or university.[25] Nathan Glazer, a student at City College of New York, who joined circa 1940–1941 and became editor of *Avukah Student Action*, recalled: "We were generally allied on campus issues with the anti-Stalinist Left—the socialists and the Trotskyites."[26]

After World War II, a sharp, inconclusive debate occurred in the AJC executive committee over whether to attack communism publicly or to combat the attempts by reactionaries and Communists to identify Jews with communism. The committee decided to focus its efforts on educating the Jewish community about the incompatibility of communism and liberalism as well as anti-Semitism in the Soviet Union.[27] In November 1945, the AJC also founded a new magazine, *Commentary,* but the anti-communism of the staff members did not, according to Glazer, "make itself sharply evident" in the journal's early years. "I seem to recall," Glazer remembered, "a hesitation in making a full-blown attack on Communism. Perhaps we were inhibited by the idea that, as a Jewish magazine, a criticism of Communism legitimately fell within our purview only when it affected Jews." In February 1948, *Commentary* began to print articles on anti-Semitism in the Soviet Union.[28]

One month later, several Jewish anti-Communists—Alfred Kohlberg, Benjamin Gitlow, George Sokolsky, Eugene Lyons, and Isaac Don Levine, among others—who were dissatisfied with the hesitant approach of the AJC founded the American Jewish League Against Communism, an organization specifically devoted to anti-communism.[29] This new group, however, failed to gain much traction or make much of an impact.

Also in 1948, the Community Relations Committee of the Jewish Federation Council (in Los Angeles) created a Commission on Communism, which, according to Paul Jacobs, "worked assiduously" to expel any affiliated Communist or Communist-front groups and expose any Communists or Communist sympathizers.[30] Two years later, the AJC created a Staff Committee on Communism to direct a concentrated campaign of anti-communism in the Jewish community. It distributed a huge amount of literature and met with other Jewish groups in attempts to convince them to purge known Communists and Communist sympathizers from their ranks. As part of this campaign, the AJC joined the American Legion's All-American Conference to Combat Communism. In addition, AJC leaders regularly consulted with congressional committee investigators regarding the questioning of Jewish Communist witnesses, and with other religious organizations (e.g., the National Council of Churches for Christ and the National Catholic Welfare Conference) to offer suggestions about the least intrusive means of investigating communism in religious organizations. Finally, the AJC supplied material to the Un-American Activities Committee's investigation of the Communist-controlled Committee to Secure Justice for the Rosenbergs.[31]

Other Jewish groups sought—rhetorically at least—a middle ground between subversive hunting and civil liberties. For example, the

National Community Relations Advisory Council, an umbrella group for several Jewish organizations, between 1953 and 1956 issued a series of what it called "Joint Program Plans for Jewish Community Relations." The 1953 plan stated that "Jewish organizations have special responsibilities for guarding against and opposing Communist purposes and methods," especially Communist efforts to infiltrate Jewish organizations. But, the report warned, "foes of our civil liberties, sometimes abetted by the well-meaning but over-zealous, are taking advantage of the campaign against Communist infiltration and subversion to promote measures which directly threaten the welfare and freedom of individuals and organizations." Jewish organizations were counseled to be on constant alert for such excessive activities.[32]

According to Naomi Cohen, the AJC and other Jewish groups, although they paid lip service to civil liberties, did not act accordingly. They did not join public campaigns against national security legislation or loyalty investigations, nor did they support clemency for the Rosenbergs.[33]

AMERICAN LEGION

The American Legion catalyzed the formation of several state legislative investigating committees and supported many national conferences on un-American activities. In 1946, the Legislative Committee of the Illinois American Legion passed a resolution calling for the establishment of a legislative committee to investigate "seditious activities." The following August, the legislature created the Seditious Activities Investigation Commission (also known as the Broyles Commission), "to investigate any activities ... suspected of being directed toward the overthrow of the Government of the United States or the State of Illinois." Two former state American Legion commanders were appointed to serve on this commission, and the Legion strongly supported the anti-Communist bills recommended by the commission.[34]

In September 1948, at the behest, and with the support, of the American Legion, California State Senator Jack Tenney convened an Interstate Legislative Conference on Un-American Activities—a two-day meeting of representatives from 10 state legislative committees, several veterans organizations, and a few patriotic societies. Karl Barslaag, the head of the American Legion's Research Department and an adviser to several of the legislative committees in attendance, proclaimed that "Communists are "para-military members of a world conspiracy, blindly and totally devoted to its service and the ruthless advancement of its interest." Government leaders, he charged, were "totally and often completely unable to grasp the nature of the Communist conspiracy or what is even worse [were] completely indifferent." William C. Sawyer, chairman of the Legion's Americanization Committee, revealed that it had resumed its file system for collecting subversive names.[35]

In February 1949, the American Legion sponsored a conference devoted to subversive activities in Indianapolis. The following year, it convened All-American Conferences in New York (January) and Chicago (May). In August 1951, the New York State American Legion passed five resolutions calling on the state legislature to, among other things, prohibit any organization on the U.S. Attorney General's list from posting bail for any person and to strip the citizenship from anyone convicted of being a Communist or Communist supporter.[36]

Perhaps the American Legion's most fascinating project was its staging of a mock Communist takeover in Mosinee, Wisconsin, on May 1, 1950. Mosinee—a town of 1,400 in the center of the state—was "seized" by "Communists." The "attack," which was sponsored by the American Legion and led by two former Communists, Joseph Kornfeder and Benjamin Gitlow, removed the town from the United States and made it part of the United Soviet States of America. The mayor and police chief were arrested, road blocks were set up, every citizen was stopped and questioned, all businesses were nationalized, and all civic organizations and political parties were banned. In addition, the library was purged, films were proscribed, and black bread and potato soup was the only meal available at the town's restaurants. At the day-ending Americanization rally, State Commander Charles L. Larson described the day's events as a "mild demonstration of totalitarianism." The event received national media attention.[37]

The American Legion's most concerted activity involved the use of its file system of subversive names to maintain and extend the blacklist and graylist mechanisms in the broadcast and motion picture industries. The Legion began to impose itself on movie studio executives in early January 1950, when William P. Laffin, Commander of Hollywood Post No. 43, sent a copy of the January 4 *Alert* edition[38] to Darryl F. Zanuck, the head of Twentieth Century-Fox. That issue focused on the studio's recent release of *Halls of Montezuma*, which, *Alert* stated, "carries the credit as writer [Michael Blankfort] and director [Lewis Milestone] of two notorious participants in Communist fronts and causes." It then listed their Communist fronts and causes, citing as its source the 1948 report of the California Fact-Finding

Committee on Un-American Activities. Zanuck sent the copy of *Alert* to Blankfort. Blankfort, a former Marine, in turn wrote Commander Laffin that he (Blankfort) would not have joined any organization that he believed was not furthering the best interests of the United States, and stated that he had, in fact, resigned from organizations when he had learned that they were no longer pursuing "American aims." Blankfort concluded: "I am not a member of any organization which has been declared subversive by the Attorney General of the United States or the F.B.I." Laffin replied: "Our files on subversives are very complete. We have offered to help 'screen' the people in your industry for the good of it. Up to now, we have been ignored, so we will let the chips fall where they may—shall we say?" He urged Blankfort to "go to Sacramento and demand a hearing before the California Un-American Activities Committee, once and for all get squared away in the eyes of your people."[39]

Later that year, at its national convention, the editors of *American Legion Magazine* were instructed to publish an article detailing all the available information on the Communist associations of people still employed in the entertainment industry.[40] The December issue featured an article entitled "Did the Movies Really Clean House?," written by J. B. Matthews. This article claimed that a number of "recently exposed communists and collaborators with communist fronts are still connected with the production of motion pictures." Matthews listed more than 50 films that, he alleged, employed these "recently exposed communists and collaborators."[41]

The next month, January 1952, the new commander of Hollywood Post No. 43 sent a letter to Mitchell Wolfson, President of the National Theater Owners of America, stating that some producers had failed "to clean their house of its UnAmerican tenants." He enclosed a resolution passed by his Post in November 1951, with a clear warning that if it were carried forward "it may directly affect your activities in the Theater." The resolution requested that state Legion headquarters arrange for Legion pickets of any theater showing a movie carrying the name or credit of any person who did not cooperate with the Un-American Activities Committee.[42]

Concerned about this and other American Legion threats, Eric Johnston asked the National Commander (Donald Wilson) and the Director of Publications (James O'Neil) to meet with him and the heads of the eight major film studios in Washington, D.C., for (in the words of a *Los Angeles Times* reporter) "an unheralded, high-level 'exploratory' talk on possible methods to eliminate the 'menace of

Communism' from movies." At the meeting, which took place in April 1952, Johnston told the film executives that he had asked Wilson to meet with them about the American Legion claim that many Communists and "Communist associates" were still working in the industry and "to discuss with them this situation freely and frankly." Wilson told the motion picture executives that the American Legion would continue what he called its "public information program," but indicated that he would also cooperate with any "earnest" steps the industry would take to improve its reputation. The executives promised to cooperate and requested that any type of information that the Legion had connecting studio employees with communism be sent to the studios, in the form of a comprehensive list. The executives also invited Wilson to send a personal representative and a writer from the *American Legion Magazine* to talk directly to the studio heads in Hollywood.[43]

Industry leaders agreed among themselves that anyone named on the American Legion list would have to write a letter defending himself or herself and explaining his or her political affiliations and activities. Each letter would then be channeled through the studios to the Legion, and the Legion would then determine whether a particular letter was satisfactory.[44] The American Legion list, bearing more than 300 names, arrived at the major studios during the summer of 1952.[45]

National, state, and local offices and posts assiduously policed the motion picture industry throughout the 1950s. Local California posts supported Howard Hughes's efforts to purge Communists from his RKO studio, deny them screen credits, and block the efforts of a group of blacklistees to make a film, *Salt of the Earth*. When the blacklist began to crumble in the latter part of the decade, the American Legion attempted to pressure movie industry leaders to fortify it.[46]

LABOR UNIONS

In terms of sheer effectiveness, the leaders of the two main national labor federations—the AFL and the CIO—dealt perhaps the most significant blows to communism at home and abroad by undercutting the working-class base of the CPUSA. The AFL had long been prominent in the ranks of domestic anti-Communists and, during the last years of World War II, had positioned itself to challenge communism in Europe. At the war's end, the AFL's leaders rejected a request by the U.S. government to allow Soviet participation in the International Labor Organization as well as a request from the British to allow the

CIO to join the Anglo-American Trade Union Committee. The reason given for the latter rejection was that Communists in the CIO would use the opportunity to disrupt and poison relations between the AFL and the British Trade Union Congress. Then, when the International Federation of Trade Unions convened a World Trade Union Conference, which included the Soviet unions and the CIO, the AFL objected and refused to join the new World Federation of Trade Unions.[47]

Meanwhile, Jay Lovestone and Irving Brown, with funding from the Central Intelligence Agency, were successfully helping to block Communists from assuming leadership of the renascent German labor confederation, and engineering splits in the French and Italian Communist-dominated labor confederations. Lovestone worked closely with Benjamin Mandel, the research director of the Committee on Un-American Activities, and with the CIA's International Organizations Division.[48]

Although the CIO joined the World Federation of Trade Unions, it had begun to move closer to the AFL's anti-Communist position. In the autumn of 1946, several leaders of CIO unions formed the Committee for Democratic Trade Unionism to fight Communists and fascists. As noted earlier in this chapter, the ACTU assisted the Reuther brothers' effort to gain control of the United Auto Workers, and James Carey's schismatic group in the United Electrical Workers union. When the Reuther forces gained complete control of the UAW in November 1947, they decisively shifted the balance of power in the CIO against the Communists and their sympathizers.[49]

In 1948, Philip Murray realigned the CIO with anti-Communist liberals and Democrats, and joined it to the AFL as a proponent of the Cold War. During the 1948 presidential campaign, Murray formally (albeit temporarily) aligned the CIO with the liberal Americans for Democratic Action. In May 1949, the CIO withdrew from the World Federation of Trade Unions, joined with the AFL to establish the International Confederation of Free Trade Unionists, and began to expel its Communist-led unions.[50]

Both federations supported the Korean War, but they did not toe the same line when it came to Senator Joseph McCarthy. The AFL wavered on how to depict McCarthy until late 1951, when its newspaper began to portray him as a "symbol of political smear tactics." Nevertheless, delegates to the AFL's 1953 convention removed the term "McCarthyism" from a resolution condemning certain types of congressional investigations.[51] The CIO, in contrast, was a consistent critic of McCarthy from the outset. Based on his review of statements by CIO newspapers, conventions, and affiliates, David M. Oshinsky concluded that "To their thinking, at least, the Wisconsinite was not a dedicated anti-Communist but rather an extreme right-wing, partisan Republican who was attempting to destroy New Deal–Fair Deal programs."[52]

Their differences over McCarthy did not block the merger talks between the two confederations, which ended successfully in February 1955. The constitution of the new AFL-CIO stated, as a basic principle, that the organization "must be and remain free from any and all corrupt influences and from the undermining efforts of communist, fascist or other totalitarian agencies." The Executive Council was given the power to investigate allegations of any violations of that principle and to suspend any affiliate found guilty of such charges.[53]

AMERICAN BAR ASSOCIATION

After World War II, the American Bar Association (ABA) created a Special Committee to Study Communist Tactics, Strategy, and Objectives; a Special Committee of Education in the Contrast Between Liberty Under Law and Communism; and a Standing Committee on Education Against Communism. These committees worked closely with the Un-American Activities Committee, the FBI, and the American Legion.

At the ABA's 1948 convention, the delegates resolved to expel any lawyer who invoked the Fifth Amendment as a vehicle for refusing to deny membership in the Communist Party or who, in any manner, "publicly or secretly aids, supports or assists the world Communist movement to accomplish its objectives in the United States." Two years later, convention delegates resolved to ask the legislatures, courts, or other appropriate authority of each state or territory and the District of Columbia "to require each member of the Bar, within a reasonable time and periodically thereafter, to file an affidavit stating whether he is or ever has been a member of the Communist Party or affiliated therewith," or of any other organization advocating the overthrow of any government. If such membership or affiliation was revealed, an investigation was planned to determine that person's "fitness for continuance as an attorney."[54]

The ABA's House of Delegates also requested all state and local bar associations to disbar "all lawyers who are members of the Communist Party or who advocate Marxism-Leninism." Moreover, it petitioned the Eisenhower administration to exclude from litigating in federal courts and administrative agencies any lawyer who was a Communist or who failed to deny being a Communist under oath. The ABA also warned its members against advising their clients to invoke the Fifth Amendment. Finally, the Special Committee to Study Communist Tactics attempted, in several ways, to destroy the National Lawyers Guild.[55]

QUASI-INSTITUTIONS

Newspaper Columnists

Conservative anti-Communist journalists, many of whom wrote for William Randolph Hearst's publications, acted in a quasi-institutional manner. They exchanged information with one another, with the FBI, with congressional investigating committees, and with those involved in policing the motion picture blacklist.

The two most vocal of these journalists, George Sokolsky and Westbrook Pegler, were strong supporters of anti-Communists in Congress—notably, Senator McCarthy. Arnold Forster, the long-time general counsel of the Anti-Defamation League, called Sokolsky "the reigning potentate of anti-Communist journalism in America, who was much more than a Hearst columnist. He served as an advisor to Hearst officialdom about the political left, a sort of father-figure to younger like-minded writers, and a mentor to certain officials fixated on the Soviet Union as an instant threat to the United States."[56]

Other anti-Communist journalists of note during this period included Howard Rushmore,[57] Frederick Woltman,[58] Victor Lasky,[59] and Victor Reisel.[60] King Features (a Hearst syndicate), the McCormick-Patterson newspapers (*New York Daily News*, *Chicago Tribune*, and *Washington Times-Herald*, in particular), and the Scripps-Howard chain prominently publicized the accusations of the various congressional investigating committees.[61]

The "China Lobby"

The epithet "China Lobby" serves as a convenient, albeit inaccurate, sobriquet for the supporters of aid to Chiang Kai-shek.[62] The main force behind the "Lobby" was actually Alfred Kohlberg, who spent the later part of his life campaigning against those parties who, in his opinion, were aiding the Communist cause in Asia. Following a trip to China in 1943, which he undertook to investigate reports of corruption and graft in Chiang's government, Kohlberg concluded that a flow of mendacious reporting from China was blinding the Roosevelt administration and the U.S. public about the true (or positive) nature of China's government and army. When he returned to the United States, none of the organizations to which he belonged accepted Kohlberg's conclusions. He then learned, from a colleague, Dr. Maurice William, that the "central source of most of the untruths" about China was the Institute of Pacific Relations. Kohlberg read all the Institute's publications, followed by the *Daily Worker* and the *Communist*. Concluding that clear parallels existed between the Institute's publications and the CPUSA line, he launched a three-year crusade to expose and purge Communists from the Institute. His charges were decisively rejected at a special meeting of the Institute, but his campaign did cause contributions to the organization to slow significantly.[63]

In 1946, Kohlberg moved in a different direction. At the invitation of Father John Cronin, Kohlberg met with several ex-FBI agents and Benjamin Mandel. They decided to establish a magazine, titled *Plain Talk*, which would be devoted to the fight against communism, and they chose Isaac Don Levine to edit the new publication. Kohlberg provided the funding. Later the same year, he founded the American China Policy Association to counter the "untruths" he believed were being spread about Chiang Kai-shek. In the ensuing years, Kohlberg was solicited by McCarthy and McCarran for derogatory information about Owen Lattimore.[64] In addition, Kohlberg, Henry Luce, and a group of congressional Republicans joined together to demand unconditional support for Chiang Kai-shek, although they did not propose sending U.S. forces to the Chinese mainland to confront the Communist forces there.[65]

The main effect of this group of people, according to John Thomas, was "to change the nature of the debate from foreign policy questions to ones involving loyalty and security." In the end, they succeeded in changing the focus of the China debate from the defects of Chiang and his regime to the loyalty of those advising about, making, and implementing China policy.[66]

Academics

The influence of academic anti-Communists on public thinking about the Soviet Union grew steadily until 1959, when the so-called (by academic anti-Communists) "revisionists" began to produce books critical of the Cold War and those books that had approved it.

(See Chapter 11.) For the first decade of the Cold War, the bulk of academic writings on the subject of communism had focused on the Soviet Union,[67] categorizing it as a "totalitarian" state. Although these writers were not, for the most part, activists, their works made a significant contribution to the anti-Communist cause by giving a scholarly imprimatur to a number of tendentious conclusions.

One of the first such books was an anthology—a compilation of writings critical of all aspects of the Soviet Union. Its second section was titled "From Dictatorship to Totalitarian Society (1928–1939)"; in his introduction to the third section, the editor stated that the Soviet totalitarian state now "threatening the entire world" was the "grotesque End Product" of three decades of suppression and terror.[68] By this time, according to Stephen J. Whitfield, "the concept of totalitarianism had already become a staple of American intellectual and political discourse."[69]

The major work in this line of thought was Hannah Arendt's *Origins of Totalitarianism*, completed in the autumn of 1949 and published in 1951. The last third of Arendt's massive tome was devoted to modern totalitarian states. Her scholarly conclusions fit nicely into the Manichaean warnings of conservative and institutional anti-Communists. According to her analysis, totalitarian movements, by their nature, aim for an eventual world conquest. Consequently, even after they have seized power, they continue to struggle "for total domination of the total population of the earth." Their drive to eliminate "every competing nontotalitarian reality is inherent in the totalitarian regimes themselves." They use the state they have seized as the vehicle for their "long-range goal of world conquest," because if they do not pursue global rule as their ultimate goal, "they are only too likely to lose whatever power they have already seized." In effect, Arendt posited the existence of a "totalitarian conspiracy against the nontotalitarian world."[70]

In March 1953, Arendt and dozens of other political scientists, historians, and social scientists attended a conference on the subject of totalitarianism. The participants failed, however, to reach firm agreement on the elements of totalitarianism. And though, as noted by Carl J. Friedrich, the chairman of the organizing committee, there were "emergent areas of agreement, ... they were limited in scope."[71] In fact, in the conference's first paper, George Kennan was "moved to wonder whether there is any generic phenomenon that we can identify and describe from actual experience as totalitarianism."[72] In a later discussion, he made the following key point: "I would ask the Conference members not to concentrate too heavily on what totalitarianism in some abstract sense *is*, to the exclusion of concern with what it is *becoming*. Totalitarianism is dynamic; it does not stand still."[73]

In general, those who subscribed to the totalitarian thesis disagreed with Kennan on two points. First, as did Paul Kecskemeti in the penultimate paper delivered at the conference, they identified a "Communist type of totalitarianism," notable for its "Communist cadres and masses, driving—or being manipulated—toward the strategic goal of *coup d'état*."[74] Second, as Merle Fainsod did both at the 1953 conference and in print the following year, they questioned Kennan's notion that Soviet power might be in the process of eroding from within. Fainsod, at the end of his detailed discussion of "the philosophy, as well as the anatomy, of Soviet totalitarianism," stated that "the immediate prospects for such a development are not hopeful." He saw no prospect that Soviet international or domestic policy would be fundamentally revised.[75]

In effect, the totalitarian writers believed that they had discovered a new form of state behavior ("Soviet aggressiveness," as distinct from traditional imperialism) and a new state goal (a "Sovietized world," as distinct from a Soviet sphere of influence). They also redefined the term "free world" as including democracies and non-Communist dictatorships. For example, Anthony T. Bouscaren, Associate Professor of Political Science at the University of San Francisco, stated that the Soviet Union was the bastion of world revolution, determined to impose its revolutionary will on the world. Thus, he concluded, the "basic doctrine of Soviet foreign policy is the doctrine of inevitability of war, leading to the victory of Soviet power over resisting non-Soviet states."[76] In 1954, the 39 scholars, journalists, and government officials who participated in a conference titled "The Problem of Soviet Imperialism," sponsored by Johns Hopkins University's School of Advanced International Studies, came to a similar conclusion. According to the editor of the papers presented there, "the Soviet Union proceeds unswervingly toward the goal of world communism"; "the problem is deadly serious"; and "the dangers to the free world are of great magnitude."[77]

Ex-Communist and Conservative Anti-Communism, 1945–1957

In his memoir, Lionel Abel wrote that anti-Communist intellectuals like him faced a moral problem during the first decade of the domestic Cold War: "the need we felt to support powers or policies we had in the past opposed, so as to act more effectively against other powers and other policies, to which, for reasons of principle, we had come to stand in even greater opposition."[1] Some conservative and most liberal anti-Communists faced a similar dilemma—namely, whether to support the use of methods uncomfortably similar to those used by their Communist opponents. Those who said "yes" (the types covered in this chapter, and the left-of-liberal types discussed in Chapter 9) believed that if a person sincerely wanted to strengthen national security, that individual must advocate fighting fire with fire. Those who said "no" (the civil libertarian anti-Communists discussed in Chapter 10) believed that using such methods would compromise democratic values, undermine national security, and lead the country toward fascism or some equivalent tyranny. Those who said "on occasion" (the liberals discussed in Chapter 9) tried to find a middle ground between enhancing national security and protecting civil liberties.

EX-COMMUNISTS

Ex-Communists advanced the anti-Communist cause in two significant ways. First, they provided, in their memoirs and interviews, a stream of anecdotal evidence that Communists were as "treacherous," "deceitful," and "ruthless" as the official anti-Communists said they were.

Second, the testimonies of a few dozen of them before congressional investigating committees, administrative hearings, and court trials facilitated these processes and kept alive the "subversive" threat. Their fingers never seemed to stop pointing; their memories appeared limitless.

Two ex-Communists, in particular—Louis Budenz and John Lautner—seemed constantly to be on one witness stand or another: Budenz testified 33 times in 12 years, Lautner 25 times in 4 years.[2] Herbert L. Packer, who subjected the testimonies of Budenz and Lautner to an extensive analysis, concluded that two factors tended to intersect in the testimony of Budenz: "a readiness to elevate hearsay to the status of authoritative facts and an expansive disregard for the niceties of actual Party affiliation." As for Lautner, Packer concluded that his testimony was basically "reliable," and he "rarely revealed the fervent commitment to Communism, or the equally fervent rejection of it, that was so often evident in the testimony of [other ex-Communists]." Nor did Lautner pursue "an extra-testimonial career as an ex-Communist."[3]

Other anti-Communist observers of Budenz's testimonies offered less generous descriptions than Packer did. For example, Senator Dennis Chavez (Democrat–New Mexico) called Budenz an outright liar, stating on the floor of the Senate: "Budenz is constitutionally unable to give a straight answer, justifying his foul means by the perverted ends he seeks. I do not think he knows truth from falsehood anymore."[4] The columnist Joseph Alsop wrote that being a congressional witness had become Budenz's avocation and predicted that, in all likelihood, "he will continue mass-producing treason charges so long as the Senatorial demand continues." Alsop accused Budenz of having developed the "highly novel technique of the belated recollection and the hearsay accusation of treason."[5] Finally, Richard H. Rovere described Budenz as "the man with the latex memory."[6] Rovere also blamed ex-Communist witnesses for the prevalence of what he called "a somewhat distorted view of the dimensions of the problem of domestic Communism." Moreover, he condemned the Department of Justice for giving these individuals the opportunity "to exert a considerable influence on public opinion and public policy on matters in which they have a special, if not an eccentric, outlook."[7]

In 1953, one prominent ex-Communist professional witness, Harvey Matusow, brought disrepute to these ranks. Matusow had joined the Communist Party in 1947, and he became an FBI informant in 1950. Expelled from the Party that year, he transformed himself into a professional witness, testifying before House and Senate investigating committees, state investigating committees, and the Subversive

Activities Control Board, as well as at two trials (the 1952 trial of second-tier Communist leaders in New York City, *United States v. Elizabeth Gurley Flynn*, et al., and the Clinton Jencks perjury trial). Matusow also served, for a short time, as a consultant to Senator Joseph McCarthy's subcommittee. But in August 1953, he signed a book contract with Cameron & Kahn, which planned to publish his confession that he had regularly lied. A few weeks before the book was launched, Matusow signed two affidavits avowing that he had lied about two witnesses in the New York case and the Jencks case. In turn, a Senate subcommittee opened an "investigation," subpoenaing Matusow, Kahn, and Cameron. Its report charged that Matusow "suddenly became an important figure in a stepped-up Communist drive against security, investigative, and enforcement agencies of the United States Government, and against ex-Communists helping those agencies."[8] Matusow was indicted by the Department of Justice and convicted of perjury, but the judge in the Jencks case refused to order the FBI to turn over its reports to the defense, and he denied Jencks a retrial. (That decision was eventually overturned by the U.S. Supreme Court.) The judge in the Flynn case, however, ordered a retrial of the two defendants against whom Matusow had testified.[9]

Whittaker Chambers, the most famous ex-Communist, leaving Federal Court, November 18, 1949. (Library of Congress)

Some ex-communistic anti-Communists, such as Whittaker Chambers and Frank S. Meyer, spoke to the FBI on several occasions and testified a few times. They did not become professional witnesses, however, and they gravitated toward conservatism and publication of their views in *National Review*.[10] Chambers, in fact, held himself aloof from all but one conservative battle: Alger Hiss's conviction for perjury. Chambers believed that the Hiss case was "the heart of the anti-Communist fight" in the United States, and suggested that "by it most of the rest stands or falls." If that case were in any way compromised or impaired, he told William F. Buckley, Jr., the whole anti-Communist front would collapse. When Buckley asked Chambers to supply a blurb for the book he co-wrote defending McCarthy, Chambers declined. He gave as his reason the relentless attack by the Hiss forces on the anti-Communist front and their ceaseless effort to discredit Chambers. Chambers wrote: "I am not really a free agent . . . I am the witness on whom to a great degree, it still all swings. [My conduct, my associations, my reactions] are a kind of public trust. They call for the most vigilant intelligence and careful judgment." If he were to associate himself publicly with McCarthy, Chambers continued, he would aid the Communists, by giving them a pretext for confusing the Hiss case with McCarthy's activities and "rolling it all into a snarl with which to baffle, bedevil, and divide opinion."[11]

In fact, Chambers was privately critical of McCarthy's judgment and his propensity for sensationalism. Likewise, he was critical of the anti-Communist right, because "A distaste for Communism and socialism is not a program." The right, he continued, lacked a program because it had not faced historical reality; it did not understand what the struggle with communism is all about or how it works. Chambers believed that he alone spoke "always from the fastness of my cold and remote foreknowledge." He also believed that he alone understood that a valid program for the right must be based on counter-revolutionary, not conservative, principles.[12] Perhaps for that reason, he at first refused Buckley's invitation to join the staff of *National Review*. (In late 1954, Chambers did join the American Committee for Cultural Freedom, and in 1957 he joined the editorial staff of *National Review*.)[13]

A very small number of ex-Communists became liberal anti-Communists. The most famous among them, *New York Post* editor James Wechsler, had been a member of the Young Communist League in the late 1930s, but had later publicly renounced his membership. Since then he had spoken to the FBI on several occasions, and he had written extensively and critically about the Communist Party.

Nevertheless, Wechsler's credibility as an anti-Communist was questioned by Senator McCarthy in the spring of 1953. McCarthy implied that Wechsler was not a true ex-Communist, stating that he used his newspaper "to attack and smear anybody who actually was fighting communism." When Wechsler pointed out that a McCarthy aide, Howard Rushmore, was also an ex-Communist who could be working for the Communists within McCarthy's own committee, McCarthy replied, "[T]here is a big difference between you and him. . . . He does not spend his time, you see, trying to smear and tear down the people who are really fighting communism."[14] (For more on Wechsler, see Chapter 10.)

CONSERVATIVE ANTI-COMMUNISM

Conservative anti-communism had gained followers and fervency toward the end of World War II, fueled by reports of how the Soviet armed forces were behaving as they advanced through Eastern Europe and by the books and articles published by exiled and *émigré* scholars. Its main target, however, had not changed; it still focused on "Communist infiltration" of the U.S. government. The former chairman of the Special Committee on Un-American Activities, Hamilton Fish, who had been defeated for reelection in 1944, weighed in with a book designed "to arouse all Americans . . . to the menace of international and revolutionary Communism," which he called "the most powerful and evil force in the world today." He asserted that "a veritable array of young radicals, left wingers, fellow travelers, and Communists" currently held important positions in the executive branch of the government, and suggested that an "unholy alliance" existed between the Democratic Party, the Communist Party, and CIO-PAC. To deal with this threat, Fish called for the creation of "a nationwide, nonpartisan, anti-Communist organization to combat the activities and propaganda of the Communists in America by educational methods."[15]

Other conservatives shifted their focus to the links between the CPUSA and the Soviet Union. In March 1947, William C. Bullitt told the Committee on Un-American Activities that the CPUSA "was, in the first place, an agency of the Soviet Government for the purpose of weakening the United States for the ultimate assault that the Soviet Government intends to make on the United States."[16] One year later, James Burnham told the Committee that the CPUSA must be outlawed, because it, as "the extension of [the] great Communist empire," posed "a clear, present, and powerful threat" to the United States.[17]

Despite these warnings, it took several years for conservative anti-Communists to mobilize effectively, and they, like conservatives as a whole, never found a unified voice. The conservative Peter Viereck attributed this failure to conservatism having become "among the most unpopular words in the American vocabulary." To be praised as a conservative had "become an insuperable political handicap."[18] In addition, conservatives were a varied lot. Like most of the other types of anti-Communists, conservative anti-Communists could be placed on a bell curve, with opportunists and ambition at one tail (McCarthy) and true believers at the other (William F. Buckley, Jr.). Conservative anti-Communist politicians (e.g., John Foster Dulles, Richard M. Nixon, and Robert A. Taft) combined a little of both.[19]

The most well-known conservative anti-Communists treated anti-communism as an agenda item, subordinate to their other concerns, to be wielded publicly only when needed. For example, former President Herbert Hoover was mainly concerned with what he called, in February 1946, "the tide of statism which is sweeping three-quarters of the world—whether it be called Communism, Fascism, Socialism or the disguised American mixture of Fascism and Socialism called 'Managed Economy' now being transformed into further ambiguity, the 'Welfare State.' " Although later that year he urged Republicans to "dig out" and "expose" Communist infiltration of the U.S. government, Hoover told the 1948 Republican Party convention that the present difficulty facing the United States was not so much Communists as "fuzzy-minded people [totalitarian liberals] who think we can have totalitarian economics in the hands of bureaucracy, and at the same time personal liberty for the people and representative government in the nation."[20] The man who replaced Hoover as the postwar spokesperson for traditional conservatism, Senator Robert A. Taft (Republican–Ohio), mainly focused on his campaign to keep the United States from engaging in wars and alliances. He especially opposed permanent, global confrontation with the Soviet Union.[21]

Further complicating the process were the divisions among congressional Republicans. In April 1950, Senator Taft complained that the differences in the Republican Party regarding the Truman administration's foreign policy were so great that it was hard for it "to take a combative position" on any particular aspect of it.[22] John W. Malsberger has documented a divide between those he labeled "Old Guard obstructionists" and " 'new' conservatives" that opened in 1938, and then widened markedly after the election of 1948. The views of the former group were rooted in the values of the nineteenth-century, preindustrial world and loathing for the New Deal; the latter were more attuned to the political contingencies of the post-Depression, postwar world.[23] Athan G. Theoharis agreed that there was a divide, but he perceived it as a threefold one, among "extremists," "partisans," and "moderates." The "extremists" were constant and sharp critics of the foreign policies of Roosevelt and Truman, but the "partisans" less so; the "moderates" could be won over to bipartisanship.[24]

Anti-Communist conservatives, however, concurred that communism could only be defeated by strengthening the religious and moral fiber of U.S. citizens and casting blame for the Cold War on "liberals" (by which they meant the members and supporters of the Roosevelt and Truman administrations). The religious moral element stoked the anti-liberal element. Most conservative anti-Communists saw the world in black and white: they divided it into two irreconcilable camps (free and Communist), and spoke in absolute terms about each camp. Liberals, in contrast, were accused of seeing the world in various shades of gray, being blind and deaf to communism, and speaking about Communists in an equivocating and apologetic manner. Frank S. Meyer, for example, was, according to his biographer, "ferociously" anti-liberal because liberals had failed to understand the errors of their past and disavow their tragic mistakes.[25]

Perhaps the best (and by far the longest) example of this antipathy is James J. Martin's two-volume (more than 1,300-page) painstaking and polemical account of the interwar liberal intellectuals who contributed to *New Republic* and *The Nation*. In his Foreword to this massive work, John Chamberlain summarized the key components of the anti-liberal case: liberals flip-flopped and somersaulted over every key issue; they ignored the cruel and brutal acts of the Soviet regime; they pushed blindly for U.S. involvement in World War II, instead of allowing Germany and the Soviet Union—the two worst dictatorships—to destroy each other; and they were inexplicably "soft" toward the very "hard" Communists. In his conclusion, Chamberlain pictured liberals as greater malefactors than the Communists, because, he wrote, "The heritage of the liberal flip-flop is a universal and vastly expensive Cold War, the ever-present threat of nuclear destruction, an enormous expansion of Communist power throughout the Old World and its increasing menace to our own Hemisphere."[26]

The domestic event that united anti-Communist conservatives of all stripes was the Hiss case, which proved to be both a major turning point for intellectuals traveling the road from liberalism to conservatism and a catalyst that hardened the positions of many politicians who had already arrived at their conservative destination. Hiss's conviction for perjury confirmed everything conservative anti-Communists had been saying about Roosevelt's domestic and foreign policies. For Ralph de Toledano, the testimony of Whittaker Chambers and the Hiss perjury case "ended one era and began another. . . . For me, the anti-Communist battle assumed a new geography," by redefining the struggle in political and theological terms. It was also "a litmus taste for liberalism. In the acid bath of history the true blue 'liberals' have come out a disconcerting pink. . . . [T]heir terrified reaction to the indictment and conviction of Alger Hiss has negated their liberalism and equated them with the Communists whom they ostensibly disdain." Both, he said, pursued "utter conformity, employed a "double standard," and held their respective isms above patriotism and self-interest above truth.[27]

A few years later, Peter Viereck sharply criticized liberals for failing "to expose and fight Stalinist totalitarianism with exactly the same vigor" as they had displayed toward Nazism. They failed to do so, he suggested, because they confused the proscription of Communists and communism with the elimination of indispensable dissent. According to Viereck, liberals did not seem to realize that "the most fruitful and challenging dissent" in the United States came from conservatives and "ornery, crotchety reactionaries." He accused those liberal intellectuals who continued to act as Communist apologizers of being "partly guilty of causing that vicious McCarthyite anti-intellectualism which they wrongly base on anticommunist fervor." Moreover, those liberal intellectuals who called themselves "noncommunist," rather than anti-Communist, committed treason against intellectuals by "evading the basic moral choice of this decade."[28]

It is interesting to note that two of the more prominent efforts to cohere conservatism during the early 1950s did not base their efforts on anti-communism. In October 1950, the first issue of *The Freeman*, edited by John Chamberlain and Henry Hazlitt, stated that the journal would be devoted "to the cause of traditional liberalism and individual freedom," and that "one of its foremost aims" would be "to clarify the concept of individual freedom and apply it to the problems of our time."[29] Four years later, Russell Kirk did not include anti-communism in his outline of "the general principles upon which conservatives ought to endeavor to form their opinions of particular issues and make their decisions in particular circumstances." In fact, Kirk rejected the notion that there was an active, threatening Communist conspiracy currently fomenting in the United States, and he expressed disquiet over the "babel" of voices promoting such a conspiracy.[30]

The task of consolidating the various strains of conservatism around a militantly anti-Communist, anti-liberal ideology fell to William F. Buckley, Jr., a true believer in the Communist conspiracy thesis. Buckley had begun his public anti-communism while he was a student at Yale University. In his editorials for the *Yale Daily News*, he supported the 1948 trial and conviction of Communist Party leaders and regularly wrote about the threat posed by the Soviet Union.[31] Nevertheless, in his 1951 book *God and Man at Yale*, Buckley did not identify himself as a conservative because, he said, a conservative is "uncomfortably disdainful of controversy" and lacks "the energy to fight his battles."[32] One year later, however, he announced what he called a new brand of conservatism, one that would be based on "hard thinking" about survival, "the most important issue of the day." Buckley called on traditional conservatives to recognize that Soviet aggressiveness posed a threat to the security of the United States and, as a result of that recognition, to join with him "to rearrange, sensibly, our battle plans; and this means we have to accept Big Government for the duration." That is, conservatives must learn to live with "a totalitarian bureaucracy," involving a very large armed force, atomic energy, central intelligence, war production boards, and centralization of power in Washington, D. C., even with Truman at its head.[33] Shortly thereafter, Buckley began to think about creating a new conservative periodical, to unite the various voices on the right. The first edition of this journal, *National Review*, appeared in November 1955. The magazine offered, according to Garry Wills (who worked there for a few years), "a deliberately rootless kind of conservatism" focused almost exclusively on "Liberalism (capitalized)" as the enemy.[34]

But *National Review* also published sharp criticism of the "New Republicanism" of the Eisenhower administration. In fact, William S. Schlamm argued that conservatives should not vote for Eisenhower in 1956 because, for conservatives, "There is an inexorable system of political priorities; and the supreme priority goes to an Administration's conduct in the war against Communism. If, on this decisive ground, the Administration's tragic failure is conceded, no other consideration can bail it out."[35]

THREE CONSERVATIVE POLITICIANS

For their part, conservative politicians did not seem to worry much about doctrinal coherence. Instead, they were motivated by pragmatic concerns. Three of the most prominent of these individuals offer interesting contrasts in style and method.

Robert A. Taft

Senator Robert A. Taft was a fervent anti-Communist who proved unable to devise a consistent set of policies regarding domestic or foreign communism. He saw himself as a pillar of conservative integrity, but he desperately wanted to be elected President of the United States. Although Taft opposed the Soviet Union and the spread of communism, he did not want the United States to try to defeat these forces by increasing military spending or by extending the powers of the executive branch. Thus he voted for aid to Greece and Turkey, but with reservations; he voted for the European Recovery Program, but tried to cut funding for it; he voted against the North Atlantic Treaty and sought cuts in the military assistance program; he approved the sending of U.S. troops to Korea, but rejected a tax to finance the operation and wage and price controls.[36] Taft was consistent only in his antagonism toward the CIO and CIO-PAC. In his campaigns, he regularly red-baited them, and he co-sponsored the Taft-Hartley Act—a key piece of legislation that reduced the power of organized labor.

In his book *A Foreign Policy for Americans*, probably written to promote his presidential aspirations, Taft painted a scary picture of Soviet purpose, but did not offer a particularly strong counteroffensive. The Russians, he wrote, "[combined] with great military and air power a fanatical devotion to communism not unlike that which inspired the Moslem invasion of Europe in the Middle Ages." As a result, they had been able to create, in many countries, "fifth-column" adjuncts to their planned military attacks. In their battle to eliminate the appeal of Communist ideology, Taft stated, the people of the United States had to reestablish their belief in liberty, and support the campaign of the U.S. government on behalf of liberty. The government, in turn, must send in undercover agents to Communist-controlled countries to build a love for freedom among the people living there, encourage and build up the forces in friendly and neutral countries prepared to

Senator Robert A. Taft meeting with Senator Arthur Vandenberg, January 1939. (Library of Congress)

fight communism, and "eliminate from the United States Government all those who are directly or indirectly connected with the Communist organization." In sum, Taft wrote, the war against global communism could be won only "in the minds of men."[37] He died in July 1953, before the Cold War reached its peak.

John Foster Dulles

John Foster Dulles, who seemed, during his tenure as Secretary of State (1953–1959), the epitome of conservative anti-communism, actually came late to that position. In fact, one of his biographers stated: "It is difficult to explain precisely why such a substantial swing in mood and attitude occurred."[38] Indeed, although Dulles had been deeply involved in the creation and operations of the United Nations, he had not blamed the Soviets for the problems besetting the new organization.

For whatever reason, in the long two-part article he wrote for *Life* magazine in June 1946, Dulles changed his position and suggested that the people of the United States could no longer rest their hopes for a peaceful world "on any genuine reconciliation of our faith with that now held by Soviet leadership." Rather, the people of the United States would have to find a way to convince Soviet leaders to "abandon the intolerant methods" they were presently employing. While he did not accuse Soviet leaders of being blindly driven by their Communist ideology, Dulles did comment that they carried out their foreign policy "in a rigid, mechanistic and uncompromising way." But, Dulles continued, Soviet leaders were "shrewd and realistic politicians"; thus, if Americans demonstrated "that our freedoms have such vigor and worth that to uproot them is an impossible task, we can expect that they will, as a matter of expediency, desist from methods which cannot succeed and which probably will provoke disaster." According to Dulles, the most significant demonstration of their resolve that the people of the United States could make was "at the religious level"; second was the building of military strength; and third was the sending of economic aid to countries susceptible to Communist control. He noted that the United Nations could be, in limited ways, useful.[39]

John Foster Dulles, Secretary of State, 1953–1959. (Library of Congress)

For several years, Dulles wavered between partisanship and ambition, between political practicality and ideological moralizing. He testified against the Mundt-Nixon anti-Communist bill because, he
stated, the Communist Party was "such a nebulous thing."[40] In addition, during the presidential campaign of 1948, he advised Republican
candidate Thomas Dewey not to red-bait Truman and to sidestep
espionage and subversive issues. Two years later, however, in his
own senatorial campaign against Herbert Lehman, Dulles red-baited
ferociously. Although he disagreed with the Truman administration's
hands-off policy vis-à-vis Asia, he petitioned U.S. Secretary of State
Dean Acheson for a place in the Department of State. While there, he
composed a book he titled *War or Peace*, which indicated that his opinion of Soviet leadership had changed. War, he now wrote, "is prob-
able," and he blamed this likelihood on Soviet leaders, whom he
characterized as "a domestic group fanatical in their acceptance of a
creed that teaches world domination and that would deny those personal freedoms which constitutes our most cherished political and
religious heritage." This war could only be avoided, Dulles stated, if
the people of the United States mobilized "the moral and spiritual
potentialities, which we usually reserve for war."[41]

Although Dulles privately supported Truman's decision to send
U.S. troops to Korea, he publicly stated, following the entry of troops
from the People's Republic of China into the war, that he had advised
against the sending of U.S. combat troops. He then sent a memo to two
Republican senators advocating the use of Formosa as a base for
covert and open warfare against the People's Republic of China as
well as an increased level of "subversive activities" within the Warsaw
Bloc countries. By the winter of 1952, according to Townsend Hoopes,
Dulles had emerged as "an advocate of [an] uncompromising anti-
Communist crusade, seeking to build upon the national mood of anxiety a sense of moral urgency and missionary zeal." Hoopes thinks that
this new position was a combination of conviction, ambition, the
immediate tactical requirements of maneuvering within Republican
politics, and "a felt power of advocacy" (the preacher-prophet element
of Dulles's personality). His speeches on behalf of Eisenhower during
the campaign were "filled with inflammatory right-wing oratory."[42] In
an article for *Life* magazine, Dulles advocated "a policy of boldness,"
combining moral fervor and military power, to deal with Communist
aggression. "*There is,*" he emphatically wrote, "*one solution and only
one: that is for the free world to develop the will and organize the means to
retaliate instantly against every aggression by Red armies, so that if it*

occurred anywhere, we could and would strike back where it hurts, by means of our choosing."[43]

During his tenure as Secretary of State, while Dulles continued to speak like an anti-Communist ideologue, he acted like a pragmatist. To neutralize the Republican right, he publicly used terms such as "massive retaliation" and spoke of going to the "brink" of war with Communist states; in contrast, in his dealings within the Eisenhower administration, he advocated neither approach.[44] In fact, he came to believe in and promote the idea that international communism would be defeated by its internal contradictions.[45]

Richard M. Nixon

Richard M. Nixon was not propelled into the front ranks of conservative anti-communism until 1948, when he took seriously Whittaker Chambers's testimony to the Committee on Un-American Activities regarding Alger Hiss. In his 1946 campaign for the House of Representatives, Nixon had identified himself as a "practical liberal,"[46] and had focused his attacks on the CIO-PAC, in effect linking his opponent, Jerry Voorhis, to what Nixon called "the Moscow–PAC–Henry Wallace line." Once elected, he was influenced by John F. Cronin regarding the role of Communists in labor unions, and Karl Mundt regarding Communist "subversion." Nixon was appointed to the House Education and Labor Committee, where he continued to argue that radical union leaders in the CIO were trying to destroy free trade unionism in the United States. He had also been selected to serve on the Committee on Un-American Activities, but there is some evidence that he was hesitant to accept the appointment. Nevertheless, while serving on that committee, Nixon became a strong supporter of Chambers and the leader of the investigation of Hiss. By the end of 1947, he had become a convinced anti-Communist, and he maneuvered to place his name on Mundt's bill to curb the activities of the Communist Party in the United States.[47]

Though the conviction of Alger Hiss was not, for Nixon, the religious icon that it was for Chambers, it became his launching pad to political fortune. Shortly after the guilty verdict in Hiss's trial was announced, Nixon, in a speech to the House of Representatives titled "The Hiss Case—A Lesson for the American People," etched the case in historical granite. According to him, the Hiss case represented a vast conspiracy of Communist infiltration of the U.S. government and a "story of inexcusable inaction" on the part of officials in the Roosevelt and Truman administrations. (Nixon specifically exempted the FBI and J. Edgar Hoover from that accusation.) To ensure that such a situation never recurred, Nixon recommended much greater support for the FBI and the Committee on Un-American Activities, a complete overhaul of the federal government's loyalty program, and the development of "an extensive educational program which will teach the American public the truth about communism."[48] The speech was printed as a pamphlet and widely distributed.

In his 1950 campaign for the U.S. Senate, Nixon, like most Republican candidates that year, focused on his opponent's "softness" toward Communists and fellow travelers in the U.S. government. He said of his opponent, Helen Gahagan Douglas, "If she had her way, the Communist conspiracy would never have been exposed, and Alger Hiss would still be influencing the foreign policy of the United States."[49] During his short term as a U.S. Senator, he focused mainly on international issues, but did not put forth a consistent, coherent position.[50]

As the vice-presidential candidate in 1952, during his "Checkers Speech," Nixon stated: "I say that a man who, like Mr. [Adlai] Stevenson, has pooh-poohed and ridiculed the Communist threat in the United States ... isn't qualified to be President of the United States."[51] As vice-president, he became the Eisenhower administration's designated McCarthy tamer.

THE CONSERVATIVES' MCCARTHY PROBLEM

Although publicly the vast majority of conservatives supported McCarthy, privately many thought that his style was antithetical to conservatism and anti-communism. For example, in April 1950, Isaac Don Levine urged McCarthy to be truthful in his anti-Communist campaign. When McCarthy insisted that one must fight Communists with their own weapons, Levine decided that McCarthy was "a boon to the Stalinist camp."[52] Peter Viereck was unusual in his sharp public criticism—published, it should be noted, after McCarthy's loss of political influence. In his contribution to Daniel Bell's anthology on the American Right, Viereck strongly criticized McCarthyism, stating that it had not been anti-Communist, but rather a "radical anti-conservatism," a "leftist instinct behind a *self-deceptive* rightist veneer." It had constituted, in fact, a "coalition of nationalism, Asian-firstism and Europe-last isolationism," as well as "a midwest hick-Protestant revenge" against the elitist east, and an attack on those traditionalists who favored government by law.[53]

Far more typical was the strident tone adopted by a writer for *Human Events*, in late December 1954, who bemoaned the death of McCarran, the condemnation of McCarthy, the Democratic control of the congressional investigating committees, and the eminence of those "Fair Deal [i.e., liberal] columnists," who had instigated the anti-McCarthy campaign. These events had opened the United States to "a campaign of re-education designed to convince the customers that Alger Hiss was just a bad dream; that Harry Dexter White was the victim of a cowardly attack mainly because he was dead at the time; and that the notion that our Government had been infiltrated by spies and traitors is a Nixonian phantasy."[54]

A different tone was used in the apologia of William F. Buckley, Jr., and L. Brent Bozell. Their book is an interesting one, in which the overblown rhetoric and polemical, anti-liberal venting of William S. Schlamm's preface stands in marked contrast to the reasonably objective analysis of Buckley and Bozell. Although it purported to examine McCarthy's "record," this book focused almost entirely on the 1950 Tydings subcommittee hearings. While the authors criticized McCarthy in many places, they concluded that his overall record had been *"extremely good"* (their emphasis). Yes, they stated, McCarthy was guilty, on occasion, of gratuitous sensationalism and reckless exaggerations; nevertheless, his was the only program of action against those in the United States who were aiding the enemy. He and his aides were "doing their level best to make our society inhospitable to Communists, fellow-travelers, and security risks in the government." Although Buckley and Bozell credited McCarthy with mobilizing the attack against Communist infiltration, they also lamented his failure to present "an articulate philosophy of national mobilization" for the United States' war against communism.[55]

Ralph de Toledano also offered a conservative apology for McCarthy, stating that despite all his faults, McCarthy had "succeeded in making the public take heed where our intellectual onslaughts had failed." Because, in de Toledano's estimation, McCarthy had accomplished this important task, conservatives, who sorely needed "direction, leadership, and an *élan vital*, ... shut their eyes to the essential nature of Joe McCarthy's political roots, drowning their doubts in the emotion of the movement."[56] Similarly, Max Eastman framed his apologia for McCarthy in terms of "a temperamental failure to do in a mature and skillful way what desperately needs doing if free civilization is to be saved."[57]

James Burnham referred to himself as an "anti-anti-McCarthyite." In April 1952, as a member of the board of the American Committee for Cultural Freedom (see Chapter 9), he had blocked a proposed resolution condemning both communism and "certain types of anti-communism." Two years later, when he resigned from the committee, he wrote in his letter of resignation: "In my opinion those anti-communists who consider themselves anti-McCarthyites have fallen into a trap. They have failed so far to realize that they are, in political reality, in a united front with the Communists, in the broadest, most imposing united front that has ever been constructed in this country."[58]

Republican leaders rarely spoke out against McCarthy, impelled by both their hope that McCarthy could lead the way to national political power and their fear of splitting the party. For example, Taft, who was the Republican leader in the Senate, underwent, in Richard Rovere's estimation, "a prolonged manic period" from 1950 to 1952, "when he stooped to encouraging and echoing McCarthy." Rovere had been following Taft closely since 1948, and thought of him as "a man of principle" and a committed civil libertarian. He quoted Taft as saying, after McCarthy's speech to the Senate defending the charges he had made at Wheeling, "It was a perfectly reckless performance."[59] But one month later, Taft told a group of reporters that while he had no particular faith in the accuracy of McCarthy's claims, he had urged McCarthy to go ahead anyway and had advised him "to keep talking, and if one case doesn't work out, proceed with another."[60] In fact, Taft did publicly criticize McCarthy's attack on George Marshall in late 1951, but early the next year he gave the senator a strong public endorsement. Switching course yet again, following the election of 1952, Taft blocked McCarthy from becoming chair of the Internal Subcommittee and tried to limit McCarthy's investigative powers by giving the Internal Subcommittee sole responsibility for investigating communism and subversion.[61]

For his part, President Eisenhower, who loathed McCarthy, chose not to confront his nemesis publicly, because he feared doing so would divide his party. He was convinced he could defeat McCarthy by ignoring him. In fact, it was a small group of moderate anti-Communists in the Eisenhower administration who began the planning for the campaign that led to the Army-McCarthy hearings and McCarthy's fall from grace.[62]

As a U.S. Senator, Nixon had neither publicly criticized nor embraced McCarthy. In 1950, Nixon had told McCarthy: "Now the important thing—when it comes to this field [anti-communism]—is one rule I would urge you to follow: always understate, never over-state your case." Although he loaned some of his files on communism to McCarthy during the Tydings subcommittee hearings, Nixon rejected McCarthy's help in his 1950 Senate campaign. As vice-president, however, Nixon was assigned the uncomfortable role of McCarthy taming, and he became obsessed with preventing an open break between McCarthy and the Eisenhower administration. Nixon participated in at least five conferences designed to temper McCar-thy's zeal, and Nixon later said: "Frankly, we tried to mediate with McCarthy until we were blue in the face." In his response to Adlai Ste-venson's charge that the Republican Party was "half McCarthy, half Eisenhower," Nixon, by indirection, both praised and chastised McCarthy. Nixon stated: "Men who have in the past done effective work exposing Communism in this country have, by reckless talk and questionable methods, made themselves the issue, rather than the cause they believe in so deeply," thereby diverting attention from the danger of communism to themselves.[63] Nixon later told de Toledano, "McCarthy's intentions were right, but his tactics, were, frankly, so inept at times that eventually he probably did our cause more harm than good."[64]

When he became Secretary of State, Dulles tried to placate the ultra-anti-Communist Republicans in Congress. He dismissed two of the old "China hands"—John Carter Vincent and John Paton Davies, Jr.—even though he found no evidence that they were disloyal. He provided no protection to the hundreds of department employees under investigation by the zealous ex-FBI agent, Scott McLeod, the Assistant Secretary of State for Security Affairs, who defined loyalty and security very narrowly and who had very close connections with McCarthy and other Senate anti-Communists.[65] According to H. W. Brands, Jr., Dulles was determined to avoid the acrimony stirred up in Congress by his predecessor, Dean Acheson, and, fearing his own past connection to Alger Hiss, made a concerted effort not to provoke Republicans in Congress.[66]

THE HYPER-INDIVIDUALISTS

Hyper-individualists, though they were viscerally opposed to communism as an extreme form of the collectivism they abhorred, did not expend much energy opposing communism or supporting investigations and exposés of Communists. Thus they were not preoccupied with anti-communism. Nevertheless, the most famous of these hyper-individualists, Ayn Rand, bears examination.

Rand was born in pre-revolution Russia and emigrated in 1926. A fierce opponent of the Soviet regime, Rand filtered most of her anti-communism through her books and letters. In neither, however, did she regularly comment on foreign or domestic events. Her main anti-Communist effort was accomplished in a book she began writing in 1930, which was published six years later as *We the Living*. In her preliminary notes for that book, Rand noted that the proposed manuscript was intended to show that in the Soviet Union there was "a 'red' angle on all activities," an ever-present threat of the secret police, and an obsession with "mass" manifestations.[67] In 1934, she wrote to a friend:

> [T]he quality which I hoped would make it [*We the Living*] saleable . . . was the fact that it was the *first* story written by a Russian who knows the living conditions of the new Russia and who has actually lived under the Soviets in the period described. . . . My book is, as far as I know, the first one by a person who *knows* the facts and also can *tell* them.[68]

A few months later, she noted, "[T]he time is certainly ripe for an anti-Red novel."[69]

The success of *We the Living* opened for Rand the opportunity to deliver a series of lectures and speeches about the Soviet Union. In those lectures, one goal interested her above all others—to publicize what she called "the greatest, most urgent conflict of our times: the individual against the collective. . . . No country on earth offers such a startling and revealing view of the conflict as Soviet Russia."[70] And yet, during that same period, when she was trying to sell her screen story "Red Pawn," Rand downplayed its political (anti-Soviet) aspects.

At some point in 1940, Rand penned a 5,000-word polemic aimed at all those who had not become dedicated anti-totalitarians. Titled "To All Innocent Fifth-Columnists," it sent a clear message: "you are against Totalitarianism—or you are for it. There is no intellectual neutrality." According to Rand, the United States was than [then] under the control of "intellectual Totalitarianism," and those opposed to it, those in favor of "Americanism," must form an organization.[71] The essay was not published, nor did its author invest much effort in founding an organization. Nevertheless, from then on, Rand's letters sound a constant theme: the need for someone to author a profound ideology of capitalism. In July 1941, she stated: "Our side has no 'ideology,' no clear-cut, consistent system of belief, no *philosophy* of life."[72] Once again, she spoke about the need for an organization to educate people about the philosophy of individualism. Two years later, Rand offered her newly published novel, *The Fountainhead*, as the ideal vehicle to spread that philosophy. She wrote DeWitt Emery, head of the National Small Business Men's Association: "If the book goes over big, it will break the way for other writers of our side. If it's allowed to be killed by the Reds—our good industrialists had better not expect anyone else to stick his neck out in order to try to save them from getting their throats cut."[73] So-called conservatives, she wrote, did little good, because they (unlike Rand) wrote in vague, general, and compromising terms, wielding "a feather duster where a meat ax is necessary."[74]

Rand's most direct public statement of the principles of "Americanism" was contained in her "Screen Guide for Americans," which she wrote in 1947 for *Vigil*, the publication of the Motion Picture Alliance for the Preservation of American Ideals.[75] It listed 13 "don'ts," including smearing the free enterprise system, industrialists, wealth, the profit motive, success, the independent man, and American political institutions. The same essay warned against glorifying failure and depravity, and deifying the "common man" and the collective. It was republished in *Plain Talk*, and Rand urged Emery to reprint it as a pamphlet for his libertarian Foundation for Economic Freedom, suggesting that it would help mobilize the public to demand "the production of movies preaching Americanism."[76]

That same year, Rand testified as a friendly witness before the Committee on Un-American Activities. During this appearance, she was disappointed that the committee members did not allow her to make a full statement about the dangers of Communist propaganda. Most of Rand's testimony focused on the "Communist propaganda" she claimed was depicted in *Song of Russia* (MGM, 1943). That movie, she stated, in presenting to the American people an untrue picture of the Soviet Union, had mirrored Nazi propaganda techniques by lying to the people for their own good. In addition, she concluded—in an interesting variation on the ex-Communist theme—only people such as herself, who had lived under a totalitarian dictatorship, could really understand its nature.[77]

A few years later, Rand criticized the studio heads and Hollywood conservatives for failing, as of December 1950, to end the "pink" control of movies. She accused them of being ignorant, muddled, politically confused, and inconsistent. According to Rand, conservative movie makers, in particular, had failed to put up an "ideological battle in the studios. They have confined themselves mainly to denouncing *persons,* not ideas—and, as a consequence, the Pinks have won by default."[78]

When she moved to New York in 1953, Rand frequented gatherings of conservatives, notably those hosted by J. B. Matthews. Although she liked Joseph McCarthy (and detested Dwight Eisenhower), she did not publicly back the congressional investigations or investigators,[79] and her extreme individualism, atheism, and anti-statism distanced her from most conservatives, including Hayek, Kirk, and Buckley.[80]

AN ODD DUCK

Roy Cohn, one of the most active official anti-Communists, consorted with conservative anti-Communists and acted and talked like them, but he does not fit comfortably into that category. Anthony Lewis, who knew him from their high school years, told Cohn's biographer:

> One of the mysteries of Roy Cohn, the thing I don't really fully understand and I'd be very surprised if anybody did, is the degree to which his right-wing posture was a genuine ideological belief or something else. I never knew. . . . His family was a standard machine-Democratic family. . . . I don't remember his taking any conservative position at school. . . . When he became this Communist hunter, I just was surprised.[81]

Rovere noted that "Cohn appears to have had no opportunity to develop the compulsive hatreds that lead many to the adoption of McCarthyism as a way of life," but "one need only observe him and his deportment to see that he is sort who takes things hard. His dark eyes are flinty and bright. He has a studied toughness of manner."[82]

Cohn, in fact, identified himself, prior to 1949, as a Democratic liberal. He went directly from law school to the New York office of the U.S. District Attorney. According to him, his work on the Alger Hiss case and his discussions with FBI agents assigned to it "had plenty to do with turning my skepticism about American Communism into a conviction that our nation faced a real and serious menace from the domestic branch of Joe Stalin & Co."[83] He later did some work on the prosecution of the CPUSA leaders, William Remington (see Chapter 10), and the Rosenbergs, and he launched a grand jury investigation of U.S. employees of the United Nations.

Later, with the assistance of George Sokolsky, Cohn secured a job in the Department of Justice, where he worked on the Owen Lattimore case. Sokolsky also introduced him to McCarthy, who appointed Cohn as chief counsel to the Permanent Subcommittee on Investigations in January 1953. Cohn's career as a public anti-Communist came to an end in July 1954, when he was forced by members of McCarthy's own committee to resign.

CONCLUSION

Because anti-communism fit more neatly into the conservative agenda than into the agendas of other types of anti-communism, conservatives, despite their disagreements and division, became formidable allies of official and institutional anti-Communists. Reciprocally, conservatism, as a political force, was strengthened by anti-communism. However, anti-communism did not make conservatism more coherent as a doctrine or ideology.

Liberal and Left-of-Liberal Anti-Communism, 1945–1957

LIBERAL ANTI-COMMUNISM

Postwar liberalism is as difficult to define as conservatism, and equally as varied. In 1948, Albert Einstein noted that the meaning of the term liberalism had "become so watered down as to cover most diverse views and attitudes."[1] Lionel Trilling called it "a large tendency rather than a concise body of doctrine.[2] Harry K. Givertz lamented that the term, as currently used (in 1950), "has come to have contradictory meanings. Everywhere men are dividing into camps over issues raised by liberalism, with only the haziest knowledge of the ground upon which they have pitched their tents."[3] Raymond English, a "confessed conservative," wrote in a 1952 essay that "no American admits that he is, still less claims to be a Conservative"; in fact, because "the word 'conservative' is traumatically repulsive," every person in the United States claims to be a liberal, "with as large a capital 'L' as possible." The result, English concluded, was "almost perfect political confusion," with people thinking and talking about themselves as liberals, while acting and subconsciously believing they were conservatives. "America," he concluded, "is a nation of Conservative fellow-travelers."[4] In his 1955 book, Arthur A. Ekirch, Jr., noted: "Historically liberalism is not easy to define, but even this difficulty pales into insignificance in comparison with the extraordinary contemporary confusion over the term."[5] Louis Hartz agreed that liberalism was a broad and vague term in the 1950s, "clouded as it is by all sorts of modern social reform connotations."[6]

Although it is probably impossible to speak with precision about something as amorphous as "liberal" anti-communism, between 1946 and 1950 a significant number of self-identified liberals clearly moved from a position of indifference toward the Communist "threat" to concern about it to active enlistment in the crusade against it.[7] As they did so, they had to bend liberalism to make it fit the demands of this crusade.

John Ehrman has located the beginnings of this liberal move (to what he calls the "vital center ideology") in a series of articles written in 1946 by Arthur Hays Sulzberger, Joseph and Stewart Alsop, Arthur Schlesinger, Jr., and Reinhold Niebuhr.[8] One of their main motifs was the deleterious effect of communism on liberalism. Schlesinger, for example, accused the CPUSA of engaging "in a massive attack on the moral fabric of the American left," dividing and neutralizing it.[9] Two years later, Robert Bendiner wrote: "If the Communists are a menace at all in this country, it is not to the government in any immediate sense but to the entire liberal movement, political and cultural, which they have recently penetrated with such success."[10]

Whereas anti-Communist liberals, for the most part, expressed approval for the congressional investigating committees and loyalty oath programs, they tended to be more concerned than were other anti-Communists with the adequacy of these programs' procedural safeguards.[11] They also tried to make clear, when they were protesting the lack of due process or fairness to the Communists involved in particular cases, that they were not also taking the side of those Communists. An excellent example of this dance was first offered by the Committee for the First Amendment, which had been formed by liberals in the motion picture industry in 1947, after the Committee on Un-American Activities had issued more than 50 subpoenas to industry members. The leaders of the Committee for the First Amendment, Philip Dunne and William Wyler, admonished the members to criticize the Committee on Un-American Activities and defend the motion picture industry, but not to support, align themselves with, or have any contact with the "unfriendly" witnesses, most of whom were Communists.[12] Similarly, the ACLU hesitated to enter high-profile cases involving alleged subversives. When this organization did become involved, directly or indirectly, in the Communist issue, it included in its legal brief a statement affirming its opposition to communism.[13]

In retrospect, one can identify three varieties of liberal anti-Communists: those burned by their association with Communists (e.g., Philip Dunne and Melvyn Douglas), those with a visceral and ideological antipathy toward the doctrine and its practitioners (e.g., Arthur Schlesinger, Jr.),[14] and those who feared being labeled "soft" on communism (e.g., Senator Hubert Humphrey). All were members of the flagship of liberal anti-communism, Americans for Democratic Action (ADA), which replaced the Union for Democratic Action in January 1947.

The130 founders of ADA blamed the Communists for the defeats suffered by Democratic candidates in the election of 1946, and they sought a means to save the New Deal, both by defending the Democratic Party from attacks by the right and the left and by resisting efforts to create a third party behind Henry Wallace.[15] In its first statement of principles, the ADA founders wrote: "We reject any association with Communists or sympathizers with communism in the United States as completely as we reject any association with Fascists or their sympathizers." One of the group's founders, James Loeb, Jr., in a letter to *New Republic*, announced that the ADA is "a declaration of liberal independence from the stifling and paralyzing influence of the Communists and their apologizers in America."[16] Although most ADA members were not enamored of Truman, the organization, for lack of an alternative, moved ever closer to his administration, and it unreservedly condemned the Wallace campaign.[17] Penn Kimball, a journalist who was then working for the election of Chester Bowles as governor of Connecticut, told the ADA's Arthur Schlesinger, Jr.: "ADA is obsessed with its Communist problem to the neglect of all the great fascist and war-making forces which are the real enemies of liberals."[18]

Although Reinhold Niebuhr did not play an active role in the new organization, one of its founders, Schlesinger, had deeply imbibed key aspects of Niebuhr's thinking. Several years later, Schlesinger would say of Niebuhr: "His penetrating reconstruction of the democratic faith—in the context of Roosevelt's brilliant invocation of democratic resources against the perils of depression and war—absorbed and mastered the forces of disillusion and preserved the nerve of action," while "his searching realism gave new strength to American liberal democracy."[19] Those themes echoed throughout Schlesinger's signal contribution to what one could call Niebuhrian (pragmatic or non-idealistic) liberalism: *The Vital Center*.[20] Schlesinger proclaimed, in the book's foreword, that mid-twentieth-century liberalism

> has been fundamentally reshaped by the hope of the New Deal, by the exposure of the Soviet Union, and by the deepening of our knowledge of men. The consequence of this historical re-education has been an unconditional rejection of totalitarianism and a reassertion of the

ultimate integrity of the individual. This awakening constitutes the unique experience and fundamental faith of contemporary liberalism.[21]

Schlesinger stated that this faith would be effective only if it was an activist one that accepted "the limitations and possibilities of the real world" and realized that political decisions "are made in practical circumstances with real consequences." The establishment of the ADA, he believed, marked "perhaps as much as anything the watershed at which American liberalism began to base itself once again on a solid conception of man and history."[22] According to Allen Yarnell, ADA-style postwar liberalism was based on three principles: Communists and liberals could not work together in the same organization, liberals must speak with one voice, and that voice must oppose a third party on the left.[23]

The question for the historian is whether these liberal principles (and this liberal organization and its fellow travelers) made a significant impact on anti-communism in the United States. Richard Gid Powers has argued that "*Vital Center* liberals" were "the architects of the free world's defense against Communism,"[24] and David Plotke credits what he calls "progressive liberals" with shaping the Cold War state.[25] Nevertheless, it is difficult, if not impossible, to identify any influential "*Vital Center*" or "progressive" liberals in the Truman administration; to argue that the administration was indebted to liberals for any of its laws, executive orders, or institutional innovations; or even to label the administration's Cold War foreign policy as "liberal."[26] John Lewis Gaddis credits the conservative George Kennan with providing "the intellectual rationale" for the Truman administration's view of international events, while Paul Y. Hammond credits General George C. Marshall with being the chief "instigator" of the administration's foreign policy.[27] Other "instigators"—including Averill Harriman, Dean Acheson, Paul Nitze, Charles Bohlen, and the Undersecretaries of State and Defense who worked on aid to Greece and Turkey, the European Recovery Program, and the North Atlantic Treaty—also do not fit comfortably under the "*Vital Center* liberal" mantle. They were, in the main, experienced lawyers, business men, and civil servants who had become convinced that negotiated agreements with the Soviet Union were no longer possible. In addition, Republican Senator Arthur Vandenberg was regularly consulted, and, in fact, authored the Senate Resolution approving a North Atlantic mutual defense organization. Finally, the votes for these programs came from the entire spectrum of anti-communism. Aid to Greece and Turkey passed the Senate 67-23, and the House 287-107; the

Economic Cooperation Act (Marshall Plan) passed by even larger majorities, 69-17 in the Senate and 318-75 in the House. In addition, the Senate approved the North Atlantic Treaty by a vote of 82-13. Even the National Security Act, which enormously strengthened the power of the state in seeming direct conflict to conservative principles, received strong bipartisan support. Liberals and conservatives in Congress parted company only on foreign policy (prior to the Korean War, that is) and on China-related issues.

Benjamin O. Fordham, for his part, has argued convincingly that there was no Cold War or anti-Communist consensus. He notes that many Cold Warriors opposed massive military spending but supported stringent measures against domestic radicals; many supported the former and resisted the latter; and some supported both. Fordham sees the policies that emerged as the result of "a bargaining process between the administration and Congress, rather than some substantive relationship between the policies."[28] Thus, instead of thinking and writing in terms of "liberal" antecedents and authorship, perhaps one should follow the lead of Michael J. Hogan, who posits the emergence of "a new ideology of national security," shaped by a new breed of "national security managers," and emerging from a hotly contested debate between liberals and conservatives, Democrats and Republicans, the legislative and executive branches, and civilians and the military.[29]

"*Vital Center* liberals" also did little to configure the course or alter the speed of anti-communism at home. They were, in fact, late, reluctant, and halting recruits to that crusade. According to Alonzo L. Hamby, prior to 1949 liberals of all types, with only a few exceptions, placed the burden of proof upon the accuser, demanded fair hearings, and, in some cases, "passionately identified themselves" with those accused.[30] In fact, according to Alan Barth, many liberals had, by the time of Alger Hiss's perjury trial, developed "so strong a sense of identification with him that they could not escape the feeling that they themselves—or at least what they believed in—were in some measure on trial with him."[31] James Wechsler, in an editorial he wrote for the *New York Post*, shortly after Hiss's conviction, stated:

> Hiss's performance, as described by Chambers, became a ruthless caricature of [the liberals'] wide-eyed romanticism during the Popular Front years; it revealed that the grand illusion contained the seeds of treason. To many who had accepted the premises of the united-front epoch, the conclusion that Hiss was guilty was unbearable; they had to believe he was innocent...or confess that they might have been guilty of the same terrible folly—"There but for the grace of God..."[32]

Most liberals, following Hiss's trial and conviction, believed Hiss was guilty of perjury, and they attempted to understand what that meant for liberals. Schlesinger stated liberals should not feel compromised by Hiss's conviction, and, he predicted that "the Hiss affair will probably trail off into dark oblivion."[33] Conversely, Leslie A. Fiedler argued that the Hiss case was, or should be, a signal to liberalism "to leave the garden of its illusion," which he defined as the belief that "mere liberal principle" is, in itself, a guarantee against evil; that the wrongdoer is always the other—" 'they' and not 'us' "; and to eschew the notion that those who were identified as "left," "progressive," and "socialist" were magically shielded from practicing deceit and abusing power.[34]

Diana Trilling thought the Hiss case might be useful if "it helps us detach the wagon of liberalism from the star of the Soviet Union and if it gives liberals a sounder insight into the nature of a political idea." According to this author, liberals must learn that "political ideas are political acts, and acts of political power," and that liberals must take responsibility for their political ideas. At the same time, liberals must not ally themselves, willy-nilly, with "undesirable allies." Trilling proposed a new credo for the anti-Communist liberal, who must maintain

> a very delicate position which neither supports a McCarthy nor automatically defends anyone whom a McCarthy attacks. He decries witch-hunts. He demands that there be no public accusations without proper legal evidence. . . . But he does not make the mistake of believing that just because the wrong people are looking for Soviet agents in the American government, there are none. He does not deceive himself that whoever a McCarthy names is ipso facto an innocent liberal.[35]

Thus, as a result of the Hiss case, many liberals sought a firmer middle ground on which they could stand to expose Communist infiltration of institutions, thereby demonstrating that they were not "soft" on communism, but without simultaneously becoming too "hard" against the rights of Communists.[36] Niebuhr had tried, in a series of lectures given in 1949 and 1951, to advocate this balance. He urged liberals to act responsibly by disavowing the "pretentious elements" in their traditional dream of managing history without attending to the problem of power and to recognize "the values and virtues which enter into history in unpredictable ways and which defy the logic either liberal or Marxist planners had conceived for it." He also called on intellectuals "to resist unscrupulous efforts to obscure all shades and distinctions on the left."[37] In a later article, Niebuhr warned those liberals who extended to Communists the tolerance of traditional liberalism's hospitality to all forms of dissent that they were as "undiscriminating as the Right, which was eager to identify every form of dissent with disloyalty or even with treason."[38] Later, however, as a result of his fear of various governmental investigations into his political past and the stroke he suffered in the spring of 1952, Niebuhr became more militantly anti-Communist. He railed against mercy for the Rosenbergs, joined the American Committee for Cultural Freedom's red-baiting campaign against the Emergency Civil Liberties Committee, praised the Senate Internal Security Subcommittee as a responsible alternative to McCarthy's Permanent Subcommittee on Investigations and the House Committee on Un-American Activities, and, in a slipshod manner, accused more than one dozen Protestant clergymen of being fellow travelers.[39]

For other anti-Communist liberals, the responsible middle required opposition to the methods of Joseph McCarthy. In a book sponsored by the American Committee for Cultural Freedom, liberals James Rorty and Moshe Decter endeavored to demonstrate that an "effective anti-Communist campaign" and the activities of McCarthy were separate animals. According to these authors, an effective anti-Communist campaigner must always keep in sight the key objective: "to eliminate Communism from any role it may have in the conduct of our public affairs." In doing so, the individual—unlike McCarthy—would use tactics and a strategy that did not either divide the ranks of genuine anti-Communists or polarize the democratic community, and would neither "wantonly" injure the processes of constitutional government nor "spread disunity at home and in the free world." In sum, Rorty and Decter's middle ground was built on a proposal to depoliticize the Communist issue by means of a strengthened, determined national unity.[40] They did not, however, explain how this depoliticized national unity could be achieved.

The difficulty of trying to occupy this middle ground was noted by the socialist anti-Communist Irving Howe in his description of the 1954 ADA convention. According to Howe, most of the delegates were caught between a desire to take a strong stand in favor of civil liberties and the belief that as "responsible" liberals they had to take into consideration the national security issue. "The result was a dizzying rhythm, one step forward, one step backward."[41] This "rhythm" became obvious when the convention had to confront Senator Humphrey's Communist control bill, which was extremely unpopular. The delegates did not pass any resolutions critical of Humphrey, but they did pass one urging President Eisenhower to veto the bill. In addition, one member wrote to

Hubert H. Humphrey, the point man of liberal anti-communism in the Senate. (Library of Congress)

Humphrey, warning him that he should not take this resolution "as an expression of fundamental disagreement with you and your colleagues."[42]

The ADA had also responded in a consistently tepid manner to other acts of official anti-Communists that, prior to 1947, liberals would have viewed as severe violations of civil liberties. McAuliffe cites as examples the ADA's responses to the Internal Security Act and the *Dennis* decision. Likewise, she does not perceive this organization as having mustered a very strong opposition to either McCarran or McCarthy.[43] Steven Gillon cites as a reason for these weak responses a conflict among ADA liberals, who were regularly torn between their approval of the objectives of loyalty investigations and their disapproval of investigators' procedures. They were equally divided between their desire to combat the "evils" of communism and their belief that Communists should enjoy the protection of civil liberties. ADA members found, that even when they took a firm anti-Communist stance (e.g., the ADA's approval of the firing of teachers found to be Communist or fascist), their organization still came under attack from conservatives as being proto-Communist.[44] David Plotke concluded that when it came to dealing with domestic communism, such "progressive liberals" "ignored crucial distinctions—between political associations and conspiracies, and between radical views

and illegal practices." In addition, "they initiated or tolerated procedures they could not reasonably defend."[45]

The middle ground also proved a slippery slope for the American
Civil Liberties Union. The ACLU, according to Samuel Walker,
entered the Cold War deeply divided between a faction, led by Norman Thomas and Morris Ernst, determined to keep the organization
free of any taint of communism; a group of First Amendment absolut-
ists; and a confused and uncertain centrist group.[46] Another divide,
between the national board and the affiliates, also quickly opened. It
first appeared in Chicago, where the local affiliate refused to cooperate
with the national board's inquiry into alleged Communist "infiltration." When the board threatened to disaffiliate the Chicago section,
it responded by disaffiliating itself.[47] Eight years later, the board and
affiliates also divided over a statement of principle that reflected the
thinking of Ernst and Thomas. Following a year of acrimonious
debate, the statement was rewritten to more sharply define domestic
communism as a defensible "political agitation movement" and an
indefensible "part of the Soviet conspiracy." It also reaffirmed the
exclusion from any ACLU office of persons who belonged to a party
"under the control or direction of any totalitarian government."[48]

The ACLU did challenge the federal loyalty program, and, during the
hearings on the Mundt-Nixon bill, ACLU attorney Arthur Garfield Hays
proclaimed his opposition to any laws affecting the Communist Party
both because the people of the United States did not need laws "to save
them from bad propaganda or bad thinking" and because the Communists did not present a danger within the United States.[49] Although the
ACLU also challenged the U.S. Attorney General's list, some contempt
of Congress citations, and blacklisting, it became very defensive after its
experience with filing briefs challenging the prosecution and conviction
of Communist leaders under the Alien Registration Act. The organization began including a disclaimer in its briefs stating that the ACLU
was "opposed to any governmental or economic system which denies
fundamental civil liberties and human rights. It is therefore opposed to
any form of the police state or the single-party state, or any movement
in support of them whether fascist, Communist, or known by any other
name."[50] Mary McAuliffe also does not give high marks to the ACLU
for its behavior during this era, suggesting that members were more concerned with the rival Emergency Civil Liberties Committee (ECLC) than
with the "red scare."[51]

Two smaller liberal organizations, however, took a strong stand
against McCarthy. In 1952, Freedom House issued a statement charging

the senator with having created an "atmosphere of fear and uncertainty." Two years later, it produced and widely distributed a 45-minute film that combined the kinescopes of Edward R. Murrow's two broadcasts exposing McCarthy's demagoguery.[52] In addition, in 1953, Maurice Rosenblatt, one of the directors of the National Committee for an Effective Congress, organized a series of meetings to develop a new strategy to deal with McCarthy and established an informal research organization, the Clearing House, to gather data about the senator to be distributed to members of Congress. The Clearing House helped fuel the effort to remove J. B. Matthews from his post as counsel to the McCarthy subcommittee, and it initiated and widely distributed a study by pollster Louis Bean to demonstrate that McCarthy's impact on the 1952 elections was seriously overestimated. It became fully engaged in the summer of 1954, when Senator Ralph Flanders called on the Clearing House to provide him with evidence to support his anti-McCarthy resolution. The Clearing House did organize a loose coalition of liberal and labor organizations to support Flanders's resolution, but, according to Robert Griffith, its aid was less than overwhelming, and most of the money for this effort was raised by Paul G. Hoffman, a liberal Republican.[53]

Finally, the approximately two dozen liberal Democrats in the United States Senate found the middle ground to be a slippery slope. In 1950, eight Senate liberals, led by Harley Kilgore (Democrat–West Virginia), tried to derail the Mundt-Nixon-McCarran internal security bill, by substituting for it a bill establishing preventive detention of suspected subversives in case of an internal security emergency. According to Paul H. Douglas (Democrat–Illinois), they did so for three reasons: (1) to offer an affirmative substitute; (2) "to change the focus of public attention from Communist speech and association (which were not the greatest dangers) to the genuine problems of sabotage and espionage"; and (3) to put into place procedures for the release of those detained when the dangers of sabotage and espionage had abated.[54] Humphrey, one of the co-sponsors of the legislation, stated that the substitute bill was much tougher than McCarran's "cream-puff special." But when the liberals were outmaneuvered, and their substitute was first rejected by the Senate (by a vote of 23–50) and then joined to McCarran's bill (stripped of most of its procedural safeguards), only three of the original sponsors voted against it (along with four others), and seven liberal Democrats, Humphrey included, voted for it. Douglas wrote that he and Humphrey voted for the bill "with heavy hearts," because they feared that opposing it would earn for them a pro-Communist label. However, when Truman vetoed the bill, Douglas, Chavez, and Humphrey changed their positions and voted to sustain the president's veto.[55] One year later, during the debate over the McCarran-Walter bill, Humphrey and Lehman again offered a substitute, with similar content but including greater due process. McCarran did not allow public hearings on the bill, and it was rejected by the Senate.[56]

Only Herbert Lehman (New York) and William Benton (Connecticut) spoke out against McCarthy from the floor of the Senate, and, prior to the 1954 Army-McCarthy hearings, only Benton introduced and pursued an investigation of McCarthy.[57] In the opening days of the 1954 session of Congress, when McCarthy requested an appropriation of $214,000 for his subcommittee, only two southern liberals, Allen Ellender (Democrat–Louisiana) and J. William Fulbright (Democrat–Arkansas) voted against it.[58] Finally, in 1954, Humphrey and three other senators introduced a bill to derail a proposed amendment to the Internal Security Act, calling for the registration of "Communist-infiltrated" organizations, with one stripping the Communist Party of all its rights and liberties.[59] Humphrey's substitute, titled "a bill to outlaw the Communist Party," made it a crime to become a member of the Party. During his discussion of his amendment, Humphrey repeatedly stated that it "gets at the heart of the evil," the "center of the problem."[60] (The bill was approved 85-1, with Lehman's the only dissenting vote.) McCarran responded by incorporating this amendment into his own bill, and, after a series of legislative maneuvers, the final version, known as the Communist Control Act, passed unanimously in the Senate and with only two nay votes in the House of Representatives.[61]

The only notable effort by a Senate liberal to rein in official anticommunism came after the vote against McCarthy. On January 18, 1955, Humphrey and John Stennis (Democrat–Mississippi) introduced S. J. Res. 21, which sought to establish a Commission on Government Security to the Committee on Government Operations. On June 27, Humphrey called this resolution "an indispensable first step in the direction of establishing a well-reasoned, effective, orderly, uniform, and consistent security program which reconciles the need of security with the protection and preservation of basic American traditions, rights, and privileges." It passed unanimously.[62]

In the House of Representatives, liberals were equally ineffective. No liberal asked for a roll call vote on the 1951 and 1952 appropriations for the Un-American Activities Committee; only 2 representatives voted against it in 1953; and one negative vote was recorded in 1954.[63] Finally, although 113 members had voted against overriding Truman's veto of the McCarran-Walter Act, only 2 voted against the Communist Control Act of 1954.

In retrospect, one can see that liberal anti-communism was undermined by the failure of many liberals to face squarely two pertinent questions posed to them by Sidney Hook. The first, in 1949, came in response to a statement that one must overlook the "sins of Russia" and focus on the dangers in the United States, because one could do nothing about the first, but had a responsibility toward the second. Hook queried his correspondent: "When you and your fellows were asked to protest against the sins of Franco, Hitler, Mussolini, Chiang Kai-shek, the Greek government, etc., did you reply then that 'the sins of other countries' are not our responsibility? Why is it only when you are asked to condemn Soviet terror do you make this response?"[64]

Two answers were likely, though neither would have satisfied Hook or the conservatives. A liberal might have said, "Although both fascist and Communist regimes brutalized their citizens, the goals of fascist regimes (national purification and aggrandizement) seemed irrational, whereas the goals of the Soviet Union (progress toward the final emancipation of the human race) appeared rational and desirable." In addition, the liberal might argue that Stalinism was inconsistent with Marxism and that perhaps post-Stalinists could redirect the revolution, whereas fascism was consistent with the racist, anti-Semitic, and nationalist themes that had bred it.

The second question posed by Hook strikes at the heart of the liberals' rejection of criticism of the Soviet Union, because such criticism aided the fascist and reactionary cause. Hook asked one of his correspondents: "What is your evidence that my criticisms of communism have helped Fascists and reactionaries?"[65] In fact, no such evidence was available to liberals, then or now.

LEFT-OF-LIBERAL ANTI-COMMUNISM

Those caught in the twilight zone separating "liberals" from Communists and fellow travelers also experienced great difficulty formulating a coherent thesis incorporating anti-communism. For example, in early 1948, Dwight Macdonald, Mary McCarthy, and Nicola Chiaramonte created the Europe-America Groups, in an effort to provide an alternative to the obsession with Stalinism of other New York intellectuals. Such zealotry, Macdonald wrote in a letter to Victor Serge, "simply makes one into the image of what one fights." Ultimately, however, this attempt to find an international third way for the independent intelligentsia of the democratic left collapsed after one year.[66]

The editorial staff of *Partisan Review* did not try to consolidate the left-of-liberal forces, contenting themselves instead with issuing harsh criticism of Communists and liberals. Their basic position was stated in a 1946 polemical editorial, "The 'Liberal' Fifth Column," written by a newcomer to the magazine, William Barrett. He opened this piece with a quotation from *New Republic*, criticizing the Truman administration's get-tough policy toward the Soviet Union. Barrett termed that statement to be advocacy for a policy "to sell out [the peoples of Europe] into Stalinist slavery." Such a statement, he continued, showed "that we have in our midst a powerfully vocal lobby willing to override all concerns of international democracy and decency in the interests of a foreign power." He accused the liberals, who wrote for *PM*, *The Nation*, and *New Republic*, of constructing this "Fifth Column." Barrett always put quotation marks around the word "liberal", because, he stated, liberals were "obviously usurping a name which they have despoiled of every vestige of its original meaning." They had also corrupted logic and morals, and embarked on a policy of appeasement, and, as a result, could "only be described as Russian patriots."[67]

Partisan Review also expressed its delight at the dilemmas faced by liberals over Hiss and McCarthy. Philip Rahv, in his review of Whittaker Chambers's *Witness*, wrote:

> The importance of the Hiss case was precisely that it dramatized [the Popular Front] mind's struggle for survival and its vindictiveness under attack. That mind is above all terrified of the disorder and evil of history, and it flees the hard choices which history so often imposes. It fought to save Hiss in order to safeguard its own illusions and to escape the knowledge of its own gullibility and chronic refusal of reality.[68]

Moreover, according to Barrett,

> [McCarthy] only confirmed them [the liberals] in their own sense of self-righteousness, which is one of the liberal temptations anyway. Where there might have been an opportunity to do some soul-searching, and to rethink their position particularly with regard to its pro-Soviet leanings, Liberals could now easily throw out the accusation of "McCarthyism" at any critic of those tendencies and the result is that Liberals have continued in these attitudes.[69]

When it came to the Hiss case, William Phillips, *Partisan Review*'s co-editor, in his review of *Witness*, condemned liberals, without actually naming them, for their "political ignorance." The Hiss case, Phillips wrote, demonstrated that the chief menace of communism emanates not "from the small and shabby Communist Party itself, but from its ability to exploit the social conscience of those who still think of Communists simply as the exponents of a high-minded and respectable social philosophy." According to Phillips, the defenders of Hiss had failed to grasp that he was a typical Communist—one who, in an idealist and humanist guise, lied and deceived.[70]

Others in this twilight zone, led by Sidney Hook and Melvin Lasky, proved more effective. Lasky, who had been a member of the League for Cultural Freedom and Socialism and a writer for *New Leader,* had been the only anti-Soviet voice at a German Writers Congress (October 1947). He proposed to the U.S. military authorities in Berlin that they sponsor an "American-edited and American-written" periodical "to address, and to stimulate, the German-reading intelligentsia of Germany and elsewhere, with the world-view of American thinkers and writers." The "unafraid self-critical tone" of these contributors would be, Lasky promised, "a living demonstration of how the democratic mind works." Aided by a subsidy from the military authorities, the first issue of Lasky's periodical, *Der Monat: Eine Internationale Zeitschrift für Politik und geistiges Leben,* was published in October 1948. It was, he later said, modeled on *Partisan Review,* aimed at corralling the "wayward intelligentsia."[71]

Lasky was also at the center of the non-Communist left's counter-offensive against the Soviet attempt to rebuild a popular front of artists and intellectuals for "peace," which was embodied in a series of international conferences held in Wroclaw (Poland), New York, and Paris in 1949. With the help of another subsidy from U.S. military authorities in Berlin, Lasky sent out invitations to a variety of ex-Communists and anti-Stalinists, asking them to attend a Congress for Cultural Freedom in June 1950. The purpose was to unite and mobilize anti-totalitarian intellectuals.[72] Almost all the participants were liberals or democratic socialists, but there was a clear divide between the British, French, and Italian participants, who wanted to fight communism by emphasizing the political and cultural achievements of the West, and the U.S. contingent, who preferred direct confrontation with every form of communism.[73] Nevertheless, the delegates agreed to establish an International Congress for Cultural Freedom (ICCF). Its founding manifesto, mainly written by Arthur Koestler, devoted 3 of its 14 points to totalitarianism. Part Eleven read: "We hold that the theory and practice of the totalitarian state are the greatest challenge to which man has been called on to meet in the course of civilized history."[74] Interim funding for the ICCF was provided by the American Federation of Labor, but the Central Intelligence Agency provided the permanent subsidies.[75] During the remainder of the decade, the ICCF sponsored a series of international gatherings as well as several prominent anti-Communist journals (e.g., *Preuves, Encounter*).

Lasky's U.S. counterpart, Sidney Hook, referred to himself as a "democratic socialist," with the emphasis on "democratic."[76] Following the signing of the German-Soviet Nonaggression Treaty, Hook had become one of the most regular exposers and accusers of fellow travelers, apologists, and front groups, as well as a determined organizer of anti-Communist groups. He had joined Macdonald's Europe-America Groups with the intent of taking control of the organization and making it more anti-Communist. When that effort failed, Hook formed the Friends of Russian Freedom in early 1949 with the goal of creating a Russian Institute to serve displaced Russians, though the group actually did little more than issue a manifesto. When he learned about the Cultural and Scientific Conference for World Peace, planned to be held in New York City later that year, he first attempted to participate. When his proposed topic was rejected, and he discovered that no person critical of the Soviet Union or the CPUSA had been invited, Hook called a meeting of former New York City members of the prewar Committee for Cultural Freedom, and they founded the Ad Hoc Committee for Intellectual Freedom (later renamed Americans for Intellectual Freedom) to expose the Communist control of that conference and attempt to counteract its message.[77] He also participated in the less successful counter-meeting to the Paris "peace" conference, where he met with Lasky. In 1951, Hook established the U.S. affiliate of the ICCF, the American Committee for Cultural Freedom (ACCF), which, in his words, was dedicated to the exposure of "Stalinism and Stalinist liberals" wherever they might be found.[78]

In 1950 and 1951, Hook made perhaps his seminal contributions to anti-communism, in the form of two articles published in the *New York Times Magazine*. In the introductory note to the reprinted version of the articles (in an ACCF-sponsored pamphlet), Hook forthrightly stated his anti-Communist credo: "Whoever says he is neither for nor against Communism is really saying that he is not opposed to total cultural terror, to judicial frameups, to slave-labor camps, to absolute regimentation of thought, to international aggression and mass murder." In effect, according to Hook, to be genuinely for freedom, one must be genuinely anti-Communist. In his view, anti-communism, did not mean suppression of Communist ideas; those ideas, he insisted, were simply a form of heresy. Anti-communism did, however, require advocacy of severe constraints on the CPUSA, because the Communist movement was a conspiracy, and conspirators pose much greater threats to freedom than heretics.[79] Hook also stated that he and the ACCF were "against attempts to use legitimate anti-Communism as a pretext for irresponsible attacks on liberal ideas and movements."[80]

The ACCF proved to be, in the words of Irving Kristol, "a heterogeneous group of intellectuals whose common cause turned out not to be common enough." They shared, in Christopher Lasch's estimation, "a conspiratorial view of Communism," a belief "that the Communist conspiracy had spread throughout practically every level of American society," and the need to maintain a "running fire on 'antianticommunism.' "[81] For example, ACCF members tended to be more militantly opposed to the National Lawyers Guild and the Emergency Civil Liberties Committee[82] than they were to threats to civil liberties in the United States. In spring 1952, the members divided over Dwight Macdonald's proposal that the committee publish a pamphlet exposing and condemning the "abuses of anti-Communism" and McCarthyism, both of which threatened cultural freedom. In the end, the Hook faction defeated the motion, and the committee accepted a compromise offered by Daniel Bell, resolving to attack "unprincipled and exaggerated innuendos and outright lies as techniques of political discourse."[83] Norman Podhoretz, who was much too young to have participated in the ideological battles that had shaped the members of the ACCF, nevertheless found himself in strong agreement with their arguments. While they could not be accused of being "soft" on McCarthyism, he said, "there [could] be little question" that ACCF members "were more concerned with fighting what they took to be the misconceptions of the nature of Soviet Communism than with fighting the persecution to which so many people were being subjected in the early fifties; and it shames me to say that I shared fully in their brutal insensitivity on this issue."[84]

The ACCF was regularly criticized by liberals. For example, Arthur Schlesinger, Jr., wrote in 1952 that "I cannot go along with those who profess a belief in culture, on the one hand, and refuse to condemn McCarthy."[85] An even more pointed critique came in February 1955, when executive director Sol Stein, in the name of the ACCF Executive Committee, criticized an anonymously authored article that had condemned the Senate Internal Security Subcommittee's treatment of Owen Lattimore. David Riesman, who had recently resigned from the ACCF, called Stein's letter an example of the ACCF's "vindictive pursuit of the shrinking minority of 'liberals' who haven't learned," and he found infamous the decision "to put the whole weight of the Committee for Cultural Freedom behind the pursuit of an already beleaguered man [Lattimore], living in limbo and not permitted to teach classes." Schlesinger wrote that the ACCF should be able to find better things to do than to harass Lattimore. Richard Rovere, for his part, stated that the Internal Security Subcommittee should be condemned: it was "a mess and a menace" and its hearings were responsible for confusing the debate over China policy.[86] These sentiments were echoed by ICCF Executive Director Michael Josselson in a 1956 letter he wrote to the ACCF, in which he stated that the American Committee seemed "to recognize only one weapon in the fight against Communism: denunciation." In addition, the Secretariat in Paris did not think that the American Committee was sufficiently critical of McCarthy.[87]

CONCLUSION

The dissonance on the anti-Communist left was sharp. Liberals were criticized by, and in turn criticized, those to the left of them. Some moderates, such as Hannah Arendt, cast a pox on both their houses. In *The Origins of Totalitarianism* (1951), she criticized what she termed "liberal rationalization" and "liberal wheedling"—that is, the propensity to explain away the truly incredible and awful aspects of totalitarianism by "common sense" conclusions.[88] Arendt was even more critical of Sidney Hook. In June 1949, she wrote that "the Red Hunt" in the United States "is going full steam. . . . The repulsive aspect of it is that someone like Hook, for example, if he is at odds with [Jean-Paul] Sartre, whom he can't fit into the formula Stalinist versus anti-Stalinist, will then declare that Sartre is a 'reluctant Stalinist.' "[89] Four years later, she accused Hook of behaving "shabbily" when he co-authored, on behalf of the Committee for Cultural Freedom, a letter calling Albert Einstein irresponsible for urging intellectuals to refuse to testify before congressional investigating committees.[90]

Civil-Libertarian Anti-Communism, 1945–1957

Civil-libertarian anti-Communists usually did not join groups, nor did they try to mobilize popular support for their position. Indeed, they did not even compose a united front (although some supported others, via forewords or favorable reviews). They mainly used their public statements, books, and articles to advocate on behalf of what I have labeled, for lack of a better term, civil-libertarian anti-communism. The term "anti-anti-Communists" does not seem appropriate for this group, for three reasons: it is too narrow, it is too slippery, and it carries polemical baggage. It is too narrow, because it implies that the person so designated is both a dedicated anti-Communist and an opponent of overly zealous anti-Communists, whereas few civil libertarians expended much time and energy demonizing the CPUSA or the Soviet Union. It is also slippery, because it provided a cover for those like James Burnham, who were steadfast anti-Communists and tepid critics of individuals such as Joseph McCarthy, who were prime targets of the civil libertarians. Finally, it was used as a polemical weapon by liberals such as Arthur Schlesinger, Jr., who applied it to "those who think it is fine to be anti-fascist, anti-Republican, or anti-Democratic but who squirm and wince when someone in exactly the same sense is anti-Communist. All form of baiting are okay for 'anti-anti-Communists' except red-baiting." Schlesinger did not mean to imply that all "anti-anti-Communists" are "pro-Stalinist," but he sarcastically noted that they "just have a feeling that a Communist is a rather noble, dedicated fellow who deserves special consideration in a harsh and reactionary world."[1]

The people in this category ran the political gamut from the conservative law professor Zechariah Chafee, Jr., to the Catholic Socialist

Michael Harrington. They were neither admirers of nor apologists for the Soviet Union or the Communist Party, but some of them did not bother to qualify their criticism of zealous anti-communism with condemnations of the CPUSA or the Soviet Union. They agreed that there was a "Communist issue," but they believed that the existing ideals, values, and institutions of the United States, and the common sense of the country's citizens, provided adequate protection against the "threat of Communist subversion." Perhaps that position was best stated by the 26 lawyers (Chafee among them) who opposed a loyalty oath for lawyers passed by the American Bar Association in September 1950 (see Chapter 7). Their opposing brief included the following statement:

> The existing means of discovering and punishing illegal or professionally improper conduct, by presenting specific charges and supporting evidence, are ample, in our belief, to meet any danger to our Government or disgrace to our profession. National and local law enforcement agencies, courts, bar associations, and grievance committees are fully alert to existing dangers from communists in our midst, whether avowed or concealed.[2]

The civil libertarians also agreed that the dangers of anti-communism, as exemplified by loyalty programs and oaths, congressional investigating committees, and anti-Communist legislation, outweighed the dangers of communism. This position was well stated by Alan Barth:

> The institutions of liberty are under attack. They are threatened by an aggressive totalitarianism abroad ... In some measure, too, the institutions are threatened by agents of that totalitarianism at home. They are threatened most of all, however, by well-meaning and patriotic but frightened Americans, who have come to think of liberty as a liability rather than an asset.[3]

Finally, they believed that the relatively small number of actual Communists in the United States offset the Communist Party's subversive ideology and purported rigid discipline. They did not believe that a Communist was transformed by his or her ideology and discipline into a super-human person with the strength of a thousand non-Communists. Many of them also had an experience in common: they were accused, by anti-Communists, of aiding communism by their criticisms of anti-communism.

THE CONSERVATIVE LAW PROFESSOR: ZECHARIAH CHAFEE, JR.

Chafee was the dean and doyen of this group. A professor at Harvard Law School (1916–1956), and a self-proclaimed "student of free speech," he was a critic of all three "red scares." He refused to join any permanent organizations or committees, but he served on several commissions and committees, and he signed a number of petitions.[4]

Chafee wrote his first article on free speech for *New Republic* in November 1918, criticizing the May 1918 amendment to the Espionage Act of 1917, which criminalized any opposition to any war. Speech in wartime should, he argued, "be free unless it is clearly liable to cause direct and dangerous interference with the conduct of the war."[5] He followed this publication with two law review articles on the subject of free speech. In the first, published in June 1919, Chafee undertook an extended discussion of the history of restrictions on free speech and proposed that the courts use a balancing test (akin to the clear-and-present danger test, enunciated by Justice Oliver Wendell Holmes, Jr., in *Schenck v. United States*, 249 U. S. 47, 1919) to arbitrate between "two very important social interests, in public safety and the search for truth."[6] The second law review article was very different in tone. It sharply criticized the trial judge in *United States v. Abrams* (1918) and the Supreme Court's majority opinion upholding the results of that case (250 U. S. 616, 1919). Chafee warned: "The danger of the majority view is that it allows the government, once there is a war, to embark on the most dubious enterprises, and gag all but very discrete protests against these nonwar activities." He ended with a spirited defense of the First Amendment as the basis for "the attainment and spread of truth, not merely as an abstraction, but as the basis of political and social progress."[7] When Chafee signed a petition urging President Wilson to grant amnesty to the defendants in the *Abrams* case, J. Edgar Hoover ordered his agents to compile a dossier on the professor.[8]

Chafee used revised versions of both law review articles as chapters in his first book, *Freedom of Speech*, which was intended as a source book for lawyers engaged in freedom of speech cases. The other chapters discussed opposition to the war, the laws against sedition and anarchy, deportations, trials of socialists, and schools. In a short section on Communists, Chafee posed the two most important, and regularly ignored, questions involving sedition charges: "(a) When does an organization advocate force and violence? (b) If it does so, can all its members be justly subjected to painful consequences?" He answered that there is "no sure test of what a party does advocate," and that even if some of a party's tenets do advocate force and violence, "it does not necessarily follow that all its members are supporters of violence. . . . The idea that guilt is not necessarily personal, but can result from mere association is absolutely abhorrent to every American tradition or conception of social justice."[9] Referring to the two newly formed Communist parties, he suggested that, objectionable as their purposes might be, those purposes were altogether compatible with the absence of force and violence.[10]

Two decades later, Chafee's *Free Speech in the United States* (published in 1941) vastly expanded his earlier book and made it less technical. The key portion was his condemnation of the Alien Registration Act for promulgating "the most drastic restrictions on freedom of speech ever enacted in the United States during peace." For the first time, he continued, guilt by association "was introduced into a federal criminal law." He also stated that "much as we dislike" Communists, the many state laws excluding the Communist Party from the ballot were "unwise." He rejected these measures because he believed, contrary to anti-Communist ideologues, that the minds of rank-and-file Party members "are not made up for life" and there is "a good chance of reconciling them to American ways."[11] In his conclusion, Chafee stated that the Alien Registration Act created only the illusion of loyalty. Genuine loyalty, can be created only by cultivating freedom, discouraging fear, allowing the discontented to talk openly, refusing to encourage people to spy on one another, and letting time and counter-arguments remedy objectionable ideas.[12]

Chafee became one of the strongest critics of the third "red scare." In fact, in January 1950, he received a letter from President Truman commending him for his opposition to the internal security bill then making its way through Congress.[13] The following year, in a speech, delivered at Swarthmore College, Chafee stated: "Never in our lifetimes have American citizens spewed such virulence against American citizens or shown such terror-stricken eagerness to shelter themselves behind novel barricades from the oft-heralded wickedness of their own fellow-countrymen." He also criticized the propensity to identify so completely Communists in the United States "with the aggressors in the Kremlin." Remember, he wrote, "they are not only Communists; they are American Communists too. . . . We shall reduce their harmlessness much more successfully if, for a while, we stop being terrified by abstract phrases about a vast international conspiracy and just think of these people as an American problem," and Communists as "American problem children." He again condemned guilt by association, which he defined as the punishing of people not for doing wrong but "merely for fear that they might do something wrong."[14] And, in his book *Blessings of Liberty*, Chafee accused the government of constructing a howitzer to kill a swarm of gnats:

It is not enough that Communists are pestiferous people or indulge in big talk about taking over our government. The question is whether they are within a million miles of doing so. Where *inside this country* are the facts which justify the establishment of unheard-of regulatory machinery, the expenditure of large sums of money in its operation, and the severe punishment of American citizens because somebody or other has not filled out a piece of paper?[15]

When he was warned by Schlesinger, among others, that an organization he was co-sponsoring, the National Committee to Defeat the Mundt Bill, was a "Communist-controlled outfit," Chafee responded: "These people were the first in the field to write me and I felt it my duty to throw in my lot with a group on the spot which would do its best to kill these measures."[16] Five years after the bill became law, he noted: "Nothing has happened during the five years since September 1950 [when it became law] to make this law any more necessary to preserve us from internal dangers through revolutionary violence or other unlawful action." Certainly, he wrote, there ought to be effective legal protection against spying and sabotage by Communists, but the United States had a great deal of it without this act. The only way to preserve the existence of the free institutions of the United States, Chafee concluded, was to make them "a living force. To ignore them in the very process of purporting to defend them, as frightened men urge, will leave us little worth defending."[17]

Chafee also wrote a laudatory foreword to Alan Barth's *The Loyalty of Free Men*. In it, Chafee urged Congress to reform the procedures of its investigating committees, President Truman to eliminate the loyalty program, and all parties to put an end to the "persistent probing of the patriotism of professors and schoolteachers."[18] The following year, Senator McCarthy during his attack on Senator William Benton, charged that Benton, during his tenure as Assistant Secretary of State for Public Affairs (1945–1947), had surrounded himself with "a motley, Red-tinted crowd." Among those seven, labeled by McCarthy as "fellow travelers, Communists, and complete dupes" who were "dangerous to America" was Chafee.[19]

THE LIBERAL EDITORIAL WRITER: ALAN BARTH

Alan Barth was an editorial writer for the *Washington Post* (1942–1972) who specialized in civil liberties issues. In one of his first articles on the subject, a review of Harold D. Lasswell's *National Security and Individual Freedom*, Barth wrote that individual freedom was presently "being jettisoned in the name of national security as though it were burdensome cargo on a foundering ship of state." He chastised Lasswell for being too meticulously objective and failing, as a result, to "sound a tocsin" and convey to his readers "the sense that they are already suffering profoundly from the malady" that his book sought to cure. "Before therapy can begin," Barth concluded, "the country must be awakened to the unreasoning fear in which it is now gripped. That fear may end up destroying national security and individual freedom alike."[20]

By the time he wrote *The Loyalty of Free Men*, Barth had developed a more moderate tone. In the Introduction, Chafee wrote: "Mr. Barth is well aware of the objectionable nature of American Communists ... But, instead of treating them like Gorgons who must not be looked at, he tries to understand what Communists are really like."[21] As a result of his conclusion that Communists did not pose a serious threat to the United States, Barth focused on the threat posed by the hunt for them. As a result of that hunt, he wrote, based largely on "groundless and neurotic fears," the freedom of the people of the United States and their security had not been protected, but rather had been steadily eroded. In addition, he accused the proponents of anti-communism of committing a fatal error when "they confuse loyalty with orthodoxy."[22]

In his discussion of the "Communist problem," Barth agreed that Communists were enemies of American values and tools of a foreign government, but insisted that those facts did not make Communists a threat to the nation. "It is a fundamental misapprehension to suppose that they are powerful simply because they are abhorrent." As he pointed out, Communists' numbers were too small, their "infiltrations" could be met in rational ways, and their ideology could not be effectively impeded by any law or administrative procedure.[23] Barth also sharply criticized what he called "the cult of loyalty in the United States," the Committee on Un-American Activities, the government's loyalty program, the FBI, official secrecy on many aspects of scientific inquiry, and the attacks on academic freedom. He closed with a chapter titled "The Utility of Freedom," in which he strongly insisted on the value of freedom as the *sine qua non* "for the security of the United States."[24]

In a subsequent article, Barth labeled as "disastrous folly" the invitations that university presidents were issuing to Congressional investigations and their firing of professors who invoked the Fifth Amendment.[25] He also questioned the reliability of FBI reports as the basis of most investigations, prosecutions, and dismissals.[26]

In 1955, Barth wrote another book, *Government by Investigation*, that extensively and critically analyzed congressional investigating committees. These committees, he stated, had "become roving satrapies unrestrained by their parent bodies," using legislative trials as "a device for condemning men without the formalities of due process," and concerned only with "punishing people for 'disloyalty' and 'fellow-traveling.' "[27] In his review of this book, Paul R. Hays, professor of law at Columbia Law School and a self-admitted anti-Communist, stated that Barth was unsound in his legal analysis and remiss in his "astonishing underestimation of Communist influence in this country."[28]

THE EX-COMMUNIST, LIBERAL JOURNALIST: JAMES WECHSLER

The only ex-Communist among the civil-libertarian anti-Communists, and perhaps this category's most outspoken critic of McCarthy, Wechsler was also the only member of this group to be subpoenaed by a congressional investigating committee. While he was a student at Columbia University, Wechsler joined the Young Communist League (YCL). He also was a leading figure in the American Student Union, a meld of various strata of the left. Eventually Wechsler began to experience doubts about communism, which were bolstered by his reading of Eugene Lyons's *Assignment in Utopia*, the purge trials, reports from Spain, and his own misgivings about the Soviet system following a trip he took there in the summer of 1937. He resigned from the YCL at the end of 1937 and wrote for, in succession, *The Nation*, *PM*, and the *New York Post*; he became the *Post's* chief editorial writer in 1949.[29] Wechsler also wrote five books during the period covered by this book: *Revolt on the Campus* (1935); *War: Our Heritage* (with Joseph Lash, 1937); *War Propaganda and the United States* (with Harold Lavine, 1940); *Labor Baron: A Portrait of John L. Lewis* (1944); and *The Age of Suspicion* (1953).

Following the signing of the German-Soviet Nonaggression Treaty, Wechsler became increasingly anti-Communist. Even so, he managed to maintain a dispassionate voice when discussing the Communist Party.[30] He fought against Communist factions at *PM* and in the New York chapter of the American Newspaper Guild, yet was among a group of American Civil Liberties Union members who condemned the 1940 resolution refusing board or staff positions to those who supported "totalitarian dictatorships."[31] In 1946, Wechsler resigned from *PM* because the editor, Ralph Ingersoll, though not himself a Communist, "continuously yielded to communist pressure."[32] He then joined Americans for Democratic Action and, a few years later, the American Committee for Cultural Freedom.

Wechsler firmly believed that Communists "must be excluded from government," but at the same time he strongly reaffirmed "their rights to raise hell through the public channels of democratic debate" because, he wrote, "Ideas are not the enemy." He stated that the national security program must distinguish between "communism as an idea and the Communist parties as battalions of Soviet espionage and sabotage," and he criticized Truman's loyalty program as being "alternately unsatisfactory and inadequate" on the matters of procedural safeguards and the criteria used to distinguish nonconformists from conspirators.[33]

Under his direction, the *New York Post* hired Arthur Schlesinger, Jr., Max Lerner, and Murray Kempton; thus, Wechsler noted, the newspaper "editorially reflected the attitudes of anti-communist liberals in America."[34] Its 17-part series, "Smear, Inc.: Joseph McCarthy's One-Man Mob," published in September 1951, brought Wechsler to the attention of the senator, who began to attack him on the floor of the Senate. Following one such speech in May 1952, Wechsler responded with a letter defending himself and his newspaper, which Senator Herbert Lehman inserted into the *Congressional Record* on June 9, 1952. Wechsler complained that McCarthy, instead of challenging the factual bases of the articles, "has chosen to make a personal attack on the editor of the *Post* and to imply that only a subversive newspaper could have published this series." In fact, Wechsler stated, "the *Post* is a militantly anti-communist newspaper," and its editor had "actively and publicly opposed communist totalitarianism" since he left the YCL.[35]

Ten months later, Wechsler received a subpoena ordering him to appear at a closed hearing of McCarthy's Permanent Subcommittee on Investigations, ostensibly to testify about those of his books that Roy Cohn had found in his investigation of overseas Department of State libraries. In reality, it rapidly became clear that he had been called before the Subcommittee to face the wrath of McCarthy. Though in many instances Wechsler gave as good as he got, perhaps he ultimately gave too much. When McCarthy asked if there were any current or former YCL members working at the *Post*, Wechsler replied: "I am going to answer that question, because I believe it is a citizen's responsibility to testify before a Senate committee whether he likes the committee or not. . . . [and] because I recognize your capacity for misstatement or misinterpretation of a failure to answer." He then answered: "To my knowledge there are no Communists on the staff of the *New York Post* at this time."[36]

Noting that Wechsler had not answered his question, McCarthy elicited from Wechsler four names, all of which Wechsler qualified with their anti-Communist credentials. He then stated that during an interview with FBI agents in 1948, he had been asked the same question, and he had given them a list of "half a dozen" people who had been in his YCL group. In that and other interviews with FBI agents, Wechsler said he was asked about "men in Government," and that he had always given "truthful responses" to the best of his ability.[37] He was then ordered to submit a list, under oath, of all Communists and Young Communists that "you know as such." To which order, Wechsler replied, "I am here as a responsive but not a friendly witness."[38]

Wechsler also testified that he would not hire a Communist journalist, because "I could not trust their devotion to truth above their adherence to a party line." He also stated that he opposed legislation that punished people for advocacy or outlawing propaganda as such, but he had no quarrel with legislation that punished people for unlawful acts or for government prosecutions of Communist leaders who acted as agents of a foreign government.[39] On several occasions, McCarthy stated his belief that Wechsler remained a crypto-Communist, whose break with the CPUSA was a "phony" one. "Your record," McCarthy told him, "has been not to fight communism. You have fought every man who has ever tried to fight communism, as far as I know. Your paper, in my opinion, is next to and almost paralleling the *Daily Worker*."[40]

Wechsler reappeared, on May 5, 1953, with his list and a request, stated several times, that it not be made part of the record because it could do the people he listed "irresponsible harm." Wechsler then repeated the main themes of his first appearance: he made the list because he did not want to give the "false impression" that he had resisted the order of an "appropriate" government agency, and so as not to obscure his "long, affirmative public record of anti-Communist activity and writing." He reiterated his accusation that his subpoena "raised grave question of freedom of the press," and represented "a reprisal against a newspaper and its editor for their opposition" to McCarthy's methods. McCarthy, in turn, accused Wechsler of being the ringleader of those who assassinated the character of ex-Communists who testified against their former comrades, as well "the chief ringleader in smearing" every chairman of the Committee on Un-American Activities.[41] Although Wechsler later wrote that he had received "editorial support" for his testimony from other newspapers,[42] editorial support was divided, and the committee appointed by the American Society of Newspaper Editors to review the transcripts of the hearings did not reach a consensus about whether McCarthy had tried to intimidate the press.[43]

Wechsler's testimony dogged him thereafter. In his chapter on Wechsler, titled "The Liberal Informer," Victor S. Navasky recounts that when Lillian Hellman, in her memoir *Scoundrel Time* (1976), labeled Wechsler a "friendly witness," he threatened to sue her. She notified him that in future editions, she would refer to him as a "cooperative" witness. Navasky labeled him an "unfriendly informer."[44]

TWO LIBERAL ATTORNEYS: ABE FORTAS AND JOSEPH L. RAUH, JR.[45]

Abe Fortas belonged to the National Lawyers Guild for a short time during the 1930s, was investigated for membership in two other left-wing groups, and refused to join Americans for Democratic Action because it excluded Communists. In early 1946, he joined with Thurman Arnold, his former teacher and prominent New Dealer, to form a law firm. They were soon joined by Paul A. Porter. The firm, Arnold, Fortas and Porter, immediately became involved in loyalty dismissals. Their first case concerned the firing of Morton Friedman from the War Manpower Commission for alleged disloyalty. When a Federal District Court sustained the dismissal, Fortas applied for a writ of *certiorari*. In his brief, Fortas wrote:

> [T]his assault on freedom will not stop with a Government employee. Assaults upon freedom have a habit of growing beyond a stated objective. They quickly attack not merely a manifestation, but freedom itself. So this crusade, once under way, will not stop with its victims in the federal service. It will spread and is now spreading over this country, blighting our democracy and bringing fear and distrust to American homes throughout the nation.[46]

The petition was denied.

When the Truman loyalty program was announced, Fortas told his partners that their firm must take on these cases, "because if we don't, no one else will."[47] Fortas was concerned that the loyalty program lacked procedural safeguards and that government power over individuals had shifted from courts and judges to congressional committees and bureaucratic boards. The only stipulation made by Arnold, Fortas and Porter, when considering whether to accept a loyalty case, was that the client could not be nor have been a Communist. During the height of the Cold War, somewhere between 20 and 50 percent of the firm's cases consisted of loyalty cases, including those of the scientist Edward U. Condon and Owen Lattimore.[48] Twice Arnold, Fortas and Porter took cases to the U.S. Supreme Court, hoping that the loyalty program would be declared unconstitutional, but the Court split 4-4 on the first case, thereby upholding the dismissal of their client, and dismissed the second case on a technicality.[49] They also successfully represented 10 of the people accused by the McCarthy subcommittee of spying at Fort Monmouth. When the writer Lillian Hellman received a subpoena, she approached Fortas to represent her, but, for a variety of reasons, he sent her to Joseph Rauh as soon as he decently could.[50]

Rauh, soon after World War II ended, opened his own law firm and became general counsel of the National Committee for Civilian Control of Atomic Energy. As a result, he became the subject of FBI surveillance, which grew more intense until, in September 1947, the agents admitted they could find nothing linking him to the Communist Party.[51] Rauh was one of the founders of Americans for Democratic Action, and he deplored the influence of Communists in liberal organizations. Nevertheless, he believed that the CPUSA was a spent force, and he opposed the Alien Registration Act and the federal loyalty program. He decided to fight the Truman administration's loyalty program "and its yielding to [J. Edgar] Hoover," because, he stated, "I'm against the idea of testing anybody's loyalty. . . . There was no possible justification for the Truman executive order." He accepted as many loyalty cases as his private practice could handle. Rauh later commented: "The people running the program didn't realize how outrageous not having confrontation [of accusers by the accused] was."[52] He represented William Remington, who had been a member of the Young Communist League during the 1930s, in his libel suit against Elizabeth Bentley; his appeal of the Loyalty Board decision against him; and his perjury trials. Although Remington was convicted of perjury, Rauh later stated: "The Remington Case is the best illustration of how the climate had become. It shows the degree of governmental wrongdoing; the government's actions are much worse than anything Remington, a lowly employee in the Commerce Department, could possibly have done."[53]

As a result of his experiences arguing loyalty board cases, Rauh concluded that the assurance of employee loyalty was being purchased at an "incalculable cost . . . in human values." The largest of these costs was the use of irresponsible informers and "publicity-seeking ex-Communists" to gain wider acceptance of guilt-by-association.[54]

Rauh was on the civil liberties side in most instances when a choice had to be made, save one: as an unpaid aide on civil rights and civil liberties to Senator Paul H. Douglas, he helped draft the preventive-detention substitute for the Mundt-Nixon-McCarran bill.[55] That was a rare aberration, however. In 1950, as a member of the ADA board, Rauh joined with Wechsler to propose a resolution calling the conviction of the Communist Party leaders (*Dennis* case) a violation of free speech, because, they argued, there is no evidence that the CPUSA was an advocate of violence. The board voted against them. In addition, according to Rauh, his suggestion that the ADA support bail for the convicted leaders "was not well received," especially by the political types, notably Hubert Humphrey.[56]

In 1952, Rauh represented Lillian Hellman when she was subpoenaed by the Committee on Un-American Activities.[57] In 1953, in a debate with Roy Cohn on NBC's *American Forum on the Air*, Rauh sharply criticized McCarthy's investigation into communism at Fort Monmouth, New Jersey.[58] Three years later, he represented playwright Arthur Miller in his appearance before the Committee on Un-American Activities and his subsequent trial for contempt of Congress.

In 1954, Rauh became involved in a strange incident. A man named Paul Hughes had tried and failed to convince McCarthy's staff and the FBI that he had discovered treasonous activity at an Air Force base. He then approached Clayton Fritchey, the editor of *Democratic Digest*, and Rauh, telling them that he was a secret member of McCarthy's staff and that he had become disgusted with, and wanted to expose, them. Fritchey paid him $2,300 and Rauh paid him $8,500 to compile a report. Rauh then gave the 94-page report to Philip Graham, the publisher of the *Washington Post*. The reporters assigned to the story wrote 12 articles before any fact-checking occurred. The fact-checkers quickly discovered that Hughes's report was fiction and the story was killed, but no one involved reported Hughes's falsifications to the Department of Justice. The following year, Hughes was indicted for perjury in another case and told the Department of Justice that Rauh and the others had bribed a government witness. Hughes was also indicted for perjury on that accusation. Rauh, who was forced to testify at Hughes's trial, in January 1956, stated that he had trusted Hughes and regarded him as "a man who was exposing America's leading assaulter of civil rights." When the judge queried Rauh about the propriety of using spies, Rauh replied that he did not believe in using them, but only did so in this instance, because he was "trying to uncover illegal activity." McCarthy was also called to testify, and he told the court that Rauh did not have a reputation "for truthfulness and honesty." He told reporters outside the courtroom: "The Hughes case looks like a conspiracy between Rauh and the Democrats, the ADA and the Committee for a More Effective Congress [sic] to do a good smear job on me." (The jury failed to reach a verdict on both counts of perjury and Hughes was acquitted.)[59]

In 1955, after being elected national chairman of ADA, Rauh announced that the organization "intended to fight for the freedom of expression of all ideas, including Communists' ideas."[60] Later he told attendees at an ADA summer workshop that they were living in a historic year, when the tide in the United States had turned back toward civil liberties and "sanity" had returned. Nevertheless, he stated, McCarthyism had left deep scars on the country, including "a surprising climate of acceptance of things totalitarian." According to Rauh, a mopping-up operation was required to place limits on national security programs and congressional investigations.[61]

THE IRREVERENT PHYSICIST: ALBERT EINSTEIN

Albert Einstein was a democratic socialist, an anti-fascist, and a militant pacifist, who just fits into the category of civil-libertarian anti-Communists because, although he disliked the Soviet system and avoided organizations and conferences dominated by Communists, he made very few public condemnations of the Soviet Union or domestic Communists.[62] In fact, he always attempted to place the excesses of the Soviet leaders into a historical context and to see them as human beings. Nevertheless, in 1932, Einstein refused to sign an appeal to a peace conference because it included a "glorification of the Soviet Union," and he objected to the conference because it was "entirely under Russian-Communist domination."[63] In addition, his wife told a newspaper reporter that Einstein had declined invitations to lecture in Russia because he did not want to give the impression that he was in sympathy with the Soviet regime.[64] Even so, he did not condemn the purge trials, and he stated that the Russians were "driven into the unfortunate [1939 Nonaggression] pact with Germany."[65] During World War II, Einstein voiced strong sympathy for the Soviet Union, and at the peak of the Cold War, he wrote: "Despite the evil methods of the Russians, I regard as completely false the point of view that would represent them or treat them as common criminals."[66]

After the war, Einstein became an opponent of nuclear testing and the arms race. In an article he wrote in 1947, he condemned what he

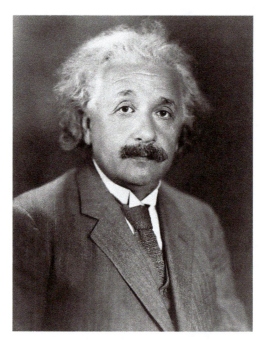

Albert Einstein, the world-famous physicist, who became a determined critic of congressional investigating committees in the early 1950s. (Library of Congress)

termed "the military mentality" in the United States, because, among other things:

> The general insecurity that goes hand in hand with this results in the sacrifice of the citizen's civil rights to the supposed welfare of the state. Political witch-hunting, controls of all sorts (e.g., control of teaching and research, of the press, and so forth) appear inevitable, and for this reason do not encounter that popular resistance which, were it not for the military mentality, would provide a protection.[67]

Einstein supported the presidential campaign of Henry Wallace, and he helped organize the Cultural and Scientific Congress for World Peace (New York City, March 1949). However, as the congress took shape, Einstein came to doubt that is would serve the cause of international understanding, given that "it is more or less a Soviet enterprise and everything is managed accordingly."[68] In 1951, when W. E. B. DuBois was indicted for violating the Foreign Agents Registration Act, Einstein volunteered to appear as a character witness, and he joined with those seeking the commutation of the death penalty against the Rosenbergs. He also signed a letter condemning anti-Semitism in the Soviet bloc countries.[69]

Einstein fully inserted himself onto the battlefield of the domestic Cold War in 1953, via a letter he wrote to William Frauenglass, a New York City high school teacher who was facing dismissal for refusing to testify before the Senate Internal Security Subcommittee. In the letter, Einstein wrote:

> The problem with which the intellectuals of this country are confronted is very serious. The reactionary politicians have managed to instill suspicion of all intellectual efforts into the public by dangling before their eyes a danger from without. Having succeeded so far, they are now proceeding to suppress the freedom of teaching and to deprive of their positions all those who do not prove submissive, i.e., to starve them.

The only way for intellectuals to confront this evil, Einstein stated, was by following "the revolutionary way of Gandhi's. Every intellectual who is called before one of the committees ought to refuse to testify, i.e., he must be prepared for jail and economic ruin, in short for the sacrifice of his personal welfare in the interest of the cultural welfare of his country." The refusal to testify "must be based on the assertion that it is shameful for a blameless citizen to submit to such an inquisition and that this kind of inquisition violates the spirit of the Constitution." When the letter was read to him by a reporter, Einstein confirmed that he had written it and indicated that, if subpoenaed, he would refuse to testify.[70] Two days later, McCarthy stated that anyone who gave advice of that sort "is himself an enemy of America." It was, the Senator continued, "the same advice that has been given by every Communist lawyer that ever appeared before our committee."[71]

That same year, Einstein congratulated George Wucinich (U.S. Army, retired) for his defiant testimony before the Senate Internal Security Subcommittee. When an engineer named Albert Shadowitz was subpoenaed by McCarthy's subcommittee, Einstein advised him not to cooperate with it or any other committee of the same nature.[72] Shadowitz invoked the First Amendment and "Professor Einstein" and was cited for contempt, but the indictment was dismissed on a technicality. In March 1954, Einstein repeated the remarks he made to Frauenglass in a letter to be read at a conference on the meaning of academic freedom, organized by the Emergency Civil Liberties Committee, on the occasion of his seventy-fifth birthday.[73] Finally, in April 1954, Einstein congratulated union official Emmanuel Fried for refusing to testify before a subcommittee of the Un-American Activities Committee.[74] He also wrote to Corliss Lamont: "Party membership is a thing for which no citizen is obliged to give an accounting."[75]

Earlier that year, Einstein, in a letter to the Decalogue Society of American Lawyers, had warned that "The fear of communism has led to practices which have become incomprehensible to the rest of civilized mankind and exposed our country to ridicule."[76] And he told Norman Thomas: "I believe America is incomparably less endangered by its own Communists than by the hysterical hunt for the few Communists that are here.... In my eyes, the 'Communist conspiracy' is principally a slogan used in order to put those who have no judgment and who are cowards into a condition which makes them entirely defenseless."[77]

THE CATHOLIC SOCIALIST: MICHAEL HARRINGTON

Harrington was born in St. Louis, attended Holy Cross College, Yale Law School (for one year), and the University of Chicago.[78] After several years of drifting, he joined the Catholic Worker Movement, and became the associate editor of the *Catholic Worker* (1951–1952). He joined the Young People's Socialist League (of the Socialist Party) in March 1952, and began to fret about the Worker Movement's failure to build an active mass base. After leaving the Movement, he began to read Marx and Lenin, and was hired as the organizational director of the Workers Defense League.[79] He also came under FBI surveillance.

In 1953, the New York section of the Young People's Socialist League, unhappy with the parent group's support of the Korean War, began to meet with the Young Socialist League (of the Independent Socialist League, a Trotskyist splinter group, headed by Max Shachtman). Eventually, the two groups merged. "We were," Harrington recalled, "determined, but unhysterical anti-Communists ... In fact, we were principled anti-Communists, we fought the persecution of Communists at every step, and we were hounded by the authorities for our pains."[80] He referred to himself as an "anti-Stalinist radical."[81]

Harrington wrote regularly for *The New International* (a Trotskyist publication), *Anvil* (an antiwar periodical), and *Commonweal* (a liberal Catholic magazine). In August 1953, he boldly stated his credo: though "it has been conclusively proved that the [Communist] Party has been used as a center for espionage activity[,] in coping with this situation, we have perhaps endangered our safety more than a spy could ever do—we have rent the basic fabric of our constitutional protection of the guilty." This danger had manifested itself in several ways, he suggested, but the two most critical had been the loose definition of the conspirator and the types of tribunals doing the accusing.

"Together, they amount to a profound trend, for their extension is almost always justified on the basis that 'the conspirator has no rights.' " Harrington concluded with the ringing statement that the rights of the conspirator and those of the innocent man were exactly the same.[82]

In his criticism, Harrington spared none of the sides in the domestic Cold War. He blamed the CPUSA for causing the decline of left-wing radicalism in the United States through its assiduous loyalty to the twistings and turnings of the Comintern line; he condemned McCarthy for his personification of right-wing radicalism and dema-goguery; and he accused the "new conservatism," as exemplified by Russell Kirk, of having a propensity to "appalling reaction."[83] Harrington was particularly harsh toward liberals. He cited, in particular, Hubert Humphrey's role in the enactment of the Communist Control Act as "the spectacle of an abject capitulation of liberalism to illiberalism." In fact, he argued, because of liberals' guilt over their tardy recognition of "Stalinist infiltration into the very center of United States policy and power," they had become the captives of their critics, moved far to the right, and created "the major institutions of the American witch hunt." The approach of these liberals toward civil liberties, he charged, "is based primarily upon the proposition, 'I am a better Red hunter than you.' "[84] In a subsequent article, Harrington accused liberals of having used McCarthy as a "ritual scapegoat" for their own purposes. Instead of fighting McCarthy, he said, liberals had served as unwitting collaborators in his rise to prominence. They had, in the name of anti-communism, attempted "to atone for their past sins of naïveté toward the Soviet Union and co-operation with the American Communists in various united-front activities," and in doing so had turned their backs on civil liberties.[85]

Harrington also strongly opposed Sidney Hook's brand of anti-communism. In an article for *Dissent*, Harrington accused the ACCF of "enthusiastically" and frequently laying itself open "to the pressures and shaping influences" of the Department of State. As a result, it had transformed itself from an organization devoted to the defense of cul-tural freedom to a propaganda agency for the United States. Moreover, he said, Hook and the ACCF had become too focused on exposing and condemning fellow travelers, when it should have been concerned with the steadily eroding civil liberties in the United States.[86]

In late 1954, Harrington was hired by John Cogley, editor of *Commonweal*, as his assistant on the Fund for the Republic's study on blacklisting. Cogley later wrote that Harrington "knew the ins and outs of the Communist Party better than any noncommunist of my acquaintance."[87] Harrington hired the remainder of the staff, vetting all of them by consulting with anti-Communists in the Los Angeles area, and carefully screening all of their contributions. The main researcher, Elizabeth Poe Kerby, who had first suggested the book idea to Robert Hutchins, the head of the Fund, was under constant suspicion, because she knew many blacklisted people, and they trusted her. In fact, Kerby's article, "The Hollywood Story," was the basis for, and the heart of, Cogley's *Report on Blacklisting*.[88]

After completing his work for Cogley, Harrington looked back at the previous decade, concluding that it was not just "ten years of gratuitous administrative hysteria," but rather a decade of "marked fundamental institutional changes in regard to civil liberties." It was a time when many people were disposed to define "all Stalinist activity" (and, by extension, all radical activity) as "conspiratorial." As a result, "it followed that police methods were justified in dealing with distasteful or hateful ideas, "an area of exception to the Bill of Rights was created," and a "quasi-judicial structure of boards, congressional committees and government agencies" was established. It is only now, when "the hysteria and the insanely repeated points of disorder" of McCarthy have receded," that "the proper, the well-fed and softspoken voice of repression, the *legitimized* institutions of unfreedom" have become evident.[89]

Following the publication of *Report on Blacklisting*, the Committee on Un-American Activities opened, in July 1956, an investigation into it. Harrington was not subpoenaed, but staff director Richard Arens closely questioned Cogley about Harrington's associations. The following day, newspaper reporter Frederick Woltman told the Committee that Cogley and Harrington were not Communists, but "they are very mixed up."[90] Five months later, Woltman, as part of his campaign against the Fund for the Republic, wrote an article stating that Harrington was "currently active in a revolutionary Marxist movement [the Young Socialist League] cited as subversive by the Attorney General." In a letter to the FBI, Chairman Francis Walter wrote that he was contemplating issuing subpoenas to some of the *Report's* researchers. The FBI approved the idea, but, for reasons unknown, Walter refrained from following through on his plans.[91]

Undaunted by these threats, Harrington called for "a principled defense of the rights of Stalinists" and "opposition to all the self-defeating undemocratic forms of anti-Stalinism, such as the notion that the way to deal with anti-libertarian Stalinists is to infringe upon their (and everyone else's) civil liberties." Although the CPUSA's fundamental character had not changed, he said, it still must be fought *"democratically."*[92] Harrington also urged democratic anti-Communists to undertake a dialogue with those Communists who had criticized the Soviet invasion of Hungary, but only "as long as they maintain their newly won independence of thought."[93]

CONCLUSION

As can be seen from the attacks and criticisms of McCarthy, Schlesinger, and Hook, among others, the civil-libertarian brand of anti-communism did not sit well with the other types of anti-Communists discussed in previous chapters. Perhaps the most detailed (and polemical) bill of particulars against civil-libertarian anti-communism was written by Irving Kristol, then managing editor of *Commentary*, and soon to be co-editor of *Encounter* (sponsored by the Congress of Cultural Freedom). In his critique, he specifically targeted the "liberal" critics of McCarthy, among which he included Chafee and Barth.[94]

Once one gets past the snide and polemical style to the substance, one finds several counts in Kristol's indictment. First, he indicated that these "liberals" did not understand communism, but rather treated it as if it were part of a political continuum, just to the left of liberalism and democratic socialism. In fact, Kristol insisted, "the antithesis of 'left' and 'right' no longer suits" current political realities, because communism was a counter-revolutionary doctrine, much as Nazism and fascism were. Second, liberals were mistaken in their belief that "an excess of anti-Communism" would gather into "a wave of 'conformism' that will drown out all free thought." Communists and fellow travelers were not free thinkers, Kristol said; they were part of a conspiratorial movement. Thus to grant them a right to silence "is to concede the right to conspiracy."

According to Kristol, no "liberal" defense of the civil liberties of Communists or fellow travelers could be taken seriously until that "liberal" defender demonstrated that he or she "knew" what communism *was* and what Communists and fellow travelers *were* (my emphasis). Communism, according to Kristol, was "an organized subversive movement" that posed "a threat to the consensus on which civil society and its liberties are based." Communists and fellow travelers were sworn to advance that movement in any way they could. Only when this "knowledge" was attained by the liberal defender might he, "if he so desires, defend the expediency in particular circumstances, of allowing them [Communists] the right to do be what they *are*" (my emphasis).[95]

Here, again, we arrive at the heart of the matter: a true anti-Communist *knows* what a Communist *is*, what a Communist *is capable of*, and the *threat* he or she represents to the nation. Anyone who speaks or acts otherwise does not *know* these *obvious facts*. Such people are to be exposed and criticized, because they, too, in their ignorance or delusion, represent a threat to national security.

The Decline and Periodic Revivals of Domestic Anti-Communism

During the late 1950s, the national mood changed, registering increasing impatience with continued loyalty oaths, security checks, and congressional investigations. According to Richard M. Fried, public support for Cold War pageantry subsided and the national consensus that had supported it began ebbing.[1] In the 1960 presidential election, neither the Republican nor the Democratic platform mentioned domestic communism. Eisenhower, in his 1961 farewell address, warned not of the danger to freedom represented by communism, but rather of the danger of "the conjunction" of two of the institutions he helped build to defeat Soviet communism: "an immense military establishment and a large arms industry." The weight and undue influence of this "military-industrial complex" might, he said, "endanger our liberties or democratic processes."[2] Four days later, the new president, John F. Kennedy, made no mention of the threat of domestic communism in his inaugural address, describing instead "the common enemies of man: tyranny, poverty, disease and war."[3]

Kennedy's election was one of three events in 1960 that dealt sharp blows to anti-communism as a domestic political weapon. The others were the publicity attending the mass protest against the Committee on Un-American Activities in San Francisco and the beginning of the end of the motion picture blacklist (following Otto Preminger's announcement that Dalton Trumbo, one of the Hollywood Ten, would receive screen credit for *Exodus*). Although Kennedy was an international Cold Warrior, his youth, humor, and energy produced a fresh political wind that invigorated criticism and diminished fear of reprisal. In addition, the number of college students had increased enormously, and many of them were unimpressed by the "logic" of anti-communism and unintimidated by the Communist-hunting apparatus of the domestic Cold War.

Nevertheless, the Committee on Un-American Activities, the Senate Subcommittee on Internal Security, evangelical Protestants, conservative Republicans, the American Legion, the FBI, and a new organization, the John Birch Society, soldiered on. Most of the individual anti-Communists discussed in the preceding pages remained anti-Communist, but many of them—notably, those belonging to liberal organizations—subordinated their animus to other issues or muted it altogether.

OFFICIAL ANTI-COMMUNISM

Congressional Investigating Committees

The Committee on Un-American Activities, though its funding and staffing remained high, authored no legislation after 1950, and the number and substance of, and the national interest in, its hearings and reports declined steadily. Walter Goodman labels many of the hearings that were scheduled between 1957 and 1960 as "frivolous" and "ludicrous."[4] While contempt citations continued to be issued, only a few witnesses were convicted and imprisoned. Increasingly, people inside and outside the hearing room protested the committee's existence. The largest, and most significant, protest occurred in San Francisco, in May 1960, when the Committee on Un-American Activities subpoenaed witnesses to testify to the current activities of the Communist Party in northern California. This hearing was held in the midst of a college-student community that was becoming highly politicized, protesting capital punishment, racial segregation, and administrative hearings about teachers' loyalty. On May 13, the second day of the hearings, several thousand protestors gathered around City Hall, the site of the hearings. Early in the afternoon, the police turned high-pressure hoses on the demonstrators and arrested more than 60 people. To counter the adverse publicity, the Committee on Un-American Activities hired a commercial firm to put together a film from the newsreel footage, which it titled *Operation Abolition*. Hundreds of prints of this carefully edited version of events circulated,[5] but it did little to improve the committee's image.

The years 1961–1966 were, according to Goodman, "the lean years." There were far fewer hearings, and most of the organizations subpoenaed to appear were small, short-lived, and lacking in influence.[6] There was, however, one notable exception: in 1965, the Committee on Un-American Activities returned to Samuel Dickstein's original intention and opened an investigation into the Ku Klux Klan. The committee was renamed the House Internal Security Committee in 1969; it was finally abolished in 1975.

The Senate Subcommittee on Internal Security continued to hold hearings and publish massive reports and indices, but it shifted its emphasis on the domestic Communist threat from what Communists were doing to what communism was. Its report on the 16th Communist Party Convention (February 1957) stated: "It is obvious . . . that the Communist Party, U.S.A., still adheres to the Soviet Union." The Communist Party, it said, was still "attempting to hoodwink the American public into believing" it was currently independent of Moscow. In fact, the report stated, the CPUSA was a "disciplined agent of Moscow" and "an integral part of the worldwide Communist conspiracy," and it had successfully fooled "important segments of the American press" about both of these facts. The report did not, however, comment on the mass exodus from the Communist Party that was in process.[7] Ten years later, another report, updating the connections between the CPUSA and the Soviet Union, noted: "It seems fantastic that prominent figures in American life have found it possible to ignore the facts about the CPUSA." It went on to list "the numerous evidences of the continuing relationship of the CPUSA as a tool and a pawn of the Soviet Communist Party."[8] It did not, however, provide any evidence of what, exactly, this "pawn" was doing to advance its side. In 1971, the Subcommittee on Internal Security issued a nine-volume report on the extent of Communist subversion of the New Left; in 1972, it produced a two-volume, 21-year, cumulative index. The subcommittee was abolished in 1977.

When the Democrats regained control of the Senate in 1955, John McClellan (Democrat–Arkansas) became chairman of the Senate's Permanent Subcommittee on Investigations. Under his leadership, it turned its attention to labor racketeering during the remainder of the decade, to organized crime during the 1960s, and to energy issues during the 1970s.

The Executive Branch

The Kennedy administration paid little attention to domestic communism. U.S. Attorney General Robert F. Kennedy did not believe that the Communist Party, as a political organization, posed any danger to the country, and he condemned anti-Communist "vigilantes" as well as those who "in the name of fighting Communism, sow seeds of suspicion and distrust by making false or irresponsible charges, not only against their neighbors, but against courageous teachers and public officials." He also argued for the dismissal of unsupported security charges against government employees and recommended a pardon for Junius Scales, the last Alien Registration Act defendant still in federal prison.[9]

Lyndon Johnson, however, became obsessed with defeating communism in Vietnam and exposing the presence of Communists in the antiwar movement at home. It became an article of faith in the White House, FBI, and several congressional committees that the antiwar movement was a Communist production. During the spring of 1965, then-President Johnson expressed his belief that he was "the target of a gigantic Communist conspiracy" and that Communists were "taking over the country." He believed that much of the protest against and criticism of his foreign policy was being generated by Communist officials, and he was sure Communists were behind the October 1967 march on the Pentagon.[10]

In an ironic twist, the presidential candidates in the 1968 election were two of the most fervent anti-Communists of the 1950s: Richard M. Nixon and Hubert H. Humphrey. Likewise, Humphrey's opponents in the battle for the Democratic nomination, Eugene McCarthy and Robert F. Kennedy, had been "hard" anti-Communists. But the antiwar campaigns of McCarthy and Kennedy, and the fight over the peace plank at the party's national convention, demonstrated that anti-Communists no longer dominated the Democratic Party. In any event, domestic anti-communism did not figure in the election campaign.

As president, Nixon was beleaguered by the antiwar movement. He was also chagrined to learn that the Subversive Activities Control Board had held only three hearings the previous year and that the Attorney General's list had not been updated since 1955. In response, he issued an Executive Order in July 1971:

> The Subversive Activities Control Board shall, upon petition of the Attorney General, conduct appropriate hearings to determine whether any organization is totalitarian, Fascist, Communist, subversive, or whether it has adopted a policy of unlawfully advocating the commission of acts of force or violence to deny others their rights under the Constitution or laws of the United States, or any state, or which seeks to overthrow the Government of the United States or any state or subdivision thereof by unlawful means.

At the same time, the Department of Justice proposed legislation to give the board subpoena and contempt authority in connection with its new functions, and to change the board's name to the Federal Internal Security Board. Senator William Proxmire (Democrat–Wisconsin) vowed to block funding for this extended authority, and the ACLU said it would challenge the constitutionality of it.[11] The Senate did add a provision to an appropriations bill denying the use of funds to carry out the president's order, but the House rejected it, the conference committee did likewise, and the funding was approved. One year later, the Senate's refusal to provide funds was approved by both chambers; in March 1973, government funding for the board ceased.[12]

The FBI

J. Edgar Hoover (or his FBI ghost writers) produced a steady stream of reports about the continued menace of communism. In a 20-page report on the 16th Communist Party Convention, Hoover wrote that Communists were "still the masters of 'The Big Lie.' Their doubletalk, duplicity, and semantic gyrations make them the most dangerous and proficient masters of propaganda in the civilized world." The Communist Party, he warned, had applied a series of cosmetic changes to end its isolation from the public, and if those changes "succeed in further hoodwinking certain people, as it has with some success since the Convention, then it will emerge stronger than it ever was and more dangerous to the peace and security of the United States."[13] In a series of books that followed, Hoover hammered away at three themes: the CPUSA remained unswerving in its allegiance to the Soviet Union; the actual strength of the Communist Party far exceeded its membership totals; and the group's leaders had continued to fool people about the CPUSA's essential nature, which was to advance Communist domination of the world.[14] In his 1962 book, Hoover stated, in bold-faced italics: *"Because the United States is the principal deterrent to further Communist expansion, the Communist Party, USA, is, and will continue to be, a serious threat to our national security."*[15]

During those same years, Hoover developed "a close and mutually rewarding relationship" with Francis Walter, chairman of the Committee on Un-American Activities. Walter had the committee incorporate in one of its reports Hoover's 1958 statement that the CPUSA was "well on its way to achieving its current objective, which is make you believe that it is shattered and dying," and his prophesy that once that objective was achieved, "it will then proceed inflexibly toward its final goal." In return, Hoover greeted the 1960 events in San Francisco by issuing an FBI report titled *Communist Target—Youth: Communist Infiltration and Agitation Tactics*, intensifying coverage of students, and urging conservative activists to defend the Committee on Un-American Activities.[16]

Hoover also kept a watchful eye on the motion picture industry. Following the announcement by Otto Preminger, in January 1960, that blacklisted writer Dalton Trumbo would receive screen credit for his screenplay for *Exodus* and Frank Sinatra's announcement, two months later, that he had hired blacklisted writer Albert Maltz to write *The Execution of Private Slovik*, Hoover expressed his fear "that communists and fellow travelers were closing ranks in an effort to re-establish themselves in the motion picture industry." He ordered the Los Angeles office to report to him every 60 days "concerning this most important field."[17]

During the 1960s, although Hoover continued to search for and expose "Reds" (e.g., members and supporters of the Fair Play for Cuba Committee, National Committee to Abolish the House Un-American Activities Committee, and the New Left), the FBI's focus shifted to exposing organized crime and undermining the civil rights movement. The nadir of Hoover's obsession with communism was reached with the FBI's full-court press against Martin Luther King, Jr. As a result of a brief conversation King had with black Communist Benjamin Davis and King's close ties to two men who either had been members of the Communist Party or had been associated with it, field offices were ordered to pay close attention to the relationship between King's Southern Christian Leadership Conference (SCLC) and communism. In May 1962, King's name was added to Section A of the FBI's Reserve Index, designating him as a person "in a position to influence others against the national interests" or one likely to aid subversives. Three months later, a full-scale formal investigation of King and the SCLC began, and the COINTELPRO division began planting disruptive newspaper stories about both. In October 1963, a report authored by the domestic intelligence division—*Communism and the Negro Movement*—concluded that King "is knowingly, wittingly, and regularly taking advice from communists." The following month, wiretaps on King's and SCLC's telephones were installed; microphone bugging followed; damaging stories were planted; and excerpts of tapes from the wiretaps and bugs were sent to King. In late 1964, another report, also titled *Communism and the Negro Movement*, reached similar conclusions about King.[18]

Hoover's death, in 1972, removed from official anti-communism its last truly significant booster.

The Supreme Court

In June 1959, the U.S. Supreme Court, faced with the prospect of having to use the First Amendment to curtail congressional investigating committees, retreated from its 1957 decisions, drawing a tighter line around uncooperative witnesses and widening the scope of authority of the Committee on Un-American Activities. In *Barenblatt v. United States*, the Court, by a 6-3 decision, upheld a contempt citation against an Un-American Activities Committee witness who had relied on the First, Ninth, and Tenth Amendments in refusing to answer questions regarding alleged Communist activities at the institution of higher learning he attended. In the domain of national security, Justice Harlan wrote, "the House has clothed the Un-American Activities Committee with pervasive authority to investigate Communist activities in this country." Further, a First Amendment claim was deemed not as complete as a Fifth Amendment claim, because the former "always involves a balancing by the courts of the competing private and public interests at stake in the particular circumstances shown." Although Harlan spoke at length about the public interest in preserving itself against a group whose tenets "include the ultimate overthrow of the Government of the United States by force and violence," he said little about Barenblatt's private interests.[19]

Two years later, relying on *Barenblatt*, the Court upheld two other contempt citations. It ruled, in cases involving two well-known critics of the Committee on Un-American Activities, that the questions asked were pertinent to the inquiry of the committee and did not invade the First Amendment rights of the witnesses.[20] Though they were the last two witnesses before the Committee on Un-American Activities to be imprisoned for contempt of Congress, these cases, in the opinion of Harry Kalven, Jr., leave one with the impression that the Court believed that criticism of the committee "is in itself an un-American activity and hence a proper target of investigation."[21]

That same year, 1961, a closely divided Court upheld the constitutionality of the membership clause of the Alien Registration Act, by confirming the conviction of Junius Scales for knowingly being a member of an organization that advocated the overthrow, by force or violence, of the U.S. government. In addition, after a seven-year process of appeals and remands, a similarly divided Court upheld the constitutionality of the registration provisions of the Internal Security Act. This case had begun in 1954, when the Subversive Activities Control Board ordered the CPUSA to register with it as a "Communist-action" organization. The majority opinion, however, did not address the obvious question: What would be the constitutional situation of the Communist Party or any of its members if it or they refused to follow that order?[22] Four years later, a unanimous Court answered that question, ruling that the board's order for certain named individuals to register violated their Fifth Amendment rights. In 1967, the Court also declared unconstitutional the section of the Internal Security Act prohibiting Communists from working in defense facilities.[23]

UNOFFICIAL ANTI-COMMUNISM

The American Legion's determination to maintain the motion picture blacklist had not waned. It reacted angrily when blacklisted writers began winning Academy Awards and the Academy of Motion Picture Arts and Sciences rescinded its by law prohibiting blacklisted people from being nominated for or receiving Academy Awards. In June 1959, the California American Legion convened a convention to pass resolutions condemning the Academy and warning the producers it would act by every means at its command to prevent the reestablishment of Communist influence in the motion picture industry. At first, the movie executives reacted strongly against those resolutions, but when the California legionnaires decided to take their resolutions to the national convention, the producers backpedaled and dispatched B. B. Kahane (vice-president of Columbia Pictures, vice-president of the Association of Motion Picture Producers, and president of the Academy of Motion Picture Arts and Sciences) to meet with the American Legion's Americanism Committee. Kahane convinced the committee members not to adopt a strongly worded resolution condemning the industry as a whole, telling it "we're just as anxious to keep Commies out of Hollywood as you are." Instead, the American Legion praised the major studios for maintaining the blacklist, condemned the independent producers for hiring blacklisted writers, and criticized the Academy of Motion Picture Arts and Sciences. The independent producers were furious.[24]

Despite the American Legion's threats, four independent producers decided to cease using phony writers' credits, but only three held their ground. On January 19, 1960, Otto Preminger became the first producer to announce publicly that he had hired a blacklisted writer, Dalton Trumbo, for *Exodus*, and that Trumbo "naturally will get the credit on the screen that he amply deserves." The writer of the article about the *Exodus* credit also noted that Trumbo had written *Roman Holiday* (Paramount, 1953) and was working on *Spartacus*.[25] One week later, the California Department Commander wrote Preminger a letter condemning his decision.[26] A few weeks after that, National Commander Martin B. McKneally criticized Stanley Kramer for hiring a blacklisted writer and warned that the American Legion intended to employ "a war of information" against "a renewed invasion of American filmdom by Soviet-indoctrinated artists." Kramer accused the American Legion of tactics "as totally un-American as anything I can imagine," stating that he would hire any writer he pleased.[27] In March 1960, following Frank Sinatra's announcement that he had hired blacklisted writer Albert Maltz to write the script for *The Execution of Private Slovik*, the American Legion and other veterans' groups threatened to boycott the movie, and Hearst writers railed against Sinatra. They were successful: Sinatra discharged Maltz and sold the film rights.[28] In August 1960, Kirk Douglas, the producer and star of *Spartacus*, announced that Trumbo would receive screen credit for his script.

When *Exodus* premiered in Los Angeles in December 1960, the American Legion picketed the theater, carrying signs protesting Preminger's employment of Trumbo: "The Reds Are Back In Hollywood," "You're Supporting A Traitorous Commie," and "Hey, Otto, Why Don't You Employ Legal American Writers?"[29] According to Preminger, a few other picket lines appeared in other parts of the country, but the movie's box office receipts did not suffer. At the same time, the Catholic War Veterans set up a picket line at a Washington, D.C., theater showing *Spartacus*. But shortly after the presidential election, both John F. Kennedy and Robert F. Kennedy crossed the picket lines to view the movie. At the end of the movie, the picketers asked the president-elect what he thought about the movie. He said that he enjoyed it; it was a good film.[30]

Meanwhile, a new anti-Communist organization, the John Birch Society, had entered the arena. The group had been founded by Robert Welch, Jr., in December 1958 to wage war against what Welch called the global collectivist conspiracy. Virtually no institution or politician in the United States was safe from the organization's charges of involvement in this gigantic conspiracy. At its peak, the John Birch Society enrolled more than 80,000 people, opened 350 bookstores, published a newspaper (*American Opinion*), made several recruiting films, and sold hundreds of thousands of copies of Welch's *Blue Book*.[31]

Those who have studied the John Birch Society have found that fundamentalist Protestants constituted a disproportionate percentage of its membership.[32] As a result, the group had close links to most of the radical right organizations (also disproportionately fundamentalist) of the 1960s, including Dr. Fred C. Schwarz's Anti-Communist Crusade. At its peak, the Anti-Communist Crusade had a paid staff of 30 and an annual income in excess of $1 million, sold or distributed more than 1 million copies of Schwarz's book *You Can Trust the Communists*, broadcast programs on radio and television, and organized numerous anti-Communist schools. The central message of the book and the Crusade was that knowledge is power and "ignorance is evil and paralytic." Members of the Anti-Communist Crusade accused the Communists of succeeding by rallying to their side "multitudes who are completely unaware that they are serving the Communist cause." Schwarz alleged that all previous anti-Communist programs "have completely failed to halt Communism. The Communists are riding high. Their program is in top gear. They are going from strength to strength." What was required, he wrote, was a moral and spiritual revival in the United States, based on the motivation, knowledge, and organization offered by the Anti-Communist Crusade.[33]

The John Birch Society and the Anti-Communist Crusade also contributed to the efforts made by certain corporations and businesses that had become "energetically" re-engaged in the campaign to educate Americans about the nature and threat of communism. Alan F. Westin attributed this renewed concern with communism to the businessmen's realization that the Communist world was here to stay, and that it was the responsibility of businesses to take the lead in educating people about it. Westin estimated that firms had spent, since 1958, more than $25 million on these programs. In addition to the John Birch Society and Schwarz material, which Westin labeled as "nonsense" anti-communism, these corporations distributed "responsible" literature and films, including Harry and Bonaro Overstreet's *What We Must Know About Communism*.[34] The Overstreets had written their book to counteract the satisfaction of the people of the United States "with half-truths [about communism] where nothing less than whole truths would serve" to halt the nation's "widespread mental and emotional drift in a world where the adversary has not been drifting."[35]

Conservative anti-Communists continued to pay lip service to domestic anti-communism, but their focus had shifted to the foreign arena. *National Review,* for example, after printing two articles on the subject in early 1957, and devoting several pages to eulogizing Joseph McCarthy in May 1957, moved on to other concerns.[36] Later, the Sharon Statement—the founding document of Young Americans for Freedom, written at William F. Buckley, Jr.'s house in September 1960—devoted only one sentence to communism: "That the forces of international Communism are, at present, the greatest threat to [our] liberties."[37] One of the largest conservative groups, the Committee of One Million, focused its efforts on preventing recognition of the People's Republic of China and blocking it from replacing Taiwan on the United Nations Security Council.

Even so, the domestic anti-Communist bogey was never far from reach. For example, in 1960, when news reached Marvin Liebman, secretary of the Committee of One Million, that Macmillan was about to publish a book critical of the "China Lobby," he proposed the publication of a counter-book to be titled *Red China Lobby,* that would document this "lobby's" infiltration of the Department of State, academic community, religion, mass media, and United Nations. When Liebman turned the project over to Forrest Davis, Davis assured Liebman he would identify the "Communist line" behind the campaign to grant concessions to the People's Republic.[38]

Liberal journals and organizations also dropped their anti-communism. An article in *Commentary* noted, on the eve of the 16th CPUSA convention, "no course seems likely to stem the party's decline."[39] Moreover, in 1971, the American Civil Liberties Union altered its 1940 resolution, which had excluded members of totalitarian organizations from its governing bodies or staff. The new resolution simply noted the ACLU's opposition "to any governmental or economic system which denies fundamental civil liberties and human rights." Five years later, the organization rescinded the 1940 exclusion of the now-deceased Elizabeth Gurley Flynn.[40]

REVIVALS

Despite the waning interest in anti-communism demonstrated by the U.S. public and many previously vigilant organizations, the specter of Communist subversion remained a latent element in the political culture of the United States, and it was periodically invoked, by former anti-Communists, to counter "disturbing" leftist trends. In one instance, a new group of anti-Communist historians mounted a strong defense of traditional anti-communism.

The Campaign Against Cold War "Revisionism"

The "Cold War revisionist" label was applied to a series of books and articles that questioned the motives of U.S. Cold War foreign-policy makers, while not condemning outright those of Soviet leaders. William Appleman Williams led the way in 1959 with his *Tragedy of American Diplomacy*. In this book, Williams argued that the United States had been, from the outset, an assertive, expansionist, and empire-minded country. His graduate seminar at the University of Wisconsin provided, in the words of Jonathan M. Wiener, "the intellectual arena in which New Left history in the United States first developed,"[41] and some of his students and admirers began publishing *Studies on the Left: A Journal of Research, Social Theory, and Review*. Denna Frank Fleming's two-volume *The Cold War and Its Origins* followed in 1961, and Gar Alperovitz's *Atomic Diplomacy* in 1965.

Disturbed by this trend, Arthur Schlesinger, Jr., wrote a letter to the *New York Review of Books* in 1966, responding to Alperovitz's review of Allen Dulles's *The Secret Surrender*. Alperovitz had written the following words: "the Cold War cannot be understood simply as an American response to a Soviet challenge, but rather as the insidious interaction of mutual suspicions, blame for which must be shared by all."[42] Schlesinger, declaring it was time to "blow the whistle before the current outburst of revisionism goes much further," stated that "Stalin's rigid theology" guaranteed that "no American policy could have won basic Soviet confidence, and every American initiative was poisoned from the outset."[43] One year later, Schlesinger wrote a long article for *Foreign Affairs* reviewing the events from 1941 to 1947, which came to the same conclusion as his letter had: not even the most rational U.S. policy could have averted the Cold War, given that Soviet leaders were "possessed by convictions both of the infallibility of the Communist world and of the inevitability of a Communist World." In a footnote, Schlesinger also stated: "The fact that in some aspects the revisionist thesis parallels the official Soviet argument must not, of course, prevent consideration of the case on its merits, nor raise questions about the motives of the writers, all of whom, so far as I know, are independent-minded scholars."[44]

Schlesinger also endorsed a book critical of Cold War revisionism, written by one of Williams's former students. Robert James Maddox examined the use of documents by seven revisionist or New Left historians. He accused all of them of revising "the evidence," producing "New Left fictions," and doing "violence to the historical record."

His book provoked a hot battle between "traditionalists" and "revisionists."[45] The two sides resumed the battle in 1978 and 1983, when another type of "revisionism" appeared, one challenging strongly held beliefs of the Old Left. Allen Weinstein concluded that Alger Hiss was, in fact, guilty of perjury,[46] and Ronald Radosh and Joyce Milton proclaimed that Julius Rosenberg was, indeed, a Soviet spy.[47] On this occasion, however, these books were warmly welcomed by the older generation of "traditionalists" and rejected by the newer generation of revisionists and some of the Old Left. The latter, according to Paul Hollander, had converted the fate of the Rosenbergs "into the message that anticommunism is and *always* has been an irrational and destructive attitude."[48]

Neoconservatism

This "persuasion" was the work of a small group of intellectuals, some of whom had been left-of-center liberals and all of whom had been anti-Communists.[49] They maintained their anti-communism in their attacks on critics of the Vietnam War and supporters of détente with the Soviet Union, all of whom they identified with the New Left. In their campaign against these "appeasers," neoconservatives recycled two conservative anti-Communist preoccupations: the decline in the nation's traditional values and the growth of the "welfare state." One segment of this new political orientation, spearheaded by Irving Kristol, began publishing *The Public Interest* in the fall of 1965. The first editorial, written by Kristol and Daniel Bell, promised that this journal would be dedicated to non-ideological essays on public policy issues.[50] Nevertheless, as the years went by and the contributors' critiques of government programs increased, the journal did become ideologically opposed to the "welfare state." In addition, in 1968, a special issue, devoted to "The Universities," contained a series of articles critical of student activism. Kristol later wrote that "the student rebellion and the rise of the counterculture, with its messianic expectations and its apocalyptic fears [made us realize] we had been cultural conservatives all along."[51]

Kristol, who is regularly called the "godfather" of this persuasion, defined neoconservatives as "disenchanted liberals" who were responding to what they perceived as the dual crises—of authority and of the culture—consuming the United States and other Western democracies. These crises, Kristol believed, were caused by contemporary liberalism and by what he called the "collectivist imperative," which "feeds on itself and most especially (and more significantly) on its own failures." Kristol also was concerned that "the ever-mounting passion for appeasement evident in liberal circles" was undermining effective resistance to "the imperialist designs of communist totalitarianism."[52] He and his cohort believed that the United States had drifted from its traditional values and that it could halt and reverse this process only by demonstrating a renewed emphasis on the Communist "threat" and a recognition of the collectivist threat posed by anti-liberal Third World governments and liberation movements.

The other neoconservative segment, consisting of regular contributors to *Commentary*, focused from the beginning on the New Left, seeing in its adherents reincarnations of Communists past. Irving Howe spied, in the fall of 1968, "a rising younger generation of intellectuals" and New Left activists who were apologists for authoritarianism and who promiscuously brandished the phrase "liberal fascism." Specifically, Howe criticized Herbert Marcuse on this basis.[53] Five months later, Theodore Draper authored two articles that equated the Communists' use of "social fascism" in Weimar Germany with the "new anti-liberal version" of it being used by a "new revolutionary generation" in the United States. Draper stated that an updated version of "social fascism" had reappeared in the writings of Herbert Marcuse and had "encouraged the New Left [and the Black Panther Party] to cultivate intolerance and court repression."[54] These themes were echoed by *Commentary* editor Norman Podhoretz in a speech he delivered to a Socialist Party gathering in June 1970, in which he castigated the New Left and the counterculture for their hatred of the United States.[55] In an editorial that appeared a few months later, Podhoretz acknowledged that he, and others like him, had become "deradicalized," refusing "to acquiesce in the surly tyranny of the activist temper in its presently dominant forms."[56] In the December issue of *Commentary*, another editorial by Podhoretz and articles by three other writers sharply critiqued the counterculture.[57]

The Revival of Academic Anti-Communism
(or the Advent of "Re-revisionism")

Insofar as a starting point may be assigned for this revival, it might be the moment when Ronald Radosh, nearing the end of his journey from communism to anti-communism, began his collaboration with Harvey

Klehr,[*] who had already arrived at that destination.[58] While working on their book on the *Amerasia* case,[59] the pair, in 1985, wrote an article in which they listed the organizations and individuals who were supporting the sending of young people from the United States to Moscow where they would attend a youth festival sponsored by the World Federation of Democratic Youth. Those supporters, Klehr and Radosh wrote, "should know that neither the cause of peace nor the legitimate criticism of U.S. policies is served by endorsing a propaganda show celebrating the cause of international communism."[60]

Three years later, Klehr, in his *Far Left of Center*, which was commissioned by the Anti-Defamation League of B'nai Brith, described and analyzed every component of the "radical left" in the United States, from the Communist Party to the Institute for Policy Studies. In the introduction to this book, Klehr noted that part of his "concern about the politics and views of the extremist left stems from its hostility to the interests of Jews."[61] In his discussion of these very small organizations, Klehr reiterated the traditional anti-Communist belief that numbers are not determinative in threat assessment. He wrote: "while many of the Marxist-Leninist groups in this country are quite small, they often have an impact far out of proportion to their size because of their ability to convince well-meaning people to support their activities in connection with some of the causes they exploit, ranging from peace to civil rights." The danger posed by the far left, he continued, posed a danger "that is overlooked or minimized to the peril of security and best interests of the American public."[62] He did not, however, document the exact nature of that peril.

One year later, Klehr's tone changed from dispassionate analysis to heavy-handed condescension, when he co-authored an article describing a three-day conference on "Anticommunism and the U.S.: History and Consequences." The authors might have been striving for witty sarcasm, but their comments were too sneering to allow them to reach that plateau. They described many of the 1,200 participants in the 1989 conference as having "just crept out of the woodwork," and their mood as "idiotically happy." After they ridiculed many of the speakers and their statements, the authors then condemned their places of origin: "They [the participants] fluttered back to their nesting places in academia, the alternative press, college campuses, the Rainbow

---

[*]I have never met or communicated with Harvey Klehr and his frequent collaborator John Earl Haynes. As far as I know, they have never harmed anyone I know. Admittedly, we are located on different points of the ideological spectrum, but the critiques that follow do not stem from any political animosity. Put simply, one cannot write a critical history of anti-communism without directly confronting their very large body of work.

Coalition, senior centers, progressive unions, and Communist Party headquarters, dedicating to wiping out that nasty word [anti-communism]."[63]

Other events in the late 1980s, including the protests in Eastern Europe and Beijing's Tiananmen Square, caught the attention of a new generation of anti-Communist writers, who used their books and articles to insist that the older generation of anti-Communists had been correct about the nature of communism and that the "New Left revisionists" had been wrong.

One of the first books in this wave was written by Guenter Lewy. While he acknowledged that the current Communist Party did not play a significant role in the United States and no longer posed a threat to national security, Lewy expressed concern over the current (read "New Left") trend of thinking about the older Communist Party and what it represented. According to him, the combination of the emergence of the New Left in the 1960s and a "belated reaction to the demagogic antics of Senator Joseph McCarthy and his supporters in the 1950s" had led "a substantial part of the American intellectual community" to adopt "a self-conscious anti-anti-communism that appears to be no less reflexive than the often unthinking anticommunism of the 1950s it has replaced." These intellectuals were preoccupied, Lewy asserted, with emphasizing the positive contributions of the Communist Party and the negative aspects of anti-communism, and their "exculpatory explanations" had merely served "to conceal the harsh essence of the Communist ideology." As a result, the Communist Party had achieved a new aura of respectability and its front groups were again attracting significant numbers of non-Communists. Lewy saw in the hidden agendas of these front groups a worrisome distortion of public discourse on important topics and an interference with the free interchange of ideas necessary to a democracy. He also questioned the morality of Communists, criticized "the profound lack of moral integrity" in the intellectuals who were or are sympathetic to Communists, and labeled anti-communism "a moral imperative."[64]

A few years later, Paul Hollander noted, unhappily, that 1960s activists had evolved from "anticommunist to anti-anticommunist and sometimes to procommunist." They had, in fact, commenced the "idealization" and "romanticization" of former Communists.[65] This charge of "romanticization" is particularly prevalent in my area of specialization, the motion picture blacklist. A series of "re-revisionist" writers have criticized the "revisionists" (me included) for extolling the blacklisted motion picture workers who resisted the Committee on Un-American Activities. The "re-revisionists" allege that this praise served to glorify die-hard, unapologetic Stalinists. In other words, according to the "re-revisionists" all unrepentant members of the Communist Party were too morally compromised, by their Party membership, to act in any praiseworthy manner whatsoever; they were not, that is, complex human beings, capable of making individual, arguably righteous, decisions about political, and social matters, but rather brainwashed robots, forever incapacitated from making moral judgments. [66]

The substantive basis for "re-revisionism" was provided by the opening of the Soviet archives and the release of the Venona cables (nearly 3,000 decrypted messages sent by Soviet spies in the United States to the Soviet Union). In a series of books, John Earl Haynes and Harvey Klehr made the case that the documents they collected and translated demonstrated, once and for all, the covert nature of the CPUSA and its umbilical attachment to the Soviet Union. Only by understanding the nature of the Communist Party as revealed in these documents, they asserted, "can one appreciate American anti-communism and the internal tensions generated by its conflict with communism."[67] Whereas they once believed that only a few Communist Party members had spied, they now knew hundreds had betrayed their country "out of ideological affinity for the Soviets." Nevertheless, these authors took a step too far when they reached the following conclusion: "By abetting Soviet espionage, these Communists and the CPUSA itself laid the basis for the anti-Communist era that followed World War II. The investigations and prosecutions of the American Communist movement undertaken by the federal government in the late 1940s and early 1950s were premised on an assumption that the CPUSA had assisted Soviet espionage."[68] In fact, as the previous pages have indicated, the domestic Cold War had multiple origins, and would have occurred even without the revelations of Soviet espionage.

One year later, two self-professed anti-Communists, Herbert Romerstein and Eric Breindel, took a much harder line in their book on the Venona cables. They wrote: "A central goal of this book is to correct the conventional wisdom regarding American Communism—to challenge the falsehood inherent in the claim that Party members were left-wing heretics rather than disloyal conspirators. For Communists, true patriotism meant helping to make the world a better place by advancing the interests of the Soviet Union in any way possible." Romerstein and Breindel were emphatic in their unproven assertion that "this bizarre view of loyalty informed the thinking of every [Communist Party] member." In their conclusion, they accused all Communists of being "traitors" who devoted "a significant part" of their energy "to infiltrating the American government to obtain information useful to the Soviet Union."[69]

These books sparked a critical counterattack by several old and new leftists, most of whom took the position that the documentation was too selective and the Soviet contributors' notes on archival material were suspect. Haynes and Klehr, in stark contrast to their attempt to be objective in their choice and use of documents, reacted subjectively to those who disagreed with their conclusions. In a 2003 book, they angrily asserted that their experience, of their work either being criticized or ignored, served "as an illustration of how an alienated and politicized academic culture misunderstands and distorts America's past" and misshapes "cultural memories to fit the ideological biases of the [left-wing] academic establishment." Their anger led them into many logical traps, not the least of which was their denial of their own ideological biases. They argued that all critics of anti-communism are revisionists, and all revisionists are leftists—ergo all critics of anti-communism are leftists; or that Communist historians are part of a rigid mental world tightly sealed from outside influences—ergo all Communist historians cannot be trusted to deal objectively with historical evidence. In terms of the excluded middle, they posited the arena of Cold War historians as pitting "traditionalists" against "revisionists," and claimed that in the world of the latter, all radicalism is good and all opposition to it is "foul." In addition, Haynes and Klehr made assertions unsupported by evidence—to wit, that academic culture has been "alienated and politicized by the left," that "radical academics thoroughly changed the ideological atmosphere of the scholarly world," and that revisionists have taken "control of the history of American communism." Finally, although Haynes and Klehr have subjected the work of "leftists, revisionists, and academic radicals" to a thorough critique, they have not done the same for the work of the "traditionalists."[70]

In an interview following the book's publication in 2003, Haynes categorized most of the people who did not fall on their ideological swords after the opening of the Soviet archives and the publication of Soviet documents as living "in a different reality from that of the rest of us. . . . They see the present and the past through a special lens. . . . They care not at all about the facts of history, only about the politics of the future." Klehr, in that same interview, characterized unrepentant historians as veterans of the New Left, who were trying to "rehabilitate an earlier American radical movement." He agreed with Haynes that many of them have "a disconnect with reality ... [T]hey retreat into a fantasy world." Both authors were critical of "liberal and left" opinion leaders and foundations, whom they described as displaying indifference to the "criminals of the Communist regime" and documenting their crimes, and of "the liberal gatekeepers in professional journals and the media," who ignored their book. Nevertheless, said Haynes, "we are intellectually on the offensive."[71]

These and other writers in this new wave of anti-communism, like their predecessors, have sought to indict all those who belonged to the Communist Party as well as those who worked for the same goals as Communists did (or viewed them in a positive light). Those types, the charges read, "knew" or should have "known" about the "crimes" committed by Communist regimes (famines, purges, terrors, assassinations, imprisonments), and they should have been appalled by them. This new wave finds it difficult to understand how anyone who professes concern about democracy and freedom could be, in Klehr's words, "anything but hostile to communism."[72] Their indictment, however, violates some of the basic principles of logic.

The main logical error is the hasty generalization that results, such as "All Communists rigidly and unquestioningly adhere to orthodox Leninist-Stalinist doctrine," "All Communists lie," and so on. As with all hasty generalizations, these statements are easily shown to be false, but anti-Communists assert them confidently as if they were obvious truths.[73] These writers do not seem to have asked themselves, "What could possibly count as counter-examples to these assumptions?" Instead, they simply assume the truth of these generalizations and then proceed to draw conclusions on the basis of them. Because the generalizations they employ in their premises are false, the conclusions that they infer from these premises are all unsound. Examples of such conclusions are "All Communists lie, and Comrade X is a Communist, so Comrade X lies"; "All Communists incarnate the will of the Party, and Comrade X is a Communist, so Comrade X incarnates the will of the Party"; and "No non-dupe could associate with Communists, and X has associated with Communists, so X is a dupe." The critics also employ several false analogies, most grievously when they compare the relatively small percentage of Communists in the United States with the even smaller percentage of Bolsheviks in prerevolutionary Russia, to imply that zealotry and discipline—not numbers—constitute the key issue.

Klehr and Haynes commit a similar syllogistic error in their 1992 book recounting the history of the CPUSA. They refer regularly to "American Communists," implying that there was just one type. This implication reflects their belief that the Communist Party was "not merely a collection of people who shared membership in a social organization. It was a Leninist party." Thus those individuals who remained Party members, in these authors' judgment, had to have fully accepted "the requirement of a Leninist organization."[74] In syllogistic form, they are basically saying: "X was a member of the Communist Party, and the Communist Party is a Leninist organization, so X must have imbibed and practiced all the elements of Leninism demanded by Party leaders."

Anti-communists also err when they conflate the possession of information with the possession of genuine knowledge. Instead of claiming that Communists "should have and could have known" about the evils perpetrated by the leaders of the Soviet Union, anti-Communists should, logically, have said that Communists "should have been better informed." But there is a deeper epistemological problem here, because anti-Communists really seem to be saying, "Because of the information available to them, Communists should not have believed in communism, the Soviet Union, or Stalin." That implicit accusation reveals a misunderstanding of the relation between knowledge and belief and the nature of a belief system.

Most philosophers who write about epistemology agree that knowledge is justified true belief, and that justified or reliable beliefs must be solidly grounded in adequate evidence or reasoning.[75] When a conflict occurs between a belief system and a new piece of information, the believer, who wishes to maintain a coherent belief system, will not jettison the belief system, but rather will undergo a process of reassessment by weighing the validity of the new evidence. In the world of political beliefs, a conflict usually arises when a believer is confronted with an observation about a political event, which is contrary to or seems to contravene his or her belief system. An observation does not constitute hard evidence, however; in most cases, someone else's observation carries less weight than one's own direct observation does. In addition, receptivity to testimony regarding the evidentiary value of the conflicting observation rests on the believer's appraisal of the testifier's morals, motives, and evidence-gathering procedures.[76]

People build and conserve belief systems to avoid an unpleasant state of doubt or uncertainty. Such belief systems are inherently unstable, because they are based on unproved assumptions (about the world and human nature). Although these assumptions are unproven, they are treated by believers as either self-evident axioms or else are simply taken on faith, and many believers proceed to draw logical conclusions from these assumptions. That is, they construct a belief system containing the inferred implications that, in their minds, logically follow from the assumptions originally adopted. They will say (aloud or to themselves), "If this assumption (e.g., "communism is the best available social arrangement") is true, then this inference (e.g., "the builders of a Communist state are good") is also true.

Belief systems cannot endure unless they are coherent—unless, that is, none of the beliefs negate each other. But lack of negation is still not enough, because it is logically possible for a belief system to be perfectly coherent (contain no inconsistencies) and contain false beliefs. Thus, although coherence is a necessary condition for truth, it is not a sufficient one. Also, because the structure of a belief system is more like a web than an arch, removing one particular belief does not automatically topple the belief system.

When confronted with an observation that on its face appears to conflict with his or her belief system, the believer will typically attempt to determine whether that conflicting observation, even if true, creates an impossible situation for his or her belief system as a whole. In many (perhaps most) cases, the believer may reasonably conclude that it does not. For example, testimony from an anti-Communist that Stalin's policy to exterminate the *kulaks* (wealthy farmers) caused the Ukrainian famine of 1932–1933 can, even if accepted as true, be met with one or all of the following belief-system-saving hypotheses by a Communist: "*Kulaks* were counter-revolutionaries"; "Famines occur regularly in agricultural-based economic systems"; "The transition from an autocracy to a people's democracy causes many deaths"; and "Leaders of newly formed revolutionary governments base their policies on the greatest good of the greatest number."

In short, the following questions should have been asked by anti-Communists: Were members of the CPUSA culpable for the Stalinist killing machine? For the expansion of the Soviet empire? For Soviet espionage? Clearly, they were not involved in the first two events, although hundreds were involved in spying. Did they know (were they told or "informed") about "the crimes of Stalinism"? Perhaps they might have known (been told or "informed"), because there was certainly evidence available that convinced many people, including those who had been originally friendly to the Bolshevik Revolution.

Does failure to acknowledge the truth of information that sub-sequently becomes impossible to deny make one culpable after the fact? It depends on the plausibility or trustworthiness of such information *at the time* it is received and the weight it is given relative to beliefs that are held *at that time.*

The thousands of people who flocked to the world's Communist parties during the 1930s fervently believed that the Depression had economically and socially devastated the United States. They believed that capitalism had not only bred the catastrophe but also failed to buffer its impact. They believed that other democratic capitalist countries had been taken over by political systems (Italian Fascism and German Nazism) that seemed far more threatening to human freedom than communism. They believed there to be rank racial and sexual injustice in the United States. They believed that rivalries between capitalist countries had caused World War I and that similar rivalries threatened to engender a second world war. They believed that, in the face of massive opposition from the democracies, the Soviet Union had "succeeded" in overcoming or alleviating many of the problems that afflicted the United States. They believed that the Communist Party (CPUSA) offered an escape from triviality and provided a means to achieve self-fulfillment; that it provided a disciplined, collective means of confronting the economic and political disasters of the 1930s; and that it was the only effective movement in the United States pursuing the type of radical social change they sought. They believed that most of the negative information regarding the Soviet Union came from their political enemies and rivals. They also knew (were not just informed or believed) that to criticize the Communist Party would mean certain expulsion, and they believed that expulsion or resignation equaled political ineffectiveness.

With this knowledge, they weighed the alleged "evils" of Soviet communism against the known evils of German Nazism, Italian Fascism, racism, and other isms, while also taking into consideration the ideologies of those criticizing the Soviet Union. Using the same scales as their political foes, but applying different ideological weights, they came out with a different result. They concluded that their comrades, their leaders, the Communist movement, their causes, their ends, and themselves were all essentially good. As it turns out, they were right about themselves, their causes, and many of their goals; but they were wrong about the quality of their leaders and about the effects of linking their aspirations to the national interests of the Soviet Union. Nevertheless, they committed no crime, their judgments were not evil, and their judgments did not have evil consequences. It is not a crime to arrive at political conclusions that may, at some future time, under very different circumstances, be judged to be mistaken, blind, misguided, or uncritical. Certainly, one could commit crimes as the result of an unsound conclusion that one had reached (as did German Nazis, Italian Fascists, and Soviet Communists), but this step is not one that the vast majority of Communists in the United States took.

In retrospect, it is possible to compile a long list of poor judgments made by Communists in the United States, including, first and foremost, their submission to Soviet policies. Nevertheless, their biggest misjudgment, by far, was their belief that the First Amendment to the U.S. Constitution gave them the right to make those other mistakes in their political judgments, free of penalty and post hoc aspersions.

The current aspersion of Communists in the United States stems from two unshakable beliefs held by anti-Communists: that the lens through which they view political events is the only accurately focused one and that anti-communism is the only morally correct world view. However, their belief system is based on several very shaky assumptions: that they possess all the relevant information about the subject, that they are conscious of all its permutations, and that they are not hindered in any way by bias, subjectivity, and ideology. They seem to be unaware of the many-sided nature of human experience as well as the many-truth claims derivable from any person's partial, limited, and incomplete experience. Like the six blind men and the elephant, they confuse a partial set of facts and subjective conclusions with truth.[77] Likewise, in their moral certainty, they mistake an assertion for a truth. They claim a privileged access to the meta-realms of moral law, which they cannot demonstrate. They might be advised to heed the words of James A. Miller, who, in his discussion of Plato, wrote: "The man who deludes himself into thinking that he has achieved real knowledge of the true, the just, and the good is liable to be a very poor judge of what is really true, just and good, since the [Platonic] Forms exist independently of any earthly embodiment, and perhaps beyond mortal comprehension."[78]

Conclusion

One of the leitmotifs of this book has been the assertion that the "Communist threat" to the United States was overblown, to a large degree because hyped anti-communism served the agendas of a significant number of official and unofficial anti-Communists. In fact, if one examines the domestic internal security "threat" to the United States posed by Communists and communism at the end of World War II, one finds that it took three forms, only one of which was genuine. A Communist-led revolution or disruption was patently ludicrous, and only a tiny percentage of people feared it could happen.[1] Communist "infiltration" of government and civic organizations had, as noted in Chapters 5 through 9, been curtailed. Indeed, in mid-1949, Arthur Schlesinger, Jr., stated that outside the area of espionage, "it is hard to argue that the CPUSA in peacetime represents much of a threat to American security."[2] One year later, Herbert Hoover told President Truman: "I doubt if there are any consequential card-carrying Communists in the Government, or if there are, they should be known to the FBI."[3] The third "threat"—espionage and theft of government documents—was authentic, but was it so threatening that a domestic Cold War was necessary to combat it? My answer is a firm "no."

That negative response is based on several factors. First, the number of Communist spies in the federal government was relatively small. John Earl Haynes and Harvey Klehr, using the Venona cables, identified "349 citizens, immigrants, and permanent residents of the United States who had a covert relationship with the Soviet intelligence agencies," and another 139 who were not identified in the Venona cables.[4]

Ten years later, Haynes and Klehr, in collaboration with Alexander Vassiliev, estimated that the total number of Americans who assisted Soviet intelligence agencies "exceeds five hundred."[5]

The second reason is that several U.S. government agencies had been, since the end of the war, clearly focused on stopping espionage. According to Haynes and Klehr, World War II had been the crucible of the espionage problem, because the "hastily created wartime agencies ... hired large numbers of people under procedures that bypassed normal Civil Service hiring practices."[6] During the war, there was little coordination among counterintelligence agencies, and the FBI did not display much concern about this particular problem until the defections of Igor Gouzenko and Elizabeth Bentley.[7] In fact, Weinstein and Vassiliev concluded, "the end of World War II's Soviet-American alliance and the defections of Gouzenko and Bentley combined to end most of the spying that had provided the USSR's leaders with a cornucopia of policy and technical secrets from the United States during the war."[8] Indeed, the most damaging breach of security—the nuclear information leak—could not be repeated. Finally, the federal loyalty program had gone into effect in mid-1947, and by 1948 the FBI was keeping those named in the Venona cables under close surveillance.

Thus, though Klehr, Haynes, and Vassiliev are correct when they conclude that "a genuine threat" existed, they are not correct when they state that the hunt for Communist spies was not a witch hunt but rather "a rational, if sometimes excessively heated, response" to that threat.[9] A rational response would have been closer to that of the United Kingdom (see Introduction), or more akin to the treatment of Japanese Americans in Hawaii following the Japanese attack on Pearl Harbor and the order to evacuate all Japanese Americans from the west coast of the United States and incarcerate them in "relocation" camps. When the Roosevelt administration demanded that the same program be followed in Hawaii, General Delos Emmons, the Army commander there, fearing the cost and disruption it would cause, stalled long enough to convince the executive branch that the security problem on the islands could be effectively handled by the arrest of those who had been identified as security threats. Thus, instead of 118,000 people being shipped to internment camps in the United States, approximately 1,800 were so treated, while another 1,500 were arrested and incarcerated in Hawaii.[10]

Finally, with the exception of a small but vocal number of conservative and Republican critics of the Truman administration, the public did not seem, until the end of 1948, to be deeply concerned about spying, despite several publicized arrests of spies and revelations of spy rings. Although very few Gallup Polls focused on spying per se, one taken in August/September 1948, directly after Bentley and Whittaker Chambers testified before the Committee on Un-American Activities, indicated concern but not panic. Seventy-four percent of respondents stated that they believed the investigations were not simply politically motivated, but that there was some substance to them; 79 percent wanted Congress to continue to investigate.[11]

To be sure, the dozens of polls taken between 1945 and 1957, asking about domestic communism, registered a very high level of intolerance for Communists,[12] but not an enormous fear of them. For example, a survey of the Gallup Polls from 1946 to 1956 indicate that when people were asked which kinds of issues concerned them most, the internal "threat" of communism was not mentioned. In the summer of 1954, a survey group of more 6,000 people were asked: "How great a danger do you feel American Communists are to this country at the present time?" Nineteen percent said "very great," 24 percent said "great," and 38 percent said "some." But when that 81 percent was then asked to specify the danger, their answers revealed a very diverse threat assessment: 8 percent replied "sabotage," 8 percent said "espionage," and 28 percent feared that Communists would convert others to their ideology, thereby spreading their ideas. Stouffer concluded from the data and interviews, "A picture of the average American as a person with the jitters, trembling lest he find a Red under the bed, is clearly nonsense."[13]

John Earl Haynes offers one other argument that must be confronted: the mobilization of the United States for the Cold War "required an anti-Communist consensus," which could not have been achieved in the presence of a political party "with the institutional power" possessed by the CPUSA in the late 1940s. Had the CPUSA not been "harassed, prosecuted, persecuted, isolated, and reduced to an insignificant force," the United States would have found it difficult to maintain its 40-year commitment to the Cold War. Thus, he concluded, "For all its sporadic ugliness, excesses, and silliness, the anticommunism of the 1940s and 1950s was an understandable and rational response to a real danger to American democracy."[14] Haynes's statements are all based on surmise, not empirical evidence. There is no evidence to indicate that a defensive mobilization against the Soviet Union could not have been achieved without the domestic Cold War; there is no evidence to back his statement regarding the "institutional power" of the CPUSA. Enough evidence of Soviet activities deemed harmful to the United States did exist to maintain the public's commitment to an anti-Soviet foreign policy, however. Finally, a mountain of evidence demonstrates that harassment, prosecution, persecution, and isolation were not limited to members of the CPUSA.

It is difficult to escape the conclusion that the domestic Cold War was an elite-driven enterprise and that the elites were not really scared about Communist spying or infiltration. Such a conclusion explains the central anomaly of the domestic Cold War: the more the internal Communist threat receded, the louder the warnings about it became. By 1950, when McCarthy and McCarran dominated Washington, D.C., the federal loyalty program was expanding, and draconian internal security laws were being passed, the CPUSA was in dire straits, reeling from the prosecution and imprisonment of its top leaders and the hemorrhaging of members[15]; most of the main atomic spies had been or were about to be arrested; few Communists remained in government service; and organized labor had been purged of its "Communists." To be sure, there were genuine fears. For example, Republicans feared they might never again win the presidency. Key members of the Truman administration feared, after the election of 1946, that FBI Director J. Edgar Hoover, congressional Republicans, and right-wing journalists would hammer at continued administration "inaction" vis-à-vis national security and undermine Truman's reelection bid in 1948. Liberals feared that if they did not respond in a "hard" manner to the "Communist threat," their credibility would be destroyed. The leaders of many organizations feared that the "Communist issue" would divide and weaken their organizations.

Those who took seriously and promoted the overblown "threat," such as James Burnham, acknowledged the difficulty of estimating "the damage, past or still to come, from underground subversion" in the United States. But Burnham was not shy about listing the damage-causing events of "underground" subversives in the United States. According to his accounting, they aided the Communist victories in Yugoslavia and China, provided political cover for Soviet advances in all parts of the world, and gave away nuclear technology.[16] In other words, in Burnham's audit, subversive types had already, and would continue to, damage the United States more than the hunt for them did or would do.

To counter this argument, those who believe in the lesser-threat thesis could provide a more empirically verifiable list of damage-causing actions by subversive-hunters: FBI wiretaps, bugging, black-bag jobs, and infiltrations; loyalty investigations; due-process violations by congressional investigating committees; blacklists; and the purge programs of a host of nongovernment and civic organizations. These acts led to the firing of thousands of people from their jobs, most of which were not relevant to national security concerns. Thousands more employees resigned under duress or fear. Hundreds of individuals were jailed or deported on the flimsiest of legal grounds. In addition, a list of (admittedly unverifiable) damages could also be compiled: opinions and critiques not offered, movies not made, books not published, government jobs not sought, and expert opinions withheld. In 1954, Harold Taylor, a professor of philosophy and president of Sarah Lawrence College, wrote that the attacks on intellectual freedom, the media, government service, and education were, if not successful in securing the dismissal of those attacked, "successful in producing a timidity, in some cases amounting to paralysis, in social thought and creative work. Deeper than this is the more dangerous effect on the national life of creating so great a fear of subversion by communists that we have become rigid, paranoiac, dogmatic, and overaggressive."[17] In the reckoning of these auditors, the damage caused by subversive-hunting far outweighed the damage actually done by subversives. Indeed, Stanley I. Kutler suggests that "We will never fully tally the incidence of official wrongdoing and attempts at repression" during those years.[18]

If the country as a whole did not benefit from the domestic Cold War, then who, among the types of anti-Communists discussed in this book, did? In the category of official anti-communism, the FBI gained by far the most. It became a much larger bureaucracy, in terms of employees, budget appropriations, and hegemony over loyalty issues. Likewise, the Committee on Un-American Activities did exceptionally well for over a decade, increasing the publicity for its members, its appropriations, the number of its investigations, its witnesses indicted and tried for contempt of Congress, and the lists of uncooperative witnesses it provided to the nation's employers in its annual reports. For five years, Senator Joseph McCarthy's political influence thrived on his anti-communism. Among the institutional anti-Communists, the American Legion benefited, as it was able to wield substantial influence over the hiring decisions of the major studios in the motion picture industry. Similarly, Protestant fundamentalists used the issue to good advantage. Some ex-Communists achieved fame and some monetary gain. Finally, conservative coherence into an influential political force (beginning in the early 1960s) undoubtedly owed a large debt to anti-communism.

In contrast, the Catholic Church, as an institution, probably did not derive significant benefits from the anti-communism efforts, and the labor movement was clearly damaged by the purges and schisms engendered by anti-Communists. Liberals and liberalism never recovered from the domestic Cold War. Although Democratic party liberals enjoyed a brief and brilliant Indian summer during the first few years of the Johnson administration, the president's decision to escalate U.S. involvement in Vietnam revealed how deeply divided liberals still were.

In sum, the numbers of those who benefited are far surpassed by the numbers of those harmed by the domestic Cold War. It is far from clear that the assemblage of anti-Communists discussed in this book can be said to have confronted and disposed of an actual threat to the internal security of the United States.

Afterword

Can It Happen Again? Or, Is Anti-Terrorism the New Anti-Communism?

Given the events of the first decade of the twenty-first century, one has to ask: Is there something in the political culture of the post–World War II United States that requires the construction of a fearful specter to instill fear in the populace and make it amenable to, or uncritical of, the growth of the national security apparatus and the scope of its activities? Anti-communism served this need well for almost eight decades, and it seems to have left behind a "framework of beliefs, core values, and patterns of behavior"[1] that needs an international "threat" to sustain it.

After the Soviet Union collapsed, there remained a strong anti-Russian attitude, necessitating, it was argued, an extension of the North Atlantic Treaty Organization to the very borders of the new Russia. In addition, a chorus of voices began to be heard advocating a unilateral, world-policing role for the post–Cold War United States. Perhaps the most significant statement of this view was made by the Project for the New American Century, in its Statement of Principles (June 1997). It asked, rhetorically, Does the United States "have the vision to build upon the achievements of the past decades? Does the United States have the resolve to shape a new century favorable to American principles and interests?" And the answer was that it must: the people of the United States "need to accept responsibility for America's unique role in preserving and extending an international order friendly to our security, our prosperity, and our principles."[2]

Four years later, as if on command, the international order became distinctly unfriendly, and the United States was confronted with the reality of Al Qaeda terrorism. That reality became a specter— international terrorism—in the speeches of President George W. Bush, which were reminiscent of those used by Harry Truman in 1947. Bush spoke about terrorism as "a threat to our way of life." He avowed that "civilization, itself, . . . is threatened." Moreover, he claimed that any person or entity "that supports, protects, or harbors terrorists" or that has "ties to terrorist groups and seeks or possesses weapons of mass destruction" represented "a grave danger to the civilized world—and will be confronted."[3] In fact, Joshua Muravchik, a neoconservative writer, compared the criticism that Bush's approach to terrorism received to that which met Truman's announcement of his policy of containment of the Soviet Union. According to Muravchik, "It was only because such voices were spurned that the world was eventually delivered from the shadow of Soviet tyranny." The moral of the story, according to Muravchik, was that Bush must not waiver.[4]

An examination of the writings of the proponents of anti-terrorism (many of whom were anti-Communists and anti-Russians) indicates that they are functionally equivalent to the writings of Cold War anti-Communists. Daniel Pipes, two months after the September 11, 2001, attacks, called attention to "the danger within":

> The Muslim population in this country is not like any other group, for it includes within a substantial body of people—many times more numerous than the agents of Osama Bin Laden—who share with the suicide attackers a hatred of the United States and the desire, ultimately, to transform it into a nation living under the strictures of militant Islam. Although not responsible for the atrocities in September, they harbor designs for this country that warrant serious and urgent attention.[5]

Two months later, Pipes specifically identified "militant Islam" as the new enemy of the United States,[6] and in February 2002, Norman Podhoretz called the war against it "World War IV." He offered a series of syllogisms to support this declaration: Because "Islam has become an especially fertile breeding ground of terrorism in our time," there must be something in the religion itself that legitimizes terrorism. Because this something is "the obligation imposed by the Koran to wage holy war, or jihad, against the 'infidels,' " this "obligation" is incarnate in, or promoted by, the tyrannical leaders of Arab countries, particularly Iraq's Saddam Hussein. Thus, according to Podhoretz, no victory in this war was possible if it ended with Saddam Hussein still in power and, in fact, the United States might be forced to topple several other "tyrannies in the Islamic world" as well.[7] Both Pipes and Podhoretz insisted that this war could be won only if the people of the United States mustered the will, persistence, or "stomach" to fight it.

This demand for a sturdy will was elaborated on by one of the leading spokespeople for ultra-conservatism, William J. Bennett. He perceived, as did conservatives of the 1940s, that an external "threat" was required to catalyze people in the United States to put aside the doubts and questions that plagued them about their country and to help them distinguish good from evil and truth from falsehood. The events of September 11, 2001, in his words, represented "a moment of moral clarity—a moment when we began to rediscover ourselves as one people even as we began to gird for battle with a not yet fully defined foe"(radical Islam) that had declared war against the West in general and against the United States in particular. Bennett also emulated his conservative forebears when he accused the critics of the coming battle—naysayers, pacifists, moral relativists, and legal nitpickers—of attempting to weaken the new moral consensus and reinforce the doubts about the purposes and methods of the United States. Their seemingly principled words were, he charged, a cover for their anti-Americanism.[8] Similar sentiments were expressed the following year by David Frum and Richard Perle, who feared that "many in the American political and media elite are losing their nerve for the fight." They alleged that "the forces and the people who lulled the United States into complacency in the 1990s remain potent today." These unnamed forces and people, they said, fail to realize that "terrorism remains the great evil of our time, and the war against this evil, our generation's great cause." Just as the most fervent anti-Communists of the 1950s had proclaimed, so, too, did Frum and Perle: "There is no middle way for Americans: It is victory or holocaust."[9]

In 2007, Podhoretz argued that President George W. Bush's "global war on terror" was a euphemism. In fact, he claimed, the United States was involved in a war against Islamofascism, "the latest mutation of the totalitarian threat to our civilization." There was, in addition to this fourth world war abroad, another war at home: "the great war of ideas"—"a war so ferocious that some of us have not hesitated to describe it as nothing less than a kind of civil war." On one side are the realists and patriots; on the other side are "most libertarians and a goodly number of liberals and leftists," defeatists, doubters, and isolationists (of the right and the left). Podhoretz concluded by paraphrasing George Kennan's warning about the Soviet Union in 1947:

In 1947 we accepted the responsibilities of moral and political leadership that history "plainly intended" us to bear, and for the next forty-
two years we acted on them. . . .

Now "our entire security as a nation" . . . once more depends on
whether we are willing to accept and ready to act upon the responsibility of moral and political leadership that history has yet again so
squarely placed on our shoulders.[10]

In sum, for the current crop of foreign-specter wielders, Osama Bin
Laden and Saddam Hussein (both now dead) had replaced Josef Stalin
as the arch-fiend. Anti-terrorism and anti-"Islamofascism" had replaced
anti-communism as the enemy,[11] and there was a political split between
"soft" anti-terrorists, "hard" anti-terrorists, and anti-anti-terrorists.
A religion, rather than an ideology, had become the focal point of resistance.[12] Despite these differences, the same statements about moral abso-
lutism and national righteousness, replete with visceral metaphors, had
reappeared.

This belief—that the moral fiber and values of the nation need to be
stiffened by international policing and military interventions—poses a
danger to a democratic society. First, notions of moral regeneration are
irrational and amorphous, and they muddle what should be a rea-
soned public debate. Second, a democratic society is not like a human
organism or metal sculpture: it cannot be "cleansed" or "revitalized"
by powerful spiritual elixirs, nor can it be annealed or tempered.
There is simply no correlation between the policing/military will of
a nation's leaders and its "moral fiber." The only consistent correla-
tions are between policing/military will and increased policing/mili-
tary activity, and between increased policing/military activity and
the domestic extension of the national-security state.

Equally worrisome, though it has not yet been institutionalized, is
the clear and disturbing growth of Arabophobia and Islamophobia in
the United States. A *Time*-Abt SRI poll conducted in the summer of
2010 indicated that 46 percent of those asked believed that Islam is
more likely than other faiths to encourage violence. The journalist
who reported those results noted, "Where Americans meet Muslims,
there is evidence that suspicion and hostility are growing." That hostility
is particularly marked on a variety of web sites.[13] The hostility radiated
by the 2010 controversy that swirled around the plans to build a mosque
in New York City, two blocks from Ground Zero (i.e., the site of the
World Trade Center), worried some advocates of the war against radical
Islamist terror. Daniel Pipes, for example, noted that the Islamic center
controversy represented the "emergence as a political force" of those

who had, since September 11, 2001, acquired knowledge about radical Islamism. Although he found himself "partially elated" by what he called the "energetic push-back of recent months," he expressed one concern, regarding the "increasing anti-Islamic tone" of his teammates:

> [They] often fail to distinguish between Islam (a faith) and Islamism (a radical utopian ideology aiming to implement Islamic laws in their totality). This amounts to not just an intellectual error but a policy dead end. Targeting all Muslims is contrary to basic Western notions, lumps friends with foes, and ignores the inescapable fact that Muslims alone can offer an antidote to Islamism. As I often note, radical Islam is the problem and moderate Islam is the solution.[14]

Accompanying, and fueled by, the anti-attitudes have been the establishment of a much more intrusive set of state institutions. On October 26, 2001, the U.S. Congress passed into law the USA PATRIOT Act (Uniting and Strengthening America by Providing Appropriate Tools Required to Intercept and Obstruct Terrorism). It allowed for, among other things, indefinite detention of suspect immigrants, warrantless searches, and extensive wiretaps.[15] A new cabinet department, the Department of Homeland Security, was created in June 2002. It was designed to protect the country "against invisible enemies that can strike with a wide variety of weapons."[16] A few years later, Congress passed the Intelligence Reform and Terrorism Prevention Act, USA PATRIOT and Terrorism Prevention Reauthorization Act, and USA PATRIOT Act Additional Authorizing Amendments Act. "Enhanced" interrogation methods were approved by the Department of Justice and employed by the military and CIA. In February 2010, President Barack Obama approved a bill extending for one year the USA PATRIOT Act's provisions concerning wiretaps, seizures of records, and surveillance of certain individuals.

In March 2011, Congressman Peter King (Republican–New York), the newly installed chairman of the House Committee on Homeland Security, began a series of hearings into "The Extent of Radicalization in the American Muslim Community and that Community's Response." It was not clear from his opening remarks or the assortment of witnesses called what these hearings were designed to accomplish. It seemed, to this observer, a replay of the 1947 hearings of the Committee on Un-American Activities to investigate the extent of communism in the motion picture industry, or exposure for the sake of exposure.

So, it is happening again, albeit on a smaller scale. Another attack could, however, widen and deepen anti-terrorism into a fourth national "scare" of unprecedented proportions. The likelihood of such an attack will probably increase if the countries of the Middle East continue to experience domestic upheavals, and if the United States continues to intervene, as it recently did in Libya.

Abbreviations

ABA	American Bar Association
ACCF	American Committee for Cultural Freedom
ACLU	American Civil Liberties Union
ACTU	Association of Catholic Trade Unionists
ADA	Americans for Democratic Action
AFL	American Federation of Labor
AJC	American Jewish Committee
ALP	American Labor Party
AMPAS	Academy of Motion Picture Arts and Sciences
CIO	Congress of Industrial Organizations
CIO-PAC	CIO Political Action Committee
COINTELPRO	Counter-Intelligence Program
CPUSA	Communist Party, United States of America
CPUSSR	Communist Party, Union of Soviet Socialist Republics
ECLC	Emergency Civil Liberties Committee
FBI	Federal Bureau of Investigation
FOIA	Freedom of Information Act
ICCF	International Congress for Cultural Freedom
IPP	Independent Progressive Party
IUE	International Union of Electrical, Radio, and Machine Workers
IWW	Industrial Workers of the World
NATO	North American Treaty Organization
NCPAC	National Citizens Political Action Committee
NLRB	National Labor Relations Board
SWP	Socialist Workers Party
UAW	United Auto Workers
UE	Union of Electrical, Radio, and Machine Workers of America
WCFTR	Wisconsin Center for Film and Theater Research
YCL	Young Communist League

Notes

Introduction

1. Jean-Jacques Becker and Serge Bernstein, in their exhaustive discussion of anti-communism in France, wrote that anti-communism lacks "positive content," lacking even "a foundation for any common attitude towards a regime, society, or the values to which [anti-Communists] aspire." It is, they conclude, an attitude that has defined itself by its opposition to the ideology it fights, stoked mainly by fear and loathing of Communist ideology. Thus anti-communism in France waxed and waned in direct proportion to the perceived strength and weakness of communism. *Histoire de l'anti-communisme en France* (Paris: Olivier Orban, 1987), 1:9–10. John Earl Haynes has called anti-communism "a stance rather than a movement." *Red Scare or Red Menace? American Communism and Anticommunism in the Cold War Era* (Chicago: Ivan R. Dee, 1996), 3.

2. Lynn Boyd Hinds and Theodor Otto Windt, Jr,. have argued that the Cold War was a "rhetorical war," and that its anti-Communist ideology "developed in rhetorical fits and starts" in the years following the end of World War II. *The Cold War as Rhetoric: The Beginnings, 1945–1950* (New York/Westport, CT: Praeger, 1991), 25.

3. Charles Owen Rice, "Confessions of an Anti-Communist," *Labor History*, 30, no. 3 (Summer 1989): 449.

4. Paul Jacobs, *Is Curly Jewish? A Political Self-Portrait Illuminating Three Turbulent Decades of Social Revolt, 1955–1965* (New York: Atheneum, 1965), 169.

5. Richard Hofstadter calls this phenomenon "the big leap from the undeniable to the unbelievable." "The Paranoid Style in American Politics," in his *The Paranoid Style in American Politics and Other Essays* (New York: Knopf, 1965), 38.

6. Albert Einstein to Norman Thomas, March 10, 1954, in *Einstein on Politics: His Private Thoughts and Public Stands on Nationalism, Zionism, War, Peace, and the Bomb*, ed. David E. Rowe and Robert Schulmann (Princeton, NJ/Oxford, UK: Princeton University Press, 2009), 501.

7. Robert Hewison, *In Anger: Culture in the Cold War, 1945–60* (London: Weidenfeld and Nicolson, 1981), 25; Dominic Sandbrook, *Never Had It So Good: A History of Britain from Suez to the Beatles* (Boston: Little, Brown, 2005), 218; David Kyniston, *Austerity Britain, 1945–51* (New York: Walker, 2008), 341.

8. Richard Thurlow, *The Secret State: British Internal Security in the Twentieth Century* (Oxford, UK/Cambridge, MA: Blackwell, 1994), 287–88.

9. Steve Parsons, "British 'McCarthyism' and the Intellectuals," in *Labour's Promised Land? Culture and Society in Labour Britain, 1945–51*, ed. Jim Fyrth (London: Lawrence and Wishart, 1995), 225, 231.

10. Eleanor Bontecou, "The English Policy as to Communists and Fascists in the Civil Service," *Columbia Law Review*, 51, no. 5 (May 1951): 565–66. See also, her *The Federal Loyalty Security Program* (Ithaca, NY: Cornell University Press, 1953).

11. H. H. Wilson and Harvey Glickman, *The Problem of Internal Security in Great Britain, 1948–1953* (Garden City, NY: Doubleday, 1954), 33, 37, 68–69, 71, 75–77.

12. Herbert H. Hyman, "England and America: Climates of Tolerance and Intolerance—1962," in *The Radical Right* (updated and expanded version of *The New American Right*), ed. Daniel Bell (Garden City, NY: Doubleday, 1963), 240, 246, 248.

13. Merrily Weisbord, *The Strangest Dream: Canadian Communists, the Spy Trials, and the Cold War* (Toronto: Lester and Orpen Dennys, 1983), 27–29, 102.

14. Reg Whitaker and Gary Marcuse, *Cold War Canada: The Making of a National Insecurity State, 1945–1957* (Toronto/Buffalo, NY: University of Toronto Press, 1994), 7–8.

15. The Gouzenko story is well told in Whitaker and Marcuse, *Cold War Canada*, 27–110, and in Amy Knight, *How the Cold War Began: The Gouzenko Affair and the Hunt for Soviet Spies* (Toronto: McClelland and Stewart, 2005).

16. Hyman, "England and America," 238–39.

17. Robert Teigrob, *Warming Up to the Cold War: Canada and the United States' Coalition of the Willing, from Hiroshima to Korea* (Toronto/Buffalo, NY: University of Toronto Press, 2009), 229; Weisbord, *The Strangest Dream, passim*, but especially 193–99.

18. Whitaker and Marcuse, *Cold War Canada*, 165–68, 190, 194.

19. Ibid., 195–97, 204–5.

20. Quoted in Peter Richardson, *American Prophet: The Life and Work of Carey McWilliams* (Ann Arbor, MI: University of Michigan Press, 2005), 197. In his memoir, written much later, McWilliams located the cause of that paradox in "the fact that socialism has always been an inadmissible heresy in American eyes," a "taboo" that made the United States susceptible to a series

of "red scares." *The Education of Carey McWilliams* (New York: Simon and Schuster, 1979), 314.

21. Jean-Paul Sartre, "The Chances of Peace," *The Nation*, December 30, 1950, 696.

22. Claude Bourdet, "This Strange America," *The Nation*, December 12, 1953, 526.

23. Gordon W. Allport, *The Nature of Prejudice* (Cambridge, MA: Addison-Wesley, 1954), 185, 256.

24. Reinhold Niebuhr, "The Cause and Cure of the American Psychosis," *The American Scholar*, 25, no. 1 (Winter 1955–1956): 11–19.

25. Reinhold Niebuhr, "Social Myths in the Cold War," *Journal of International Affairs*, 1967, reprinted in Niebuhr, *Faith and Politics: A Commentary on Religious, Social and Political Thought in a Technological Age*, ed. Ronald H. Stone (New York: George Braziller, 1968), 223, 235–36. Niebuhr's social myth is very similar to Sigmund Freud's "cultural ideal." According to Freud, the satisfaction provided by a nation's cultural ideal is of "a narcissistic nature," resting on pride in what the nation has achieved. Freud concluded: "To make this satisfaction complete calls for a comparison with other cultures. . . . On the strength of these differences every culture claims the right to look down on the rest. In this way cultural ideals become a source of discord and enmity between different cultural units." Freud also notes that "the narcissistic satisfaction" provided by the cultural ideal is regularly employed to combat any hostility to that ideal that arises from within the culture. If, as Freud suggests, the cultural ideal is an "illusion" or a "wish-fulfillment," it can be easily shaken, provoking an angry social response. "The Future of an Illusion," in *The Standard Edition of the Complete Psychological Works of Sigmund Freud*, trans. and ed. James Strachey (London: Hogarth Press, 1961), 21:13. Freud also suggested that one way of maintaining social unity is to allow the aggressive instinct of individuals "an outlet in the form of hostility against intruders." *Civilization and Its Discontents*, in *The Standard Edition of the Complete Psychological Works of Sigmund Freud*,21:114. For an extensive, but to my mind, questionable psychological analysis of the exceptional nature of anti-communism in the United States, see Joel Kovel, *Red Hunting in the Promised Land: Anticommunism and the Making of America* (New York: Basic Books, 1994).

26. Daniel Bell, "Interpretations of American Politics," 3; Richard Hofstadter, "The Pseudo-Conservative Revolt," in *The New American Right*, ed. Daniel Bell (New York: Criterion, 1955), 41–42.

27. Talcott Parsons, "Social Strains in America," in Bell, *The New American Right*, 117–18, 127, 129.

28. Edward A. Shils, *The Torment of Secrecy: The Background and Consequences of American Security Policies* (Glencoe, IL: Free Press, 1956), 13, 45, 61–64, 125, 135–42.

29. Seymour Martin Lipset and Gary Marks later wrote: "Americanism . . . is an 'ism' or ideology in the same way that communism or fascism or liberalism are isms." *It Didn't Happen Here: Why Socialism Failed in the United States* (New York/London: Norton, 2000), 30.

30. Louis Hartz, *The Liberal Tradition in America* (New York and London: Harcourt Brace Jovanovich, 1955), 5, 6, 11, 12, 15, 56, 58–59, 299–303, 305. Hartz's close linkage of Locke and liberalism is no longer considered tenable. See, for example, J. G. A. Pocock and Richard Ashcraft, *John Locke: Papers Read at a Clark Library Seminar, 10 December 1977* (Los Angeles, CA: William Andrews Clark Memorial Library, UCLA, 1980).

31. Murray B. Levin, *Political Hysteria in America: The Democratic Capacity of Repression* (New York/London: Basic Books, 1971), 236–40.

32. Richard Hofstadter, "Pseudo-Conservatism Revisited: A Postscript—1962," in Bell, *The Radical Right*, 81.

33. For a detailed, historically based critique of the populism-under-strain argument, see Michael Paul Rogin, *The Intellectuals and McCarthy: The Radical Specter* (Cambridge, MA/London: MIT Press, 1967), 168–91.

34. Shils, *The Torment of Secrecy*, 41, 47, 227. The U.S. tendency to embrace conspiracy theories has been argued by Shils (45), Hofstadter (*The Age of Reform* [New York: Knopf, 1956], 72), and Samuel P. Huntington (*American Politics: The Promise of Disharmony* [Cambridge, MA/London: Belknap, 1981], 79–81. However, all of these arguments have been impressionistic rather than empirical, and none has offered a cross-cultural analysis to determine if the United States is exceptional in this regard.

35. Shils, *The Torment of Secrecy*, 77–80.

36. Hofstadter, "The Paranoid Style in American Politics," 6, 7, 39.

37. Henry David, *The History of the Haymarket Affair: A Study in Social-Revolutionary and Labor Movements* (New York: Russell and Russell, 1958), 206, 217, 528.

38. *Congressional Record*, 47th Congress, 1st Session, 13:2, March 21, 1882, 131.

39. Woodrow Wilson and Albert Fried, *A Day of Dedication* (New York: Macmillan, 1965), 224.

40. *The State of the Union Messages of the Presidents, 1790–1966* (New York: Chelsea House, 1966), 3:2571–72.

41. Speech of June 14, 1917, in *A Compilation of the Messages and Papers of the Presidents*, ed. James D. Richardson (New York: Bureau of National Literature, 1917), 16:8281.

42. On the one hand, Stanley Coben emphasizes nativism more than anti-radicalism as the leitmotif of the first "red scare." He argues that anti-radicalism supervened on a two-decade long nativist opposition to immigrants from eastern Europe, the series of revolutions in postwar eastern Europe, and the predominance of east European names on the many new radical periodicals and parties. "A Study in Nativism: The American Red Scare of 1919–20,"

Political Science Quarterly, 79, no. 1 (March 1964): 68. On the other hand, a Department of Justice spokesperson told a newspaper reporter on Armistice Day that the United States' official and unofficial intelligence networks must continue to keep a "vigilant watch over anarchists, plotters, and aliens." Quoted in Ann Hagedorn, *Savage Peace: Hope and Fear in America, 1919* (New York: Simon and Schuster, 2007), 24.

43. Distinction blurring (or confusion of categories) is a venerable tradition in U.S. anti-radical history. For other examples, see Susan Jacoby, *Freethinkers: A History of American Secularism* (New York: Metropolitan Books, 2004), 258, 280, 294. Gordon W. Allport undertook a content analysis of the *Boston Herald*, in 1920, to find synonyms for the "menace" the country faced. He counted 26 "villains," ranging from "alien" to "undesirable," and including "Bolshevik," "Communist," "radical," and "red." He concluded that "there was no agreement as to the actual source of the menace," and that "the *need* for an enemy—someone to serve as a focus for discontent and jitters—was considerably more apparent than the precise *identity* of the enemy. At any rate, there was no clearly agreed upon label." Allport labels this blurring of distinctions "syncretism," which "reflects the generality of prejudice and an emotional equating of disliked objects." *The Nature of Prejudice*, 184, 253. Lisa McGirr, in her study of conservatism in Orange County, California, noted that anti-communism there "often meant opposition to the United Nations, agricultural controls by the federal government, or any sort of planning. Anticommunism provided the symbolic glue that united conservatives with divergent priorities." *Suburban Warriors: The Origins of the New American Right* (Princeton, NJ/Oxford, UK: Princeton University Press, 2001), 36.

44. Geoffrey R. Stone, *Perilous Times: Free Speech in Wartime, from the Sedition Act of 1798 to the War on Terrorism* (New York: Norton, 2004), 222, 223.

45. Robert M. Lichtman, "J. B. Matthews and the 'Counter-Subversives': Names as a Political and Financial Resource in the McCarthy Era," *American Communist History*, 5, no. 1 (June 2006): 3.

46. Ralph S. Brown, Jr., *Loyalty and Security: Employment Tests in the United States* (New Haven, CT: Yale University Press, 1958), 313.

47. Allport, *The Nature of Prejudice*, 184.

48. A good example of this mode of thinking was provided by Gabriel A. Almond, who wrote that the basic issues and values of the United States "are under attack by an expanding Soviet Union," which is "universalist, dogmatic-absolutist, monolithic." Its leaders, he continued, practice a "permanent activism." *The American People and Foreign Policy* (New York: Harcourt, Brace, 1950), 12, 18. I. F. Stone remarked on the dilemma created by this "demonology": How does one fight against this "super-natural breed of men, led by diabolic master minds in that distant Kremlin, engaged in a Satanic conspiracy to take over the world and enslave all mankind"? "The

Costs of Anticommunism," *I. F. Stone's Weekly,* August 9, 1954, reprinted in Stone, *The Haunted Fifties* (New York: Random House, 1963), 69.

49. According to anti-Communists, all non-Communist governments were on the side of the good. For example, Congressman Richard M. Nixon (R-California) stated, in 1948, "We will expose the expansion of Communism, without regard to the character of the existing governments" supported by the United States. Quoted in Jonathan Bell, *The Liberal State on Trial: The Cold War and American Politics in the Truman Years* (New York: Columbia University Press, 2004), 182.

50. Frank Gibney, "After the Ball," *Commonweal,* 60 (September 3, 1954): 531–34. Seymour Martin Lipset and Earl Raab stated that McCarthy traded in "a kind of religious hysteria which was called anti-Communism." *The Politics of Unreason: Right-Wing Extremism in America, 1790–1970* (New York: Harper and Row, 1970), 234. For more on Cohn, see Chapter 8.

51. Irving Kristol, "Memoirs of a 'Cold Warrior,' " *New York Times Magazine,* February 11, 1968, 25. For a discussion of the Communist belief system, see Chapter 11. For an excellent discussion of competing belief systems, see Ruth Harris, *Dreyfus: Politics, Emotion, and the Scandal of the Century* (New York: Metropolitan Books, 2010).

52. Alan Barth, *The Loyalty of Free Men* (New York: Viking, 1951), 13, 241.

53. Rice, "Confessions of an Ex-Communist," 452–53.

54. Roy Brewer, transcript of unfinished oral history (1980), UCLA, University Archives, Record Series 507, box 16, 157. His emphasis. Seymour Martin Lipset noted the marked similarity between the political approaches of Communists and the radical-right component of anti-communism. "The Sources of the 'Radical Right,' " in Bell, *The New American Right,* 186. Irving Howe stated that anti-communism, like anti-capitalism, "could be put to the service of ideological racketeering and reaction." "The New York Intellectuals: A Chronicle and a Critique," *Commentary* 45 (October 1968): 37.

55. Richard Gid Powers, *Not Without Honor: The History of American Anticommunism* (New York: Free Press, 1995), 15, 17, 43, 69, 93, 98, 129–32, 426. Other writers on this subject have either omitted a set of categories or not defined them with sufficient precision. The American Friends Service Committee focused mainly on the third "red scare" and did not provide a taxonomy: *Anatomy of Anti-Communism: A Report Prepared for the Peace Education Division of the American Friends Service Committee* (New York: Hill and Wang, 1969). David Green, in a chapter titled "The Struggle for the Anti-Communist Label," employed too narrow a focus on types, and he narrowed the topic to a type of language game: *Shaping Political Consciousness: The Language of Politics in America from McKinley to Reagan* (Ithaca, NY/London: Cornell University Press, 1987), 173, 205, 206. Peter H. Buckingham provides a standard chronological history of anti-communism, without categories: *America Sees Red: Anti-Communism in America, 1870s to 1980s* (Claremont,

CA: Regina Books, 1988). George Sirgiovanni divided his discussion of anti-communism during World War II into "five general groupings": anti-Communist political figures, leaders of organized labor, prominent right-wing journalists, leading Catholics, and Protestant fundamentalists: *An Undercurrent of Suspicion: Anti-Communism during World War II* (New Brunswick, NJ/London: Transaction, 1990), 1. M. J. Heale treats anti-communism as an entity: *American Anticommunism: Combating the Enemy Within, 1830–1970* (Baltimore, MD: Johns Hopkins University Press, 1990). Joel Kovel divides anti-Communists into two types, elitist and populist: *Red Hunting in the Promised Land*. John Earl Haynes acknowledges there have been a "multitude" of anti-Communists, "with different objections to communism," but he does not provide a schematic for differentiating their styles and objectives: *Red Scare or Red Menace?*, 3. Ellen Schrecker, in her well-researched book, *Many Are the Crimes: McCarthyism in America* (Boston: Little, Brown, 1998), relies on general terms, the "anti-Communist network" or "professional anti-Communists" (43–45).

56. Powers, *Not Without Honor*, 22–23, 25.

57. I have borrowed the labels "official" and "unofficial" from Steven Englund, who devised them for his yet-unpublished history of French nationalism.

58. Clearly, these unofficial categories are not exhaustive. One could expand them to include true-believing purists (e.g., Roy Brewer, International Representative of the International Alliance of Theatrical Stage Employees, 1945–1953); de facto anti-Communists (e.g., the motion picture industry executives who initiated the industry blacklist in 1947, expanded it in 1951, and maintained it for another 10 years); FBI-recruited infiltrators (e.g., Herbert Philbrick and Matt Cvetic); and anti-Semitic anti-Communists (e.g., William Dudley Pelley and Gerald L. K. Smith). Although there has always been a strain of anti-Semitism in anti-communism, notably among Catholics and white supremacists, most anti-Communists are not anti-Semites, and I have not found any systematic association of anti-Semitism and anti-communism.

Chapter 1: Official Anti-Communism, 1919–1939

1. Arno J. Mayer, *Wilson v. Lenin: Political Origins of the New Diplomacy, 1917–1918* (Cleveland, OH/New York: Meridian Books, 1964), 70.

2. Letter to Congressman Frank Clark (Democrat–Florida), quoted in Ray Stannard Baker, *Woodrow Wilson: Life and Letters—War Leader, 1917–1918* (New York: Scribner's, 1946), 355.

3. Henry Steele Commager, ed., *Documents of American History*, 8th ed. (New York: Appleton-Century-Crofts, 1968), 2:138.

4. Baker, *Wilson—Armistice, Mar. 1–Nov. 11, 1918*, 338.

5. Robert Lansing, "Some Legal Questions on the Peace Conference" [address to the American Bar Association, Boston, September 5, 1919], in *American Journal of International Law* 13, no. 4 (October 1919): 632. He restated these points in his peroration (649–50).

6. Arno J. Mayer, *Politics and Diplomacy of Peacemaking: Containment and Counterrevolution at Versailles, 1918–1919* (New York: Knopf, 1967), 318, 329, 598.

7. Thomas A. Bailey, *America Faces Russia: Russian-American Relations from Early Times to Our Day* (Ithaca, NY: Cornell University Press, 1950; Gloucester, MA: Peter Smith, 1964), 238; Peter G. Filene, *Americans and the Soviet Experiment, 1917–1933* (Cambridge, MA: Harvard University Press, 1967), 63; George F. Kennan, *Soviet-American Relations, 1917–1920: The Decision to Intervene* (Princeton, NJ: Princeton University Press, 1958), 9.

8. Robert K. Murray, *Red Scare: A Study in National Hysteria, 1919–1920* (Minneapolis, MN: University of Minnesota Press, 1956), 33–34; "Communism and the Great Steel Strike of 1919," *Mississippi Valley Historical Review* 38, no. 3 (December 1951): 445.

9. Quoted in Melvin I. Urofsky, *Louis D. Brandeis: A Life* (New York: Pantheon Books, 2009), 551.

10. The Industrial Workers of the World (IWW) was formed in 1905 to organize the unskilled and industrial workers ignored by the AFL. It emphasized class conflict, direct action, and the destruction of the capitalist system. Its members and sympathizers were constantly attacked by vigilantes and police and jailed by authorities. The courts provided virtually no protection against this persecution. See Joyce L. Kornbluh, "Industrial Workers of the World," in *Encyclopedia of the American Left*, 2nd ed., edited by Mary Jo Buhle, Paul Buhle, and Dan Georgakas, 355–59 (New York/Oxford, UK: Oxford University Press, 1998).

11. Murray, *Red Scare*, 58–66. Six months after the strike ended, Hansen resigned his position and embarked on a year-long, nationwide series of speeches to promote "Americanism." He was paid $500 per speech and he earned a total of $38,000. Robert L. Friedheim, *The Seattle General Strike* (Seattle, WA: University of Washington Press, 1964), 173–75. Hanson also wrote *Americanism Versus Bolshevism* (Garden City, NY/London: Doubleday, Page, 1920).

12. Murray, *Red Scare*, 123–34; A. G. Gardiner, *Portraits and Portents* (New York/London: Harper and Brothers, 1926), 13–15.

13. Murray, "Communism," 452–64.

14. Ernest Freeberg, *Democracy's Prisoner: Eugene V. Debs, the Great War, and the Right to Dissent* (Cambridge, MA/London: Harvard University Press, 2008), 147, 227, 236, 240, 255. The imprisoned Debs was nominated as the Socialist Party's candidate for president. He received 919,799 votes. One year later, Harding commuted Debs's sentence.

15. For the history of the various Communist parties, see Irving Howe and Lewis Coser, *The American Communist Party: A Critical History* (Boston: Beacon

Press, 1957; New York: Praeger, 1962) and Theodore Draper, *American Communism and Soviet Russia: The Formative Period* (New York: Viking Press, 1960).

16. A few months later, Stevenson sent a report on "Bolshevism" to the New York state legislature, and he was named special counsel to a new committee established to investigate it. This New York Joint State Legislative Committee, chaired by, and named after, State Senator Clayton L. Lusk, had extraordinary powers. It instigated major raids on the Soviet Bureau (a trade organization) and the Rand School (a socialist enterprise). During the Rand raid, Stevenson told reporters that he had one objective: "names! . . . names of all the parlor Bolsheviki, I.W.W.'s, and socialists we can get hold of." Quoted in Todd J. Pfannstiel, *Rethinking the Red Scare: The Lusk Committee and New York's Crusade Against Radicalism, 1919–1923* (New York: Routledge, 2003), 13, 82. The Lusk committee's four-volume report, *Revolutionary Radicalism*, became a standard source for patriotic organizations in their campaigns against "Communist fronts." Paul L. Murphy, *The Constitution in Crisis Times, 1918–1969* (New York: Harper and Row, 1972), 28, n. 93.

17. Margaret A. Blanchard, *Revolutionary Sparks: Freedom of Expression in Modern America* (New York/Oxford, UK: Oxford University Press, 1992), 115–16, 120.

18. John Lord O'Brian, "Loyalty Tests and Guilt by Association," *Harvard Law Review* 61, no. 4 (April 1948), 602–3.

19. See Zechariah Chafee, Jr., *Free Speech in the United States* (Cambridge, MA: Harvard University Press, 1941), Appendix III. In addition, many large city governments transformed their "anarchist squads" into "red squads" and, with the support of civic federations and businessmen's organizations, targeted every type of "radicalism." Frank Donner, *Protectors of Privilege: Red Squads and Police Repression in Urban America* (Berkeley/Los Angeles, CA: University of California Press, 1990), 30–35.

20. Philip L. Cantelon, *In Defense of America: Congressional Investigations of Communism in the United States, 1919–1935* [Ph.D. dissertation] (Bloomington, IN: Indiana University, 1971), 18, 197, 224–25, 232–34. That same year, a section of the Smoot-Hawley Tariff Act gave federal courts the power to confiscate any imported material that advocated or urged "treason, insurrection or forcible resistance to any law of the United States." Robert Justin Goldstein, *Political Repression in Modern America: From 1870 to the Present* (Cambridge, MA: Schenckman, 1978), 200.

21. House Resolution 198, printed in U.S. Congress, House of Representatives, Special Committee on Un-American Activities, *Investigation of Nazi Propaganda and Investigation of Certain Other Propaganda Activities*, 73d Congress, 2d Session, November–December 1934 (Washington, DC: U.S. Government Printing Office, 1935), v; Cantelon, *In Defense of America*, 292, 299.

22. Steele appeared again in August 1938, July 1947, and May 1951. Each time he provided the committee with an extensive list of names and organizations.

23. *Investigation*, November–December 1934, 224; *Investigation*, December 17–18, 1934, 1–2.

24. Walter Goodman, *The Committee: The Extraordinary Career of the House Committee on Un-American Activities* (Baltimore, MD: Penguin Books, 1969), 10; *New York Times*, February 16, 1935, pp. 1, 4; Michael R. Belknap, *Cold War Political Justice: The Smith Act, the Communist Party and American Civil Liberties* (Westport, CT: Greenwood Press, 1977), 18–19. Four states—Arkansas, Delaware, Indiana, and Tennessee—passed laws excluding the Communist Party from the ballot. Chafee, *Free Speech in the United States*, Appendix III.

25. See M. J. Heale, *American Anticommunism: Combating the Enemy Within, 1830–1970* (Baltimore, MD: Johns Hopkins University Press, 1990), 99–121.

26. *Congressional Record*, 75th Congress, 3d Session, 83:7, May 26, 1938, 7568–70.

27. *Hollywood Reporter*, August 4, 1938, p. 1; August Raymond Ogden, *The Dies Committee: A Study of the Special House Committee for the Investigation of Un-American Activities, 1938–1944* (Washington, DC: Catholic University of America Press, 1945), 56–57. The investigator, Edward E. Sullivan, had been sent west by Dies to find evidence that labor leader Harry Bridges was receiving support from the Roosevelt administration. Prior to August 1938, no references regarding Communist activity in the motion picture industry appeared in the *Congressional Record*.

28. *Hollywood Reporter*, November 26, 1938, p. 3. In the anti-Communist book he authored several months later, *The Trojan Horse in America* (New York: Dodd, Mead, 1940), Dies did not make any charges against the motion picture industry.

29. U.S. Congress, House of Representatives, Special Committee on Un-American Activities, *Investigation of Un-American Propaganda Activities in the United States*, 75th Congress, 3rd Session, August 1938 (Washington, DC: U.S. Government Printing Office, 1938), 1:91, 94. Frey, a conservative Republican and dedicated anti-radical, and Matthew Woll, AFL vice-president and also a conservative Republican and dedicated anti-radical, were the main promoters of the AFL's anti-communism.

30. After his testimony, Matthews was appointed as the committee's chief researcher. According to Richard H. Rovere, Matthews was "an industrious fanatic" who used his position to compile a vast digest of names. Rovere claimed that Matthews wrote *The Trojan Horse in America*. "J. B. Matthews—he Informer," *The Nation* (October 3, 1942): 314–15.

31. Kenneth O'Reilly, *Hoover and the Un-Americans: The FBI, HUAC, and the Red Menace* (Philadelphia, PA: Temple University Press, 1983), 74.

32. *Los Angeles Times*, December 11, 1938, A7.

33. *Congressional Record*, 76th Congress, 1st Session, 84:1, February 3, 1939, 1127.

34. Ibid., 84:3, March 9, 1939, 1939.

35. Geoffrey R. Stone, *Perilous Times: Free Speech in Wartime, from the Sedition Act of 1798 to the War on Terrorism* (New York: Norton, 2004), note on 248, 354.

36. Stanley Coben, *A. Mitchell Palmer: Politician* (New York/London: Columbia University Press, 1963), 199–211.

37. For a discussion of the anti-Communists aspects of immigration policy and activity during the 1920s, see Nick Fischer, "The Founders of American Anti-Communism," *American Communist History* 5, no. 1 (June 2006), 72–80.

38. Goldstein, *Political Repression*, 200.

39. Athan G. Theoharis, *The FBI and American Democracy: A Brief Critical History* (University Press of Kansas, 2004), 46; Charles F. Croog, "FBI Political Surveillance and the Isolationist-Interventionist Debate, 1939–1941," *The Historian* 54, no. 3 (Spring 1992), 448–49. The Bureau of Investigation created an index of national security threats and a list of those persons to detain in case of a national security emergency.

40. Paul L. Murphy, *World War I and the Origins of Civil Liberties in the United States* (New York and London: Norton, 1979), 189.

41. Murphy, *The Constitution in Crisis*, 87.

42. *Stromberg v. California*, 283 U.S. 359, 1931. Paul L. Murphy couples *Stromberg* with *Near v. Minnesota*, 283 U.S. 697 (1931) as signifying "a quiet, legal, free-speech revolution." *The Meaning of Freedom of Speech: First Amendment Freedoms from Wilson to FDR* (Westport, CT: Greenwood, 1972), 272. In the *Near* case, by a 5-4 decision, the Supreme Court overturned a state press censorship law, holding that freedom of the press is a freedom from invasion by state action guaranteed by the due process clause of the Fourteenth Amendment.

43. *Herndon v. Lowry*, 304 U.S. 242, 1937.

44. The following year, in the Alien Registration Act, Congress explicitly made past membership a ground for deportation. The Supreme Court, in *Harisiades v. Shaughnessy*, 342 U.S. 580 (1952), upheld this ground.

45. Murphy, *The Constitution in Crisis*, 211.

Chapter 2: Unofficial Anti-Communism, 1919–1939

1. Richard Gid Powers, *Not Without Honor: The History of American Anti-communism* (New York: Free Press, 1995), 51–55; Donald F. Crosby, "American Catholics and the Anti-Communist Impulse," in *The Specter: Original Essays on the Cold War and the Origins of McCarthyism*, edited by Robert Griffith and Athan Theoharis, 20–22 (New York: New Viewpoints, 1974). Although Catholic leaders firmly believed that the Spanish Popular Front government was completely dominated by "Reds," lay Catholics were divided. An unpublished poll from the late 1930s registered 39 percent of Catholics as

pro-Franco; 30 percent as pro-Loyalist; and 31 percent as neutral. Ralph Lord Roy, *Communism and the Churches* (New York: Harper and Brothers, 1960), 114. Dorothy Day, who headed the Catholic Worker Movement, wrote: "Catholics who look at Spain and think Fascism is a good thing because Spanish Fascists are fighting for the Church against Communist persecution should take another look at recent events in Germany to see just how much love the Catholic Church can expect." William D. Miller, *Dorothy Day: A Biography* (New York: Harper and Row, 1982), 314.

2. Christopher J. Kauffman, *Faith and Fraternalism: The History of the Knights of Columbus, 1882–1982* (New York: Harper and Row, 1982), 333–35.

3. David O'Brien, *American Catholics and Social Reform: The New Deal Years* (New York: Oxford University Press, 1968), 82–83.

4. U.S. Congress, House of Representatives, Special Committee on Un-American Activities, *Investigation of Nazi Propaganda and Investigation of Certain Other Propaganda Activities*, 73d Congress, 2d Session, November–December 1934 (Washington, DC: U.S. Government Printing Office, 1935), December 18, 1934, 7:135–40.

5. Patrick McNamara, *A Catholic Cold War: Edmund A. Walsh, S.J., and the Politics of American Anticommunism* (New York: Fordham University Press, 2005), 23–24, 29, 54, 92, 93; *New York Times*, April 15, 1936, p. 23. He wrote two books during this period: *The Fall of the Russian Empire: The Story of the Last Romanovs and the Coming of the Bolsheviki* (1928) and *The Last Stand: An Interpretation of the Soviet Five-Year Plan* (1931).

6. Charles J. McFadden, *The Philosophy of Communism* (New York: Benziger Brothers, 1939), xv–xvi. In his prefacing remarks, Sheen called the book "the best treatment" of this subject in any language, and he noted that McFadden knew this subject "far better" than did CPUSA leader Earl Browder (ix).

7. Donald Warren, *Radio Priest: Charles Coughlin, the Father of Hate Radio* (New York: Free Press, 1996), 30–32.

8. Charles J. Tull, *Father Coughlin and the New Deal* (Syracuse, NY: Syracuse University Press, 1965), 188–91.

9. Quoted in David O'Brien, "American Catholics and Organized Labor in the 1930's," *Catholic Historical Review* 51, no. 3 (October 1966), 337.

10. See Francis L. Broderick, *Right Reverend New Dealer: John A. Ryan* (New York: Macmillan, 1963).

11. Mel Piehl, *Breaking Bread: The Catholic Worker and the Origin of Catholic Radicalism in America* (Philadelphia: Temple University Press, 1982), 122.

12. O'Brien, *American Catholics*, 206.

13. Miller, *Dorothy Day*, 319.

14. Douglas P. Seaton, *Catholics and Radicals: The Association of Catholic Trade Unionists and the American Labor Movement, from Depression to Cold War* (Lewisburg, PA: Bucknell University Press; London/Toronto: Associated University Presses, 1981), 18, 22–23, 55–56, 61, 75, 82, 100, 110, 142–50; Steve Rosswurm, "The Catholic Church and the Left-Led Unions: Labor Priests,

Labor Schools, and the ACTU," in *The CIO's Left-Led Unions*, edited by Steve Rosswurm, 121–24 (New Brunswick, NJ: Rutgers University Press, 1992).

15. Neil Betten, *Catholic Activism and the Industrial Worker* (Gainesville, FL: University Presses of Florida, 1976), 79, 131–33. Father Rice was a dedicated trade unionist who helped found labor schools and the Catholic Radical Alliance. He also walked the picket line during the Little Steel strike in Ohio.

16. M. J. Heale, *American Anticommunism: Combating the Enemy Within, 1830–1970* (Baltimore, MD: Johns Hopkins University Press, 1990), 118.

17. William Pencak, *For God and Country: The American Legion, 1919–1941* (Boston: Northeastern University Press, 1989), 8, 10; Stanley Coben, "A Study in Nativism: The American Red Scare of 1919–20," *Political Science Quarterly* 79, no. 1 (March 1964), 70; Robert K. Murray, *Red Scare: A Study in National Hysteria, 1919–1920* (Minneapolis, MN: University of Minnesota Press, 1956), 88.

18. Regin Schmidt, *Red Scare: FBI and the Origins of Anticommunism in the United States, 1919–1943* (Copenhagen: Museum Tusculanum Press, 2000), 105. In fact, in November, in Centralia, Washington, Legionnaires participated in a bloody attack on an IWW headquarters. Margaret A. Blanchard, *Revolutionary Sparks: Freedom of Expression in Modern America* (New York/ Oxford, UK: Oxford University Press, 1992), 116–17.

19. Rodney G. Minott, *Peerless Patriots: Organized Veterans and the Spirit of Americanism* (Washington, DC: Public Affairs Press, 1962), 58. Paul L Murphy, *The Meaning of Freedom of Speech: First Amendment Freedoms from Wilson to FDR* (Westport, CT: Greenwood, 1972), 173; Murray, *Red Scare*, 90. In return, every American Legion national convention from 1920 to 1962 condemned the ACLU as an un-American organization.

20. Norman Hapgood, ed., *Professional Patriots: An Exposure of the Personalities, Methods and Objectives Involved in the Organized Effort to Exploit Patriotic Impulses in These United States During and After The Late War* (New York: Albert and Charles Boni, 1927), 61–62.

21. Pencak, *For God and Country,*146, 157, 237–38, 243–47; Heale, *American Anticommunism*, 117; *ISMS: A Review of Alien Isms, Revolutionary Communism and their Active Sympathizers in the United States*, 2nd ed. (Indianapolis, IN: National Americanism Commission of the American Legion, National Headquarters, 1937), [5]. The American Legion and the AFL also joined forces to support the deportation of Harry Bridges, who had led the massive 1934 longshoremen' strike on the west coast and later helped organize CIO unions in California. Stanley I. Kutler, *The American Inquisition: Justice and Injustice in the Cold War* (New York: Hill and Wang, 1982), 126, 132.

22. The AFL did join this organization in August 1937, but raised strong objections when it opened negotiations with the Soviet Union's Central Council of Trade Unions. That objection became moot when the Nonaggression Treaty was signed. Philip Taft, *The A.F. of L. from the Death of Gompers to the Merger* (New York: Harper and Brothers, 1959), 235–36.

23. Bernard Mandel, *Samuel Gompers: A Biography* (Yellow Springs, OH: Antioch Press, 1963), 451, 478, 512–13.

24. Philip Taft, *Organized Labor in American History* (New York: Harper and Row, 1964), 396.

25. *Investigation of Nazi Propaganda Activities*, December 17, 1934, 7:10–11.

26. Quoted in Philip S. Foner, *The Fur and Leather Workers Union: A Story of Dramatic Struggles and Achievements* (Newark, NJ: Nordan Press, 1950), 447.

27. Taft, *The A.F. of L. from the Death of Gompers to the Merger*, 431.

28. Harvey A. Levenstein, *Communism, Anticommunism, and the CIO* (Westport, CT: Greenwood Press, 1981), 80–81, 106.

29. Benjamin Stolberg, *The Story of the CIO* (New York: Viking Press, 1938), 153. Stolberg, who had served on the Commission of Inquiry into the Charges Made Against Leon Trotsky in the Moscow Trials, charged that "Stalinism" was a danger to the CIO.

30. Alan Barth, *The Loyalty of Free Men* (New York: Viking, 1951), 210. Gabriel A. Almond, who utilized dozens of ex-Communist interviews in *The Appeals of Communism* (Princeton, NJ: Princeton University Press, 1954), concluded that the former Communists who became professional witnesses were hardly unbiased reporters of their own experience, nor were they representative of the ex-Communist population as a whole. In fact, Almond concluded, the very act of "public confession" differentiated them from the great mass of former party members, who, for a variety of reasons, remained silent (xv).

31. Quoted in David Caute, *The Great Fear: The Anti-Communist Purge Under Truman and Eisenhower* (New York: Simon and Schuster, 1978), 123–24.

32. Arthur Koestler, "The Complex Issue of Ex-Communists," *New York Times Magazine*, February 2, 1950, reprinted in Patrick Swan, ed., *Alger Hiss, Whittaker Chambers, and the Schism in the American Soul* (Wilmington, DE: Intercollegiate Studies Institute, 2003), 55.

33. Isaac Deutscher, "The Ex-Communist Conscience," *The Reporter* (April 1950), reprinted in his *Heretics and Renegades: And Other Essays* (London: Hamish Hamilton, 1955), 9–22.

34. Sidney Hook, "The Faiths of Whittaker Chambers" [1952], in his *Convictions* (Buffalo, NY: Prometheus Books, 1990), 198–99. In a diary entry, Arthur Koestler described Chambers as "sincere, but fanatical." Michael Scammell, *Koestler: The Life and Political Odyssey of a Twentieth-Century Skeptic* (New York: Random House, 2009), 375.

35. Reinhold Niebuhr, "Liberals and the Marxist Heresy," *New Republic* 129 (October 12, 1953): 14.

36. Quoted in Mary Sperling McAuliffe, *Crisis on the Left: Cold War Politics and American Liberals* (Amherst, MA: University of Massachusetts Press, 1978), 124.

37. Hannah Arendt, "The Ex-Communists," *Commonweal* 57 (March 20, 1953): 595–99.

38. Memo from Eisenhower to Attorney General Herbert Brownell, Jr., November 4, 1953, quoted in Robert P. Newman, *Owen Lattimore and the "Loss" of China* (Berkeley/Los Angeles, CA: University of California Press, 1992), 449.

39. William S. Schlamm, "Apropos Apostasy," *The Freeman* (March 26, 1951): 401.

40. Deutscher, "The Ex-Communist Conscience," 10.

41. Richard Hofstadter, "Pseudo-Conservatism Revisited: A Postscript—1962," in Daniel Bell, ed., *The Radical Right* (*The New American Right*, expanded and updated) (Garden City, NY: Doubleday, 1963), 84.

42. Michael Paul Rogin, *The Intellectuals and McCarthy: The Radical Specter* (Cambridge, MA/London, MIT Press, 1967), 58.

43. Russell G. Fryer, *Recent Conservative Political Thought: American Perspectives* (Washington, DC: University Press of America, 1986), 8, 24–25.

44. Patrick Allitt, *The Conservatives: Ideas and Personalities Throughout American History* (New Haven, CT/London: Yale University Press, 2009), 126, 129.

45. See Frederick Rudolph, "The American Liberty League, 1934–1940," *American Historical Review* 56, no. 1 (October 1950), 19–33; and George Wolfskill, *The Revolt of the Conservatives: The American Liberty League, 1934–1940* (Boston: Houghton Mifflin, 1962).

46. Louis Pizzitola, *Hearst Over Hollywood: Power, Passion, and Propaganda in the Movies* (Columbia University Press, 2002), 361–62. Matthews had been recommended to the committee by Hearst columnist George Sokolsky, and, when Matthews resigned from the committee in 1944, he became a consultant to the Hearst Publications. In that position, he fed material to columnists George Sokolsky and Westbrook Pegler, the American Legion, Senator McCarthy, and a host of other anti-Communists. George M. Lichtman, "J. B. Matthews and the 'Counter-Subversives': Names as a Political and Financial Resource in the McCarthy Era," *American Communist History* 5, no. 1 (June 2006): 12, 13, 17, 20.

47. Isaac Don Levine, *Eyewitness to History: Memoirs and Reflections of a Foreign Correspondent for Half a Century* (New York: Hawthorn Books, 1973), xi. He interviewed Krivitsky and wrote articles about him for the *Saturday Evening Post*, introduced Krivitsky to Whittaker Chambers, and set up Chambers's 1939 interview with Assistant Secretary of State Adolf A. Berle, Jr. He also assisted Soviet defector Jan Valtin with his memoir, *Out of the Night*. For more on Levine, see Eugene H. Methvin, "Isaac Don Levine: Herald of Free Russia," www.mmisi.org/ma/37_03/methvin.pdf. Accessed December 19, 2010.

48. For other examples of left-to-right hegiras, see John P. Diggins, *Up from Communism: Conservative Odysseys in American Intellectual History* (New York: Harper and Row, 1975).

49. Schmidt, *Red Scare*, 35; Hapgood, *Professional Patriots*, 98–102; Murphy, *The Meaning of Freedom of Speech*, 197–99; Murphy, "Sources and Nature of Intolerance in the 1920s," *Journal of American History* 51, no. 1 (June 1964), 67.

50. Arthur Schlesinger, Jr., *The Politics of Upheaval* (Boston: Houghton Mifflin, 1960), 619–20. The Union Party outpolled the Socialist and Communist parties in the election, but disintegrated shortly thereafter.

51. Albert Lee, *Henry Ford and the Jews* (New York: Stein and Day, 1980), 14, 28–29, 50.

52. Dilling linked up with many of the fascist, white supremacist groups of the 1930s. In 1942, along with 27 of their leaders, she was indicted under the Sedition Act and the Alien Registration Act for conspiring to cause insubordination in the military. The trial dragged on for four years before all charges were dismissed. Dilling later became a supporter of Joseph McCarthy. See Glen Jeansonne, *Women of the Far Right: The Mother's Movement and World War II* (Chicago/London: University of Chicago Press, 1996). Natalie Robins discovered, in the FBI's files on the writers she studied, that Dilling's *Red Network* accusations can be found everywhere. In fact, "in many files the language of Dilling's book is used, word for word." *Alien Ink: The FBI's War on Freedom of Expression* (New York: William Morrow, 1992), 76.

53. Henry Steele Commager, "The New Year Puts a Challenge to Us," *New York Times Magazine* (January 1, 1939): 1–2.

54. Calverton edited *Modern Quarterly* and *Modern Monthly*, which served as fora for the independent anti-Stalinist radicals and liberals. Calverton had been a socialist, had floated within the Communist cultural orbit, and then had joined the American Workers Party after the CPUSA cultural critics had harshly criticized him and his journal. See Leonard Wilcox, *V. F. Calverton: Radical in the American Grain* (Philadelphia, PA: Temple University Press, 1992).

55. Two notable examples were Eugene Lyons, *Moscow Carrousel* (1935), and William Henry Chamberlin, *The Russian Revolution, 1917–1921* (1935).

56. Roger N. Baldwin, *A New Slavery: Forced Labor—The Communist Betrayal of Human Rights* (New York: Oceana, 1953), 18–20.

57. The letter was printed in the *Daily Worker*, August 14, 1939, and reprinted in *The Nation*, August 26, 1939, p. 228. Sometime later, Sidney Hook—a founder of the Committee for Cultural Freedom—referred to the liberal signers of the letter as "totalitarian liberals." Hook to Arthur Schlesinger, Jr., June 6, 1952, in Sidney Hook, *Letters of Sidney Hook: Democracy, Communism, and the Cold War*, edited by Edward S. Shapiro, 185 (Armonk, NY/London: M. E. Sharpe, 1995).

58. John Dewey, *Liberalism and Social Action* (New York: G. P. Putnam's Sons, 1935), 62, 91, 92; Robert B. Westbrook, *John Dewey and American Democracy* (Ithaca, NY/London: Cornell University Press, 1991), 429–30, 440, 445–51, 479. Sidney Hook called *Liberalism and Social Action* "the most remarkable piece of political writing of our generation," and, after reading it, he had no doubt that Dewey was a socialist. Hook to John Chamberlain, August 30, 1935, in Hook, *Letters of Sidney Hook*, 38–39. Some years later, however, Hook labeled Dewey as "the leading anti-Communist liberal during the Roosevelt

and Truman administrations." "Liberal Anti-Communism Revisited: A Symposium," *Commentary* (September 1967): 44.

59. John Dewey, "Declaration of Purposes by the American Committee for the Defense of Leon Trotsky," March 31, 1937, in John Dewey, *The Later Works*, edited by Jo Ann Boydston (Carbondale/Edwardsville, IL: Southern Illinois University Press, 1987), 11:304–5. According to Hook, the committee had been founded for two purposes: to help safeguard Trotsky's right to political asylum and to urge the formation of a commission of inquiry into the charges made against him during the purge trials. Hook to Arthur S. Lovejoy, February 18, 1937, in Hook, *Letters of Sidney Hook*, 46.

60. Dewey, untitled news release (December 13, 1937) and interview in *Washington Post* (December 19, 1937), in Dewey, *The Later Works*, 11:328, 331–32.

61. Westbrook, *John Dewey*, 483.

62. Ibid., 486.

63. Reinhold Niebuhr, *Moral Man and Immoral Society: A Study in Ethics and Politics* (New York: Scribner's, 1960 [1932]), 163.

64. Reinhold Niebuhr, *Reflections on the End of an Era* (New York/London: Scribner's, 1934), ix, 270–71.

65. Niebuhr, *Moral Man*, xiii, 35, 212.

66. Daniel F. Rice, *Reinhold Niebuhr and John Dewey: An American Odyssey* (Albany, NY: State University of New York Press, 1993), 22, 61. Dewey, in his 1933 reply to Niebuhr's proclamation that liberalism in philosophy was a "spent force," wrote that liberalism, as used by Niebuhr, had no relation to what Dewey was proposing (31). As late as 1949, Niebuhr was still critiquing Dewey's liberalism. See *Faith and History: A Comparison of Christian and Modern Views of History* (New York: Scribner's, 1949), 83, 95, 156, 187–88.

67. Daniel D. Williams, "Niebuhr and Liberalism," in *Reinhold Niebuhr: His Religious, Social, and Political Thought*, edited by Charles W. Kegley and Robert We. Bretall, 201 (New York: Macmillan, 1956).

68. Richard Wightman Fox, *Reinhold Niebuhr: A Biography* (New York: Pantheon, 1985), 168–71.

69. Martin, *American Liberalism*, 1:11; Ralph de Toledano, *Lament for a Generation* (New York: Farrar, Straus and Cudahy, 1960), 42.

70. Richard H. Rovere, "Factions on the Far Left," *New Republic* (April 8, 1940): 468.

71. Emma Goldman, *My Disillusionment with Russia* (New York: Crowell, 1970), xli, xlii.

72. Emma Goldman, "The Tragedy of the Political Exiles," *The Nation* (October 10, 1934): 401–2.

73. Nunzio Pernicone, "Carlo Tresca," in *Encyclopedia of the American Left*, 2nd ed., edited by Mari Jo Buhle, Paul Buhle, and Dan Georgakas, 826–28 (New York/Oxford, UK: Oxford University Press, 1998). Paul Berman recently called attention to perhaps the most significant anarchist

condemnation of Soviet communism: G. P. Maximoff, *The Guillotine at Work: Twenty Years of Terror in Russia (Data and Documents)*. This 600-plus page book, published in 1940, did not, Berman noted, seem to have made an impact. "The Prisoner Intellectuals," *New Republic* (May 27, 2010): 30.

74. John Spargo, *Bolshevism: The Enemy of Political and Industrial Democracy* (New York: Harper and Brothers, 1919); Irving Howe and Lewis Coser, *The American Communist Party: A Critical History (1919–1957)* (Boston: Beacon Press, 1957; New York: Praeger, 1962), 187.

75. Quoted in Larry Ceplair, *Under the Shadow of War: Fascism, Anti-Fascism, and Marxists, 1918–1939* (New York: Columbia University Press, 1987), 192.

76. Frank A Warren, *An Alternative Vision: The Socialist Party in the 1930's* (Bloomington, IN: Indiana University Press, 1974), 147–49.

77. See Ted Morgan, *A Covert Life: Jay Lovestone, Communist, Anti-Communist, and Spymaster* (New York: Random House, 1999).

78. Constance Ashton Myers, *The Prophet's Army: Trotskyists in America, 1928–1941* (Westport, CT: Greenwood Press, 1977); Tim Wohlforth, "Trotskyism," in Buhle et al., *Encyclopedia of the American Left*, 828–31.

79. Sidney Hook, *Out of Step: An Unquiet Life in the 20th Century* (New York: Harper and Row, 1987), 186.

80. Quoted in Ceplair, *Under the Shadow of War*, 189–90.

81. The story is well told in Terry A. Cooney, *The Rise of the New York Intellectuals: Partisan Review and Its Circle* (Madison, WI: University of Wisconsin Press, 1986); see also Alan M. Wald, *The New York Intellectuals: The Rise and Decline of the Anti-Stalinist Left from the 1930s to the 1980s* (Chapel Hill, NC: University of North Carolina Press, 1987).

82. The Committee included, among others, George Novack (Trotskyist), Suzanne La Follette (libertarian), Norman Thomas (Socialist), Reinhold Niebuhr, and Sidney Hook. The Commission included an anarchist, several former Communists, and some liberals. John Dewey chaired the subcommittee that traveled to Mexico to "interview" Trotsky. The documentation of the investigation was published in two forms, both of which served as significant anti-Soviet-communist documents: *The Case of Leon Trotsky: Report of the Charges Made Against Him in the Moscow Trials by the Preliminary Commission of Inquiry into the Charges Made Against Leon Trotsky in the Moscow Trials* (New York/London: Harper and Brothers, 1937) and *Not Guilty: Report of the Commission of Inquiry into the Charges Made Against Leon Trotsky in the Moscow Trials* (New York/London: Harper and Brothers, 1938).

83. Hook, *Out of Step*, 259. For Hook's political odyssey, see Christopher Phelps, *Young Sidney Hook: Marxist and Pragmatist* (Ithaca, NY: Cornell University Press, 1997).

84. "Statement of the L.C.F.S.," *Partisan Review* 6, no. 4 (Summer 1939): 125–27. The acting secretary was Dwight Macdonald, who had flirted with the Popular Front, but became an anti-Stalinist after reading about the Soviet purge trials. He joined the Trotsky Defense Committee and, a few years later,

the Socialist Workers Party. Michael Wrezsin, *The Life and Politics of Dwight Macdonald* (New York: Basic Books, 1994), 62–63. For the background to the founding of the League, see James B. Gilbert, *Writers and Partisans: A History of Literary Radicalism in America* (New York: Wiley, 1968).

Chapter 3: The Second "Red Scare," 1939–1941

1. M. J. Heale has called that period "the Little Red Scare." *American Anticommunism: Combating the Enemy Within* (Baltimore, MD: Johns Hopkins University Press, 1990), 123.

2. *Los Angeles Times*, September 8, 1939, p. 18.

3. Geoffrey R. Stone, *Perilous Times: Free Speech in Wartime, from the Sedition Act of 1798 to the War on Terrorism* (New York: Norton, 2004) 252; William B. Gellermann, *Martin Dies* (New York: John Day, 1944), 147, 151.

4. *New York Times*, April 7, 1940, p. 1.

5. *Los Angeles Times*, September 7, 1939, p. 8; February 23, 1940, p. 7.

6. Earl Latham, *The Communist Controversy in Washington: From the New Deal to McCarthy* (Cambridge, MA: Harvard University Press, 1966), 131–40; *Los Angeles Times*, March 27, 1941, p. 2.

7. In the months between the CPUSA's endorsement of the German-Soviet Nonaggression Treaty and his conviction, Browder was denied the right to speak at Harvard and Princeton Universities, his car was stormed by a mob after a speech at Yale University, and he was hissed and jeered at the Massachusetts Institute of Technology. *Los Angeles Times*, November 29, 1939, p. 1; December 15, 1939, p. 10. In November 1940, the Department of Justice ordered the deportation of Browder's wife, Raissa, alleging that she had entered the country illegally.

8. Henry Steele Commager, ed., *Documents in American History*, 8th ed. (New York: Appleton-Century-Crofts, 1968), 2:433.

9. Quoted in Stanley I. Kutler, *The American Inquisition: Justice and Injustice in the Cold War* (New York: Hill and Wang, 1982), 136.

10. Paul L. Murphy, *The Constitution in Crisis, 1918–1969* (New York: Harper and Row, 1972), 215–17.

11. Athan G. Theoharis and John Stuart Cox, *The Boss: J. Edgar Hoover and the Great American Inquisition* (Philadelphia, PA: Temple University Press, 1988), 172.

12. Steven Fraser, *Labor Will Rule: Sidney Hillman and the Rise of American Labor* (New York: Free Press, 1991), 460.

13. Athan Theoharis, *Chasing Spies: How the FBI Failed in Counterintelligence But Promoted the Politics of McCarthyism in the Cold War Years* (Chicago: Ivan R. Dee, 2002), 12.

14. Ever since he led the West Coast waterfront strike of 1934, Bridges, an Australian, had been a target of anti-Communists, who regularly called for

his deportation. Secretary of Labor Frances Perkins resisted until 1939, when, at the express order of President Roosevelt, she ordered a special hearing. It concluded that Bridges was not a Communist. In 1940, following the passage of the Alien Registration Act, U.S. Attorney General Jackson sent Hoover to the West Coast, to personally oversee another investigation. Hoover's report concluded that Bridges was a Communist, and Hoover leaked that conclusion to the press. Jackson ordered a new deportation hearing. Following its report, the new U.S. Attorney General, Francis Biddle, ordered Bridges to be deported. Stone, *Free Speech*, 99–109, 208–10. In the case of *Bridges v. Wixon*, the Supreme Court overturned the order. (326 U.S. 135, 1945), and, eight years later, in *Bridges v. United States*, 346 U.S. 209, the Court overturned his conviction for perjury during his deportation hearings. The editors of the *Annals of Communism* series have stated that they have discovered in the Soviet archives documents "definitely establishing Bridges' membership in the CPUSA." Harvey Klehr, John Earl Haynes, and Fridrikh Igorevich Firsove, *The Secret World of American Communism* (New Haven, CT/London: Yale University Press, 1995), fn. 24, p. 104. Be that as it may, one has to wonder whether Bridges's threat to the national security of the United States merited two deportation hearings, three trials, and two appellate proceedings. See Kutler, *The American Inquisition*, 118–51.

15. Robert Justin Goldstein, *Political Repression in America: From 1870 to the Present* (Cambridge, MA: Schenkman, 1978), 245–47; Kenneth O'Reilly, *Hoover and the Un-Americans: The FBI, HUAC, and the Red Menace* (Philadelphia, PA: Temple University Press, 1983), 62; Robert Justin Goldstein, *American Blacklist: The Attorney General's List of Subversive Organizations* (Lawrence, KS: University Press of Kansas, 2008), 19. Seven months later, more than 30 (mainly pro-Axis) organizations were added (Ibid., 25). This list, along with the indices of the annual reports of the Committee on Un-American Activities, would provide future blacklisters with all the material they needed for their work.

16. Art Preis, *Labor's Giant Step*, (New York: Pioneer, 1964), 138–43. The Communist Party, claiming that the SWP was a "Trotskyite Fifth Column" and that its members were "agents of fascism," supported the indictment (and, by implication, the use of the Alien Registration Act against political parties). According to Paul Jacobs, a former Trotskyist, the "bitter distrust of the Communists" harbored by Trotskyists and Socialists was reinforced by this episode: "the Communists were absolutely ferocious in their demands that patriotism required jailing the Trotskyists, and when they were convicted, the Communists lamented the fact that the sentences were not severe enough." *Is Curly Jewish? A Political Self-Portrait Illuminating Three Turbulent Decades of Social Revolt, 1935–1965* (New York: Atheneum, 1965), 111–12. It should also be noted that, with the exception of an article by I. F. Stone in *The Nation*, no liberal periodicals criticized the government's use of the Alien Registration Act in this case. Harvey A. Levenstein, *Communism, Anticommunism, and the CIO* (Westport, CT: Greenwood Press, 1981), 133.

17. Alexander Stephan, *"Communazis": FBI Surveillance of German Émigré Writers*, translated by Jan Ven Heurck (New Haven, CT/London: Yale University Press, 2000).

18. Goldstein, *Political Repression*, 255–58. The two best-known state investigating committees were the Joint Legislative Committee to Investigate the Educational System of the State of New York (also known as the Rapp-Coudert committee, 1940–1941) and the Joint Fact-Finding Committee on Un-American Activities in California (also known as the Tenney committee, 1941). Edward L. Barrett, Jr., *The Tenney Committee: Legislative Investigation of Subversive Activities in California* (Ithaca, NY: Cornell University Press, 1951).

19. William Z. Foster, *History of the Communist Party of the United States* (New York: International Publishers, 1952), 391; Goldstein, *Political Repression*, 258. In any event, Browder's vote total declined from 80, 160 (in 1936) to 46, 251 (in 1940).

20. *Los Angeles Times*, July 4, 1939, p. A3; July 19, 1939, p. A2; August 16, 1939, p. 1.

21. Douglas P. Seaton, *Catholics and Radicals: The Association of Catholic Trade Unions and the American Labor Movement, from Depression to Cold War* (Lewisburg, PA: Bucknell University Press, 1981), 154–55, 157, 164; Steve Rosswurm, "The Catholic Church and the Left-Led Unions: Labor Priests, Labor Schools, and the ACTU," in *The CIO's Left-Led Unions*, edited by Steve Rosswurm, 125–26 (New Brunswick, NJ: Rutgers University Press, 1992); Neil Betten, *Catholic Activism and the Industrial Worker* (Gainesville, FL: University Presses of Florida, 1976), 136–37. Richard H. Rovere noted several striking resemblances between the ACTU and the Communists. Both focused on local unions; both were controlled by a foreign entity; both were millennial in their outlook and approach. Finally, the ACTU had, on occasion, "made alliances no less cynical." For example, in the New York Newspaper Guild, it worked "both sides of the street and some of the corners." Richard H. Rovere, "Labor's Catholic Bloc," *The Nation* (January 4, 1941): 12–14.

22. Fraser, *Labor Will Rule*, 434. Following the North American strike of June 1941, Hillman recommended to President Roosevelt that he create a board to investigate subversives in the defense industry (466).

23. Victor G. Reuther, *The Brothers Reuther and the Story of the UAW: A Memoir* (Boston: Houghton Mifflin, 1976), 221; Levenstein, *Communism, Anticommunism, and the CIO*, 88–89, 94.

24. Fraser M. Ottanelli, *The Communist Party of the United States: From Depression to World War II* (New Brunswick, NJ: Rutgers University Press, 1991), 200–203.

25. Len De Caux, *Labor Radical: From the Wobblies to the CIO* (Boston: Beacon Press, 1970), 347–51, 361, 380–81.

26. Alan Brinkley, *The Publisher: Henry Luce and His Century* (New York: Knopf, 2010), 289–91.

27. Sam Tanenhaus, *Whittaker Chambers: A Biography* (New York: Modern Library, 1998), 159–62.

28. Entry dated March 18, 1952, Adolf A. Berle, *Navigating the Rapids, 1918–1971*, edited by Beatrice Bishop Berle and Travis Beal Jacobs, 2:598 (New York: Harcourt Brace Jovanovich, 1973). Berle stated that he reported everything Chambers said to President Roosevelt's appointment secretary, and that he (Berle) mentioned the matter to the president. It is apparent from Berle's three journal entries referring to the meeting with Chambers that Berle had heard several similar accounts of spies in the government and that he believed that the Foreign Agents Registration Act would solve the problem. Nevertheless, in 1941, he did inform the FBI of Chambers's list. Jordan A. Schwarz, *Liberal: Adolf A. Berle and the Vision of an American Era* (New York: Free Press, 1987), 299. Levine repeated Chambers's story to others who had access to Roosevelt—Loy Henderson (head of the State Department's Russian Section), Senator Warren R. Austin (Republican–Vermont), William Bullitt (former Ambassador to the Soviet Union), labor leader David Dubinsky, and Walter Winchell. When Winchell mentioned it to the president, Roosevelt angrily dismissed the matter. Isaac Don Levine, *Eyewitness to History: Memoirs and Reflections of a Foreign Correspondent for Half a Century* (New York: Hawthorn Books, 1973), 197–99.

29. Max Eastman, "The Communist Constitution," *The Nation* (June 4, 1938): 655. The constitution had been discussed at the Tenth Party Convention of the CPUSA, in May 1938.

30. James Burnham, *The Managerial Revolution: What Is Happening in the World* (New York: John Day, 1941), 7, 152. Although he stated that the New Deal was not yet totalitarian, he noted that it was moving in that direction, following a pattern closer to Nazism than Stalinism (257, 270).

31. James Loeb, Jr., quoted in *Atlantic Blog*, "Whatever Happened to the Americans for Democratic Action?", December 9, 2004, www.atlanticblog .com/archives;00178.html.

32. Richard Wrightman Fox, *Reinhold Niebuhr: A Biography* (New York: Pantheon, 1985), 190, 193–94,197–98. According to Fox, UDA was "a haven for former radicals in transit toward the liberalism of the Democratic Party. . . . [A] halfway house for anti-fascists eager to defend Britain and groping for a non-Socialist yet still progressive vantage point on domestic issues" (200).

33. Arthur Schlesinger, Jr., "Reinhold Niebuhr's Role in American Political Thought," in *Reinhold Niebuhr: His Religious, Social, and Political Thought*, by Charles W. Kegley and Robert W. Bretall, 150 (New York: Macmillan, 1956).

34. Goldstein, *Political Repression*, 262; Richard W. Steele, *Free Speech in the Good War* (New York: St. Martin's Press, 1994), 72. ACLU general counsel Morris Ernst was the main supporter of this purge. At about the same time, Ernst met with Dies and Hoover to arrange a *démarche* between the committee, which had accused the ACLU of being a "Communist front," and the ACLU, which had a lawsuit in the works against Dies. In 1941, Ernst worked with J. Edgar Hoover on an unsuccessful plan to force isolationist and archconservative organizations to register their officers, directors, and financial

supporters with the Internal Revenue Service. For the next 30 years, Ernst and Hoover regularly corresponded, and Ernst provided the FBI with considerable ACLU material. In addition, between 1948 and 1952, Ernst wrote numerous articles, speeches, and books extolling the FBI, including one for *Reader's Digest* titled "Why I No Longer Fear the FBI" (December 1950). Harrison E. Salisbury, "The Strange Correspondence of Morris Ernst and J. Edgar Hoover, 1939–1964," *The Nation* 239 (December 1, 1984), 575–89.

35. John P. Diggins, *Up from Communism: Conservative Odysseys in American Intellectual History* (New York: Harper and Row, 1975), 186; Tim Wohlforth, "Trotskyism," in *Encyclopedia of the American Left*, 2nd ed., edited by Mary Jo Buhle, Paul Buhle, and Dan Georgakas, 829 (New York/Oxford, UK: Oxford University Press, 1998).

36. Ted Morgan, *A Covert Life: Jay Lovestone, Communist, Anti-Communist, and Spymaster* (New York: Random House, 1999), 137.

37. W. A. Swanberg, *Norman Thomas: The Last Idealist* (New York: Scribner's, 1976), 238.

38. *Partisan Review*, Fall 1939, 125.

39. Sidney Hook, *Out of Step: An Unquiet Life in the 20th Century* (New York: Harper and Row, 1987), 262.

40. James Wechsler, "Stalin and Union Square," *The Nation* (September 30, 1939): 342–43.

41. Among those present at these meetings were Max Lerner, Granville Hicks, Richard Rovere, Joseph Lash, Paul Sweezy, Malcolm Cowley, I. F. Stone, and Leo Huberman. For a discussion of what occurred at these meetings, see Granville Hicks, *Part of the Truth* (New York: Harcourt, Brace and World, 1965), 187–88; and Richard Rovere, *Final Reports: Personal Reflections on Politics and History in Our Time* (Garden City, NY: Doubleday, 1984), 67.

42. Richard H. Rovere, "Factions on the Far Left," *New Republic* (April 8, 1940): 470.

43. Totalitarianism (*totalitarismo*) was first used by Giovanni Gentile in his study of Italian fascism, *Origine e Dottrina del Fascismo* (1929). A small number of writers during the 1930s had, in various ways, made the same association: conservatives Charles Beard, Herbert Hoover, and William Henry Chamberlin; and liberals Archibald MacLeish, Walter Lippmann, Elmer Davis, and Arthur Garfield Hays. See Les K. Adler and Thomas G. Paterson, "Red Fascism: The Merger of Nazi Germany and Soviet Russia in the Image of Totalitarianism, 1930s–1950s," *American Historical Review* 75, no. 4 (April 1970): 1046–64.

44. Frist Morstein Marx, "Totalitarian Politics," *Symposium on the Totalitarian State: From the Standpoint of History, Political Science, Economics and Sociology, Proceedings of the American Philosophical Society* 82, no. 1 (February 23, 1940): 1–38.

45. Peter F. Drucker, *The End of Economic Man: A Study of the New Totalitarianism* (London: William Heinemann, 1939), 233. It is interesting to note that

John Dewey, in a chapter titled "Totalitarian Economics and Democracy," discussed only the Marxist variant: *Freedom and Culture* (New York: Capricorn, 1963 [1939]).

46. Walter Goodman, *The Committee: The Extraordinary Career of the House Committee on Un-American Activities* (Baltimore, MD: Penguin Books, 1969), 110–16.

Chapter 4: World War II

1. Arthur M. Schlesinger, Jr. and Roger Bruns, *Congress Investigates: A Documented History, 1792–1974* (New York: Chelsea House, 1975), 2951.

2. U.S. Congress, House of Representatives, Special Committee on Un-American Activities, *Investigation of Un-American Propaganda Activities in the United States*, 78th Congress, 2d Session, September and October 1944, Appendix—Part IX, *Communist Front Organizations*.

3. Kenneth O'Reilly, *Hoover and the Un-Americans: The FBI, HUAC, and the Red Menace* (Philadelphia, PA: Temple University Press, 1983), 90.

4. When both houses of Congress approved an appropriations bill with a rider denying salaries to three employees, it was ruled an unconstitutional bill of attainder and overturned by the Supreme Court. *The Committee: The Extraordinary Career of the House Committee on Un-American Activities* (Baltimore, MD: Penguin Books, 1968), 140–42, 149–50.

5. Robert M. Lichtman, "J. B. Matthews and the 'Counter-Subversives': Names as a Political and Financial Resource in the McCarthy Era," *American Communist History* 5, no. 1 (June 2006): 7–9.

6. Michael J. Ybarra, *Washington Gone Crazy: Senator Pat McCarran and the Great American Communist Hunt* (Hanover, NH: Steerforth Press, 2004), 363–64. The ultra-conservative McCarran, a staunch opponent of the New Deal, regularly gave speeches warning about Communist subversion of education and referring to Communists as "domestic termites" (184, 238).

7. At the state level, the Joint Fact-Finding Committee on Un-American Activities in California initiated an investigation of the hiring practices of the University of California and sharply criticized UCLA's liaison with the Hollywood Writers' Mobilization and their jointly sponsored 1943 Writers' Congress.

8. Robert Justin Goldstein, *American Blacklist: The Attorney General's List of Subversive Organizations* (Lawrence, KS: University Press of Kansas, 2008), 28, 38.

9. Larry Ceplair, *The Marxist and the Movies: A Biography of Paul Jarrico* (Lexington, KY: University Press of Kentucky, 2007), 83–84.

10. *Bridges v. Wixon*, 326 U.S. 135 (1945), 145–46.

11. *Schneiderman v. United States*, 320 U.S. 118 (1943), AT 119–20.

12. Ibid., 122–23, 135–36, 154–55, 157. By a 6-3 vote (with Chief Justice Harlan Fiske Stone and Associate Justices Felix Frankfurter and Owen Roberts dissenting), the lower court's decision upholding the deportation order was reversed.

13. Sam Tannenhaus, *Whittaker Chambers: A Biography* (New York: Modern Library, 1998), 203–4.

14. Quoted in Gary Dean Best, *Herbert Hoover: The Postpresidential Years, 1933–1964* (Stanford, CA: Hoover Institution Press, 1983), 2:279.

15. George C. Herring, Jr., *Aid to Russia: Strategy, Diplomacy, the Origins of the Cold War* (New York/London: Columbia University Press, 1973),121, 123, 165, 222–23.

16. *New York Times*, October 31, 1944, p. 14.

17. Friedrich A. Hayek, *The Road to Serfdom* (Chicago: University of Chicago Press, 1944), 2, 6. Because Hayek feared the power of the state more than he did the power of corporate monopolies, business organizations purchased his book in large numbers. Theodore Rosenof, "Freedom, Planning, and Totalitarianism: The Reception of F. A. Hayek's *Road to Serfdom,*" *Canadian Review of American Studies* 5, no. 2 (Fall 1974), 150. In addition, a condensed version was published in *Reader's Digest*, which sold more than 1 million copies, and a comic-book version in *Look* magazine, which was reprinted as a pamphlet and distributed by General Motors. Jennifer Schuessler, "Hayek: The Back Story," *New York Times Book Review* (July 11, 2010): 27.

18. William L. O'Neill, *The Last Romantic: A Life of Max Eastman* (New York: Oxford University Press, 1978), 219, 220, 226.

19. Will Brownell and Richard N. Billings, *So Close to Greatness: A Biography of William C. Bullitt* (New York: Macmillan, 1987), 278. During his tenure as Ambassador to the Soviet Union (1935–1936), Bullitt had grown steadily more rancorous toward communism. In a report sent to Washington, D.C., in April 1936, he specifically stated that Soviet activity was ideologically driven: "The problem of relations with the Government of the Soviet Union is . . . a subordinate part of the problem presented to Communism as a militant faith determined to produce world revolution and the 'liquidation' . . . of all non-believers." A few months later, he told J. Edgar Hoover that Soviet leaders were making "every effort to put spies in all government agencies" (184–86).

20. William C. Bullitt, "The World from Rome: The Eternal City Faces a Struggle Between Christianity and Communism," *Life* (September 4, 1944): 100, 106, 109.

21. *Life*, July 30, 1945, 20.

22. O'Reilly, *Hoover and the Un-Americans*, 87–88.

23. Douglas P. Seaton, *Catholics and Radicals: The Association of Catholic Trade Unions and the American Labor Movement, from Depression to Cold War* (Lewisburg, PA: Bucknell University Press, 1981), 168, 171, 179.

24. Charles Owen Rice, "New Communist Line," *Pittsburgh Catholic*, June 26, 1941, reprinted in Charles J. McCallester, ed., *Fighter with a Heart: Writings of Charles Owen Rice, Pittsburgh's Labor Priest* (Pittsburgh, PA: University of Pittsburgh Press, 1996), 64.

25. Rice, "The Tragic Purge of 1948," *Blueprint for the Christian Reshaping of America*, February 1977, in McCallester, *Fighter with a Heart*, 65, 96.

26. Joshua B. Freeman and Steve Rosswurm, "The Education of an Anti-Communist: Father John F. Cronin and the Baltimore Labor Movement," *Labor History* 33, no. 2 (Spring 1992): 232, 235.

27. John T. Donovan, *Crusader in the Cold War: A Biography of Fr. John F. Cronin, S.S. (1908–1994)* (New York: Peter Lang, 2005), 16–17, 19–20, 23, 33–35.

28. Fulton J. Sheen, "War and Revolution," January 3, 1943, www.fultonsheen.com/Fulton-Sheen-articles/War-and-Revolution.cfm?articl=2; "The Thing We Are Fighting Against," www.fultonsheen.com/Fulton-Sheen-articles/The-Thing-We-Are-Fighting-Against.cfm?articl=2. Accessed December 6, 2010.

29. Patrick McNamara, *A Catholic Cold War: Edmund A. Walsh, S.J., and the Politics of American Anticommunism* (New York: Fordham University Press, 2005), 105, 199–20.

30. Harvey A. Levenstein, *Communism, Anticommunism, and the CIO* (Westport, CT: Greenwood Press, 1981), 169–70.

31. Philip Taft, *The A.F. of L. from the Death of Gompers to the Merger* (New York: Harper and Brothers, 1959), 342–47. Brown had most recently worked for the U.S. government, in Europe, as director of the Labor and Manpower Division of the Foreign Economic Administration.

32. Steven M. Gillon, *Politics and Vision: The ADA and American Liberalism, 1947–1985* (New York/Oxford, UK: 1987), 11; Niebuhr quoted in Arthur M. Schlesinger, Jr., *A Life in the Twentieth Century: Innocent Beginnings, 1917–1950* (Boston/New York: Houghton Mifflin, 2000), 263–64. Liberals did, however, reunite with Communists in new organizations, creating, in effect, a wartime popular front. Among the most prominent were the Hollywood Writers' Mobilization, CIO-PAC, National Citizens Political Action Committee, and Independent Voters Committee of Artists, Writers and Scientists for the Re-Election of President Roosevelt.

33. Aaron Levenstein, in collaboration with William Agar, *Freedom's Advocate: A Twenty-Five Year Chronicle* (New York: Viking, 1965), 10–11, 20–21, 37, 97.

34. David Dubinsky and A. H. Raskin, *David Dubinsky: In Life with Labor* (New York: Simon and Schuster, 1977), 272–76.

35. William L. O'Neill, *A Better World: The Great Schism, Stalinism and the American Intellectuals* (New York: Simon and Schuster, 1982), 44–45.

36. Ibid., 77; Sidney Hook, *Out of Step: An Unquiet Life in the 20th Century* (New York: Harper and Row, 1987), 313.

37. Hugh Wilford, *The New York Intellectuals: From Vanguard to Institution* (Manchester, UK/New York: Manchester University Press, 1995), 138–40.

38. David J. Dallin, *Soviet Russia's Foreign Policy, 1939–1942*, translated by Leon Denner (New Haven, CT: Yale University Press, 1942), 385; *Russia and Postwar Europe*, translated by F. K. Lawrence (New Haven, CT: Yale University Press, 1943), 177, 194; *The Real Soviet Union*, rev. ed., translated by Joseph Shaplen (New Haven, CT: Yale University Press, 1947 [1944]), 312.

39. See, for example, W. L. White's account of his six-week trip to the Soviet Union during the summer of 1944: *Report on the Russians* (New York: Harcourt, Brace, 1944). Although White noted that the leaders of the Soviet Union would, like leaders of other countries, move into any geopolitical vacuums, he stated that for the present the country "needs no more territory, but badly needs several decades of peace. She is, however, still plagued with suspicions of the capitalist world, and needs to be dealt with on a basis of delicately balanced firmness and friendliness" (309).

40. Barrington Moore, Jr., "The Communist Party of the USA: An Analysis of a Political Movement," *American Political Science Review* 39, no. 1 (February 1945): 31, 41.

Chapter 5: Official Anti-Communism, 1945–1948

1. Doris Kearns Goodwin, *Wait Till Next Year: A Memoir* (New York: Simon and Schuster, 1997), 10.

2. *Time*, December 31, 1945, 15, 17. According to Paul Boyer, a "primal fear of extinction" cut across all social strata, politics, and ideologies. *By the Bomb's Early Light: American Thought and Culture at the Dawn of the Atomic Age* (New York: Pantheon Books, 1985), 21.

3. James A. Wechsler, *The Age of Suspicion* (New York: Random House, 1953), 203.

4. John Houseman, "Today's Hero: A Review," *Hollywood Quarterly* 2, no. 2 (January 1947); 161. A few months later, movie director Irving Pichel stated his belief that "the unity of the war years has vanished" and that U.S. society was replete with "aggressions and strains." "Areas of Silence," *Hollywood Quarterly* 3, no. 1 (Autumn 1947): 52, 53. Continuing this Hollywood motif, director Joseph Losey claimed that he saw "an inevitable Third World War coming out of Hiroshima" as well as "the complete unreality of the American dream." Michel Ciment, *Conversations with Losey* (London/New York: Methuen, 1985), 84, 96.

5. John M. Fenton, *In Your Opinion . . . : The Managing Editor of the Gallup Poll Looks at Polls, Politics, and the People from 1945 to 1960* (Boston and Toronto: Little, Brown, 1960), 38, 43.

6. Eric F. Goldman, *The Crucial Decade—and After: America, 1945–1960* (New York: Vintage, 1960), 5, 12.

7. William H. Chafe, *The Unfinished Journey: America Since World War II*, 4th ed. (New York/Oxford, UK: Oxford University Press, 1999), 31, 79.

8. Seymour Martin Lipset and Earl Raab, *The Politics of Unreason: Right-Wing Extremism in America, 1790–1970* (New York: Harper and Row, 1970), 210–11.

9. John Lewis Gaddis, *The Cold War: A New History* (New York: Penguin, 2005), 6, 27.

10. See Melvin P. Leffler, *A Preponderance of Power: National Security, the Truman Administration, and the Cold War* (Stanford, CA: Stanford University Press, 1992), 56–59; Robert L. Messer, *The End of an Alliance: James F. Byrnes, Roosevelt, Truman, and the Origins of the Cold War* (Chapel Hill, NC: University of North Carolina Press, 1982), 120.

11. The Soviet Union's domestic cold war was authored by Stalin but orchestrated by the Soviet party's chief ideologue, Andrei Zhdanov. Hence, it came to be known as the *Zhdanovschina*.

12. The best summary of these spy cases is John Earl Haynes and Harvey Klehr, *Early Cold War Spies: The Espionage Trials That Shaped American Politics* (Cambridge, UK: Cambridge University Press, 2006.

13. Fenton, *In Your Opinion*, 84, 85. The percentage of those who, during the war, believed that the Soviet Union would continue to cooperate after the war had peaked at 55 percent in February 1945, but had declined to 41 percent by October of the same year (80).

14. Ira Katznelson, Kim Geiger, and Daniel Kryder have argued that this cross-party conservative coalition functioned only "in the single area of labor policy." "Limiting Liberalism: The Southern Veto in Congress, 1933–1950," *Political Science Quarterly* 108, no. 2 (Summer 1993): 286. These authors did not, however, examine whether it also functioned in the area of anti-communism, or the ways in which anti-communism might have tied businessmen and Congressmen together. In fact, in July 1950, a representative of the Americans for Democratic Action noted that "a strong Republican–Southern Democrat coalition" supported passage of the Internal Security Act. Quoted in William W. Keller, *The Liberals and J. Edgar Hoover: Rise and Fall of a Domestic Intelligence State* (Princeton, NJ: Princeton University Press, 1989), 38, fn. 33.

15. I. F. Stone, commenting on these publications in 1952, wrote that one could see "that behind the antics of Congressional witch-hunters, responsible businessmen have been working in an intelligent and organized fashion." "The Master Plan for American Thought Control," [*The Daily Compass?*], March 13, 1952, reprinted in Stone, *The Truman Era* (New York: Monthly Review Press, 1953), 81.

16. "Communists Within the Labor Movement" included a confidential appendix listing union and locals most influenced by Communists. See Donald F. Crosby, "American Catholics and the Anti-Communist Impulse" and Peter H. Irons, "The Cold War Crusade of the United States Chamber of Commerce," both found in Robert Griffith and Athan Theoharis, eds., *The Specter:*

Original Essays on the Cold War and the Origins of McCarthyism (New York: New Viewpoints, 1974), 28, 79–80, 85.

17. Robert Griffin, "The Selling of America: The Advertising Council and American Politics, 1942–1960," *Business History Review* 57, no. 3 (Autumn 1983): 388–412. See also Richard M. Fried, *The Russians Are Coming! The Russians Are Coming!* (New York/Oxford, UK: Oxford University Press, 1998), 29–50.

18. According to Christopher L. Tomlins, the conservative/business bloc's opposition to unions was based on its belief that the CIO represented the major obstacle against the bloc's campaign to rescind New Deal legislation: *The State and the Unions: Labor Relations, Law, and the Organized Labor Movement in America, 1880–1960* (Cambridge, UK: Cambridge University Press, 1985), 247–49. In June 1947, after several failed attempts, Congress passed, and then repassed over President Truman's veto, the Taft-Hartley Act. It included section 9(h), requiring labor unions to certify that none of their officers were members of the CPUSA. Failure to do so would result in loss of access to the National Labor Relations Board. There was remarkably little debate over this section, and only a few members of Congress specifically criticized it. See National Labor Relations Board, *Legislative History of the Labor Management Relations Act, 1947* (Washington, DC: U.S. Government Printing Office, 1959). According to Tomlins, the National Labor Relations Board members not only approved of 9(h), because it provided a tool to remove Communist influence from the labor movement, but also developed a device of their own—a "schism" doctrine. This device allowed non-Communist dissidents to challenge incumbent leaders if the union they led had been expelled from a parent body on grounds of Communist domination. The National Labor Relations Board, by this device, encouraged raids on Communist-led unions (*The State and the Unions*, 295–96, 323).

19. *Congressional Record*, 79th Congress, 1st Session, 91:1, January 3, 1945, 13. Sixteen months later, an appropriation of $75,000 was approved by a vote of 240-81. Ibid., 79th Congress, 2nd Session, 92:11, May 17, 1946, 108.

20. Rankin had been regularly criticized by the Hollywood Writers' Mobilization and the Hollywood branch of the Independent Citizens Committee of the Arts, Sciences and Professions. Rankin was also a virulent anti-Semite; Walter Goodman believes that his animus toward Hollywood was fed by the large number of eminent Jews in the movie industry. Walter Goodman, *The Committee: The Extraordinary Career of the House Committee on Un-American Activities* (Baltimore, MD: Penguin Books, 1969), 167. For a list of the hearings and reports during the period 1945–1956, see Goodman, *The Committee*, 500–12.

21. Special Agent in Charge, Los Angeles (SACLA) to Director, July 2, 1945; Hoover to Clyde Tolson and D. M. Ladd, July 4, 1945; D. M. Ladd to E. A. Tamm, July 3, 1945, Freedom of Information Act (FOIA) photocopies,

secured by Dirk Richardson, and donated to the Margaret Herrick Library, Academy of Motion Picture Arts and Sciences. Henceforth cited as FOIA.

22. *Congressional Record*, 79th Congress, 1st Session, 91:6, July 9, 1945, 7386. The FBI believed that Rankin's announcement was prompted by an event sponsored by the Screen Cartoonists Guild, to honor *New Masses* cartoonist William Gropper. On that occasion, Gropper and two other writers for the magazine proclaimed that Hollywood would become a citadel of future propaganda and cultural activity. The *Los Angeles Examiner* had devoted two hyperbolic front-page articles to that occasion. D. M. Ladd to Director, July 9, 1945, FOIA; *Los Angeles Examiner*, June 10 and June 11, 1945.

23. *Los Angeles Examiner*, June 12, 1945, p. 1.

24. U.S. Congress, House of Representatives, Committee on Un-American Activities, *Investigation of Un-American Propaganda Activities in the United States*, 79th Congress, 2d Session, November 22, 1946, 6, 24, 43.

25. *Los Angeles Times*, December 3, 1946, p. 2, and December 4, 1946, p. 1.

26. Eric Bentley, ed., *Thirty Years of Treason: Excerpts from Hearings before the House Committee on Un-American Activities, 1938–1968* (New York: Viking, 1971), 73. In her book *Stalin and German Communism: A Study in the Origins of the State Party* (Cambridge, MA: Harvard University Press, 1948), Fischer alleged that Hanns, a composer for the movie studios, and Bertolt Brecht formed the nucleus of a Communist literary and artistic group in Hollywood (615, n. 6). In 1943, the Committee had been told that Gregory Kheifets, the Soviet vice-consul in San Francisco (and a Soviet secret police agent), had traveled to Hollywood to meet with Hanns and Bertolt Brecht. Gregg Herken, *Brotherhood of the Bomb: The Troubled Lives and Loyalties of Robert Oppenheimer, Ernest Lawrence, and Edward Teller* (New York: Henry Holt, 2002), 90–92, 214–215.

27. *New York Times*, April 20, 1946, p. 16.

28. *Los Angeles Times*, May 29, 1946, p. 2.

29. David Greenberg, *Nixon's Shadow: The History of an Image* (Norton, 2003), 25; Ralph de Toledano, *Nixon* (New York: Henry Holt, 1956), 44.

30. George H. Gallup, *The Gallup Poll: Public Opinion, 1953–1971* (New York: Random House, 1972), 1:557, 590, 605.

31. David Caute, *The Great Fear: The Anti-Communist Purge Under Truman and Eisenhower* (New York: Simon and Schuster, 1978), 27.

32. Jonathan Bell, *The Liberal State on Trial: The Cold War and American Politics in the Truman Years* (New York: Columbia University Press, 2004), 43.

33. *New York Times*, February 11, 1947, p. 22.

34. U.S. Congress, House of Representatives, Committee on Un-American Activities, *Investigation of Un-American Propaganda Activities in the United States, Hearings Before the Committee on Un-American Activities, on HR 1884 and HR2122, Bills to Curb or Outlaw the Communist Party of the United States*, 80th Congress, 1st Session, March 24–27, 1947, 35–46.

35. Ibid., 244, 246, 264, 290–91, 293–96, 302.

36. *Variety*, March 29, 1948, pp. 1, 10.

37. Daniel J. Leab, " 'The Iron Curtain' (1948): Hollywood's First Cold War Movie," *Historical Journal of Film, Radio and Television* 8, no. 2 (1988),158–59.

38. SACLA to Director, October 22, 1948, FOAI.

39. For a discussion of these and the other anti-Communist films that followed, see Michael Barson and Steven Heller, *Red Scared: The Commie Menace in Propaganda and American Culture* (San Francisco: Chronicle Books, 2001).

40. *Variety*, May 7, 1947, p. 1; Robert E. Stripling, *The Red Plot Against America* (Drexel Hill, PA: Bell Publishing, 1949), 72.

41. *Hollywood Reporter*, May 7, 1947, p. 1; May 9, pp. 1, 3; May 16, p. 1; May 19, p. 1.

42. *Congressional Record*, 80th Congress, 1st Session, 93:11, June 6, 1947, A2687–88.

43. For the details of the Committee's hearings into the "Communist Infiltration of the Motion Picture Industry," see Larry Ceplair, "The Film Industry's Battle Against Left-Wing Influences from the Russian Revolution to the Blacklist," *Film History* 20, no. 4 (2008), 399–411.

44. For a detailed discussion of American Business Consultants and Aware, see David Everitt, *A Shadow of Red: Communism and the Blacklist in Radio and Television* (Chicago: Ivan R. Dee, 2007). See also Larry Ceplair and Steven Englund, *The Inquisition in Hollywood: Politics in the Film Community, 1930–1960* (Garden City, NY: Anchor Press/Doubleday, 1980), 386; Larry Ceplair, *The Marxist and the Movies: A Biography of Paul Jarrico* (Lexington, KY: University Press of Kentucky, 2007), 279, n. 11. In 1955, a group of former FBI agents founded the Mid-Western Research Library (later renamed American Security Council). It provided dues-paying corporations with information about the political associations of prospective employees. The company amassed files on more than 1 million people, co-sponsored an annual series of national military-industrial conferences, and launched an Institute for American Strategy to teach anti-communism. Sara Diamond, *Roads to Disunion: Right-Wing Movements and Political Power in the United States* (New York/London: Guilford Press, 1995), 46–47.

45. The Office of Policy Coordination had been created on September 1, 1948, and placed under the immediate supervision of the Department of State's Policy and Planning Staff. It functioned as the covert political arm of the Department of State until 1953, and, according to Tim Weiner, it rapidly became "bigger than the rest of the agency combined." Its first head was Frank Wisner, who funneled a great deal of money to the International Congress for Cultural Freedom (see Chapter 9). Burton Hersh, *The Old Boys: The American Elite and the Origins of the CIA* (New York: Scribner's and Maxwell Macmillan, 1992), 228; Tim Weiner, *Legacy of Ashes: The History of the CIA* (New York: Doubleday, 2007), 32.

46. Peter L. Steinberg, *The Great "Red Menace": United States Prosecution of American Communists, 1947–1952* (Westport, CT/London: Greenwood Press, 1984), 4, 12–13.

47. Ellen Schrecker, *Many Are the Crimes: McCarthyism in America* (Boston: Little, Brown, 1998), 42. Mandel, who had been expelled from the CPUSA in 1929 as a "Lovestonite," served as research director of the Committee from 1939 to 1945 and again from 1947 to 1951, when he moved over to the Senate Internal Security Subcommittee. Baarslag was research director of the Legion's National Americanism Commission, and he would later join the staff of McCarthy's subcommittee.

48. Ibid., 208–12.

49. Caute, *The Great Fear*, 113–14.

50. William C. Sullivan, *The Bureau: My Thirty Years in Hoover's FBI* (New York/London: Norton, 1979), 45.

51. Clark Clifford with Richard Holbrooke, *Counsel to the President: A Memoir* (New York: Random House, 1991), 177–79.

52. Memorandum dated February 14, 1947, is reprinted in Athan G. Theoharis, *The Truman Presidency: The Origins of the Imperial Presidency and the National Security State* (Stanfordsville, NY: Earl M. Coleman, 1979), 255; Robert J. Donovan, *Conflict and Crisis: The Presidency of Harry Truman, 1945–1948* (New York: Norton, 1977), 292–93.

53. Henry Steele Commager, *Documents in American History*, 8th ed. (New York: Appleton-Century-Crofts, 1968), 2:527–29. These loyalty boards employed approximately 6,000 people. It is estimated that some 13 million employees (or more than 20 percent of the national work force) fell under the shadow of a loyalty program between 1947 and 1955. Among U.S. government employees, more than 5 million were investigated, 2,700 were discharged, and 12,000 resigned. Those numbers do not include those who were investigated and discharged by the 42 states and some 2,000 city and county governments, which had their own loyalty oath programs. Geoffrey R. Stone, *Perilous Times: Free Speech in Wartime, from the Sedition Act of 1798 to the War on Terrorism* (New York: Norton, 2004), 340–41, 348, 350–51. Truman did try to maintain control over the raw data compiled by the loyalty boards. He issued a directive on March 13, 1948, prohibiting any document under the control of the Employment Loyalty Program from being sent to Congress. Robert J. Donovan, *Tumultuous Years: The Presidency of Harry S. Truman, 1949–1953* (New York: Norton, 1982), 162–63. Truman also tried to give the Civil Service Commission the predominant role in loyalty investigations, but J. Edgar Hoover prevailed on Congress to award the bulk of the authority and funding to the FBI. Steinberg, *The Great "Red Menace,"* 28.

54. Steinberg, *The Great "Red Menace,"* 40, 41, 47. A few months later, Clark told the Committee on Un-American Activities that he would continue to use the deportation statutes "to remove from among us those aliens who believe in a foreign ideology" (91).

55. Between then and October 1955, when the last names were added, nearly 300 organizations were listed. According to Robert Justin Goldstein, the list "quickly became a massively publicized, quasi-official blacklist that

was utilized in an almost unlimited variety of punitive fashions by govern-ments and private groups." Of the functioning groups on the list, nearly 70 percent were weakened or disappeared within five years of the list's appearance (*American Blacklist*, 62, 63, 66). The Department of Justice never publicly explained the criteria for selection, but in July 1949 Clark told a Senate Subcommittee chaired by Pat McCarran: "Some [of the listed organiza-tions] clearly were organized for the purpose of fostering American policy favorable to the current policy of a foreign state; others are designed to pro-mote the defense of specific individuals or to serve generally as legal defense of legal aid groups for Communists, or others who cases can be rendered into causes celebres [*sic*] to serve the ends of Communism; others again are designed to teach Communist dogma and tactics." U.S. Congress, Senate, Hearings Before the Subcommittee on Immigration and Naturalization of the Committee of the Judiciary, *Communist Activities Among Aliens and National Groups*, 81st Congress, 1st Session, Part 1, May–August 1949, (Wash-ington, DC: U.S. Government Printing Office, 1950), 321–22.

56. Quoted in Benjamin O. Fordham, *Building the Cold War Consensus: The Political Economy of United States National Security, 1949–1951* (Ann Arbor, MI: University of Michigan Press, 1998), 144–45.

57. *To Secure These Rights: The Report of the President's Committee on Civil Rights* (Washington, DC: U.S. Government Printing Office, 1947), 48–49, 164–65.

58. The decision to support a third party, arrived at slowly and reluctantly by CPUSA leaders, proved disastrous for the Communist Party. It destroyed what remained of the wartime popular front; it further divided the Commu-nist Party from its base in organized labor, which did not support the IPP; and it involved the CPUSA in a campaign that it did not fully control, a cam-paign that seemed in constant disarray. As Communist involvement grew more noticeable, the liberal exodus from IPP increased, and Wallace, who had not sought the Communist Party's support, became increasingly antago-nistic toward it.

59. Thomas G. Paterson, *Meeting the Communist Threat: From Truman to Reagan* (New York/Oxford, UK: Oxford University Press, 1988), 84; Kenneth O'Reilly, *Hoover and the Un-Americans: The FBI, HUAC, and the Red Menace* (Philadelphia, PA: Temple University Press, 1983), 176. The FBI regularly sent the White House its information on the Wallace campaign. Fordham, *Building the Cold War Consensus*, 108.

60. Lauren Kessler, *Clever Girl: Elizabeth Bentley, The Spy Who Ushered in the McCarthy Era* (New York: HarperCollins, 2003), 155–56, 179. See also Kathryn S. Olmstead, *Red Spy Queen: A Biography of Elizabeth Bentley* (Chapel Hill, NC: University of North Carolina Press, 2002).

61. Press conference, August 5, 1948, *Public Papers of the Presidents of the United States, Harry S. Truman, 1948* (Washington, DC: U.S. Government Print-ing Office, 1965), 432.

62. Address in Oklahoma City, September 28, 1948, Ibid., 609–10.

63. Kirk H. Porter and Donald Bruce Johnson, eds., *National Party Platforms, 1840–1964* (Urbana, IL/London: University of Illinois Press, 1966), 430, 436.

64. Ibid., 451–52.

65. *Los Angeles Times*, October 2, 1948, pp. 1, 2.

Chapter 6: Official Anti-Communism, 1949–1957

1. Henry Steele Commager, ed., *Documents on American History*, 8th ed. (New York: Appleton-Century-Crofts, 1968), 2:553–54.

2. *New York Times*, February 6, 1950, p. 20.

3. *Los Angeles Times*, February 8, 1950, p. 1.

4. A reconstructed version of McCarthy's Lincoln's Birthday address (the original having been lost), in Irwin Unger and Robert R. Tomes, eds., *American Issues: A Primary Source Reader in United States History*, 2d ed. (Upper Saddle River, NJ: Prentice Hall, 1999), 2:241–42.

5. *Los Angeles Times*, March 8, 1950, p. 16.

6. Quoted in Peter L. Steinberg, *The Great "Red Menace": United States Prosecution of American Communists, 1947–1952* (Westport, CT/London: Greenwood Press, 1984), 181.

7. *Public Papers of the Presidents of the United States: Harry S. Truman, 1950* (Washington, DC: U.S. Government Printing Office, 1965), 271–72.

8. Caroline H. Keith, *"For Hell and a Brown Mule": The Biography of Senator Millard E. Tydings* (Lanham, MD: Madison Books, 1991), 3–11, 36. Tydings was a conservative, and he had been one of the Democrats whose reelection Roosevelt had opposed in 1938.

9. Robert J. Donovan, *Tumultuous Years: The Presidency of Harry S. Truman, 1949–1953* (New York: Norton, 1982), 169, 174.

10. U.S. Congress, Senate, Committee of Foreign Relations, *State Department Loyalty Investigations*, 81st Cong., 2nd Sess., July 20, 1950, excerpted in Unger and Tomes, *American Issues*, 2:245–47.

11. *Congressional Record*, 81st Congress, 2d session, 96:6, June 1, 1950, 7804–05. The five other concurring senators were Charles W. Tobey (New Hampshire), Wayne L. Morse (Oregon), Irving M. Ives (New York), Edward J. Thye (Minnesota), and Robert C. Hendrickson (New Jersey). Smith later wrote: "Of the five, only Wayne Morse was to hold his ground and not show any subsequent misgivings about the statement or signs of retreat and partial repudiation." The mail response to her was overwhelmingly favorable, as were editorial comments in newspapers. McCarthy did not respond to Smith's statement, but he had her removed from the Permanent Subcommittee on Investigations, replacing her with Richard Nixon. Margaret Chase Smith, *Declaration of Conscience*, edited by William C. Lewis (Garden City, NY:

Doubleday, 1972), 7–11, 18–21. See also Janann Sherman, *No Place for a Woman: A Life of Senator Margaret Chase Smith* (New Brunswick, NJ/London: Rutgers University Press, 2000).

12. The National Maritime Union, which had recently purged itself of "Communists," was invited.

13. Ralph S. Brown, Jr., and John O. Fassett, "Security Tests for Maritime Workers: Due Process Under the Port Security Program," *Yale Law Journal* 62, no. 8 (July 1953): 1163–208. The authors concluded, after reviewing the processes for evaluation and appeal, that they were "shot through with inadequacies" (1179).

14. Special Message to the Congress, August 8, 1850, *Public Papers of the Presidents of the United States, Harry S. Truman, 1950*, 573–76.

15. Commager, *Documents*, 2:555–58.

16. Ibid., 2:558–59.

17. The Subversive Activities Control Board, as its first order of business, conducted a 14-month hearing to consider whether the CPUSA was a "Communist-action organization" within the meaning of the act. In April 1953, the board ordered the Communist Party to register as such. The Communist Party appealed the decision, which dragged through the courts for 12 years. Zechariah Chafee, Jr., *The Blessings of Liberty* (Philadelphia/ New York: Lippincott, 1956), 132.

18. George H. Gallup, *The Gallup Poll: Public Opinion, 1953–1971* (New York: Random House, 1972), 2:1010.

19. Richard Fried, "Electoral Politics and McCarthyism: The 1950 Campaign," in *The Specter: Original Essays on the Cold War and the Origins of McCarthyism*, edited by Robert Griffith and Athan Theoharis, 190–222 (New York: New Viewpoints, 1974).

20. Statement of the President, January 23, 1951, *Public Papers of the Presidents of the United States, Harry S. Truman, 1951*, 119.

21. Michael J. Ybarra, *Washington Gone Crazy: Senator Pat McCarran and the Great American Communist Hunt* (Hanover, NH: Steerforth Press, 2004), 502.

22. See Larry Ceplair and Steven Englund, *The Inquisition in Hollywood: Politics in the Film Community, 1930–1960* (Garden City, NY: Anchor/Doubleday, 1980), 361–97; Larry Ceplair, *The Marxist and the Movies: A Biography of Paul Jarrico* (Lexington, KY: University Press of Kentucky, 2007), 117–36.

23. Francis E. Walter (Democrat–Pennsylvania) had been selected, in 1949, to sit on the Committee on Un-American Activities. He chaired it from 1955 to 1963.

24. Commager, *Documents*, 2:583. Meanwhile, the Department of Justice launched a series of mass arrests of state CPUSA leaders in New York, California, Maryland, Pennsylvania, Hawaii, Seattle, Detroit, and St. Louis. Almost all were convicted of violating the Alien Registration Act. Steinberg, *The Great "Red Menace,"* 227, 232.

25. See David Caute, *The Great Fear: The Anti-Communist Purge Under Truman and Eisenhower* (New York: Simon and Schuster, 1978), 224–44. Aubrey

Finn, one of the lawyers who did pro bono work for the Los Angeles section of the American Committee for the Protection of the Foreign Born, told me he did not win a single one of the deportation cases he handled. Interview, March 8, 2005.

26. It did so in the face of a Gallup Poll, taken at the end of 1951, showing that only 143 of 2,987 Republican country chairmen thought that the Communist-in-government issue was the strongest argument that Republicans office seekers could use. Gallup, *The Gallup Poll*, 2:1021.

27. Kirk H. Porter and Donald Bruce Johnson, eds., *National Party Platforms, 1840–1964* (Urbana, IL/London: University of Illinois Press, 1966), 474–76, 498–500.

28. Lawrence R. Brown, "Eisenhower v. Taft: The Vital Issue," *The Freeman* (March 24, 1952): 393, 396.

29. Jeff Broadwater, *Eisenhower and the Anti-Communist Crusade* (Chapel Hill, NC/London: University of North Carolina Press, 1992), 20–25, 50–51; Geoffrey Perret, *Eisenhower* (New York: Random House, 1999), 491.

30. George Sokolsky, "The Conservative's Plight," *The Freeman* (September 9, 1952): 839. The gossip columnist Hedda Hopper wrote in her memoir that Sokolsky "wept openly on my shoulder" at the Republican convention, when Eisenhower defeated Taft for the nomination. Hedda Hopper, *The Whole Truth and Nothing But* (Garden City, NY: Doubleday, 1963), 280.

31. Gallup, *The Gallup Poll*, 2:1089, 1101. In fact, three contemporary surveys of voter attitudes concluded that the Communist-in-government issue per se played a very small role in the election of 1952. Angus Campbell, Gerald Gurin, and Warren E. Miller, *The Voter Decides* (Evanston, IL/White Plains, NY: Row, Peterson, 1954), 52; Louis Harris, *Is There a Republican Majority? Political Trends, 1952–1956* (New York: Harper and Brothers, 1954), 32; Alfred de Grazia, *The Western Public and Beyond* (Stanford, CA: Stanford University Press, 1954), 189–90. Samuel Lubell, however, stated that he found the Communist issue "of considerable importance"; *Revolt of the Moderates* (New York: Harper and Brothers, 1956), 265. Harris noted that the chief exploiters of this issue, McCarthy and William Jenner (Republican–Indiana) ran far behind Eisenhower in voting totals in their respective states (32). De Grazie predicted that, in the 1954 election, this issue would be far weaker and bring in fewer votes than "recession talk" (190).

32. McCarthy appointed J. B. Matthews as the staff director of the subcommittee, but Matthews was forced to resign when he wrote, in an article in *American Mercury*, that Protestant clergymen composed "the largest single group supporting the Communist apparatus in the United States." Donald F. Crosby, *God, Church, and Flag: Senator Joseph McCarthy and the Catholic Church, 1950–1957* (Chapel Hill, NC: University of North Carolina Press, 1978), 126. To replace him, McCarthy hired the Special Agent in Charge of the FBI's New York office, Frank P. Carr.

33. Richard H. Rovere used a different sports metaphor to describe McCarthy, referring to him as "a certain kind of American athlete: the kind who earns and revels in such sobriquets as killer and slugger; who looks ugly and talks ugly and wants to deceive no on this score." *Senator Joe McCarthy* (Berkeley/Los Angeles, CA: University of California Press, 1996 [1959]), 64.

34. Quoted in Edward R. Bayley, *Joe McCarthy and the Press* (Madison, WI/ London: University of Wisconsin Press, 1981), 193. Alan Barth noted: "It is a little thick to hear administration spokesmen denounce Senator McCarthy for imputing guilt by association when the loyalty boards, operating under a presidential order, had for two and a half years been condemning men on grounds of 'sympathetic association' with organizations arbitrarily called 'subversive' by the Attorney General." *The Loyalty of Free Men* (New York: Viking, 1951), 138. For Murrow's critiques of McCarthy, see Thomas Doherty, *Cold War, Cool Medium: Television, McCarthyism, and American Culture* (New York: Columbia University Press, 2003), 161–88.

35. Michael Paul Rogin concluded that McCarthy was a product of the normal routine of American politics, rooted in conservative Republicanism, and that McCarthyism was not a radical, mass movement, but rather one shaped by elites. *The Intellectuals and McCarthy: The Radical Specter* (Cambridge, MA/London: MIT Press, 1967), 59, 99, 216, 225.

36. For a gallery of these types, see Fred J. Cook, *The Nightmare Decade: The Life and Times of Senator Joe McCarthy* (New York: Random House, 1971), 275–97. For a small sampling of contemporary liberal anti-Communist critiques of McCarthy, see Jonathan Stout, "McCarthy by the Numbers," *New Leader* (March 18, 1950): 3; Granville Hicks, "Is McCarthyism a Phantom?," *New Leader* (June 4, 1951): 7; Robert Bendiner, "Has Anti-Communism Wrecked Our Liberties?," *Commentary* (July 1951): 12.

37. Roy Cohn, *McCarthy* (New York: NAL, 1968), 276.

38. Quoted in Rovere, *Senator Joe McCarthy*, 7. A dedicated group of conservative writers have regularly attempted to restore McCarthy's reputation and substantiate all his accusations, notably his conspiracy theories. See, in particular, William F. Buckley, Jr., and L. Brent Bozell, *McCarthy and His Enemies: The Record and Its Meaning* (Chicago: H. Regnery, 1954); Medford Evans, *The Assassination of Joe McCarthy* (Belmont, MA: Western Islands, 1970); Ann Coulter, *Treason: Liberal Treachery from the Cold War to the War on Terrorism* (New York; Crown Forum, 2003); and M. Stanton Evans, *Blacklisted by History: The Untold Story of Joe McCarthy and His Fight Against America's Enemies* (New York: Crown Forum, 2007). For a review of the last-named book and an analysis of the McCarthyism phenomenon, see Larry Ceplair, "McCarthyism Revisited," *Historical Journal of Film, Radio and Television* 28, no. 3 (August 2008): 405–14.

39. Joseph McCarthy, *McCarthyism: The Fight for America, Documented Answers to Questions Asked by Friend and Foe* (New York: Devin-Adair, 1952), 7.

40. Jack Anderson and Ronald W. May, *McCarthy: The Man, the Senator, the "Ism"* (Boston: Beacon Press, 1952), 359–60.

41. Ibid., January 3, 1953, 14.

42. *Congressional Record*, 83rd Congress, 1st Session, January 7, 1953, 99:1, 8357.

43. Dan Gillmor, *Fear, the Accuser* (New York: Abelard-Schuman, 1954), 43, 291.

44. At one of his first Cabinet meetings, President Eisenhower stated that his administration would adopt a sympathetic attitude toward congressional investigations already under way and cooperate with those committees. Robert J. Donovan, *Eisenhower: The Inside Story* (New York: Harper and Brothers, 1956), 85. Although Eisenhower stood fast against the anti-Communist senators who opposed his nomination of Charles Bohlen as Ambassador to the Soviet Union, he heeded Senator Taft's warning, given after Bohlen had been confirmed: "No more Bohlens!" (89).

45. Annual Message, February 2, 1953, *Public Papers of the Presidents of the United States, Dwight D. Eisenhower, 1953* (Washington, DC: U.S. Government Printing Office, 1960), 24.

46. Commager, *Documents*, 2:585–87.

47. Caute, *The Great Fear*, 208, 226, 229.

48. Chafee, *The Blessings of Liberty*, 134.

49. "Television Report to the American People by the President and Members of the Cabinet, June 3, 1953," *Public Papers, Dwight D. Eisenhower, 1953*, 375.

50. *Los Angeles Times*, October 24, 1953, 1. Secretary of State John Foster Dulles established an Undersecretary of State for Administration and Operations (i.e., an official departmental cleanser of subversives) and allowed it to operate without restraints. Ambassador to the United Nations Henry Cabot Lodge asked FBI Director Hoover to proceed with full-field investigations of all U.S. employees of the United Nations, and Eisenhower established an International Organizations Employees Loyalty Board.

51. For membership totals from 1939 to 1988, see Guenter Lewy, *The Cause That Failed: Communism in American Political Life* (New York/Oxford, UK: Oxford University Press, 1990), 307–8.

52. The polls were conducted by the American Institute of Public Opinion. Samuel A. Stouffer, *Communism, Conformity, and Civil Liberties: A Cross Section of the Nation Speaks Its Mind* (Garden City, NY: Doubleday, 1955), 24–45.

53. In his memoir, Eisenhower devoted 24 pages to internal security, but he does not mention anything about the spate of legislation in 1954. *Mandate for Change, 1953–1956* (Garden City, NY: Doubleday, 1963), 308–31.

54. State of the Union address, January 7, 1954, *Public Papers, Dwight D. Eisenhower, 1954*, 13.

55. *New York Times*, April 10, 1954, pp. 1, 8. It is interesting to note that the president, in a televised speech four days earlier, struck the same chords,

stating that the danger of Communist penetration should not be minimized, but the fear of it had "been greatly exaggerated." *Public Papers, Dwight D. Eisenhower, 1954,* 377. When it became clear that Congress was not going to pass the wiretapping bill, Brownell, in May 1954, lifted the ban preventing FBI agents from trespassing to plant bugs. Broadwater, *Eisenhower and the Anti-Communist Crusade,* 181.

56. Statement Upon Signing of Communist Control Act, August 1954, *Public Papers, Dwight D. Eisenhower, 1954,* 758–59.

57. *Congressional Record,* 83rd Congress, 2nd Session, 100:3, March 9, 1954, 2886–87. Coincidentally or not, that evening Edward R. Murrow 's *See It Now* broadcast a sharply critical profile of McCarthy.

58. Ibid., 100:6, June 1, 1954, 7389–90. For the televised hearings, see Doherty, *Cold War, Cool Medium,* 189–214.

59. Shortly after the election, Robert W. Welch, Jr., a faithful supporter of McCarthy, accused Eisenhower of double-crossing a number of conservative congressional candidates. This document, titled *The Politician,* implied that Eisenhower was either a Communist agent or a dupe of the Communist Party. Two years later, Welch founded the ultra-anti-Communist John Birch Society. J. Allen Broyles, *The John Birch Society: Anatomy of a Protest* (Boston: Beacon Press, 1964), 10–11.

60. *Congressional Record,* 84th Congress, 1st session, 101:1, January 14, 1955, 361. It was approved 84-0, with 12 senators not voting.

61. State of the Union address, January 6, 1955, *Public Papers, Dwight D. Eisenhower, 1955,* 14; State of the Union address, January 5, 1956, *Public Papers, Dwight D. Eisenhower, 1956,* 11.

62. Porter and Johnson, *National Party Platforms,* 542, 552.

63. Edward Alwood, *Dark Days in the Newsroom: McCarthyism Aimed at the Press* (Philadelphia, PA: Temple University Press paperback, 2007), 94–133.

64. In a harsh indictment of the Court, Michael E. Parrish wrote: "Since 1946 at least five of its members and sometimes seven had displayed a growing reluctance to include Communist or Communist 'sympathizers' within the protection of the Constitution and the Bill of Rights." "The Supreme Court and the Rosenbergs," *American Historical Review* 82, no. 4 (October 1977): 840.

65. *Barsky et al. v. United States,*167 F. 2d 250 (1948).

66. *Lawson v. United States* and *Trumbo v. United States,* 176 F. 2d, 52–53 (1949).

67. *American Communication Association v. Douds,* 339 U.S. 382, at 396, 406 (1950). The concurring/dissenting opinion of Justice Robert Jackson is of interest, because he compiled a list of the "important distinguishing characteristics" of communism" (424–31). As far as I can ascertain, the first mention of a "factual" list of characteristics of the CPUSA appeared in Murray Cohen and Robert F. Fuchs, "Communism's Challenge and the Constitution," *Cornell Law Quarterly* 34, no. 2 (Winter 1948): 183–85. Another list of "facts" concerning the Communist Party appeared in Board of Regents, University of

Washington, *Communism and Academic Freedom: The Record of the Tenure Cases at the University of Washington* (Seattle, WA: University of Washington Press, 1949), 30–33. Judge Learned Hand, in the majority opinion he wrote upholding the conviction of the CPUSA leaders, offered a "factual" definition: "The American Communist Party ... is a highly articulated, well contrived, far spread organization, numbering thousands of adherents, rigidly and ruthlessly disciplined, many of whom are infused with a passionate Utopian faith to redeem mankind. ... The violent capture of all existing governments is one creed of that [Party's] faith." *United States v. Dennis*, 183 F. 2d, 201, at 212 (1950).

68. http://www.law,umkc.edu/faculty/projects/ftrials/rosenb/ROS -SENT.HTM. Accessed June 16, 2010.

69. Harry Kalven, Jr., *A Worthy Tradition: Freedom of Speech in America* (New York: Harper and Row, 1988), 199.

70. *Dennis v. United States*, 341 U.S. 494, at 510-11 (1951). The Court also upheld the contempt citations and jail sentences of the defense attorneys, as well as the disbarment of one of them.

71. Paul L. Murphy, *The Constitution in Crisis Times, 1918–1969* (New York: Harper and Row, 1972), 300–06. Justice Jackson, in a case upholding the law allowing deportation for past membership in a subversive organization, took judicial notice of the Cold War: "We think that, in the present state of the world, it would be rash and irresponsible to reinterpret out fundamental law to deny or qualify the Government's power of deportation." *Harisiades v. Shaughnessy*, 342 U.S. 580, at 592 (1952).

72. *New York Times*, November 18, 1950, pp. 1, 9.

73. *Joint Anti-Fascist Refugee Committee v. McGrath*, 341 U.S. 123 (1951).

74. *Wiemann v. Updegraff*, 344 U.S. 183 (1952).

75. *Nugent v. United States*, 346 U.S., 1, at 13 (1953). Douglas, Black, and Frankfurter also dissented against the Court's decision to vacate the stay of execution against the Rosenbergs, issued by Douglas on June 17, 1953 (*Rosenberg v. United States*, 346 U.S. 273).

76. *United States v. Rumely*, 345 U.S. 41 (1953).

77. Robert P. Newman, *Owen Lattimore and the "Loss" of China* (Berkeley/ Los Angeles, CA: University of California Press, 1992), 436, 458, 483, 489; Stanley I. Kutler, *The American Inquisition: Justice and Injustice in the Cold War* (New York: Hill and Wang, 1982), 183–214. *Los Angeles Times*, May 3, 1953, p. A8; January 19, 1955, 7; *U.S. v. Lattimore*, 112 F. Supp. 507 (1953); *U.S. v. Lattimore*, 127 F. Supp., 405 (1955).

78. Caute, *The Great Fear*, 146–47.

79. *Schware v. Board of Bar Examiners*, 353 U.S. 232 (1957).

80. *Jencks v. United States*, 353 U.S. 672. His conviction was reversed by a 7-1 decision. The day the decision was announced, Congressman Walter introduced a bill to allow the U.S. Attorney General to withhold FBI files when, in his opinion, disclosure would not be in the public interest. The Eisenhower

administration also drafted its own bill. A compromise measure, accepting the principle that a defendant is allowed to see prior statements of a testifying government witness to check his or her truthfulness on the witness stand, was signed into law by President Eisenhower, on September 2, 1957. *New York Times*, June 5, 1957, p. 21; August 30, 1957, p. 1; September 3, 1957, p. 1.

81. *Yates v. United States*, 354 U.S., at 330.

82. Two years later, Congressman Francis Walter stated that the *Watkins* decision had been the most dangerous of the 1957 cases, because in it the Supreme Court had stated that "the Communist conspiracy" was a political party. U. S. Congress, House of Representatives, Committee on Post Office and Civil Service, *Federal Employees Security Program*, 86th Congress, 1st Session, April-June 1959 (Washington, D. C.: United States Government Printing Office, 1960), 7.

83. *Kent v. Dulles*, 357 U.S. 116 (1958).

84. *Albertson v. Subversive Activities Control Board*, 382 U.S. 70 (1965).

Chapter 7: Institutional Anti-Communism, 1945–1957

1. Christopher J. Kauffman, *Faith and Fraternalism: The History of the Knights of Columbus, 1882–1982* (New York: Harper and Row, 1982), 361–63.

2. Donald F. Crosby, *God, Church, and Flag: Senator Joseph Raymond McCarthy and the Catholic Church, 1950–1957* (Chapel Hill, NC: University of North Carolina Press, 1978), 18–19. For an extensive analysis of the FBI and the Catholic Church, see Steve Rosswurm, *The FBI and the Catholic Church, 1935–1962* (Amherst, MA: University of Massachusetts Press, 2009).

3. Donald F. Crosby, "American Catholics and the Anti-Communist Impulse," in *The Specter: Original Essays on the Cold War and the Origins of McCarthyism*, edited by Robert Griffith and Athan Theoharis, 23, 27–28, 31–33 (New York: New Viewpoints, 1974); Stephen Thernstrom, ed., *The Harvard Encyclopedia of American Ethnic Groups* (Cambridge, MA/London: Belknap Press, 1980), 800–1. Mindszenty was a Hungarian who had been jailed by the Nazis during the war and by the Communist Government in1949.

4. John T. Donovan, *Crusader in the Cold War: A Biography of Fr. John F. Cronin, S.S. (1908–1994)* (New York: Peter Lang, 2005), 41–49, 57–58, 61–69.

5. Fulton J. Sheen, *Communism and the Conscience of the West* (Indianapolis, IN/New York: Bobbs-Merrill, 1948), 11. His emphasis.

6. The Reverend D. P. Noonan, *The Passion of Fulton Sheen* (New York: Dodd, Mead, 1972), 25.

7. Sheen, *Communism*, 122–23; Noonan, *The Passion*, 24; Fulton J. Sheen, *Treasure in Clay: The Autobiography of Fulton J. Sheen* (Garden City, NY: Doubleday, 1980), 85, 86. After Louis Budenz left the Communist Party, he contacted Sheen, who oversaw his return to the Catholic Church (*Treasure*, 265–66).

8. U.S. Congress, House of Representatives, *The Ideological Fallacies of Communism*, Staff Consultations with Rabbi Andhil Fineberg, Bishop Fulton

J. Sheen, Doctor Daniel A. Poling, 85th Congress, 1st Session, September 4, September 25, and October 18, 1957 (Washington, DC: U.S. Government Printing Office, 1958), 13. Rabbi Fineberg was director of the American Jewish Committee's program against communism. and Dr. Poling was the editor of the *Christian Herald*. Each person met with Arens and one of his assistants, to be asked a series of questions on communism. All agreed on the need to educate the public, strengthen people's spiritual values, and support the Committee on Un-American Activities' work.

9. He did, however, at the request of the FBI, pen a scathing review of Max Lowenthal's critical book, *The Federal Bureau of Investigation* (New York: Harcourt, Brace, 1950). Patrick McNamara, *A Catholic Cold War: Edmund A. Walsh, S.J., and the Politics of American Anticommunism* (New York: Fordham University Press, 2005), 159–60.

10. Edmund J. Walsh, *Total Empire: The Roots and Progress of World Communism* (Milwaukee, WI: Bruce, 1951), 3, 104, 166, 171, 177, 205, 208–9, 259.

11. Douglas P. Seaton, *Catholics and Radicals: The Association of Catholic Trade Unionists and the American Labor Movement, from Depression to Cold War* (Lewisburg, PA: Bucknell University Press, 1981), 187, 192; Philip Taft, "The Association of Catholic Trade Unions," *Industrial and Labor Relations Review* 2, no. 2 (January 1949): 216–18. James B. Carey had been an organizer and the first president of the UE, but the Communist faction had voted him out as president in 1941, because he had supported a resolution condemning Communist activity and a constitutional provision allowing locals to bar Communists from union offices. James A. Wechsler, "Carey and the Communists," *The Nation* (September 13, 1941): 224–25. Murray appointed him CIO secretary, but insisted that Carey remain silent about communism. Seven years later, Carey, with ACTU support, organized his own faction, the United Electrical Members for Democratic Action.

12. Statements of electrician Margaret (Peg) Stasik and steel worker Joseph (Sonny) Robertson. According to Robertson, the ACTU "was a union within a union," holding its own private meetings and telling people that the officers were Communists or Communist sympathizers, trying to destroy the union. Bud Schultz and Ruth Schultz, eds., *The Price of Dissent: Testimonies to Political Repression in America* (Berkeley/Los Angeles, CA: University of California Press, 2001), 79, 89.

13. Ronald W. Schatz, *The Electrical Workers: A History of Labor at General Electric and Westinghouse, 1923–60* (Urbana/Chicago, IL: University of Illinois Press, 1983), 183, 194. Rice later admitted that he had not fought fair: "I was not really careful about their [Communists'] civil rights, because I had the feeling that they were a menace." He also regretted devoting so much time to a fight against people who were, in the main, "good unionists" and against unions, which "were the most democratic." Quoted in Schultz and Schultz, *The Price of Dissent*, 81–84. Rice also rued his association with the "horribly

conservative" and "the "bad sort" of anti-Communists in the Catholic Church. Charles Owen Rice, "The Tragic Purge of 1948," *Blueprint for the Christian Reshaping of Society* (February 1977), cited in Charles McCallester, ed., *Father with a Heart: Writings of Charles Owen Rice, Pittsburgh's Labor Priest* (Pittsburgh, PA: University of Pittsburgh Press, 1996), 97–98.

14. Tom Quinn, "To Swing a Union Election," in *It Did Happen Here: Recollections of Political Repression in America*, by Bud Schultz and Ruth Schultz, 120–22 (Berkeley and Los Angeles, CA: University of California Press, 1989). Fitzpatrick and Panzino were acquitted, but Quinn was convicted. The Supreme Court overturned the conviction (in *Quinn v. United States*, 349 U.S. 155).

15. Frank Emspak, *The Break-up of the Congress of Industrial Organizations (CIO), 1945–1950* [Ph.D. dissertation] (Los Angeles, CA: University of California at Los Angeles, 1972), 323.

16. Schatz, *The Electrical Workers*, 201–2.

17. Mark McCulloch, "The Shop-Floor Dimension of Union Rivalry: The Case of Westinghouse in the 1950s," in *The CIO's Left-Led Unions*, edited by Steve Rosswurm, 184 (New Brunswick, NJ: Rutgers University Press, 1992).

18. Seaton, *Catholics and Radicals*, 244; John Cooney, *The American Pope: The Life and Times of Francis Cardinal Spellman* (New York: Times Books, 1984), 191. Dorothy Day criticized Spellman for his use of force against the strikers, and Catholic Workers walked the picket lines. William D. Miller, *Dorothy Day: A Biography* (New York: Harper and Row, 1982), 404–5.

19. Crosby, *God, Church, and Flag*, 51–53, 98–99, 116–17, 140, 234–35. According to Christopher J. Kauffman, the Knights' anti-communism had lost its momentum in 1951. *Faith and Fraternalism*, 365.

20. M. J. Heale calculated that the number of Protestant evangelicals increased 10-fold during the 1950s. *American Anticommunism: Combating the Enemy Within, 1830–1970* (Baltimore, MD/London: Johns Hopkins University Press, 1990), 170–71.

21. Darren Dochuk, *From Bible to Sunbelt: Plain-Folk Religion, Grassroots Politics, and the Rise of Evangelical Conservatism* (New York/London: Norton, 2011), 139–51; Daniel K. Williams, *God's Own Party: The Making of the Christian Right* (Oxford, UK/New York: Oxford University Press, 2010), 39; William Martin, *With God on Our Side: The Rise of the Religious Right in America* (New York: Broadway Books, 1996), 37; Ralph Lord Roy, *Communism and the Churches* (New York: Harcourt, Brace, 1960), 228–29; Heale, *American Anticommunism*, 171. Several leaders of established Protestant churches, however, opposed McCarthy: Dr. Reuben Nelson (American Baptist Convention); Bishop James Pike (St. John the Divine); Francis B. Sayre, Jr. (Washington Cathedral); and the Presbyterian General Assembly. Crosby, *God, Church, and Flag*, 134–37.

22. Naomi W. Cohen, *Not Free to Desist: The American Jewish Committee, 1906–1966* (Philadelphia, PA: Jewish Publication Society of America, 1972), 126, 128–31, 213, 216.

23. Tony Michels, *A Fire in Their Hearts: Yiddish Socialists in New York* (Cambridge, MA/London: Harvard University Press, 2005), 222–248; Jules Chametzky, "Abraham Cahan," in *Encyclopedia of the American Left*, 2nd ed., edited by Mary Jo Buhle, Paul Buhle, and Dan Georgakas, 115–16 (New York/Oxford, UK: Oxford University Press, 1998).

24. Melech Epstein, *The Jew and Communism: The Story of Early Communist Victories and Ultimate Defeats in the Jewish Community, U.S.A., 1919–1941* (New York: Trade Union Sponsoring Committee, 1959), 293, 300, 302.

25. "The Avukah," *Harvard Crimson*, February 18, 1941. www.thecrimson .com/article/1941/2/18/the-avukah-pmany-a-scholar-and/. Accessed October 30, 2010.

26. Nathan Glazer, "An Excerpt from *From Socialism to Sociology*," www.pbs.org/arguing/nyintellectuals_glazer_2.html. Accessed October 30, 2010. For more on Avukah, see Robert F. Barsky, *Noam Chomsky: A Life of Dissent* (Cambridge, MA/London: MIT Press, 1997), 59–70.

27. Cohen, *Not Free to Desist*, 346–47.

28. Nathan Glazer, "*Commentary*: The Early Years," in *Commentary in American Life*, edited by Murray Freedman, 46–47 (Philadelphia, PA: Temple University Press, 2005).

29. *New York Times*, March 15, 1948, p. 7.

30. Paul Jacobs, *Is Curly Jewish? A Political Self-Portrait Illuminating Three Turbulent Decades of Social Revolt, 1935–1965* (New York: Atheneum, 1965), 162, 169; Victor S. Navasky, *Naming Names* (New York: Viking, 1980), 113–14, 120–21. On the one hand, Jacobs fought against Communists in the United Office and Professional Workers of America and the Los Angeles CIO Council. He also gathered material for the CIO, to use in its expulsion of the International Longshoremen and Warehousemen's Union. On the other hand, he fought, in several ways, against the motion picture blacklist, worked for the Fund for the Republic, and, he admitted later, rued some of the anti-Communist tactics he used and some of the anti-Communist allies with whom he associated.

31. Cohen, *Not Free to Desist*, 348–58; Marianne R. Sanua, *Let Us Prove Strong: The American Jewish Committee, 1945–2006* (Waltham, MA: Brandeis University Press, 2007), 76.

32. National Community Relations Advisory Council, *Joint Program Plan for Jewish Community Relations in 1953* (New York, 1953), 19. www.Jewish publicaffairs.org/www.e-guana.net/organizations/org/JointProgramPlan 1953-1.pdf. Accessed October 21, 2010. This double warning was repeated in the 1954 and 1955–1956 plan. A supplement to the 1955–1956 plan noted: "The climate is not friendly to McCarthyism. On the other hand, many of the procedures and mechanisms devised during the period of the 'scare' continue in force." *Guide to Program Planning*, 19. www.Jewishpublic affairs.org/www.e-guana.net/organizations/org/JointProgramPlan1956-1.pdf. Accessed October 21, 2010.

33. Cohen, *Not Free to Desist*, 351–53; Sanua, *Let Us Prove Strong*, 76.

34. Francis Biddle, *The Fear of Freedom* (Garden City, NY: Doubleday, 1951), 133–37. J. B. Matthews was appointed as the commission's investigator, but no public hearings were held, and the anti-Communist bills that group recommended were not passed by the legislature.

35. *Los Angeles Times*, September 18, 1948, p. A16; September 21, p. A1; September 22, p. A1. Richard Nixon also spoke at the conference, advocating the deportation of alien Communists.

36. *New York Times*, August 10, 1951, p. 5.

37. *New York Times*, May 20, 1950, p. 6; Richard M. Fried, *The Russians Are Coming! The Russians Are Coming!: Pageantry and Patriotism in Cold-War America* (New York/Oxford, UK: Oxford University Press, 1998), 67–86.

38. *Alert: A Weekly Confidential Report on Communism and How to Combat It* was published by the firm of Jacoby and Gibbons and Associates, Anti-Subversive Public Relations Specialists. Norman Jacoby, a newspaper reporter, and Edward Gibbons, who had worked with the International Alliance of Theatrical Stage Employees, began publishing this newsletter in November or December 1947, as *Alert Against Communism in California*. They also were members of the Los Angeles Conference of Civic Organizations to Fight Communism.

39. *Alert*, January 4, 1951; Blankfort to Laffin, January 10, 1951; Laffin to Blankfort, February 13, 1951; Blankfort to Zanuck, January 17, 1951; all in the Michael Blankfort Collection, Margaret Herrick Library, Academy of Motion Picture Arts and Sciences, Beverly Hills, CA. (Hereafter cited as AMPAS.) Milestone had been one of the Hollywood Nineteen (or "unfriendly" witnesses) who were subpoenaed by the Committee on Un-American Activities in 1947. He had not testified. Blankfort would appear before the Committee on Un-American Activities on January 28, 1952, as a "friendly" witness. He stated that he had not been a member of the Communist Party.

40. Robert P. Pitkin, "The Movies and the American Legion," *American Legion Magazine* (May 1953): 39.

41. J. B. Matthews, "Did the Movies Really Clean House?" *American Legion Magazine* (December 1951): 12–13, 49–56.

42. Edward A. Underwood to Wolfson, January 29, 1952; Resolution, November 6, 1951, in Vertical Files, American Legion folder, AMPAS; Pitkin, "The Movies and the American Legion," 39, 41.

43. *Los Angeles Times*, April 1, 1952, p. 4; James F. O'Neil to Y. Frank Freeman, April 3, 1952; Eric Johnston to Donald R. Wilson, April 21, 1952. The letters are in the Nedrick Young Collection, box 8, folder 6, Wisconsin Center for Film and Theater Research, State Historical Society of Wisconsin, Madison, WI. (Hereafter cited as WCFTR.) Deposition of Y. Frank Freeman, May 4, 1964, *IPC v. Loew's*, Herbert Biberman-Gale Sondergaard Collection, box 37, WCFTR.

44. Dore Schary, *Heyday* (Little, Brown, 1979), 238–41; Schary to Schenck, April 7 (unsent), July 10, and July 25, 1952, Dore Schary Collection, box 100, folder 4, WCFTR.

45. The lists, containing more than 300 names, are in the Dore Schary Collection, box 100, folder 5, WCFTR. For contemporary commentaries on the American Legion in Hollywood, see Phil Kerby, "The Legion Blacklist," *New Republic* (June 16, 1952): 14–15; "Hollywood Blacklist," *Frontier* (July 1952): 5–7; and Elizabeth Poe, "The Hollywood Story," *Frontier* (May 1954): 6–25.

46. Larry Ceplair, *The Marxist and the Movies: A Biography of Paul Jarrico* (Lexington, KY: University Press of Kentucky, 2007), 127–28, 202–3.

47. Philip Taft, *The A.F. of L. from the Death of Gompers to the Merger* (New York: Harper and Brothers, 1959), 243–51.

48. Ted Morgan, *A Covert Life: Jay Lovestone, Communist, Anti-Communist and Spymaster* (New York: Random House, 1999), 153–54, 197; Thomas W. Braden, "I'm Glad the CIA Is 'Immoral,' " *Saturday Evening Post* (May 20, 1967): 10–14. Braden also stated that he gave the Reuther brothers $50,000 to aid free German trade unions (10).

49. Harvey A. Levenstein, *Communism, Anticommunism, and the CIO* (Westport, CT: Greenwood Press, 1981), 204–05.

50. Eleven CIO unions, representing about one-sixth of the total membership (approximately 900,000 people), had opposed Truman's reelection. Not so coincidentally, they were the ones expelled. The UAW then launched jurisdictional raids on two of them, the United Electrical Workers and the United Farm Equipment Workers. David Plotke, *Building a Democratic Political Order: Reshaping American Liberalism in the 1930s and 1940s* (Cambridge, UK: Cambridge University Press, 1996), 243, n. 46; Kevin Boyle, *The UAW and the Heyday of American Liberalism, 1945–1968* (Ithaca, NY/London: Cornell University Press, 1995), 64.

51. David M. Oshinsky, *Senator Joseph McCarthy and the American Labor Movement* (Columbus, MO: University of Missouri Press, 1976), 118–121, 128.

52. Ibid., 103–9.

53. Henry Steele Commager, ed., *Documents of American History*, 8th ed. (New York: Appleton-Century-Crofts, 1968), 2:619.

54. Zechariah Chafee, Jr., *The Blessings of Liberty* (Philadelphia/New York: Lippincott, 1956), 158–59. As of 1955, no state had adopted this program.

55. Percival R. Bailey, "The Case of the National Lawyers Guild, 1939–1958," in *Beyond the Hiss Case: The FBI, Congress, and the Cold War*, edited by Athan G. Theoharis, 150–55 (Philadelphia, PA: Temple University Press, 1982); Jerold S. Auerbach, *Unequal Justice: Lawyers and Social Change in Modern America* (New York/London: Oxford University Press, 1977), 238; Kenneth O'Reilly, *Hoover and the Un-Americans: The FBI, HUAC, and the Red Menace* (Philadelphia, PA: Temple University Press, 1983), 343, n. 34. The Association of the Bar of the City of New York adopted a different position. It regularly appointed committees to study aspects of the domestic Cold War, and at

least three of them delivered critical reports. In 1948, for example, its Committee on the Bill of Rights recommended seven principles to govern the conduct of congressional investigations: *Report on Congressional Investigations*, 1948. Two years later, its Committee on Federal Legislation urged Congress not to enact the Mundt-Nixon bill (which became law the following year, as the Internal Security or McCarran Act): *Report on Proposed "Subversive Activities Control Act, 1949,"* 1950. Finally, in 1956, a special committee criticized the federal loyalty program for being too broad in scope and failing in various ways to protect, as well as it could, the interests of both the government and its employees: *Report of the Special Committee on the Federal Loyalty-Security Program* (New York: Dodd, Mead, 1956). Also, the Bar Association of the City of Chicago's Committee on Civil Rights strongly opposed state anti-Communist bills in 1949 and 1951. Biddle, *The Fear of Freedom*, 151, 153.

56. Arnold Forster, *Square One* (New York: Donald I. Fine, 1988), 117.

57. Rushmore, a former Communist, testified as a friendly witness at the 1947 hearings of the Committee on Un-American Activities into Communist infiltration of the motion picture industry. He later became an investigator for McCarthy, but had to resign when he could not hide his disdain for Roy Cohn. When he refused to stop criticizing Cohn in his columns, Rushmore was fired from the newspaper. Jay Maeder, "Turncoat: The Estrangements of Howard Rushmore, January 1958, Chapter 282," *New York Daily News*, February 26, 2001. www.nydailynews.com/archives/news/2001/02/26/200i _02_26_turncoat_the-estrangements_o.html. Accessed August 21, 2010.

58. Woltman was the only one of this group to change his mind on McCarthy. After 16 years of exposing Communists in his column, and after winning a Pulitzer Prize in 1948 for a series of articles on Communist infiltration, he wrote, in July 1954, a five-part series of articles in the *New York World-Telegram* (Scripps-Howard), in which he stated that McCarthy was "a major liability to the cause of anti-Communism" and an asset to communism. "About McCarthy," *Time* (July 19, 1954): 61–62.

59. Lasky assisted Woltman with his Communist-infiltration series and then co-wrote, with Ralph de Toledano, *Seeds of Treason: The True Story of the Hiss-Chambers Tragedy* (New York: Funk and Wagnalls, 1950).

60. Victor Riesel was a veteran labor reporter when he switched his syndicated column from the *New York Post* to the Hearst newspapers in 1948. He investigated "Communist infiltration" of the National Maritime Union, and provided material on other union "infiltrations" to McCarran's subcommittee. John Cogley, in an interim memorandum of his work on blacklisting in the entertainment industries, *Report on Blacklisting*, noted that once the blacklist had been institutionalized, it was "presided over by an informal 'board of directors,' " among whom were Sokolsky and Reisel. "Résumé of the Blacklisting Project," Fund for the Republic Collection, Seeley G. Mudd Manuscript Library, Princeton University, box 85, folder 12, [3].

61. Henry Luce, although he had purged most of the left-leaning writers from *Time* and *Life*, seldom associated himself with the Hearst and McCormick newspapers. In addition, he displayed an early and strong distaste for McCarthy. Alan Brinkley, *The Publisher: Henry Luce and His Century* (New York: Knopf, 2010), 342, 360. Ironically, when his employee, Whittaker Chambers, admitted in his testimony to the Committee on Un-American Activities that he had been a Communist, conservative columnists accused Luce of harboring a Communist, and Luce fired Chambers (358). At one point, McCarthy called Luce a "debased, degraded, degenerate liar." Richard H. Rovere, *Senator Joe McCarthy* (Berkeley/Los Angeles, CA: University of California Press, 1996 [1959]), 73.

62. See Charles Wertenbaker, "The China Lobby," *The Reporter* (April 15, 1952): 4–24; Philip Horton, "The China Lobby: Part II," *The Reporter* (April 29, 1952): 5–18; Ross Y. Koen, *The China Lobby in American Politics* (New York: Octagon Books, 1974); Stanley D. Bachrack, *The Committee of One Million: "China Lobby" Politics, 1953–1971* (New York: Columbia University Press, 1976).

63. John N. Thomas, *The Institute of Pacific Relations: Asian Scholars and American Politics* (Seattle, WA/London: University of Washington Press, 1974, 39–44.

64. Joseph Keeley, *The China Lobby Man: The Story of Alfred Kohlberg* (New Rochelle, NY: Arlington House, 1969), 75–77, 98–99, 196–97, 235. Keeley was an unabashed admirer of Kohlberg. *Plain Talk* was absorbed by *The Freeman* in 1950.

65. Alan Brinkley states that Luce was not as "fevered a member of the China Lobby" as Kohlberg. *The Publisher*, 341, 366.

66. Thomas, *The Institute of Pacific Relations*, 49.

67. The first fully researched, purportedly objective history of the CPUSA was written by Irving Howe and Lewis Coser, *The American Communist Party: A Critical History (1919–1957)* (Boston: Beacon Press, 1957).

68. Julien Steinberg, ed., *Verdict of Three Decades: From the Literature of the Individual Revolt Against Soviet Communism* (New York: Duell, Sloan and Pearce, 1950), 416. It included excerpts from the writings of several people who have been previous noted: Alexander Berkman, Emma Goldman, Max Eastman, Eugene Lyons, W. H. Chamberlin, Leon Trotsky, Walter Krivitsky, Louis Budenz, and Sidney Hook.

69. Stephen J. Whitfield, *Into the Dark: Hannah Arendt and Totalitarianism* (Philadelphia, PA: Temple University Press, 1980), 13.

70. Hannah Arendt, *The Origins of Totalitarianism* (New York: Schocken, 2004), 509–11, 563.

71. Carl J. Friedrich, "The Problem of Totalitarianism: An Introduction," in *Totalitarianism: Proceedings of a Conference Held at the American Academy of Arts and Sciences, March 1953*, edited by Carl J. Friedrich, 3 (Harvard University Press, 1954).

72. George F. Kennan, "Totalitarianism in the Modern World," in *Totalitarianism: Proceedings of a Conference Held at the American Academy of Arts and Sciences, March 1953*, edited by Carl J. Friedrich, 19 (Harvard University Press, 1954). In a brief remark in a later discussion, George Denicke stated his belief that "no adequate general concept [of totalitarianism] can be defined" (75).

73. Ibid., 83.

74. Paul Kecskemeti, "Totalitarianism and the Future," in *Totalitarianism: Proceedings of a Conference Held at the American Academy of Arts and Sciences, March 1953*, edited by Carl J. Friedrich, 345, 357 (Harvard University Press, 1954).

75. Merle Fainsod, *How Russia Is Ruled* (Cambridge, MA: Harvard University Press, 1954), 499–500.

76. Anthony T. Bouscaren, *Imperial Communism* (Washington, DC: Public Affairs Press, 1953), 3–4.

77. C. Groves Haines, ed., *The Threat of Soviet Imperialism* (Baltimore, MD: Johns Hopkins University Press, 1954), xv–xvi. Ten academics and 29 government officials and journalists participated.

Chapter 8: Ex-Communist and Conservative Anti-Communism, 1945–1957

1. Lionel Abel, *The Intellectual Follies: A Memoir of the Literary Venture in New York and Paris* (New York: Norton, 1984), 61.

2. Between July 1953 and April 1955, the Department of Justice paid slightly more than $43,000 to 59 internal security witnesses or consultants. Lautner was the highest paid, receiving just over $16,000. *New York Times*, August 24, 1955, p. 23.

3. Herbert L. Packer, *Ex-Communist Witnesses: Four Studies in Fact Finding* (Stanford, CA: Stanford University Press, 1962), 124, 176, 183, 185, 225. In 1954, Budenz's *The Techniques of Communism* (Chicago: Henry Regnery) was published. He described it as an "inquiry into the nature and operations of Communism as a basis for combating it" (viii).

4. *Congressional Record*, 81st Congress, 2nd Session, 96:5, May 12, 1950, 6969–73. Chavez, a Catholic, also questioned Budenz's recent conversion to Catholicism, accusing him of "investing his appearances and utterances with an added sanctity by virtue of the fact that he recently went through the forms of conversion to Catholicism."

5. Joseph Alsop, "The Strange Case of Louis Budenz," *The Atlantic* 189 (April 1952): 29, 30.

6. Richard H. Rovere, "The Adventures of Cohn and Schine," *The Reporter* (July 21, 1953): 10. After examining material from the Soviet archives and the Venona decrypts, John Earl Haynes and Harvey Klehr wrote that Budenz gave correct information about five of the people they studied. *Venona:*

Decoding Soviet Espionage in America (New Haven, CT/London: Yale University Press, 1999), 222–23, 234, 261–62. They do not comment on his overall veracity. See also Herbert Romerstein and Eric Breindel, *The Venona Secrets: Exposing Soviet Espionage and America's Traitors* (Washington, DC: Regnery, 2000), 342–44, 360.

7. Richard H. Rovere, "The Kept Witnesses," *Harper's* (May 1955): 34.

8. U.S. Congress, Senate, *Strategy and Tactics of World Communism (Significance of the Matusow Case)*, Report of the Subcommittee to Investigate the Administration of the Internal Security Act and Other Internal Security Laws, to the Committee on the Judiciary, United States Senate, 84th Congress, 1st Session, April 6, 1955, 1.

9. For an interesting account of the publication story, see Albert E. Kahn, *The Matusow Affair: Memoir of a National Scandal* (Mt. Kisco, NY: Moyer Bell, 1987). See also Robert M. Lichtman and Ronald D. Cohen, *Deadly Farce: Harvey Matusow and the Informer System in the McCarthy Era* (Urbana/Chicago, IL: University of Illinois Press, 2005).

10. Meyer, who had joined the Communist Party of Great Britain in 1930, transferred to the CPUSA in 1934, and left the Communist Party in 1945, wrote for *The Freeman, American Mercury*, and *National Review* See Kevin J. Smant, *Principles and Heresies: Frank S. Meyer and the Shaping of the American Conservative Movement* (Wilmington, DE: ISI Books, 2002).

11. Chambers to Buckley, February 7, 1954, in Whittaker Chambers, *Odyssey of a Friend: Whittaker Chambers's Letters to William F. Buckley, Jr., 1954–1961*, edited by William F. Buckley, Jr. (New York: G. P. Putnam's Sons, 1969), 50–51.

12. Chambers to Buckley, August 6, 1954 (69), November 28, 1954 (97–88), and January 7, 1955 (98), in Chambers, *Odyssey of a Friend*. Chambers never detailed his counter-revolutionary strategy.

13. His first article was "Soviet Strategy in the Middle East," *National Review* (August 31, 1957): 371–75.

14. U.S. Congress, Senate, Hearing Before the Permanent Subcommittee on Investigations of the Committee on Government Operations, *State Department Information Program—Information Centers*, 83rd Congress, 1st Session, Part 4, April 24, 1953 (Washington, DC: U.S. Government Printing Office, 1953), 272. Rushmore continued to write his newspaper column while he worked as research director for McCarthy's subcommittee. According to Wechsler: "It [was] a matter of open knowledge in the newspaper business that Mr. Rushmore ... [was] a continual news source for Mr. [Walter] Winchell." Ibid., Part 5, May 5, 1953, 297. Roy Cohn was also a regular source of information for Winchell.

15. Hamilton Fish, *The Challenge of World Communism* (Milwaukee, WI: Bruce, 1946), vii, x, 148–49, 176. Ironically, Fish provided the most extensive list of anti-Communists yet published. He "named," as "effective and constructive anti-Communists," the Catholic Church, AFL, American Legion, Veterans of Foreign Wars, Chamber of Commerce, several fraternal

organizations, Martin Dies, Walter Steele, and three newspaper chains (Hearst, McCormick, and Patterson). He then "named" 37 "uncompromising foes," including 4 newspaper columnists and 15 Congressmen (144–46).

16. U.S. Congress, House of Representatives, Committee on Un-American Activities, *Investigation of Un-American Propaganda Activities in the United States*, 80th Congress, 1st Session, March 24, 1947, 5.

17. James Burnham, testimony before the Un-American Activities Committee of the House of Representatives, February 19, 1948, excerpted in Eric Bentley, ed., *Thirty Years of Treason: Excerpts from Hearings before the House Committee on Un-American Activities, 1938–1968* (New York: Viking, 1971), 275, 276, 287. Burnham was perhaps the most influential conservative anti-Communist. He wrote four books on the subject; he was consulted by CIA official Frank Wisner about ways to challenge the Soviet-sponsored peace conferences of 1949; he was intimately involved in planning the invitation list of the counter effort, the Congress for Cultural Freedom, held in Berlin, in June 1950; and he became an intellectual mentor to William F. Buckley, Jr., who called him "the number-one intellectual influence on *National Review*." Quoted in Joshua Muravchik, "Renegades," *Commentary* (October 2002): 86. For his speech to the Congress for Cultural Freedom, see "Rhetoric and Peace," *Partisan Review* 17, no. 8 (November–December 1950): 870–71. His books were *The Struggle for the World* (New York: John Day, 1947), *The Coming Defeat of Communism* (New York: John Day, 1950), *Containment or Liberation: An Inquiry into the Aims of United States Foreign Policy* (New York: John Day, 1953), and *The Web of Surveillance: Underground Networks in the U.S. Government* (New York: John Day, 1954). According to Townsend Hoopes, *The Coming Defeat* "struck profoundly sympathetic chords in important segments of the State Department, the CIA, and among military planners in the Pentagon." *The Devil and John Foster Dulles* (Boston/Toronto: Little, Brown, 1973), 118.

18. Peter Viereck, *Conservatism Revisited: The Revolt Against Revolt, 1815–1949* (New York: Scribner's, 1949), x.

19. For other discussions of divisions in conservative ranks, see J. David Hoeveler, Jr., *The New Humanism: A Critique of Modern America, 1900–1940* (Charlottesville, VA: University Press of Virginia, 1977), 185; George H. Nash, *The Conservative Intellectual Movement in America Since 1945* (New York: Basic Books, 1976), 87–97; Ronald Lora, "Conservative Intellectuals, the Cold War, and McCarthy," in *The Specter: Original Essays on the Cold War and the Origins of McCarthyism*, edited by Robert Griffith and Athan Theoharis, 48–53 (New York: New Viewpoints, 1974); Richard Gid Powers, *Not Without Honor: The History of American Anti-Communism* (New York: Free Press, 1995),181–82.

20. Quoted in Gary Dean Best, *Herbert Hoover: The Postpresidential Years, 1933–1964* (Stanford, CA: Hoover Institution Press, 1983), 2:285, 296, 332.

21. See Ronald Radosh, *Prophets on the Right: Profiles of Conservative Critics of American Globalism* (New York: Simon and Schuster, 1975), 147–95.

22. Benjamin O. Fordham, *Building the Cold War Consensus: The Political Economy of the U.S. National Security Policy, 1949–51* (Ann Arbor, MI: University of Michigan Press, 1998), 67.

23. John W. Malsberger, *From Obstruction to Moderation: The Transformation of Senate Conservatism, 1938–1952* (Selinsgrove, PA: Susquehanna University Press; London: Associated University Presses, 2000), 12–16. In fact, in early 1950, three Republican drafted a "Declaration of Republican Principles," calling attention to the differences between the two blocs' domestic policies (218–19).

24. Athan G. Theoharis, *The Yalta Myths: An Issue in U.S. Politics, 1945–1955* (Columbia, MO: University of Missouri Press, 1970), 5–7, 70, 97. According to Theoharis, these three types united only in the years between the 1948 and 1952 elections, motivated mainly by the Hiss case and the Korean War.

25. Smant, *Principles and Heresies*, 28.

26. John Chamberlain, "Foreword," in *American Liberalism and World Politics, 1931–1941: Liberalism's Press and Spokesmen on the Road Back to War Between Mukden and Pearl Harbor*, by James J. Martin, 1:vi–viii (New York: Devin-Adair, 1964).

27. Ralph de Toledano, "The Liberal Disintegration: A Conservative View," *The Freeman* (November 13, 1950): 109, 111; *Lament for a Generation* (New York: Farrar, Straus and Cudahy, 1960), 103.

28. Peter Viereck, *Shame and Glory of the Intellectuals: Babbitt Jr. vs. the Rediscovery of Values* (Boston: Beacon Press, 1953), 6, 102, 107, 173, 175, 286.

29. "The Faith of *The Freeman*," *The Freeman* (October 2, 1950): 5. When Frank Chodorov became editor of *The Freeman*, he stated that the magazine was no more opposed to communism than it was to other forms of authoritarianism, and stressed that emphasis on the "threat" of communism diverted attention from the "the threats of equal potency" in the United States. "An Editorial Problem," *The Freeman* (September 1955): 630.

30. Russell Kirk, *A Program for Conservatives* (Chicago: Henry Regnery, 1954), 2, 4, 5, 23, 259–60.

31. John B. Judis, *William F. Buckley: Patron Saint of the Conservatives* (New York: Simon and Schuster, 1988), 67, 71.

32. William F. Buckley, Jr., *God and Man at Yale: The Superstitions of "Academic Freedom"* (Chicago: Henry Regnery, 1951), xv.

33. William F. Buckley, Jr., "The Party and the Deep Blue Sea," *Commonweal* (January 25, 1952): 392–93.

34. Garry Wills, *Confessions of a Conservative* (Garden City, NY: Doubleday, 1979), 33, 36. The left-wing anti-Communist, Dwight Macdonald, wrote a highly polemical analysis of its first 10 issues, labeling the editors and contributors "McCarthy nationalists," who, despite their "heroic" effort "to be intellectually articulate," had expressed the ideas and style "of the lumpen-bourgeoisie, the half-educated, half-successful provincials" who were "anxious, embittered, resentful." "Scrambled Eggheads on the Right:

Mr. Buckley's New Weekly," *Commentary* (April 1956): 367. For Buckley's response to Macdonald and two other liberal critics of his magazine, see "Reflections on the Failure of 'National Review' to Live Up to Liberal Expectations," *National Review* (August 1, 1956): 7–12.

35. "Should Conservatives Vote for Eisenhower?," *National Review* (October 20, 1956): 15. James Burnham argued the pro side of this question.

36. All of this information is taken from James T. Patterson, *Mr. Republican: A Biography of Robert A. Taft* (Boston: Houghton Mifflin, 1972).

37. Robert A. Taft, *A Foreign Policy for Americans* (Garden City, NY: Doubleday, 1951), 19, 114–21.

38. Ronald W. Preussen, *John Foster Dulles: The Road to Power* (New York: Free Press, 1982), 288.

39. John Foster Dulles, "Thoughts on Soviet Foreign Policy and What to Do About It," *Life* (June 3, 1946): 112–26; (June 10, 1946): 118–30. It is of interest to note that his brother, Allen Dulles, who would later be director of the Central Intelligence Agency, in his response to a draft of the *Life* articles, wrote that some issues dividing the two countries could still be negotiated and settled, and that political "maneuver and pressure"—not immediate confrontation—was the best approach. Peter Grose, *Gentleman Spy: The Life of Allen Dulles* (Boston/New York: Houghton Mifflin, 1994), 267–70.

40. Quoted in Irwin F. Gellman, *The Contender: Richard Nixon—The Congress Years, 1946–1952* (New York: Free Press, 1999), 155.

41. John Foster Dulles, *War or Peace* (New York: Macmillan, 1950), 2, 3, 253, 259, 261.

42. Hoopes, *The Devil and John Foster Dulles*, 83, 87–88, 94, 114–15, 124–25, 131.

43. John Foster Dulles, "A Policy of Boldness," *Life* (May 19, 1952): 151. His emphasis.

44. H. W. Brands, Jr., *Cold Warriors: Eisenhower's Generation and American Foreign Policy* (New York: Columbia University Press, 1988), 3, 14.

45. John Lewis Gaddis, "The Unexpected John Foster Dulles," in *John Foster Dulles and the Diplomacy of the Cold War*, edited by Richard H. Immerman, 61 (Princeton, NJ: Princeton University Press, 1990).

46. Gellman, *The Contender*, 27, 32. According to Gellman, Nixon had, at that time, only the vaguest notion of the Soviet "threat" (107).

47. Ibid., 100, 114, 119. Gellman states that Nixon's anti-Communist voice was a moderate one (161).

48. *Congressional Record*, 81st Congress, 2nd Session, 96:1, January 26, 1950, 1000, 1004, 1006–7.

49. Quoted in Herbert S. Parmet, *Richard Nixon and His America* (Boston: Little, Brown, 1990), 113, 141, 186. For a detailed account of this contest, see Greg Mitchell, *Tricky Dick and the Pink Lady: Richard Nixon Versus Helen Gahagan Douglas—Sexual Politics and the Red Scare, 1950* (New York: Random House, 1998).

50. Gellman, *The Contender*, 363, 365.

51. www.historyplace.com/speeches/nixon-checkers.htm. Accessed October 19, 2009.

52. Isaac Don Levine, *Eyewitness to History: Memoirs and Reflections of a Foreign Correspondent for Half a Century* (New York: Hawthorn Books, 1973), 177–78.

53. Peter Viereck, "The Revolt Against the Elite," in *The New American Right*, edited by Daniel Bell, 94–96, 102, 111 (New York: Criterion Books, 1955).

54. Handicapper, "These 'Liberal' Journalists," *Human Events* (December 22, 1954): np. Harry Dexter White, former Assistant Director in the Department of the Treasury, who had been nominated by Truman to serve as executive director of the International Monetary Fund, had been named by Elizabeth Bentley and Whittaker Chambers of being part of a Washington, D.C., spy ring. He denied the accusation, appeared before the Committee on Un-American Activities, and died three days later. In 1953, J. Edgar Hoover and Herbert Brownell, Jr., publicly charged Truman with ignoring FBI warnings about White.

55. William F. Buckley, Jr., and L. Brent Bozell, *McCarthy and His Enemies: The Record and its Meaning* (Chicago: Henry Regnery, 1954), 246, 277, 331. According to Judis, the authors showed a draft of the manuscript to the senator and agreed to tone down or remove some of their criticisms (*William F. Buckley*, 108). Three years earlier, Buckley had written: "If we want a full-dress investigation of the personnel of the State Department, we must support Senator McCarthy, despite some of his crass inconsistencies." "Senator McCarthy's Model?," *The Freeman* (May 21, 1951): 533. For its part, *The Freeman* printed another article criticizing McCarthy; an exchange between that author and McCarthy; and an editorial calling McCarthyism "an invention of the Communists." But, in 1954, another editorial questioned the tactics McCarthy was using in his investigation of the U.S. Army, and it had nothing to say about his condemnation by the Senate. Towner Phelan, "Modern School for Scandal," *The Freeman* (September 24, 1951): 813–17; Towner Phelan and Joseph McCarthy, "Is McCarthy Guilty of 'McCarthyism'?," *The Freeman* (February 11, 1952): 297–301; " 'McCarthyism': Communism's New Weapon," *The Freeman* (December 14, 1953): 187; untitled editorial, *The Freeman* (March 22, 1954): 437.

56. De Toledano, *Lament for a Generation*, 177, 206.

57. Max Eastman, "Facts and Logic on McCarthy," *The Freeman* (April 19, 1954): 534.

58. John P. Diggins, *Up from Communism: Conservative Odysseys in American Intellectual History* (New York: Harper and Row, 1975), 326–29.

59. Richard H. Rovere, *Senator Joe McCarthy* (Berkeley/Los Angeles, CA: University of California Press, 1996 [1959]), 135.

60. Richard Rovere, *Final Reports: Personal Reflections on Politics and History in Our Time* (Garden City, NY: Doubleday, 1984), 121–24.

61. David W. Reinhard, *The Republican Right Since 1945* (Lexington, KY: University Press of Kentucky, 1983), 77, 117. Taft's successor as Republican leader, Senator William F. Knowland (Republican–California), acted in a similar manner, publicly commending McCarthy's effort to expose and purge Communists from the U.S. government, while privately lamenting his "tendency to overstate his case." He did not, however, attempt to rein in McCarthy. Gayle B. Montgomery and James W. Johnson, *One Step from the White House: The Rise and Fall of Senator William F. Knowland* (Berkeley/Los Angeles, CA: University of California Press, 1998), 129–30.

62. William Bragg Ewald, Jr., *Who Killed Joe McCarthy?* (New York: Simon and Schuster, 1984), 66, 148, 167–72, 379. The planners, who first met on January 21, 1954, were Attorney General Herbert Brownell, Jr., Deputy Attorney General William P. Rogers, United Nations Ambassador Henry Cabot Lodge, Jr., Army legal counsel John Adams, White House Chief of Staff Sherman Adams, and congressional liaison Jerry Morgan. Prior to this meeting, Sherman Adams, Robert Cutler (Special Assistant for National Security), and C. D. Jackson (special assistant for psychological warfare) had, individually, been pushing President Eisenhower to confront McCarthy.

63. Earl Mazo, *Richard Nixon: A Political and Personal Portrait* (New York: Harper and Brothers, 1959), 140–41, 144, 148–49. Samuel Lubell dubbed Nixon the administration's go-to person "when the White House sought to take the play away from McCarthy on the 'Communist' issue." *Revolt of the Moderates* (New York: Harper and Brothers, 1956), 87.

64. Ralph de Toledano, *Nixon* (New York: Henry Holt, 1956), 171–72, 177.

65. Hoopes, *The Devil and John Foster Dulles*, 153–57. Although he did not cave in to the campaign of conservative anti-Communist Senators against the confirmation of Charles Bohlen as Ambassador to the Soviet Union, Dulles maintained a chilly distance from him (160). According to Bohlen, Dulles never questioned his loyalty, but he was very, very nervous about the confirmation process, and he did not rein in McLeod, who was, Bohlen thought, leaking material to McCarthy and others. Charles E. Bohlen, *Witness to History, 1929–1969* (New York: Norton, 1973), 309–36.

66. Brands, *Cold Warriors*, 13. Dulles had played a large role in making Hiss president of the Carnegie Endowment for International Peace; in the process, had disregarded two letters accusing Hiss of Communist affiliations: Gellman, *The Contender*, 208. Rovere called Dulles "almost gutless in the McCarthy period": *Final Reports*, 145.

67. Ayn Rand, *Journals of Ayn Rand*, edited by David Harriman (New York: Dutton, 1997), 59.

68. Letter to Jean Wick, March 23, 1934, in Ayn Rand, *Letters of Ayn Rand*, edited by Michael S. Berliner (New York: Dutton, 1995), 4. Her emphasis.

69. Letter to Jean Wick, October 27, 1934, in Rand, *Letters of Ayn Rand*, 19.

70. An autobiographical note to her publisher, February 2, 1936, in Rand, *Journals of Ayn Rand*, 65.

71. Rand, "To All Innocent Fifth Columnists," *Journals of Ayn Rand*, 348, 352.

72. Letter to Channing Pollock, July 20, 1941, in Rand, *Letters of Ayn Rand*, 54. Her emphasis.

73. Letter to DeWitt Emery, May 17, 1943, in Rand, *Letters of Ayn Rand*, 73.

74. Letter to Leonard Read, November 12, 1944, in Rand, *Letters of Ayn Rand*, 171. In a later letter to Read, Rand wrote that conservatives did not know how to defend capitalism (259). In fact, she believed that "pinks" had taken over the formerly respectable conservative journals (306).

75. According to Roy Brewer, Rand was a loner in the Motion Picture Association. Although she wrote its declaration of principles and the "Screen Guide," Brewer stated that she did not have an important impact and did not influence very many people, mainly because none of the other members shared her extreme anti-government position. Scott McConnell, ed., *100 Voices: An Oral History of Ayn Rand* (New York: NAL, 2010), 75.

76. Rand, "Screen Guide for Americans," reprinted in Rand, *Journals of Ayn Rand*, 356–66; Rand to De Witt Emery, April 17, 1948, in Rand, *Letters of Ayn Rand*, 395.

77. Ayn Rand, testimony before the Un-American Activities Committee of the House of Representatives, excerpted in Bentley, *Thirty Years of Treason*, 111–19. One of her followers, Robert Mayhew, has attempted to shore up Rand's testimony in a rather silly article and a rather long rant: "MGM's Potemkin Church: Religion in *Song of Russia*," *American Communist History* 1, no. 1 (June 2002): 91–103; *Ayn Rand and Song of Russia: Communism and Anti-Communism in 1940s Hollywood* (Lanham, MD: Scarecrow Press, 2005).

78. Letter to Henry Hazlitt, December 25, 1950, in Rand, *Letters of Ayn Rand*, 485. Her emphasis.

79. Anne C. Heller, *Ayn Rand and the World She Made* (New York: Doubleday, 2009), 245–47, 251.

80. Jennifer Burns, *Goddess of the American Market: Ayn Rand and the American Right* (New York/Oxford, UK: Oxford University Press, 2009), 104–5, 139–40. For a detailed discussion of hyper-individualism, see Brian Doherty, *Radicals for Capitalism: A Freewheeling History of the Modern American Liberation Movement* (New York: Public Affairs, 2007).

81. Quoted in Nicholas von Hoffman, *Citizen Cohn* (New York: Doubleday, 1988), 139–40.

82. Rovere, "The Adventures of Cohn and Schine," 10. Rovere also stated that Cohn's knowledge of the Communist movement, "though well short of overwhelming," greatly surpassed that of McCarthy.

83. Sidney Zion, *The Autobiography of Roy Cohn* (Secaucus, NJ: Lyle Stuart, 1988), 47.

Chapter 9: Liberal and Left-of-Liberal Anti-Communism, 1945–1957

1. Albert Einstein to John Dudzic, March 8, 1948, in David E. Rowe and Robert Schulmann, eds., *Einstein on Politics: His Private Thoughts and Public Stands on Nationalism, Zionism, War, Peace, and the Bomb* (Princeton, NJ/Oxford, UK: Princeton University Press, 2009), 454.

2. Lionel Trilling, *The Liberal Imagination: Essays on Literature and Society* (New York: Viking, 1950), x–xi.

3. Harry K. Givertz, *From Wealth to Welfare: The Evolution of Liberalism* (Stanford, CA: Stanford University Press, 1950), vii.

4. Raymond English, "Conservatism: The Forbidden Faith," *American Scholar* 21, no. 4 (Autumn 1952): 393–395. English stated that Reinhold Niebuhr's *The Children of Light and the Children of Darkness* (1944) "might have been received as a veritable manifesto of political conservatism and ... may still become such." He also labeled Arthur Schlesinger, Jr.'s *The Vital Center* as "the new conservatism of the left wing."

5. Arthur A. Ekirch, Jr., *The Decline of American Liberalism* (New York/London: Longmans, Green, 1955), ix. The "decline" in the title referred to contemporary liberals' sacrifice of the classic liberal doctrine of individual freedom to a welfare, war, and garrison state.

6. Louis Hartz, *The Liberal Tradition in America: An Interpretation of American Political Thought Since the Revolution* (New York/London: Harcourt Brace Jovanovich, 1955), 3–4.

7. Perhaps the clearest dividing line between Cold War conservative and liberal anti-Communists was their respective concept of the value of a clear and present danger test for resolving national security problems. When pricked, a conservative would probably say: "The people and the government of the United States may proscribe a political movement and its adherents if they find that movement's ideas and pronouncements inimical to the ideals of the United States, even if that movement does not represent a clear and present danger." A liberal, by comparison, would probably say: "Communism is a reprehensible doctrine and Soviet communism is a danger to the United States, but Communist agitation and propaganda do not represent a clear and present danger in the United States."

8. John Ehrman, *The Rise of Neoconservatism: Intellectuals and Foreign Affairs, 1945–1994* (New Haven, CT/London: Yale University Press, 1995), 9–12.

9. Arthur Schlesinger, Jr., "The U.S. Communist Party," *Life* (July 29, 1946): 94.

10. Robert Bendiner, "Civil Liberties and the Communists: Checking Subversion without Harm to Democratic Rights," *Commentary* 5, no. 5 (May 1948): 426.

11. See, for example, James A. Wechsler, "How to Rid the Government of Communists," *Harper's* (November 1947): 438–43; Arthur Schlesinger, Jr., "What Is Loyalty? A Difficult Question," *New York Times Magazine*

(November 2, 1947): 7, 48–51. Schlesinger also strongly opposed firing a college professor who was a Communist, Nazi, anti-Semite, or representative of the National Association of Manufacturers "solely on the basis of beliefs alone short of clear and present danger"; "The Right to Loathsome Ideas," *Saturday Review of Literature* (May 14, 1949): 17–18, 47.

12. Wyler interview, May 17, 1955, Elizabeth Poe Kerby Papers, box 3, folder 45, AMPAS. Dalton Trumbo, one of the "Hollywood Nineteen," later wrote, with this committee in mind: "The New Liberals have no stomach for liberalism itself, save on a high and almost theological plane. When the battle is actually joined on a specific issue involving the lives and rights of existing men . . . they are not to be found in the lists." *The Time of the Toad: A Study of Inquisition in America*, reprinted in *The Time of the Toad: A Study of Inquisition in America, and Two Related Pamphlets* (New York: Harper and Row, 1972), 36. In fact, after the October 1947 hearings, when the members of the Committee for the First Amendment came under strong pressure from the studio heads, the committee disintegrated. For more on the Committee for the First Amendment, see Larry Ceplair and Steven Englund, *The Inquisition in Hollywood: Politics in the Film Community, 1930–1960* (Garden City, NY: Anchor Press/Doubleday, 1980), 275–77; Philip Dunne, *Take Two* (New York: McGraw-Hill, 1980); Marsha Hunt, *The Way We Wore: Styles of the 1930s and 1940s and Our World Since Then, Shown and Recalled by Marsha Hunt* (Fallbrook, CA: Fallbrook, 1993).

13. Mary S. McAuliffe, "The ACLU During the McCarthy Years," in *The Specter: Original Essays on the Cold War and the Origins of McCarthyism*, edited by Robert Griffith and Athan Theoharis, 166–68 (New York: New Viewpoints, 1974).

14. In 1967, Schlesinger proclaimed himself "an unrepentant anti-Communist—unrepentant because there seems to be no other conceivable position for a liberal to take." "Liberal Anti-Communism Revisited: A Symposium," *Commentary* (September 1967): 68.

15. Norman Markowitz, "From the Popular Front to Cold War Liberalism," in Griffith and Theoharis, *The Specter*, 108, 111.

16. Alonzo L. Hamby, *Beyond the New Deal: Harry S. Truman and American Liberalism* (New York/London: Columbia University Press, 1973), 162–63. Robert Bendiner hailed the new organization as "something new in the history of American politics"—a left-wing organization "free of the orthodoxies of Marxism" and not "inspired by the Communists." "Revolt of the Middle," *The Nation* (January 18, 1947): 65. Some non-Communist liberals, however, worried that the members of the new organization were too obsessed with anti-communism (Hamby, *Beyond the New Deal*, 166).

17. McAuliffe, *Crisis on the Left*, 38, 44.

18. Quoted in Steven M. Gillon, *Politics and Vision: The ADA and American Liberalism, 1947–1985* (New York: Oxford University Press, 1987), 22–24. Kimball, who had written for *Time, PM,* and *New Republic,* stated that he had met

Schlesinger only once, but that when Bowles appointed William Benton to the vacant U.S. Senate seat for Connecticut and Benton asked Kimball to join his staff, Schlesinger warned Benton that Kimball was either a Communist or a fellow traveler. *The File* (San Diego, CA/New York: Harcourt Brace Jovanovich, 1983), 225. Kimball does not mention the ADA.

19. Arthur Schlesinger, Jr., "Reinhold Niebuhr's American Political Thought and Life," in *Reinhold Niebuhr: His Religious, Social, and Political Thought*, edited by Charles W. Kegley and Robert W. Bretall, 150 (New York: Macmillan, 1956). Schlesinger first heard about Niebuhr in the winter of 1940–1941, when Niebuhr spoke at Memorial Church in Harvard Yard. Schlesinger wrote, in his autobiography, that Niebuhr's "interpretations of man and history came as a vast illumination," and his arguments, unlike those of John Dewey, "had the great merit of accounting both for Hitler and Stalin and for the necessity of standing up to them." The pair did not meet until January 1947. The following year, when Schlesinger was planning to turn his article "Not Left, Not Right, But a Vital Center" into a book, he said that he "immersed" himself in Niebuhr's writings, particularly *The Nature and Destiny of Man* (1941, 1942). Arthur M. Schlesinger, Jr., *A Life in the Twentieth Century: Innocent Beginnings, 1917–1950* (Boston: Houghton Mifflin, 2000), 249–50, 511. In a 1981 commentary, Schlesinger stated: "The postwar generation premised its liberalism on Reinhold Niebuhr's mighty dictum: 'Man's capacity for justice makes democracy possible, but man's inclination to injustice makes democracy necessary.' " "A Reply," 140 (Schlesinger is quoting from *Children of Darkness*, xi).

20. It is of historical interest to note that when Schlesinger first used the term "vital center" in April 1948, it referred not to a realistic liberalism, but rather to "a democratic middle way" for the United States, akin to the "Third Force" in Western Europe. He wanted to include in this "middle way" the "non-Communist Left" and the "non-fascist Right." Because they share a common faith in a free political society," they should, according to Schlesinger, be natural comrades. "Not Left, Not Right, But a Vital Center," *New York Times Magazine* (April 4, 1948): 46–47.

21. Arthur Schlesinger, Jr., *The Vital Center: The Politics of Freedom* (Boston: Houghton Mifflin, 1949), ix. Clearly, he was referring to Niebuhr when he spoke of "the deepening of our knowledge of men." It is of interest to note that Schlesinger does not mention Dewey or Hook. In his autobiography, Schlesinger wrote that Hook overestimated the power of communism in the United States and that he allowed anti-communism to take over his life. Schlesinger, *A Life*, 507.

22. Schlesinger, *The Vital Center*, 159–60, 166.

23. Allen Yarnell, *Democrats and Progressives: The 1948 Presidential Election as a Test of Postwar Liberalism* (Berkeley/Los Angeles, CA: University of California Press, 1974), 89–92. Michael Wrezin contends that *Vital Center* liberalism "became a servant to the Democratic Party," and, consequently, "basic

liberal principles were sacrificed to political expediency." "Arthur Schlesinger, Jr, Scholar-Activist in Cold War America: 1946–1956," *Salmagundi* 63–64 (Spring–Summer 1984): 284.

24. Richard Gid Powers, *Not Without Honor: The History of American Anticommunism* (New York: Free Press, 1995), 192.

25. Plotke, *Building a Democratic Political Order*, 299, 310.

26. Indeed, it is difficult to label Harry Truman as a "liberal." Although his program included "liberal" reform elements, many of them arrived there as the result of political considerations. Truman was, in essence, a veteran politician with progressive leanings, who became the liberals' choice when they were caught between Henry Wallace and Thomas Dewey. He did not deliver on liberal hopes during his second term. James A. Wechsler labeled him "a radical George Babbitt," who, due to his background and the circumstances surrounding his presidency, was "incapable of giving continuity or new direction to the movement of liberalism." *Reflections of an Angry Middle-Aged Editor* (New York: Random House, 1960), 47, 49.

27. John Lewis Gaddis, *Strategies of Containment: A Critical Appraisal of Postwar American National Security Policy* (New York/Oxford, UK: Oxford University Press, 1982), 26; Paul Y. Hammond, *The Cold War Years: American Foreign Policy Since 1945* (New York: Harcourt, Brace and World, 1969), 30.

28. Benjamin O. Fordham, *Building the Cold War Consensus: The Political Economy of the U.S. National Security Policy, 1949–51* (Ann Arbor, MI: University of Michigan Press, 1998), 103–104.

29. Michael J. Hogan, *A Cross of Iron: Harry S. Truman and the Origins of the National Security State, 1945–1954* (Cambridge, UK: Cambridge University Press, 1998), 1–2. Truman's aide, Clark Clifford, is probably the best example of this new breed of national security manager. According to Clifton Brock, the ADA reached the peak of its influence in the1948 election. In the following years, a conservative Congress blocked liberal legislation and the ADA became "a prime conservative target." *Americans for Democratic Action: Its Role in National Politics* (Washington, D. C.: Public Affairs Press, 1962), 104, 132, 167.

30. Hamby, *Beyond the New Deal*, 383.

31. Alan Barth, *The Loyalty of Free Men* (New York: Viking, 1951), 90.

32. James A. Wechsler, "The Trial of Alger Hiss," *New York Post*, January 25, 1950, reprinted in U.S. Congress, Senate, Hearings Before the Subcommittee on Investigations of the Committee on Government Operations, *State Department Information Program*, Hearings, 83rd Congress, 1st Session, April 24, 1953, Part IV (Washington, DC: U.S. Government Printing Office, 1953), 284. See also, James A. Wechsler, "The Trial of Our Times (Cont'd)," *The Progressive*, March 1950, 5–6.

33. Arthur M. Schlesinger, Jr., "Espionage or Frame-up?," *Saturday Review of Literature* (April 15, 1950): 22–23.

34. Leslie A. Fiedler, "Hiss, Chambers, and the Age of Innocence," *Commentary* (August 1951), reprinted in Patrick Swan, ed., *Alger Hiss, Whittaker Chambers, and the Schism in the American Soul* (Wilmington, DE: Intercollegiate Studies Institute, 2003), 25.

35. Diana Trilling, "A Memorandum on the Hiss Case," *Partisan Review* (May–June 1950): reprinted in Swan, *Alger Hiss*, 30, 41, 43–44, 47–48.

36. Perhaps the first such use of this dichotomy appeared in a 1950 editorial in *New Leader*. The "softs" were those pro-Hiss liberals who were either "blind to the political relations exposed by the case" or "emotional innocents" afraid to confront the reality of the Cold War. The "hards," in contrast, employed a far more sophisticated analysis of events: "The Hards and the Softs," *New Leader* (May 20, 1950): 30–33, cited in Kenneth O'Reilly, "Liberals Values, the Cold War, and American Intellectuals," in *Beyond the Hiss Case: The FBI, Congress, and the Cold War*, edited by Athan G. Theoharis, 313 (Philadelphia: Temple University Press, 1982). In 1954, Granville Hicks, one of the "hards," further subdivided the "softs" into "fakes" (fellow travelers) and "retarded" (those who lacked an understanding of the present world situation). Mary McAuliffe defined a "hard" anti-Communist liberal as one who perceived communism as a militant, monolithic, and dangerous foe, which must be stopped no matter the cost. A "soft" anti-Communist liberal, in contrast, believed that the Soviet Union was acting from national, not ideological, interests and that the Truman administration's suspicions and bellicosity had caused the Cold War. A "hard" believed that the "hysteria" over McCarthy was misplaced; a "soft" perceived that the "hysteria" over communism was harming the United States. *Crisis on the Left*, 109–13.

37. The lectures form the basis of Reinhold Niebuhr, *The Irony of American History* (New York: Scribner's, 1962), 74, 79.

38. Niebuhr, "Liberals and the Marxist Heresy," *New Republic* 129 (October 12, 1953): 14.

39. Richard Wightman Fox, *Reinhold Niebuhr: A Biography* (New York: Pantheon Books, 1985), 242, 252–55. One year later, he retracted his accusation of one of the clergymen.

40. James Rorty and Moshe Decter, *McCarthy and the Communists* (Boston: Beacon Press, 1954), 3, 18, 50, 87.

41. Irving Howe, "The ADA: Vision and Utopia," *Dissent* 2, no. 2 (Spring 1955), 111. Howe had founded *Dissent* the previous year as a democratic socialist journal aimed at joining together "independent radicals" holding common values and ideas, among which were the defense of "democratic, humanist and radical values" and the attacking of "all forms of totalitarianism, whether fascist or Stalinist." "A Word to Our Readers," *Dissent* 1, no. 1 (Winter 1954): 3–4.

42. Gillon, *Politics and Vision*, 109.

43. McAuliffe, *Crisis on the Left*, 85, 96–97.

44. Gillon, *Politics and Vision*, 77, 79–81, 90–91, 107–109.

45. Plotke, *Building a Democratic Order*, 318–19, 334.

46. Samuel Walker, *In Defense of American Liberties: A History of the ACLU*, 2nd ed. (Carbondale/Edwardsville, IL: Southern Illinois University Press, 1999), 175. And yet, Ernst, in a book he co-authored with David Loth, stated that in the fight against communism "the bulwarks of American freedom" should not be sacrificed, "through the frantic expedient of burning the house down to get rid of the rats." *Report on the American Communist* (New York: Henry Holt, 1952), 221–22.

47. Guenter Lewy, *The Cause That Failed: Communism in American Politics* (New York/Oxford, UK: Oxford University Press, 1990), 153.

48. Ibid., 154–56.

49. Testimony before the Un-American Activities Committee of the House of Representatives, February 10, 1948, reprinted in Eric Bentley, ed., *Thirty Years of Treason: Excerpts from Hearings Before the House Committee on Un-American Activities, 1938–1965* (New York: Viking, 1971), 253, 355, 260. When closely questioned by Nixon as to his own organization's anti-Communist rules, Hays argued that they represented a response to the particular needs of his organization (264). The ACLU voted not to support the emergency detention substitute for the Mundt-Nixon bill.

50. Walker, *In Defense of American Liberties*, 186.

51. McAuliffe, *Crisis on the Left*, 106. The ECLC had been founded in 1951 by four professors, a retired banker, and I. F. Stone, "to augment the American Civil Liberties Union, but with guts enough to fight the evil of McCarthyism without fear of being sullied by the label of 'pro-Communist.' " They intended to offer free legal counsel, from the lowest to the highest courts. The ECLC and its administrators were publicly denounced as "dupes" by the anti-Communist left. D. D. Guttenplan, *American Radical: The Life and Times of I. F. Stone* (New York: Farrar, Straus and Giroux, 2009), 277–78. In November 1957, Congressman Francis Walter described the ECLC as "another Communist front," the purpose of which was "to cripple the anti-subversive programs of the Congress, to shackle or abolish the Committee on Un-American Activities, and to discredit J. Edgar Hoover and the Federal Bureau of Investigation." *Weekly Variety*, November 13, 1957, 2, 70.

52. www.freedomhouse.org/template.cfm?page=24. Accessed December 19, 2009; Aaron Levenstein, in collaboration with William Agar, *Freedom's Advocate: A Twenty-Five Year Chronicle* (New York: Viking, 1965), 199.

53. The Committee had been created by Eleanor Roosevelt in 1948, to help elect liberal candidates to Congress. For its impact on the McCarthy censure effort, see Robert Griffith, *The Politics of Fear: Joseph R. McCarthy and the Senate*, 2nd ed. (Amherst, MA: University of Massachusetts Press, 1987), 224–42, 275–85.

54. Paul H. Douglas, *In the Fullness of Time: The Memoirs of Paul H. Douglas* (New York: Harcourt Brace Jovanovich, 1972), 306–7.

55. Ibid., 308; Griffith, *The Politics of Fear*, 119–22; *Congressional Record*, 81st Congress, 2nd Session, 96:10, September 12, 1950, 14606, 14628. Six of the liberal senators who voted for the Internal Security Act signed a memorandum to their constituents and ADA members, urging them not to attack the law publicly, because to do so would help the Communists. Jonathan Bell, *The Liberal State on Trial: The Cold War and American Politics in the Truman Years* (New York: Columbia University Press, 2004), 182. On April 2, 1952, the Assistant Director of the Bureau of the Budget wrote that, pursuant to §103(a), six camps "are being placed on stand-by status," at a cost of $1,586,500. Roger Jones to Mr. Perlmeter, in Athan G. Theoharis, *The Truman Presidency: The Origins of the Imperial Presidency and the National Security State* (Stanfordsville, NY: Earl M. Coleman, 1979), 323.

56. McAuliffe, *Crisis on the Left*, 82; Sidney Hyman, *The Lives of William Benton* (Chicago/London: University of Chicago Press, 1969), 471–72.

57. Griffith, *The Politics of Fear*, 105, 152, 204 (n. 40). For the history of Benton's resolution, see 157–87. For the reasons why Benton was defeated for reelection, see 195. See also Hyman, *The Lives of William Benton*.

58. I. F. Stone, "The Silence in the Senate," *I. F. Stone's Weekly*, February 8, 1954, reprinted in Stone, *The Haunted Fifties* (New York: Random House, 1963), 20.

59. Humphrey's legislative aide, Max M. Kampelman, stated that Humphrey did so because he believed that "the liberal movement unnecessarily abandoned 'anti-communism' to the reactionaries" and because "he had a strong personal feeling that anti-subversive legislation was desirable and necessary." Quoted in William W. Keller, *The Liberals and J. Edgar Hoover: Rise and Fall of a Domestic Intelligence State* (Princeton, NJ: Princeton University Press, 1989), 35, fn. 21.

60. *Congressional Record*, 83rd Congress, 2nd Session, 100:11, August 12, 1954, 14208–9.

61. Mary Sperling McAuliffe, "Liberals and the Communist Control Act of 1954," *Journal of American History* 63 (September 1976): 352–60; McAuliffe, *Crisis on the Left*, 132–44; Griffith, *Politics of Fear*, 292–94. Griffith quotes Humphrey as stating, "I anticipated some of the rather emotional reaction from the liberal community because I was hitting somewhat of a sacred cow." But, he added, it was time for American liberals to begin to do some "20th century thinking in order to face 20th century problems" (*The Politics of Fear*, 293, n. 65). It is interesting to note that Humphrey does not mention this bill in his autobiography, *The Education of a Public Man: My Life and Politics* (Garden City, NY: Doubleday, 1976).

62. *Congressional Record*, 84th Congress, 1st Session, 101:7, June 27, 1955, 9240. In November, 12 commission members (6 Democrats and 6 Republicans) were appointed. Their 600-plus page report was published in August 1957. It acknowledged that the loyalty program that evolved from 1947 consisted of "a vast, intricate, confusing and costly complex of

temporary, inadequate, uncoordinated programs," but the report also stated that "the disloyal are dangerous and the Communist threat is both real and formidable." It strove to balance equally "the protection and safeguarding" of the rights and liberties of Americans with "the need of protecting national security from the disloyal few." It also endeavored to separate "the loyalty program from that of suitability and security," because "all loyalty cases are security cases, but the converse is not true." It recommended five pieces of legislation and three executive orders. *Report of the Commission on Government Security* [Washington, DC: U.S. Government Printing Office, 1957], xiii, xvi, xvii. www.archives.org/details/reportofcommisi1957unit. Accessed March 8, 2011.

63. McAuliffe, *Crisis on the Left*, 83, 130, 131. Congressman Emanuel Celler (Democrat–New York) wrote: "For over half a century I have opposed the Un-American Activities Committee. I have voted against appropriations for it": *You Never Leave Brooklyn: The Autobiography of Emanuel Celler* (New York: John Day, 1953), 197.

64. Hook to Talbot F. Hamlin, May 27, 1949, in Sidney Hook, *Letters of Sidney Hook: Democracy, Communism, and the Cold War*, edited by Edward S. Shapiro (Armonk, NY/London: M. E. Sharpe, 1995), 136–37. Several years later, David Riesman and Nathan Glazer concluded that anti-McCarthy liberals failed to find a firm, anti-Communist middle ground, because they had been unable to accept "Communism and the USSR as an enemy in the same way they did Fascism." Thus anti-McCarthy liberals found themselves "without an audience, their tone deprecated, their slogans ineffectual." "The Intellectuals and the Discontented Classes," in *The New American Right*, edited by Daniel Bell, 76(New York: Criterion, 1955).

65. Hook to Ed Wilson, August 14, 1950, in Hook, *Letters of Sidney Hook*, 154–55.

66. Hugh Wilford, *The New York Intellectuals: From Vanguard to Institution* (Manchester, UK/New York: Manchester University Press, 1995), 166–67, 171–73. Macdonald had gravitated from a sort-of-Trotskyist to a sort-of-anarchist-pacifist, to a complete political muddle. At every step he had been sharply critical of what he called "Stalinoids" (dupes, fellow travelers, Communist Party sympathizers) for their downplaying of the Soviet threat to Western civilization. Michael Wreszin, *A Rebel in Defense of Tradition: The Life and Politics of Dwight Macdonald* (New York: Basic Books, 1994), 198–201.

67. The editorial appeared in the Summer 1946 issue. It is reprinted in William Barrett, *The Truants: Adventures Among the Intellectuals* (Garden City, NY: Anchor Press/Doubleday, 1982), 244, 246, 249, 252, 256. Barrett wrote, in the text, "I have just reread the piece with some embarrassment, aghast at how strident it is, like a man shouting at the top of his lungs" (81). But he confessed that, as a liberal, he was then, and still remained, perplexed and disturbed by what he calls "the peculiar liberal temptation . . . to drift into compliance with pro-Russian tendencies" (83).

68. Philip Rahv, "The Sense and Nonsense of Whittaker Chambers," *Partisan Review* (July–August 1952): 478.

69. Barrett, *The Truants*, 95.

70. William Phillips, "In and Out of the Underground: The Confessions of Whittaker Chambers," *American Mercury* (June 1952): 92, 95, 99.

71. Giles Scott-Smith, "A Radical Democratic Political Offensive": Melvin J. Lasky, *Der Monat*, and the Congress for Cultural Freedom," *Journal of Contemporary History* 35, no. 2 (April 2000): 268–71.

72. Giles Scott-Smith, *The Politics of Apolitical Culture: The Congress for Cultural Freedom, the CIA and Post-War American Hegemony* (London/New York: Routledge, 2002), 31, 101. According to Michael Scammell, Arthur Koestler was the "true intellectual progenitor" of the congress. *Koestler: The Life and Political Odyssey of a Twentieth-Century Skeptic* (New York: Random House, 2009), 354.

73. Scammell, *Koestler*, 356.

74. Reprinted in Arthur Koestler, *The Trail of the Dinosaur and Other Essays* (New York: Macmillan, 1955), 179–82.

75. The only U.S. member of the first executive committee, Irving Brown, was the AFL's roving European troubleshooter and the conduit of the ICCF's CIA funds. Scammell, *Koestler*, 362.

76. Hook to Talbot F. Hamlin, May 27, 1949, and Hook to John K. Jessup, August 31, 1951, in Hook, *Letters of Sidney Hook*, 138, 165.

77. Sidney Hook, *Out of Step: An Unquiet Life in the 20th Century* (New York: Harper and Row, 1987), 384–85. He wrote that the conference, "by giving only one point of view . . . is perpetrating a fraud on the American public." Hook to Guy E. Shipler, March 16, 1949, in Hook, *Letters of Sidney Hook*, 125. Excerpts of a letter from Hook and George S. Counts to the organizers of the conference—including their request that the delegates from the Soviet Union be asked, "What has happened to the purged artists, writers, and critics of the Soviet Union?"—were included in the Committee on Un-American Activities' "review" of the conference. The Committee labeled the Cultural Conference "a supermobilization of the inveterate wheelhorses and supporters of the Communist Party and its auxiliary organizations." U.S. Congress, House of Representatives, Committee on Un-American Activities, *Review of the Scientific and Cultural Conference for World Peace, Arranged by the National Council of the Arts, Sciences and Professions, and Held at New York City, March 25, 26, and 27, 1949*, April 19, 1949 (Washington, DC: U.S. Government Printing Office, 1949). 1. This review was, in fact, another opportunity for the Committee on Un-American Activities to list hundreds of names of persons and organizations and their "Communist affiliations."

78. Quoted in McAuliffe, *Crisis on the Left*, 116.

79. Sidney Hook, *Heresy, Yes—Conspiracy, No!* (New York: ACCF, 1951), iii, iv, 5.

80. Ibid., 3. Hook divided liberals into two types. The "realistic" liberal believed in "the free market of ideas," and that this free market might be

interfered with if a speech or idea constituted "a clear and present danger to public peace or the security of the country." Such individuals could be trusted with this task because, unlike "frightened reactionaries," "realistic liberals" were capable of distinguishing heresies from conspiracies. The second type, the "ritualistic" liberal, ignored or blithely dismissed "the mass of evidence concerning the conspiratorial character of the Communist movement in all institutions in which it is active," and regarded this movement "as an unpleasant heresy just a little worse than a crotchety theory of disease or finance" (4, 8–9,11–14). In the second article, "The Dangers of Cultural Vigilantism," Hook prescribed a series of antidotes to the purge diseases spread by "frightened reactionaries." However, he failed to distinguish the "excesses" of the reactionaries from the purges of the "realistic" liberals.

81. Irving Kristol, "An Autobiographical Memoir," reprinted in Kristol, *The Neoconservative Persuasion: Selected Essays, 1942–2009*, edited by Gertrude Himmelfarb (New York: Basic Books, 2011), 332; Christopher Lasch, *The Agony of the American Left* (New York: Knopf, 1969), 82, 86–87.

82. When the ECLC held a conference on academic freedom to honor the seventy-fifth birthday of Albert Einstein, Sol Stein, the ACCF's executive director, issued a statement that expressed the organization's opposition to any exploitation of academic freedom and civil liberties "by persons who are at this late date still sympathetic to the cause of Soviet Russia." According to Stein, the ECLC was not sincerely opposed to threats to freedom anywhere in the world, nor was it sincerely concerned about the gross suppression of civil liberties and academic freedom behind the Iron Curtain. *New York Times*, March 14, 1954, p. 69.

83. Hook, *Out of Step*, 423, 425, 432; McAuliffe, *Crisis on the Left*, 116–21, 125; John P. Diggins, *Up from Communism: Conservative Odysseys in American Intellectual History* (New York: Harper and Row, 1975), 330. And yet, in a symposium sponsored by *Partisan Review*, Hook had—albeit in the context of criticizing intellectuals—criticized McCarthy for making "wild and irresponsible charges." "Our Country and Our Culture: A Symposium," *Partisan Review* 19, no. 5 (September–October 1952): 574. Two years later, in a review of Henry Steele Commager's *Freedom, Loyalty, and Dissent*, Hook noted McCarthy's "irresponsible demagogic exploitation" of the problems in the government's security programs. "Unpragmatic Liberalism," *New Republic* (May 24, 1954): 19.

84. Norman Podhoretz, *Making It* (New York: Random House, 1967), 291.

85. "Our Country and Our Culture: A Symposium," 593.

86. Brian Gilbert, "New Light on the Lattimore Case," *New Republic* (December 27, 1954); letter from Sol Stein criticizing "Gilbert," *New Republic* (February 14, 1955): 20–22; letters from Riesman, Schlesinger, and Rovere, *New Republic* (February 28, 1955): 21. Later that year, in November, when the Fund for the Republic was being criticized by anti-Communists for using its resources to fund "un-American and subversive activities," Robert M.

Hutchins, the Fund's president, met with Hook and other ACCF members. They demanded that he impose a blanket policy against the hiring of Communists, but Hutchins refused. Milton Mayer, *Robert Maynard Hutchins: A Memoir* (Berkeley/Los Angeles, CA: University of California Press, 1993), 447.

87. Peter Coleman, *The Liberal Conspiracy: The Congress for Cultural Freedom and the Struggle for the Mind of Postwar Europe* (New York: Free Press, 1989), 164–66. Josselson "invited" the ACCF to go its own way. Perhaps as a result, the American Committee suspended its operations in late 1957.

88. Hannah Arendt, *The Origins of Totalitarianism* (New York: Schocken Books, 2004), 567–68.

89. Hannah Arendt to Karl Jaspers, June 3, 1949, in Arendt and Karl Jaspers, *Correspondence, 1926–1969*, edited by Lotte Kohler and Hans Saner, translated by Robert and Rita Kimber (San Diego, CA/New York: Harcourt Brace, 1992), 137.

90. Arendt to Jaspers, July 13, 1953, in Arendt and Jaspers, *Correspondence*, 223. One year earlier, Mary McCarthy had written to Arendt: "I can't believe that these people [Hook, among others] seriously think that stalinism on a large scale is latent here, ready to revive at the slightest summons." Letter dated March 14, 1952, in *Between Friends: The Correspondence of Hannah Arendt and Mary McCarthy, 1949–1975*, edited by Carol Brightman (New York/San Diego, CA: Harcourt Brace, 1995), 5. Both women also criticized Hook et al. for their failure to criticize McCarthy. For more on Einstein's statement, see Chapter 10.

Chapter 10: Civil-Libertarian Anti-Communism, 1945–1957

1. *New York Post*, May 4, 1952, quoted in Victor S. Navasky, *Naming Names* (New York: Viking, 1980, 54.

2. "Statement of Twenty-Six Members of the American Bar Association Opposing a Loyalty Oath for Lawyers," February 1951, reprinted in Zechariah Chafee, Jr., *The Blessings of Liberty* (Philadelphia/New York: Lippincott, 1956, 177.

3. Alan Barth, *The Loyalty of Free Men* (New York: Viking, 1951), 3.

4. The biographical details are taken from Donald L. Smith, *Zechariah Chafee, Jr.: Defender of Law and Liberty* (Cambridge, MA/London: Harvard University Press, 1986).

5. Zechariah Chafee, Jr., "Freedom of Speech," *New Republic* (November 16, 1918): 66–68.

6. Zechariah Chafee, Jr., "Freedom of Speech in Wartime," *Harvard Law Review* 32, no. 8 (June 1919): 959–60, 969.

7. Zechariah Chafee, Jr., "A Contemporary State Trial: *The United States versus Jacob Abrams, et al.*," *Harvard Law Review* 33, no. 6 (April 1920): 769, 771. Abrams and three other anarchists had been convicted of violating the

Sedition Act, for writing, printing, and distributing two leaflets condemning President Wilson for his decision to send U.S. troops to intervene in the Russian civil war. The *Abrams* article almost cost Chafee his job. See Peter H. Irons, " 'Fighting Fair': Zechariah Chafee, Jr., the Department of Justice, and the 'Trial at the Harvard Club,' " *Harvard Law Review* 94, no. 6 (April 1981), 1205–36.

8. Irons, "Fighting Fair," 1222–26.

9. Zechariah Chafee, Jr., *Freedom of Speech* (New York: Harcourt, Brace and Howe, 1920), 257, 261–63.

10. Ibid., 260. Chafee's articles and books influenced the thinking on free speech of Supreme Court Justice Louis D. Brandeis. In his concurring opinion in *Whitney v. California*, Brandeis cited Chafee's thesis that the cure for dangerous speech is not more silence, but more speech: 374 U.S. 378 (1927). See also Melvin I. Urofsky, *Louis D. Brandeis: A Life* (New York: Pantheon Books, 2009), 563.

11. Zechariah Chafee, Jr., *Free Speech in the United States* (Cambridge, MA: Harvard University Press, 1941), 441, 470, 491–92. The first chapter was included in Howard Mumford Jones's anthology, *Primer of Intellectual Freedom* (Cambridge, MA: Harvard University Press, 1949), 42–64.

12. Chafee, *Free Speech*, 565.

13. Peter L. Steinberg, *The Great "Red Menace": United States Prosecution of American Communists, 1947–1952* (Westport, CT/London: Greenwood Press, 1984), 187.

14. Zechariah Chafee, Jr., "Investigations of Radicalism and Laws Against Subversion," in *Civil Liberties Under Attack*, edited by Henry Steele Commager et al., 46, 48–52, 57 (Philadelphia: University of Pennsylvania Press, 1951).

15. Chafee, *Blessings of Liberty*, 127.

16. Quoted in Smith, *Zechariah Chafee, Jr.*, 250, 252.

17. Chafee, *Blessings of Liberty*, 123, 124, 127.

18. Barth, *Loyalty of Free Men*, ix–xxxi.

19. *New York Times*, July 4, 1952, p. 5.

20. Alan Barth, "The Individual and the State," *The Nation* (December 16, 1950): 656–57.

21. Barth, *Loyalty*, x. Barth returned the compliment: The epigraph for the first chapter is a quotation from Chafee's *Free Speech in the United States*, and Barth favorably reviewed Chafee's *Blessings of Liberty*, "Beyond Law, There Is No Fair Play," *New Republic* (July 9, 1956): 19.

22. Barth, *Loyalty*, 2–3.

23. Ibid., 48.

24. Ibid., 239.

25. Alan Barth, "Congress on the Campus: A Warning to Universities," *The Nation* (April 18, 1953): 323.

26. Alan Barth, "How Good Is an FBI Report?," *Harper's* (March 1954): 25–31.

27. Alan Barth, *Government by Investigation* (New York: Viking, 1955), 23, 81, 82, 140.

28. Paul R. Hays, "Congress's Right to Investigate: Two Books Examined," *Commentary* (November 1955): 440–46. Barth's was one of several books sharply critical of congressional investigating committees that were published between 1952 and 1955. See also Robert K. Carr, *The House Committee on Un-American Activities* (Ithaca, NY: Cornell University Press, 1952); Robert K. Carr, *The Constitution and Congressional Investigating Committees: Individual Liberty and Congressional Power* (New York: Carrie Chapman Catt Memorial Fund, 1954); Telford Taylor, *Grand Inquest: The Story of Congressional Investigations* (New York: Simon and Schuster, 1955) [which Paul R. Hays treated respectfully in the above review, and Alan Barth praised unstintingly in his "The Growing Abuse of an Ancient Power," *The Reporter* (March 24, 1955): 42–43]; Harold W. Chase, *Security and Liberty: The Problem of Native Communists, 1947–1955* (Garden City, NY: Doubleday, 1955), 35.

29. Biographical information can be found in James A. Wechsler, *The Age of Suspicion* (New York: Random House, 1953) and Murray Polner, "James Wechsler: The Editor Who Challenged McCarthy," *History News Network*, January 5, 2004. hnn.us/articles/2869.html. Accessed September 12, 2010.

30. See, for example, his article on the German-Soviet Nonaggression Treaty and a CPUSA rally: "Stalin and Union Square," *The Nation* (September 30, 1939): 342–45. See also his discussion of the ouster of James Carey as president of the United Electrical Workers in 1941: "Carey and the Communists," *The Nation* (September 13, 1941): 224–25.

31. Samuel Walker, *In Defense of Civil Liberties: A History of the ACLU*, 2nd ed. (Carbondale/Edwardsville, IL: Southern Illinois University Press, 1999), 131.

32. Wechsler, *The Age of Suspicion*, 201.

33. James A. Wechsler, "How to Rid the Government of Communists," *Harper's* (November 1947): 438, 440.

34. Wechsler, *The Age of Suspicion*, 241. Schlesinger stated that Wechsler was "one of the most intelligent anti-Communists in America." "Espionage or Frame-up?," *Saturday Review of Literature* (April 15, 1950): 22.

35. James A Wechsler to Senator Herbert H. Lehman, June 4, 1952, *Congressional Record*, 82nd Congress, 2nd Session, 98:5, June 9, 1952, 812–13.

36. U.S. Congress, Senate, Hearings Before the Permanent Subcommittee on Investigations of the Committee on Government Operations, *State Department Information Program—Information Centers*, 83rd Congress, 1st Session, Part 4, April 24, 1953 (Washington, DC: U.S. Government Printing Office, 1953), 256. Six years earlier, Wechsler had stated: "I have no brief for anybody who refuses to testify before a congressional committee; no matter how foolish or fierce the committee, an American ought to be prepared to state his case in any public place at any time." Quoted in Navasky, *Naming Names*, 60.

37. *State Department Information Program—Information Centers*, 265–66.

38. Ibid., 267–68.

39. Ibid., 273, 277.

40. Ibid., 257, 276.

41. Ibid., Part 5, May 5, 1953, 290–92, 314. Wechsler brought with him several articles he had written: some critiqued the Alien Registration Act, its use to prosecute leaders of the CPUSA, J. Edgar Hoover, and the Internal Security Act; others criticized the behavior of the Communists and their lawyers at the trial and condemned the Wallace campaign for allowing Communists to dominate it. They were made a part of the record of his testimony.

42. Wechsler's account of his testimony can be found in *Age of Suspicion*, 289–319.

43. Edward Alwood, *Dark Days in the Newsroom: McCarthyism Aimed at the Press* (Philadelphia, PA: Temple University Press, 2007), 69–73; Navasky, *Naming Names*, 62. Navasky notes that when, on May 9, 1953, the editors of *National Guardian*, a left-wing journal, were subpoenaed by McCarthy's subcommittee, Wechsler and the *Post* remained silent. When one of them—Cedric Belfrage, a resident alien—invoked the Fifth Amendment and was later arrested and held for deportation, Wechsler again remained silent, because, he told Navasky, he believed Belfrage was a Communist and that people should not be silent about their affiliations (67–68).

44. Navasky, *Naming Names*, 45–46.

45. Others who could be included in this group were Thomas I. Emerson, Walter Gellhorn, Alexander Meiklejohn, and A. L. Wirin.

46. Quoted in Thurman Arnold, *Fair Fights and Foul: A Dissenting Lawyer's Life* (New York: Harcourt, Brace and World, 1965), 205.

47. Bruce Allen Murphy, *Fortas: The Rise and Ruin of a Supreme Court Justice* (New York: William Morrow, 1988), 81–82.

48. For more on the Lattimore case, see Arnold, *Fair Fights and Foul*, 214–27.

49. Laura Kalman, *Abe Fortas: A Biography* (New Haven, CT/London: Yale University Press, 1990), 131, 133, 135.

50. Ibid., 136.

51. Michael E. Parrish, *Citizen Rauh: An American Liberal's Life in Law and Politics* (Ann Arbor, MI: University of Michigan Press, 2010), 79–83.

52. Joseph Rauh interview in Griffen Fariello, *Red Scare: Memories of the American Inquisition, An Oral History* (New York: Norton, 1995), 138; oral history interview, Harry S. Truman Memorial Library and Museum, 1989, 53. www.trumanlibrary.org/oralhist/rauh.htm. Accessed September 18, 2010.

53. Fariello, *Red Scare*, 141. See also Rauh, "An Unabashed Liberal Looks at a Half-Century of the Supreme Court," *North Carolina Law Review* 69, no. 1 (December 1969): 223–24. Wechsler wrote: "In some respects, Remington's vindication ironically exposes the [loyalty] program's most glaring injustices": "The Remington Loyalty Case," *New Republic* (February 28, 1949): 18. For the history of the Remington case, see Gary May, *Un-American Activities:*

The Trials of William Remington (New York/Oxford, UK: Oxford University Press, 1994).

54. Joseph L. Rauh, Jr., "Informers, G-Men, and Free Men," *The Progressive*, May 1950, 9–11.

55. Paul H. Douglas, *In the Fullness of Time: The Memoirs of Paul H. Douglas* (New York: Harcourt Brace Jovanovich, 1972), 306.

56. Rauh oral history interview, Truman Library, 76–79.

57. This is as good a place as any to put to rest the fable first woven by Hellman, in *Scoundrel Time* (Boston: Little, Brown, 1976), and perpetuated in Parrish, *Citizen Rauh* (109), that Hellman and Rauh invented an honorable approach to the invocation of the Fifth Amendment. In fact, their tactic, known as "the diminished Fifth," whereby a witness is agreeable to admitting his or her membership in the Communist Party but not giving names of others, had been used on May 16, 1951, by Leonardo Bercovici. Bercovici stated that he was not a member of the Communist Party and then invoked the Fifth Amendment when asked specifically about several people, when his membership had ceased, and which other organizations he had joined. U.S. Congress, House of Representatives, Committee on Un-American Activities, 82nd Congress, 1st Session, *Communist Infiltration of Hollywood Motion-Picture Industry—Part 2*, testimony of Leonardo Bercovici, May 16, 1951 (Washington, DC: U.S. Government Printing Office, 1951), 441–51. Four months later, Carl Foreman employed a variation of the "diminished Fifth" in his testimony. Ibid., Part 5, September 24, 1951, 1753–71.

58. Steven M. Gillon, *Politics and Vision: The ADA and American Liberalism, 1947–1985* (New York: Oxford University Press, 1987), 106.

59. The material in this paragraph is taken from the *New York Times*, January 20, 1956, 49, and January 27, 1956, 7, and William F. Buckley, Jr., "The Liberal in Action: The Testament of Paul Hughes," in his Up From Liberalism (New Rochelle, NY: Arlington House, 1968), 101–16. In his thoroughly researched article—he read the trial transcripts—Buckley clearly took huge delight at being able to hoist Rauh on his own petard. Buckley chose as the epigraph to his essay a quotation from Rauh, condemning the use of spies and informants.

60. Gillon, *Politics and Vision*, 111.

61. Joseph L. Rauh, Jr., "The McCarthy Era Is Over," *U.S. News and World Report* (August 26, 1955): 68–70.

62. As a result of some of the causes he sponsored or organizations he joined, Einstein came under the intense scrutiny of the FBI. At various times, the FBI listed him as a member, sponsor, or endorser of 10, 33, and 73 subversive organizations, respectively. Fred Jerome, *The Einstein File: J. Edgar Hoover's Secret War Against the World's Most Famous Scientist* (New York: St. Martin's Press, 2002), xxi, 123, 173.

63. Albert Einstein to Henri Barbusse, June 6, 1932, and Einstein to German Committee Against Imperialistic War, September 9, 1932, excerpted

in David E. Rowe and Robert Schulmann, eds., *Einstein on Politics: His Private Thoughts and Public Stands on Nationalism, Zionism, War, Peace, and the Bomb* (Princeton, NJ/Oxford, UK: Princeton University Press, 2009), 423, 427.

64. *New York Times*, December 6, 1932, p. 18.

65. Albert Einstein to Max Born, 1937, and Address to Jewish Council on Russian War Relief, October 25, 1942, in Rowe and Schulmann, *Einstein on Politics*, 450, 452.

66. Albert Einstein to Sidney Hook, November 12, 1952, in Rowe and Schulmann, *Einstein on Politics*, 490.

67. Albert Einstein, "The Military Mentality," *American Scholar* 16, no. 3 (Summer 1947): 353–54, reprinted in Rowe and Schulmann, *Einstein on Politics*, 478.

68. Albert Einstein to Jacques Hadamard, April 7, 1949, in Rowe and Schulmann, *Einstein on Politics*, 482. Sidney Hook regularly tried to enlist Einstein in Hook's causes and to dissuade him from enlisting in others, particularly the Wallace campaign and this congress. In response to one of Hook's letters, Einstein told Hook: Your "views are far from objective" and your judgment is rigid and one-sided. Letter dated April 3, 1948, in Rowe and Schulmann, *Einstein on Politics*, 481.

69. *New York Times*, January 22, 1953, p. 6.

70. *New York Times*, June 12, 1953, pp. 1, 9. It should be noted that Einstein, when he was applying for a visa in December 1932, was asked by an employee of the U.S. Consulate in Berlin to state his "political creed" and the organizations to which he belonged. "What is this, an inquisition?," Einstein exclaimed, and he refused to answer. *New York Times*, December 6, 1932, pp. 1, 18.

71. *New York Times.*, June 14, 1953, p. 30.

72. Jerome, *The Einstein File*, 244; *New York Times*, December 17, 1953, p. 1.

73. *New York Times*, March 14, 1954, p. 69.

74. *New York Times*, April 20, 1954, p. 24.

75. Jerome, *The Einstein File*, 149.

76. *New York Times*, February 21, 1954, p. 5.

77. Albert Einstein to Norman Thomas, March 10, 1954, in Rowe and Schulmann, *Einstein on Politics*, 500–1.

78. The following biographical data come from Michael Harrington, *Fragments of the Century: A Serial Autobiography* (New York: Saturday Review Press/E. P. Dutton, 1973), and Maurice Isserman, *The Other American: The Life of Michael Harrington* (New York: Public Affairs, 2000).

79. It had been founded in 1936, by Norman Thomas, among others, to serve as a nonpartisan alternative to the Communist-controlled International Labor Defense.

80. Harrington, *Fragments*, 77–78.

81. Michael Harrington, *Taking Sides: The Education of a Militant Mind* (New York: Holt, Rinehart and Winston, 1985), 16.

82. Michael Harrington, "Rights of the Guilty," *Commonweal* (August 7, 1953): 435–47.

83. Michael Harrington, "Silence on the Left," *Commonweal* (October 2, 1953): 628–29 (his emphasis); "Politics in a New World," *Commonweal* (August 26, 1955): 512.

84. Michael Harrington, "Myths of U.S. Liberalism," *Commonweal* (December 17, 1954): 304–5.

85. Summarized in Harrington, *Taking Sides*, 16.

86. Michael Harrington, "The Committee for Cultural Freedom," *Dissent* 2, no. 2 (Spring 1955): 114–16. Reprinted in Harrington, *Taking Sides*, 20–33. In *Taking Sides*, Harrington took another shot at the ACCF, accusing it of having "formalized the capitulation of some liberals to a vicious, antidemocratic anti-Communism" (16).

87. John Cogley, *A Canterbury Tale: Experiences and Reflections, 1916–1976* (New York: Seabury Press, 1976), 55. It is not clear why Cogley thought that, because Harrington later noted, at that time, "I really didn't know any Communists." He had first come into contact with them when he was working on clemency for the Rosenbergs, but it was not until his work for Cogley that he had what he called his "first truly personal contacts" with them. Harrington, *Fragments*, 79; *Taking Sides*, 18.

88. For the full story of Kerby, Cogley, and Harrington, see Larry Ceplair, "Reporting the Blacklist: Anti-Communist Challenges to Elizabeth Poe Kerby," *Historical Journal of Film, Radio and Television* 28, no. 2 (June 2008): 135–52. In an unsent letter to Hutchins, Kerby stated that Harrington told her he was investigating *Frontier*, the magazine edited by Kerby's husband and the publisher of her blacklist article. Harrington told her that he had sought the opinions of Max Mont of the Jewish Labor Committee and John Despol, secretary-treasurer of the CIO California State Council—two of the staunchest anti-Communists in the Los Angeles area. Undated, typewritten letter, Elizabeth Poe Kerby Collection, box 2, folder 20, AMPAS.

89. Michael Harrington, "The Post-McCarthy Atmosphere," *Dissent* 2, no. 4 (Autumn 1955): 292–94.

90. U.S. Congress, House of Representatives, Committee on Un-American Activities, *Investigation of So-Called "Blacklisting" in Entertainment Industry: Report of the Fund for the Republic, Inc.*, 84th Congress, 2nd Session, Part I, July 10 and 11, 1956 (Washington, DC: U.S. Government Printing Office, 1956), 5179, 5243.

91. Harrington, *Fragments*, 86; Isserman, *The Other American*, 153. At the same time as the Woltman accusation, the Tenney committee of the California legislature issued a report alleging that the Young Socialist League was in the forefront of an international plot to reunite socialists and Communists of the world. *Taking Sides*, 37.

92. Michael Harrington, "New Communist Line," *Commonweal* (July 13, 1956): 365.

93. Michael Harrington, "In the United States: Communism After Hungary," *Commonweal* (February 1, 1957): 456–57.

94. Irving Kristol, " 'Civil Liberties,' 1952–A Study in Confusion: Do We Defend Our Rights by Protecting Communists?," *Commentary* (March 1952): 231–36.

95. For sharp criticisms of Kristol's article, see Richard H. Rovere, "Communists in a Free Society," *Partisan Review* 19, no. 3 (May–June 1952): 229–46; Alan F. Westin, "Our Freedom—and the Rights of Communists: A Reply to Irving Kristol," *Commentary* 14, no. 1 (July 1952): 33–40. Many years later, Kristol replied to his liberal critics, stating they "were so hysterical about McCarthy that they simply could not think straight about the issue I was addressing. My unforgivable sin, I subsequently realized, was in *not* being hysterical about McCarthy, whom I assumed to be a transient, ugly phenomenon with no political future." "An Autobiographical Memoir," in his *The Neoconservative Persuasion: Selected Essays, 1942–2009*, edited by Gertrude Himmelfarb (New York: Basic Books, 2011), 331.

Chapter 11: The Decline and Periodic Revivals of Domestic Anti-Communism

1. Richard M. Fried, *The Russians Are Coming! The Russians Are Coming!: Pageantry and Patriotism in Cold-War America* (New York/Oxford, UK: Oxford University Press, 1998), 139. In 1958, Ralph S. Brown, Jr. wrote, that in his opinion, the Communist Party "is now so weak as to be insignificant as a politically subversive force." *Loyalty and Security: Employment Tests in the United States* (New Haven, CT: Yale University Press, 1958), 312.

2. Delivered January 17, 1961, reprinted in Richard Hofstadter and Beatrice Hofstadter, eds., *Great Issues in American History: From Reconstruction to the Present Day, 1864–1981*, rev. ed. (New York: Vintage, 1982), 544.

3. Ibid., 549.

4. Walter Goodman, *The Committee: The Extraordinary Career of the House Committee on Un-American Activities* (Baltimore, MD: Penguin Books, 1969), 402–4.

5. Ibid., 429–32. The ACLU countered with *Operation Correction*, a documentary using the same footage but with a very different narrative.

6. Ibid., 434.

7. U.S. Congress, Senate, Subcommittee to Investigate the Administration of the Internal Security Act and Other Internal Security Laws of the Committee on the Judiciary, *The 16th Convention of the Communist Party, U.S.A.: Interim Report*, 85th Congress, 1st Session, June 13, 1957 (Washington, DC: U.S. Government Printing Office, 1957), v, 10.

8. U.S. Congress, Senate, Subcommittee to Investigate the Administration of the Internal Security Act and Other Internal Security Laws of the

Committee on the Judiciary, *Communist Party, U.S.A.: Soviet Pawn*, 90th Congress, 1st Session (Washington, DC: U.S. Government Printing Office, 1967), v, 19.

9. Arthur M. Schlesinger, Jr., *A Thousand Days: John F. Kennedy in the White House* (Boston: Houghton Mifflin, 1965), 699.

10. Robert Dallek, *Flawed Giant: Lyndon Johnson and His Times, 1961–1973* (New York/Oxford, UK: Oxford University Press, 1998), 281, 352, 489–90. He was not dissuaded even by a CIA report that found "no significant evidence that would prove Communist control or direction of the United States peace movement or its leaders" (490).

11. *New York Times*, July 16, 1971, p. 12.

12. *New York Times*, July 20, 1971, p. 1; *Los Angeles Times*, May 20, 1972, p. 2. Nixon did, however, sign the act repealing the emergency detention provisions of the Internal Security Act.

13. Quoted in *The 16th Convention of the Communist Party, U.S.A.: Interim Report*, 2.

14. These themes are repeated in *Masters of Deceit: The Story of Communism in America and How to Fight It* (New York: Henry Holt, 1958); *One Nation's Response to Communism* (Washington, DC: Federal Bureau of Investigation, 1960); *A Study of Communism* (New York: Holt, Rinehart and Winston, 1962); and *On Communism* (New York: Random House, 1969). *Masters of Deceit* sold 441,000 copies in hardcover and 1.75 million in softcover, making it, by far, the biggest-selling anti-Communist book:*Alice Payne Hackett, 70 Years of Best Sellers, 1895–1965* (New York and London: Bowker, 1967), 17, 46.

15. Hoover, *A Study of Communism*, 157.

16. Goodman, *The Committee*, 416–17, 431; Athan G. Theoharis and John Stuart Cox, *The Boss: J. Edgar Hoover and the Great American Inquisition* (Philadelphia, PA: Temple University Press, 1988), 320–28.

17. Director to SACLA, April 14, 1960, Dalton Trumbo FBI file, in possession of Nancy Escher.

18. David J. Garrow, *The FBI and Martin Luther King, Jr.* (New York: Penguin Books, 1981), 25–26, 49, 53, 73, 101, 131. It is interesting to note that the first report had been widely distributed until Robert F. Kennedy intervened to have it recalled. President Johnson approved the distribution of the second report.

19. *Barenblatt v. United States*, 360 U.S. 109 (1959), at 117–18,126, 128–29.

20. *Wilkinson v. United States*, 365 U.S. 399 (1961) and *Braden v. United States*, 361 U.S. 431 (1961). See also Robert Sherrill, *First Amendment Felon: The Story of Frank Wilkinson, His 132,000-Page FBI File, and His Epic Fight for Civil Rights and Liberties* (New York: Nation Books, 2005).

21. Harry Kalven, Jr., *A Worthy Tradition: Freedom of Speech in America* (New York: Harper and Row, 1988), 511.

22. *Scales v. United States*, 367 U.S. 203 (1961); *Communist Party v. Subversive Activities Control Board*, 367 U.S. 1 (1961).

23. *Albertson v. Subversive Activities Control Board*, 382 U.S. 70 (1965); *United States v. Robel*, 398 U.S. 258 (1967). Congress repealed the registration provision in 1967, but sustained the Board's power to designate organizations as "Communist-action" or "Communist-front" groups. When the Board then listed individual members of these groups, a federal appeals court ruled that the Board had violated those persons' First Amendment rights. Kalven, *A Worthy Tradition*, 639–40, n. 45.

24. Reply Affidavit of Nedrick Young, in *Nedrick Young et al. v. Motion Picture Association of America, et al.*, Civil Action No. 4989-60, 41–42 (a copy is in the Nedrick Young Collection, WCFTR); Murray Schumach, "Hollywood Blues," *New York Times*, September 6, 1959, section 2, p. 7; Howard Suber, *The Anti-Communist Blacklist in the Hollywood Motion Picture Industry*, Ph. D. dissertation (Los Angeles, CA: University of California, Los Angeles,1968), 134. John Howard, chairman of the Counter-Subversive Commission of the California American Legion told Elizabeth Poe Kerby that Kahane "was lying through his teeth" when he told Ameican Legion leaders in Minneapolis that the major studios were firing all the Communists. Interview of October 28, 1960. Elizabeth Poe Kerby Collection, box 1, folder 2, AMPAS. That same year, Myron C. Fagan, one of the most indefatigable anti-Communist film-industry sentinels, issued another of his incendiary publications: "Urgent Warning to All Americans: The Reds Are Back in Hollywood!!!" This screed took the form of an open letter to "Dear Fellow-Patriot." Fagan then issued a smaller tract, "Red Stars—No. 3," in which Americans were urged "TO SAVE AMERICA FROM THE COMMUNIST CONSPIRACY—DON'T PATRONIZE RED!!!" It contained the names of more than 200 actors, actresses, writers, directors, producers, and composers, only some of whom had been Communists. Both publications, issued by the Cinema Educational Guild in June 1959, are in the General AMPAS File, box 6, Communist Charges—1959, AMPAS.

25. *New York Times*, January 20, 1960, pp. 1, 8; *Los Angeles Times*, January 20, 1960, p. 2; *Hollywood Reporter*, January 20, 1960, p. 1.

26. *Los Angeles Herald-Express*, January 26, 1960. Clipping in Dalton Trumbo's FBI file, in possession of Nancy Escher.

27. *New York Times*, February 8, 1960, pp. 1, 35; *Los Angeles Times*, February 9, 1961, p. B1. Kramer had, a few years earlier, hired the blacklisted writer Nedrick Young to co-write *The Defiant Ones*. Young, writing under the name "Nathan Douglas," and his co-writer, Harold Smith, won the 1958 Academy Award for best story and screenplay. Unlike previous blacklisted winners (Carl Foreman, Michael Wilson, and Dalton Trumbo), Young and Smith were allowed to accept their award. As per their agreement with the Academy, however, they did not say anything about the blacklist. Committee on Un-American Activities chairman Frances Walter stated that he planned to hold hearings to examine Preminger's hiring decision (*Los Angeles Examiner*, February 2, 1960. Clipping in Dalton Trumbo's FBI files, in possession of Nancy Escher). Walter did not do so.

28. Jack Salzman, *Albert Maltz* (Boston: Twayne, 1978), 130–31.

29. *Los Angeles Times*, December 22, 1960, p. 2.

30. Bruce Cook, *Dalton Trumbo* (New York: Scribner's, 1977), 276–78.

31. Alan F. Westin, "The John Birch Society: Fundamentalism on the Right," *Commentary* (August 1961): 93–104; Benjamin R. Epstein and Arnold Forster, *The Radical Right: Report on the John Birch Society and Its Allies* (New York: Random House, 1967), 88, 206, 214. In late 1965, the editors of *National Review* accused Welch of undermining the anti-Communist movement; "The John Birch Society and the Conservative Movement," *National Review* (October 19, 1965): 915–16.

32. Fred W. Grupp, Jr., "The Political Perspectives of Birch Society Members," in *The American Right Wing*, edited by Robert A. Schoenberger, 91 (New York: Holt, Rinehart and Winston, 1969).

33. Dr. Fred Schwarz, *You Can Trust the Communists (. . . to do exactly as they say!)* (Englewood Cliffs, NJ: Prentice-Hall, 1960), 102, 126, 163–64, 181. A study of the attendees of one of Schwarz's schools indicated that they viewed communism as "a shorthand symbol for unacceptable trends" and anti-communism as a means of expressing their resentment. Raymond E. Wolfinger, Barbara Kaye Wolfinger, Kenneth Prewitt, and Sheila Rosenhack, "America's Radical Right: Politics and Ideology," in *Ideology and Discontent*, edited by David E. Apter, 263–64, 282, 288 (New York: Free Press of Glencoe, 1964). See also Alan F. Westin, "Anti-Communism and the Corporations," *Commentary* (December 1963): 482; Fred C. Cook, "Radio Right: Hate Clubs of America," *The Nation* (May 25, 1964): 524, 526. According to Cook, at least 6,600 radical-right programs were broadcast weekly on1,300 radio and television stations (or approximately 20 percent of stations nationally). In February 1962, Billy Ray Hargis convened many of the leading radical-right activists to form the Anti-Communist Liaison.

34. Alan F. Westin, "Anti-Communism and the Corporations," *Commentary*(December 1963): 479–87.

35. Harry Overstreet and Bonaro Overstreet, *What We Must Know About Communism* (New York: Norton, 1958), 9. Although the book was written with the assistance of the FBI, this role was not mentioned in the acknowledgments. After it was published, the book was warmly approved by Hoover, but fiercely attacked by a member of the John Birch Society: Edward Janisch, "What We Must Know About Overstreet," *American Opinion* (October 1959): 35–46. Google.com/site/ernie124102/jbs-2. Accessed February 23, 2011. "Ernie" is a self-described "conspiracy buff," who has been collecting Freedom of Information Act materials on that subject for nearly 30 years. Google.com/site/ernie124102/home.

36. Ralph de Toledano, "It's Still the Soviet Party," *National Review* (January 5, 1957): 11–12;Towner Phelan, "Rebirth of the Popular Front?," *National Review* (February 23, 1957): 183–84.

37. *National Review* (September 24, 1960): 173.

38. Stanley D. Bachrack, *The Committee of One Million: "China Lobby" Politics, 1953–1971* (New York: Columbia University Press, 1976), 170–72. Macmillan decided not to publish the book on the China Lobby, which had been written by Ross Y. Koen. It took 14 years for Koen to find another publisher for *The China Lobby in American Politics.* Davis and Robert Hunter's book, *The Red China Lobby,* was published in 1963.

39. Maurice J. Goldbloom, "The American Communists Today," *Commentary* (February 1957): 134.

40. Guenter Lewy, *The Cause That Failed: Communism in American Political Life* (New York/Oxford, UK: Oxford University Press, 1990), 160, 163.

41. Jonathan M. Wiener, "Radical Historians and the Crisis in American History, 1959–1980," *Journal of American History* 76, no. 2 (September 1989): 405.

42. Gar Alperovitz, "The Double Dealer," *New York Review of Books* (September 8, 1966): 4.

43. Arthur Schlesinger, Jr., letter to the editors, *New York Review of Books* (October 20, 1966): 37.

44. Arthur Schlesinger, Jr., "Origins of the Cold War," *Foreign Affairs* 46, no. 1 (October 1967): 23, 24, fn. 3. The author of an earlier, critical article on the subject had refrained from that sort of innuendo. Irwin Unger forthrightly stated that New Left historians "are not the captives of an official ideology": "The 'New Left' and American History: Some Recent Trends in United States Historiography," *American Historical Review* 72, no. 4 (July 1967): 1241.

45. Robert James Maddox, *The New Left and the Origins of the Cold War* (Princeton, NJ: Princeton University Press, 1973), 10–11, 161, 164. The Schlesinger letter and article and the Maddox book are cited and discussed in Paul M. Buhle and Edward Rice-Maximin, *William Appleman Williams: The Tragedy of Empire* (New York/London: Routledge, 1995), 186–96. My discussion of them is based on my independent reading of them.

46. Allen Weinstein, *Perjury: The Hiss-Chambers Case* (New York: Knopf, 1978).

47. Ronald Radosh and Joyce Milton, *The Rosenberg File: A Search for the Truth* (New York: Holt, Rinehart and Winston, 1983). Radosh later wrote: "When the book was published, I never received an iota of public support from the democratic socialist intellectuals. . . . And of course, the hard Left . . . were all of one mind: I had become the new enemy." This reaction led him, in his words, "to consider the ultimate heresy: perhaps the Left was wrong not just about the Rosenberg case, but about most everything else." *Commies: A Journey Through the Old Left, the New Left and the Leftover Left* (San Francisco: Encounter Books, 2001), 161, 171.

48. Paul Hollander, *Anti-Americanism: Critiques at Home and Abroad, 1965–1990* (New York/Oxford, UK: Oxford University Press, 1992), 19. His emphasis.

49. Every writer I have consulted on this subject, whether favorable, unfavorable, or neutral, agrees that former anti-Communists were the founders of neoconservatism: Lewis A. Coser and Irving Howe, eds., *The New*

Conservatives: A Critique from the Left, rev. ed. (New York/Scarborough, ON: New American Library, 1976); Peter Steinfels, *The Neoconservatives: The Men Who Are Changing America's Politics* (New York: Simon and Schuster, 1979), 276; Gary Dorrien, *The Neoconservative Mind: Politics, Culture, and the War of Ideology* (Philadelphia, PA: Temple University Press, 1993), 17; John Ehrman, *The Rise of Neoconservatism: Intellectuals and Foreign Affairs* (New Haven, CT/London: Yale University Press, 1995), 34; and Mark Gerson, *The Neoconservative Version: From the Cold War to the Culture Wars* (Lanham, MD/New York: Madison Books, 1996), 31.

50. *The Public Interest* 1, no. 1 (Fall 1965): 3–5.

51. Irving Kristol, "An Autobiographical Memoir," in his *The Neoconservative Persuasion: Selected Essays, 1942–2009*, edited by Gertrude Himmelfarb (New York: Basic Books, 2011), 341.

52. Irving Kristol, *Reflections of a Neoconservative: Looking Back, Looking Ahead* (New York Basic Books, 1983), 75–76; *Neoconservatism: The Autobiography of an Idea* (New York/London: Free Press, 1995), 31, 193–94, 486.

53. Irving Howe, "The New York Intellectuals: A Chronicle and a Critique," *Commentary* (October 1968): 44–45.

54. Theodore Draper, "The Ghost of Social Fascism," *Commentary* (February 1969): 29, 40; "The Specter of Weimar," *Commentary* (December 1971): 48–49.

55. Thomas L. Jeffers, *Norman Podhoretz: A Biography* (Cambridge, UK: Cambridge University Press, 2010), 151.

56. Norman Podhoretz, "Laws, Kings, and Cures," *Commentary* (October 1970): 31. In that same issue, Nathan Glazer echoed the "deradicalization" theme, citing the "young radical guerrillas now engaged in the sabotage of social organization," their fierce "hatred of the free world," and their "style of absolutist thinking." "On Being Deradicalized," *Commentary* (October 1970): 78–80.

57. Norman Podhoretz, "The New Hypocrisy," and Robert A. Nisbet, Roger Starr, and David L. Bromwich, "The Counter-Culture and Its Apologists," *Commentary* (December 1970): 5–6, 40–59. Neoconservatism was also promoted in the editorial pages of the *Wall Street Journal*. A smaller revival occurred in the 1990s, around the issue of multiculturalism. In his 1992 book on the subject, Arthur Schlesinger, Jr. charged that "self-styled multiculturalists" (i. e., the products of the counterculture) were attacking "the common American identity" and advancing "the fragmentation of American life." Schlesinger, *The Disuniting of America* (New York/London: 1992), 119, 123, 130. Four years later, Samuel Huntington, in his book describing the Islamic threat to the West, expressed concern that the "concentrated and sustained onslaught" of multiculturalists on the moral, cultural, and political strength of the United States was undermining its ability to resist this threat. He approvingly quoted Schlesinger on the subject. Huntington, *The Clash of Civilizations and the Remaking of World Order* (New York: Simon and Schuster, 1996), 304–5.

58. For Radosh's account of his political journey, see his *Commies*. For Klehr, see *Communist Cadre: The Social Background of the American Communist Party Elite* (Stanford, CA: Hoover Institute Press, 1978) and *The Heyday of American Communism: The Depression Decade* (New York: Basic Books, 1984).

59. Harvey Klehr and Ronald Radosh, *The Amerasia Spy Case: Prelude to McCarthyism* (Chapel Hill, NC/London: University of North Carolina Press, 1996). Actually, as their text makes clear, it was a leak case, not a spy case.

60. Harvey Klehr and Ronald Radosh, "Redfest '85,' " *New Republic* (August 12–19, 1985): 16–17.

61. Harvey Klehr, *Far Left of Center: The American Radical Left Today* (New Brunswick, NJ/Oxford, UK: Transaction Books, 1988), xii. It is possible that Klehr and the Anti-Defamation League were responding to the two-decade-long battle to allow Jewish people to leave the Soviet Union. The organizations that sought to save Soviet Jewry had been criticized by many groups on the left. The Soviet Jewish émigrés, for their part, swelled the ranks of anti-communism in the United States and passionately opposed the policies of détente and peaceful coexistence.

62. Ibid.

63. David Evanier and Harvey Klehr, "Anticommunism and Mental Health," *American Spectator* 22, no. 2 (February 1989): 28–30.

64. Guenter Lewy, *The Cause That Failed: Communism in American Political Life* (New York/Oxford, UK: Oxford University Press, 1990), vii–ix, 295–99, 302, 305.

65. Hollander, *Anti-Americanism*, 20–22.

66. See, for example, Kenneth Lloyd Billingsley, *Hollywood Party: How Communism Seduced the American Film Industry in the 1930s and the 1940s* (Rocklin, CA: Forum, 1998); Robert Mayhew, *Ayn Rand and Song of Russia: Communism and Anti-Communism in 1940s Hollywood* (Lanham, MD: Scarecrow Press, 2005); Ronald and Allis Radosh, *Red Star Over Hollywood: The Film Colony's Long Romance with the Left* (San Francisco: Encounter Books, 2005); Richard Schickel, "Still Seeing Red," *Los Angeles Times*, September 16, 2007, M4; Alan Canty, *Communism in Hollywood: The Moral Paradoxes of Testimony, Silence, and Betrayal* (Lanham, MD/Toronto: Scarecrow Press, 2009).

67. Harvey Klehr, John Earl Haynes, and Kyrill M. Anderson, *The Soviet World of American Communism* (New Haven, CT/London: Yale University Press, 1998), 356. See also Harvey Klehr, John Earl Haynes, and Fridrikh Igorevitch Firsov, *The Secret World of American Communism* (New Haven, CT/London: Yale University Press, 1995).

68. John Earl Haynes and Harvey Klehr, *Venona: Decoding Soviet Espionage in America* (New Haven, CT/London: Yale University Press, 1999), 7, 333–35.

69. Herbert Romerstein and Eric Breindel, *The Venona Secrets: Exposing Soviet Espionage and America's Traitors* (Washington, DC: Regnery, 2000), xv, 448.

70. Harvey Klehr and John Earl Haynes, *In Denial: Historians, Communism and Espionage* (San Francisco, CA: Encounter Books, 2003), 8.

71. Jamie Glazov, "An Interview with John Earl Haynes and Harvey Klehr," *History News Network*, December 1, 2003. hnn.us/articles/1832.html. Accessed March 21, 2011.

72. Klehr, *Far Left of Center*, xii.

73. Particularly good examples of this tendency may be found in the letters of Sidney Hook and the writings of Hilton Kramer. Hook insisted that the thoughts and actions of all Communist Party members in the world were dictated to them by the Communist Party leadership. Hook to L. O. Kattsoff, November 7, 1949, and to Ernest H. Kantorowicz, December 12, 1950, in Sidney Hook, *Letters of Sidney Hook: Democracy, Communism, and the Cold War*, edited by Edward S. Shapiro (Armonk, NY: M. E. Sharpe, 1995), 141, 154–55. Kramer, in September 1984, described "the true Stalinist mind, which is impervious alike to documentary evidence and moral discrimination." In November 1997, he wrote, "it was in the nature of Stalinism for its followers to lie about everything that impinged upon their political allegiance." Hilton Kramer, *The Twilight of the Intellectuals: Culture and Politics in the Era of the Cold War* (Chicago: Ivan R. Dee, 1999), 50, 73.

74. Harvey Klehr and John Earl Haynes, *The American Communist Movement: Storming Heaven Itself* (New York: Twayne, 1992), 5. It is interesting to note that Klehr, 18 years earlier, had written: "There was nothing unique or peculiar about Communists as people. They came out of all environments, had all sorts of motives for becoming members, and differed greatly in their commitment to the cause"; *The Heyday of American Communism*, 416.

75. The discussion that follows is based on the remarks of W. V. Quine and J. S. Ullian, *The Web of Belief*, 2nd ed. (New York: Random House, 1978), especially pp. 9–34; several articles on the nature of belief by C. S. Peirce; and conversations with my wife, Christine Holmgren, a professor of philosophy.

76. Pierre Rigoulot stated, in his discussion of the sources of "knowledge" ("connaissances") in France of Soviet concentration camps, "It would be prudent [to assess the quality, precision, rigor, literary value, and diffusion of textual information] before pointing an accusatory finger at those who 'knew but preferred to close their eyes.' " *Les Paupières Lourdes: Les Français face au goulag— aveugelements et indignations* (Paris: Editions Universitaires, 1991), 9. When Haynes and Klehr state that many people in the 1930s and 1940s "knew very well the nature of communism's threat to democracy," they, too, fall into this epistemological trap (*In Denial*, 83).

77. This short statement of perspective is based on the Jain theories of *anek~ntav~da* and *nayav~da*. I am indebted to Christine Holmgren for her explication of them, but the condensation is my own.

78. James A. Miller, *Examined Lives: From Socrates to Nietzsche* (New York: Farrar, Straus and Giroux, 2011), 69.

Conclusion

1. Samuel A. Stouffer, *Communism, Conformity, and Civil Liberties: A Cross Section of the Nation Speaks Its Mind* (Garden City, NY: Doubleday, 1955), 59.

2. Arthur Schlesinger, Jr., "The Life of the Party: What It Means to Be a Communist," *Saturday Review of Literature* (July 16, 1949): 36. Virtually every objective person who has examined the United States in the late 1940s has concluded that communism was a spent force or, in the words of Senator Daniel Patrick Moynihan, "a defeated ideology." Quoted in Allen Weinstein and Alexander Vassiliev, *The Haunted Wood: Soviet Espionage in America—The Stalin Era* (New York: Random House, 1999), 340.

3. Herbert Hoover to Harry S. Truman, November 20, 1950, in Athan G. Theoharis, *The Truman Presidency: The Origins of the Imperial Presidency and the National Security State* (Stanfordsville, NY: Earl M. Coleman, 1979), 368.

4. John Earl Haynes and Harvey Klehr, *Venona: Decoding Soviet Espionage in the United States* (New Haven, CT/London, Yale University Press, 1999), 9, 339–82.

5. John Earl Haynes, Harvey Klehr, and Alexander Vassiliev, *Spies: The Rise and Fall of the KGB in America* (New Haven, CT/London: Yale University Press, 2009), 541.

6. Haynes and Klehr, *Venona*, 331.

7. Robert Louis Benson and Michael Warner, eds., *Venona: Soviet Espionage and the American Response, 1939–1957* (Washington, DC: National Security Agency and Central Intelligence Agency, 1996), xvi, xviii, xix.

8. Weinstein and Vassiliev, *The Haunted Wood*, xxi–xxiv, 340.

9. Haynes, Klehr, and Vassiliev, *Spies*, xv, 548.

10. Stetson Conn, Rose C. Engelman, and Bryon Fairchild, *Guarding the United States and Its Outposts* (Washington, DC: U.S. Army, 1964), 206—14; Greg Robinson, *By Order of the President: FDR and the Internment of Japanese Americans* (Cambridge, MA/London: Harvard University Press, 2001), 146–55.

11. George H. Gallup, *The Gallup Poll: Public Opinion, 1935–1971* (New York: Random House, 1972),1:587.

12. Substantial majorities of those polled between 1936 and 1953 consistently favored restrictions on the freedom of Communists to function in the United States. Herbert H. Hyman and Paul B. Sheatsley, "Trends in Public Opinion on Civil Liberties," *Journal of Public Issues* 9, no. 3 (1953): 16. It is interesting to note that a study of the electorate conducted 35 years later found that 70 percent of those surveyed still strongly identified themselves as anti-Communist. The next largest self-identifier was religion. Norman Ornstein, Andrew Kohut, and Larry McCarthy, *The People, the Press, and Politics: The* Times Mirror *Study of the American Electorate* (Reading, MA: Addison-Wesley, 1988), 113.

13. Stouffer, *Communism, Conformity, and Civil Liberties*, 76, 87, 158. No Gallup polls on domestic communism were taken in 1956.

14. John Earl Haynes, *Red Scare or Red Menace? American Communism in the Cold War Era* (Chicago: Ivan R. Dee, 1996), 199–200.

15. In addition, on July 2, 1951, only seven of the convicted Communist Party leaders surrendered to federal authorities. Four of them joined the four who had ducked the original subpoenas in the group's underground leadership: *New York Times*, July 3, 1951, p. 1. According to Irving Howe and Lewis Coser, this action produced "panic" among Communist Party members who had raised the forfeited bail funds ($80,000) from their organizations and "lost the Party sympathy among people who doubted the propriety or usefulness of the government prosecutions." *The American Communist Party: A Critical History* (Boston: Beacon Press, 1957; New York: Praeger, 1962), 483.

16. James Burnham, *The Web of Subversion: Underground Networks in the United States Government* (New York: John Day, 1954), 218–21.

17. Harold Taylor, *On Education and Freedom* (New York: Abelard-Schuman, 1954), 245.

18. Stanley I. Kutler, *The American Inquisition: Justice and Injustice in the Cold War* (New York: Hill and Wang, 1982), 244.

Afterword

1. Mel Gurtov, *Superpower on Crusade: The Bush Doctrine in US Foreign Policy* (Boulder, CO/London: Lynne Rienner, 2006), 8. In fact, for some observers, anti-terrorism is simply anti-communism updated. In his 2007 book, Dinesh D'Souza blamed "the cultural left and its allies in Congress, the media, Hollywood, the nonprofit sector, and the universities" (the left wing of the Democratic party, ACLU, NOW, People for the American Way, Planned Parenthood, Human Rights Watch, and moveon.org) for causing the events of September 11, 2001. In his view, they "are the primary cause of the volcano of anger toward America that is erupting from the Islamic world." Because the Muslims who carried out the September 11 attacks were the products of this "visceral rage," terrorism cannot be defeated unless the cultural left is defeated. According to D'Souza, one way to do so is to "expose the domestic insurgency." D'Souza proceeded to name 113 individuals and 16 organizations that he considered to be "secretly allied with [the radical Muslim] movement to undermine" the George W. Bush administration's war on terror. But, he assured his readers, he was "in no sense saying that the left is disloyal." *The Enemy at Home: The Cultural Left and Its Responsibility for 9/11* (New York/London: Doubleday, 2007), 1–2, 23, 274, 288–90.

2. Project for the New American Century, "Statement of Principles," June 3, 1997. www.newamericancentury.org/statementofprinciples. Accessed March 2, 2011. The signers are an interesting group, consisting of family members from the ranks of traditional neoconservative (Norman Podhoretz, his wife Midge Decter, and their son-in-law Elliott Abrams; and William Kristol)

and those who would be architects of the post–September 11 war on terror (Dick Cheney, Paul Wolfowitz, and I. Lewis Libby).

3. Speeches of September 20, 2001, November 11, 2001, and October 29, 2002, reprinted in John W. Dietrich, ed., *The George W. Bush Foreign Policy Reader: Presidential Speeches with Commentary* (Armonk, NY/London: M. E. Sharpe, 2005), 53, 56, 97.

4. Joshua Muravchik, "The Bush Manifesto," *Commentary* (December 2002): 30.

5. Daniel Pipes, "The Danger Within: Militant Islam in America," *Commentary* (November 2001): 19. Steven Emerson followed this warning with two books on the topic: *American Jihad: The Terrorists Living Among Us* (New York: Free Press, 2002) and *Jihad Incorporated: A Guide to Militant Islam in the United States* (Amherst, NY: Prometheus Books, 2006).

6. Daniel Pipes, "Who Is the Enemy?," *Commentary* (January 2002): 22.

7. Norman Podhoretz, "How to Win World War IV," *Commentary* (February 2002): 27–29.

8. William J. Bennett, *Why We Fight: Moral Clarity and the War on Terrorism* (New York/London: Doubleday, 2002), 2, 20–21, 78, 141.

9. David Frum and Richard Perle, *And End to Evil: How to Win the War on Terror* (New York: Random House, 2003), 4, 5–6, 9.

10. Norman Podhoretz, *World War IV: The Long Struggle Against Islamofascism* (New York/London: Doubleday, 2007), 2, 5, 8, 15, 216. The quotations are taken from "X" [George Kennan], "The Sources of Soviet Conduct," *Foreign Affairs* (July 1947).

11. It is interesting to contemplate why the enemy is labeled "Islamofascist" rather than "Islamocommunist" or "Islamofascistcommunist." Paul Berman has traced the fascist and totalitarian roots of what he calls "Islamism," though he does note that there is also an admixture of leftist terrorist methods in it. Berman prefers to identify the enemy as "Muslim totalitarianism" and the war against it as a war against terror, totalitarianism, and nihilism. *Terror and Liberalism* (New York/London: Norton, 2003), 112, 208, 210.

12. John W. Dower has noted several threads linking United States attitudes against its enemies, from Pearl Harbor to the war against Saddam Hussein: The enemy is always determined and in the throes of a ruthless ideology or agenda; the enemy has no legitimate grievance against the United States; it is always a matter of us or them; if one is not for us, one is against us; we must not lose heart and abandon the good fight. *Cultures of War: Pearl Harbor/Hiroshima/9-11/Iraq* (New York/London: Norton/The New Press, 2010), 12, 14, 70, 86.

13. Bobby Ghosh, "Does America Have a Muslim Problem," *Time* (August 19, 2010). www.time.com/time/national/0,8599,2011798-2,00.html. Accessed March 11, 2011.

14. Daniel Pipes, "Americans Wake Up to Islamism," *National Review* (September 7, 2010). www.nationalreview.com/articles/245737/americans-wake-islamism-daniel-pipes. Accessed March 5, 2011.

15. While the PATRIOT Act was being debated, Arthur Schlesinger, Jr. voiced his concern that Congress was showing "alarming signs of abdicating its Constitutional role, by failing to hold a thoroughgoing debate on the effects the war on terror will have on the Bill of Rights. "Democracy in Wartime," *New York Times*, October 3, 2001, A23. It is interesting to note that three years later, in a chapter titled "Patriotism and Dissent in Wartime," Schlesinger made no mention of Congress's much greater abdication during the third "red scare." *Wartime and the American Presidency* (New York/London: Norton, 2004), 69–82.

16. "The Department of Homeland Security," June 2002, 8. www.DHS.gov/xlibrary/assets/book.pdf. Accessed February 24, 2011.

Bibliography

Abel, Lionel. *The Intellectual Follies: A Memoir of the Literary Venture in New York and Paris*. New York: Norton, 1984.

Adler, Les K., and Thomas G. Paterson. "Red Fascism: The Merger of Nazi Germany and Soviet Russia in the Image of Totalitarianism, 1930s–1950s." *American Historical Review* 75, no. 4 (April 1970): 1046–64.

Acheson, Dean. *Present at the Creation: My Years in the State Department*. New York: Norton, 1969.

Allitt, Patrick. *The Conservatives: Ideas and Personalities Throughout American History*. New Haven, CT/London: Yale University Press, 2009.

Allport, Gordon W. *The Nature of Prejudice*. Cambridge, MA: Addison-Wesley, 1954.

Almond, Gabriel A. *The American People and Foreign Policy*. New York: Harcourt, Brace, 1950.

Almond, Gabriel A. *The Appeals of Communism*. Princeton, NJ: Princeton University Press, 1954.

Alperovitz, Gar. *Atomic Diplomacy*. New York: Simon and Schuster, 1965.

Alperovitz, Gar. "The Double Dealer." *New York Review of Books* (September 8, 1966): 4.

Alsop, Joseph. "The Strange Case of Louis Budenz." *The Atlantic* 189 (April 1952): 29–33.

Alsop, Joseph, and Stewart Alsop. "Tragedy of Liberalism." *Life* (May 20, 1946): 68–76.

American Friends Service Committee. *Anatomy of Anti-Communism: A Report Prepared for the Peace Education Division of the American Friends Service Committee*. New York: Hill and Wang, 1969.

Anderson, Jack, and Ronald W. May. *McCarthy: The Man, the Senator, the "Ism."* Boston: Beacon Press, 1952.

Arendt, Hannah. *Correspondence, 1926–1969*. Edited by Lotte Kohler and Hans Saner. Translated by Robert and Rita Kimber. San Diego, CA/New York: Harcourt Brace, 1992.

Arendt, Hannah. "The Ex-Communists." *Commonweal* 57 (March 20, 1953): 595–99.

Arendt, Hannah. *The Origins of Totalitarianism.* New York: Schocken, 2004.

Arendt, Hannah, and Mary McCarthy. *Between Friends: The Correspondence of Hannah Arendt and Mary McCarthy, 1949–1975.* Edited by Carol Brightman. New York/San Diego, CA: Harcourt Brace, 1995.

Arnold, Thurman. *Fair Fights and Foul: A Dissenting Lawyer's Life.* New York: Harcourt, Brace and World, 1965.

Association of the Bar of the City of New York, Commission on the Bill of Rights. *Report on Congressional Investigations.* New York, 1948.

Association of the Bar of the City of New York, Commission on the Bill of Rights. *Report of the Special Committee on the Federal Loyalty-Security Program.* New York: Dodd, Mead, 1956.

Association of the Bar of the City of New York, Commission on the Bill of Rights, Committee on Federal Legislation. *Report on Proposed "Subversive Activities Control Act, 1949" (S. 2311, 81st Congress).* New York, 1950.

Auerbach, Jerold S. *Unequal Justice: Lawyers and Social Change in Modern America.* New York/London: Oxford University Press, 1977.

Bachrack, Stanley D. *The Committee of One Million: "China Lobby" Politics, 1953–1971.* New York: Columbia University Press, 1976.

Bailey, Percival R. "The Case of the National Lawyers Guild, 1939–1958." In *Beyond the Hiss Case: The FBI, Congress, and the Cold War,* ed. by Athan G. Theoharis, 129–75. Philadelphia, PA: Temple University Press, 1982.

Bailey, Thomas A. *America Faces Russia: Russian-American Relations from Early Times to Our Day.* Ithaca, NY: Cornell University Press, 1950; Gloucester, MA: Peter Smith, 1964.

Baker, Ray Stannard. *Woodrow Wilson: Life and Letters—War Leader, 1917–1918.* New York: Scribner's, 1946.

Baldwin, Roger N. *A New Slavery: Forced Labor—The Communist Betrayal of Human Rights.* New York: Oceana, 1953.

Barrett, William. *The Truants: Adventures Among the Intellectuals.* Garden City, NY: Anchor Press/Doubleday, 1982.

Barsky, Robert F. *Noam Chomsky: A Life of Dissent.* Cambridge, MA/London: MIT Press, 1997.

Barson, Michael, and Steven Heller. *Red Scared: The Commie Menace in Propaganda and American Culture.* San Francisco: Chronicle Books, 2001.

Barth, Alan. "Beyond Law, There Is No Fair Play." *New Republic* (July 9, 1956): 19.

Barth, Alan. "Congress on the Campus: A Warning to Universities." *The Nation* (April 18, 1953): 322–24.

Barth, Alan. *Government by Investigation.* New York: Viking, 1955.

Barth, Alan. "The Growing Abuse of an Ancient Power." *The Reporter* (March 24, 1955): 42–43.

Barth, Alan. "How Good Is an FBI Report?" *Harper's* (March 1954): 25–31.

Barth, Alan. "The Individual and the State." *The Nation* (December 16, 1950): 656–57.

Barth, Alan. *The Loyalty of Free Men.* New York: Viking, 1951.

Barrett, Edward L., Jr. *The Tenney Committee: Legislative Investigation of Subversive Activities in California*. Ithaca, NY: Cornell University Press, 1951.

Bayley, Edward R. *Joe McCarthy and the Press*. Madison, WI/London: University of Wisconsin Press, 1981.

Becker, Jean-Jacques, and Serge Bernstein. *Histoire de l'anti-communisme en France*. Paris: Olivier Orban, 1987.

Belknap, Michael R. *Cold War Political Justice: The Smith Act, the Communist Party and American Civil Liberties*. Westport, CT: Greenwood Press, 1977.

Bell, Daniel, ed. *The New American Right*. New York: Criterion, 1955.

Bell, Daniel. *The Radical Right* (updated and expanded version of *The New American Right*). Garden City, NY: Doubleday, 1963.

Bell, Jonathan. *The Liberal State on Trial: The Cold War and American Politics in the Truman Years*. New York: Columbia University Press, 2004.

Bendiner, Robert. "Civil Liberties and the Communists: Checking Subversion without Harm to Democratic Rights." *Commentary* 5, no. 5 (May 1948): 423–31.

Bendiner, Robert. "Revolt of the Middle." *The Nation* (January 18, 1947): 65–66.

Bennett, William J. *Why We Fight: Moral Clarity and the War on Terrorism*. New York/London: Doubleday, 2002.

Bentley, Eric, ed. *Thirty Years of Treason: Excerpts from Hearings before the House Committee on Un-American Activities, 1938–1968*. New York: Viking, 1971.

Benson, Robert Louis, and Michael Warner, eds. *Venona: Soviet Espionage and the American Response, 1939–1957*. Washington, DC: National Security Agency and Central Intelligence Agency, 1996.

Berkman, Alexander. *The Bolshevik Myth (Diary 1920–1922)*. New York: Boni and Liveright, 1925.

Berle, Adolf A. *Navigating the Rapids, 1918–1971*. Edited by Beatrice Bishop Berle and Travis Beal Jacobs. New York: Harcourt Brace Jovanovich, 1973.

Berman, Paul. "The Prisoner Intellectuals." *New Republic* (May 27, 2010): 30–31.

Berman, Paul. *Terror and Liberalism*. New York/London: Norton, 2003.

Best, Gary Dean. *Herbert Hoover: The Postpresidential Years, 1933–1964*. Stanford, CA: Hoover Institution Press, 1983.

Betten, Neil. *Catholic Activism and the Industrial Worker*. Gainesville, FL: University Presses of Florida, 1976.

Biddle, Francis. *The Fear of Freedom*. Garden City, NY: Doubleday, 1951.

Billingsley, Kenneth Lloyd. *Hollywood Party: How Communism Seduced the American Film Industry in the 1930s and the 1940s*. Rocklin, CA: Forum, 1998.

Blanchard, Margaret A. *Revolutionary Sparks: Freedom of Expression in Modern America*. New York/Oxford, UK: Oxford University Press, 1992.

Board of Regents, University of Washington. *Communism and Academic Freedom: The Record of the Tenure Cases at the University of Washington*. Seattle, WA: University of Washington Press, 1949.

Bohlen, Charles E. *Witness to History, 1929–1969*. New York: Norton, 1973.

Bontecou, Eleanor. "The English Policy as to Communists and Fascists in the Civil Service." *Columbia Law Review* 51, no. 5 (May 1951): 564–86.

Bontecou, Eleanor. *The Federal Loyalty-Security Program*. Ithaca, NY: Cornell University Press, 1953.

Bourdet, Claude. "This Strange America." *The Nation* (December 12, 1953): 526.

Bouscaren, Anthony T. *Imperial Communism*. Washington, DC: Public Affairs Press, 1953.

Boyer, Paul. *By the Bomb's Early Light: American Thought and Culture at the Dawn of the Atomic Age*. New York: Pantheon Books, 1985.

Boyle, Kevin. *The UAW and the Heyday of American Liberalism, 1945–1968*. Ithaca, NY/London: Cornell University Press, 1995.

Braden, Thomas W. "I'm Glad the CIA Is 'Immoral.' " *Saturday Evening Post* (May 20, 1967): 10–14.

Brands, H. W., Jr. *Cold Warriors: Eisenhower's Generation and American Foreign Policy*. New York: Columbia University Press, 1988.

Brewer, Roy. *Transcript of Unfinished Oral History*. 1980, University of California at Los Angeles, University Archives, Record Series 507, box 16.

Brinkley, Alan. *Liberalism and Its Discontents*. Cambridge, MA: Harvard University Press, 1998.

Brinkley, Alan. *The Publisher: Henry Luce and His Century*. New York: Knopf, 2010.

Broadwater, Jeff. *Eisenhower and the Anti-Communist Crusade*. Chapel Hill, NC/London: University of North Carolina Press, 1992.

Brock, Clifton. *Americans for Democratic Action: Its Role in National Politics*. Washington, D. C.: Public Affairs Press, 1962.

Broderick, Francis L. *Right Reverend New Dealer: John A. Ryan*. New York: Macmillan, 1963.

Brown, Lawrence R. "Eisenhower v. Taft: The Vital Issue." *The Freeman* (March 24, 1952): 393–96.

Brown, Ralph S., Jr. *Loyalty and Security: Employment Tests in the United States*. New Haven, CT: Yale University Press, 1958.

Brown, Ralph S., Jr., and John O. Fassett. "Security Tests for Maritime Workers: Due Process Under the Port Security Program." *Yale Law Journal* 62, no. 8 (July 1953): 1163–208.

Brownell, Will, and Richard N. Billings. *So Close to Greatness: A Biography of William C. Bullitt*. New York: Macmillan, 1987.

Broyles, J. Allen. *The John Birch Society: Anatomy of a Protest*. Boston: Beacon Press, 1964.

Buckingham, Peter H. *America Sees Red: Anti-Communism in America, 1870s to 1980s*. Claremont, CA: Regina Books, 1988.

Buckley, William F., Jr. *Did You Ever See a Dream Walking?: American Conservative Thought in the Twentieth Century*. Indianapolis, IN/New York: Bobbs-Merrill, 1970.

Buckley, William F., Jr. "A Dilemma of Conservatives." *The Freeman* (August 1954): 51–52.

Buckley, William F., Jr. *God and Man at Yale: The Superstitions of "Academic Freedom."* Chicago: Henry Regnery, 1951.

Buckley, William F., Jr. "McLiberal's McCarthyism." *The Freeman* (February 9, 1953): 355–56.

Buckley, William F., Jr. *Miles Gone by: A Literary Autobiography*. Washington, DC: Henry Regnery, 2004.

Buckley, William F., Jr. "The Party and the Deep Blue Sea." *Commonweal* (January 25, 1952): 392–93.

Buckley, William F., Jr. "Reflections on the Failure of 'National Review' to Live Up to Liberal Expectations." *National Review* (August 1, 1956): 7–12.

Buckley, William F., Jr. "Senator McCarthy's Model?" *The Freeman* (May 21, 1951): 531–33.

Buckley, William F., Jr. *Up from Liberalism*. New Rochelle, NY: Arlington House, 1968.

Buckley, William F., Jr., and L. Brent Bozell. *McCarthy and His Enemies: The Record and Its Meaning*. Chicago: H. Regnery, 1954.

Budenz, Louis. *The Techniques of Communism*. Chicago: Henry Regnery, 1954.

Buhle, Mary Jo, Paul Buhle, and Dan Georgakas, eds. *Encyclopedia of the American Left*, 2nd ed. New York/Oxford, UK: Oxford University Press, 1998.

Buhle, Paul M., and Edward Rice-Maximin. *William Appleman Williams: The Tragedy of Empire*. New York/London: Routledge, 1995.

Bullitt, William C. *The Great Globe Itself: A Preface to World Affairs*. New York: Scribner's, 1946.

Bullitt, William C."A Report to the American People on China." *Life* (October 13, 1947): 35–36, 139–54.

Bullitt, William C. "The World from Rome: The Eternal City Faces a Struggle Between Christianity and Communism." *Life* (September 4, 1944): 94–109.

Burnham, James. *The Coming Defeat of Communism*. New York: John Day, 1950.

Burnham, James. *Containment or Liberation: An Inquiry into the Aims of United States Foreign Policy*. New York: John Day, 1953.

Burnham, James. *The Managerial Revolution: What Is Happening in the World*. New York: John Day, 1941.

Burnham, James. "Rhetoric and Peace." *Partisan Review* 17, no. 8 (November–December 1950): 870–71.

Burnham, James. *The Struggle for the World*. New York: John Day, 1947.

Burnham, James. *The Web of Surveillance: Underground Networks in the U.S. Government*. New York: John Day, 1954.

Burnham, James, and William S. Schlamm. "Should Conservatives Vote for Eisenhower?" *National Review* (October 20, 1956): 12–15.

Burns, Jennifer. *Goddess of the American Market: Ayn Rand and the American Right*. New York/Oxford, UK: Oxford University Press, 2009.

Campbell, Angus, Gerald Gurin, and Warren E. Miller. *The Voter Decides*. Evanston, IL/White Plains, NY: Row, Peterson, 1954.

Cantelon, Philip L. *In Defense of America: Congressional Investigations of Communism in the United States, 1919–1935* [Ph.D. dissertation]. Bloomington, IN: Indiana University, 1971.

Canty, Alan. *Communism in Hollywood: The Moral Paradoxes of Testimony, Silence, and Betrayal*. Lanham, MD/Toronto: Scarecrow Press, 2009.

Carr, Robert K. *The Constitution and Congressional Investigating Committees: Individual Liberty and Congressional Power*. New York: Carrie Chapman Catt Memorial Fund, 1954.

Carr, Robert K. *The House Committee on Un-American Activities.* Ithaca, NY: Cornell University Press, 1952.

The Case of Leon Trotsky: Report of the Charges Made Against Him in the Moscow Trials by the Preliminary Commission of Inquiry into the Charges Made Against Leon Trotsky in the Moscow Trials. New York/London: Harper and Brothers, 1937

Caute, David. *The Great Fear: The Anti-Communist Purge Under Truman and Eisenhower.* New York: Simon and Schuster, 1978.

Celler, Emanuel. *You Never Leave Brooklyn: The Autobiography of Emanuel Celler.* New York: John Day, 1953.

Ceplair, Larry. "The Film Industry's Battle Against Left-Wing Influences from the Russian Revolution to the Blacklist." *Film History* 20, no. 4 (2008): 399–411.

Ceplair, Larry. *The Marxist and the Movies: A Biography of Paul Jarrico.* Lexington, KY: University Press of Kentucky, 2007.   ʹ

Ceplair, Larry. "McCarthyism Revisited." *Historical Journal of Film, Radio and Television* 28, no. 3 (August 2008): 405–14.

Ceplair, Larry. "Reporting the Blacklist: Anti-Communist Challenges to Elizabeth Poe Kerby." *Historical Journal of Film, Radio and Television* 28, no. 2 (June 2008): 135–52.

Ceplair, Larry. *Under the Shadow of War: Fascism, Anti-Fascism, and Marxists, 1918–1939.* New York: Columbia University Press, 1987.

Ceplair, Larry, and Steven Englund. *The Inquisition in Hollywood: Politics in the Film Community, 1930–1960.* Garden City, NY: Anchor Press/Doubleday, 1980.

Chafe, William H. *The Unfinished Journey: America since World War II,* 4th ed. New York/Oxford, UK: Oxford University Press, 1999.

Chafee, Zechariah, Jr. *The Blessings of Liberty.* Philadelphia/New York: Lippincott, 1956.

Chafee, Zechariah, Jr. "A Contemporary State Trial: *The United States versus Jacob Abrams, et al.*" *Harvard Law Review* 33, no. 6 (April 1920): 747–74.

Chafee, Zechariah, Jr. "Freedom of Speech." *New Republic* (November 16, 1918): 66–68.

Chafee, Zechariah, Jr. *Freedom of Speech.* New York: Harcourt, Brace and Howe, 1920.

Chafee, Zechariah, Jr. "Freedom of Speech in Wartime." *Harvard Law Review* 32, no. 8 (June 1919): 932–73.

Chafee, Zechariah, Jr. *Free Speech in the United States.* Cambridge, MA: Harvard University Press, 1941.

Chafee, Zechariah, Jr. "Investigations of Radicalism and Laws Against Subversion." In Commager, *Civil Liberties Under Attack,* 46–57.

Chamberlin, William Henry. *America's Second Crusade.* Chicago: Henry Regnery, 1950.

Chamberlin, William Henry. *Beyond Containment.* Chicago: Henry Regnery, 1953.

Chamberlin, William Henry. *The Evolution of a Conservative.* Chicago: Henry Regnery, 1959.

Chamberlin, William Henry. *The Russian Enigma: An Interpretation*. New York: Scribner's, 1944.

Chamberlin, William Henry. *The Russian Revolution, 1917–1921*. New York: Macmillan, 1935.

Chamberlin, William Henry. *The World's Iron Age*. New York: Macmillan, 1941.

Chase, Harold W. *Security and Liberty: The Problem of Native Communists, 1947–1955*. Garden City, NY: Doubleday, 1955.

Chodorov, Frank. "An Editorial Problem." *The Freeman* (September 1955): 630.

Ciment, Michel. *Conversations with Losey*. London/New York: Methuen, 1985.

Chambers, Whittaker. *Odyssey of a Friend: Whittaker Chambers's Letters to William F. Buckley, Jr., 1954–1961*. Edited by William F. Buckley, Jr. New York: G. P. Putnam's Sons, 1969.

Chambers, Whittaker. "The Revolt of the Intellectuals." *Time* (January 6, 1941): 58–59.

Chambers, Whittaker. *Witness*. (New York: Random House, 1952).?

Clifford, Clark, with Richard Holbrooke. *Counsel to the President: A Memoir*. New York: Random House, 1991.

Coben, Stanley. *A. Mitchell Palmer: Politician*. New York/London: Columbia University Press, 1963.

Coben, Stanley. "A Study in Nativism: The American Red Scare of 1919–20." *Political Science Quarterly* 79, no. 1 (March 1964): 52–75.

Cogley, John. *A Canterbury Tale: Experiences and Reflections, 1916–1976*. New York: Seabury Press, 1976.

Cogley, John. *Report on Blacklisting*. New York: Fund for the Republic, 1956.

Cohen, Murray, and Robert F. Fuchs. "Communism's Challenge and the Constitution." *Cornell Law Quarterly* 34, no. 2 (Winter 1948): 182–219.

Cohen, Naomi W. *Not Free to Desist: The American Jewish Committee, 1906–1966*. Philadelphia, PA: Jewish Publication Society of America, 1972.

Cohn, Roy. *McCarthy*. New York: NAL, 1968.

Coleman, Peter. *The Liberal Conspiracy: The Congress for Cultural Freedom and the Struggle for the Mind of Postwar Europe*. New York: Free Press, 1989.

Colodny, Len, and Tom Schactman. *The Forty Years War: The Rise and Fall of the Neocons, from Nixon to Obama*. New York: Harper, 2009.

Commager, Henry Steele, ed. *Documents of American History*, 8th ed. New York: Appleton-Century-Crofts, 1968.

Commager, Henry Steele. *Freedom, Loyalty, Dissent*. New York: Oxford University Press, 1954.

Commager, Henry Steele. "The New Year Puts a Challenge to Us." *New York Times Magazine* (January 1, 1939): 1–2, 12.

Commager, Henry Steele. "To Secure the Blessings of Liberty." *New York Times Magazine* (April 9, 1939): 4, 16.

Commager, Henry Steele. "Washington Witch-Hunt." *The Nation* (April 5, 1947): 385–88.

Commager, Henry Steele, et al. *Civil Liberties Under Attack*. Philadelphia, PA: University of Pennsylvania Press, 1951.

Conn, Stetson, Rose C. Engelman, and Bryon Fairchild. *Guarding the United States and Its Outposts*. Washington, DC: U.S. Army, 1964.

"Control of Communist Activities." *Stanford Law Review* 1, no. 1 (November 1948): 85–107.

Cook, Bruce. *Dalton Trumbo*. New York: Scribner's, 1977.

Cook, Fred J. *The Nightmare Decade: The Life and Times of Senator Joe McCarthy*. New York: Random House, 1971.

Cook, Fred J. "Radio Right: Hate Clubs of America." *The Nation* (May 25, 1964): 524–26.

Cooney, John. *The American Pope: The Life and Times of Francis Cardinal Spellman*. New York: Times Books, 1984.

Cooney, Terry A. *The Rise of the New York Intellectuals: Partisan Review and Its Circle*. Madison, WI: University of Wisconsin Press, 1986.

Coser, Lewis A., and Irving Howe, eds. *The New Conservatives: A Critique from the Left*, rev. ed. New York/Scarborough, ON: New American Library, 1976.

Cosgrove, John E. "Constitutional Law: Communism's Criminality." *Notre Dame Lawyer* 23, no. 4 (May 1948): 577–91.

Coulter, Ann. *Treason: Liberal Treachery from the Cold War to the War on Terrorism*. New York: Crown Forum, 2003.

Courtois, Stéphane, et al. *The Black Book of Communism: Crimes, Terror, Repression*. Translated by Jonathan Murphy and Mark Kramer. Cambridge, MA/London: Harvard University Press, 1999.

Crick, Bernard. "The Strange Quest for an American Conservatism." *Review of Politics* 17, no. 3 (July 1955): 359–76.

Croog, Charles F. "FBI Political Surveillance and the Isolationist-Interventionist Debate, 1939–1941." *The Historian*, 54, no. 3 (Spring 1992): 441–58.

Crosby, Donald F. "American Catholics and the Anti-Communist Impulse." In Griffith and Theoharis, *The Specter*, 18–39.

Crosby, Donald F. *God, Church, and Flag: Senator Joseph McCarthy and the Catholic Church, 1950–1957*. Chapel Hill, NC: University of North Carolina Press, 1978.

Dallek, Robert. *Flawed Giant: Lyndon Johnson and His Times, 1961–1973*. New York/Oxford, UK: Oxford University Press, 1998.

Dallin, David J. *The Real Soviet Union*, rev. ed. Translated by Joseph Shaplen. New Haven, CT: Yale University Press, 1947 [1944].

Dallin, David J. *Russia and Postwar Europe*. Translated by F. K. Lawrence. New Haven, CT: Yale University Press, 1943.

Dallin, David J. *Soviet Russia's Foreign Policy, 1939–1942*. Translated by Leon Denner. New Haven, CT: Yale University Press, 1942.

David, Henry. *The History of the Haymarket Affair: A Study in Social-Revolutionary and Labor Movements*. New York: Russell and Russell, 1958.

Davis, Forrest, and Robert Hunter. *The Red China Lobby*. New York: Fleet, 1963.

De Caux, Len. *Labor Radical: From the Wobblies to the CIO*. Boston: Beacon Press, 1970.

De Grazia, Alfred. *The Western Public and Beyond*. Stanford, CA: Stanford University Press, 1954.

De Toledano, Ralph. "It's Still the Soviet Party." *National Review* (January 5, 1957): 11–12.

De Toledano, Ralph. *Lament for a Generation*. New York: Farrar, Straus and Cudahy, 1960.

De Toledano, Ralph. "The Liberal Disintegration: A Conservative View." *The Freeman* (November 13, 1950): 109–11.

De Toledano, Ralph. *Nixon*. New York: Henry Holt, 1956.

De Toledano, Ralph, and Victor Lasky. *Seeds of Treason: The True Story of the Hiss-Chambers Tragedy*. New York: Funk and Wagnalls, 1950.

Deutscher, Isaac. *Heretics and Renegades: And Other Essays*. London: Hamish Hamilton, 1955.

Dewey, John. *Freedom and Culture*. New York: Capricorn, 1963 [1939].

Dewey, John. *The Later Works, Vol. 11*. Edited by Jo Ann Boydston. Carbondale/Edwardsville, IL: Southern Illinois University Press, 1987.

Dewey, John. *Liberalism and Social Action*. New York: G. P. Putnam's Sons, 1935.

Diamond, Sara. *Roads to Disunion: Right-Wing Movements and Political Power in the United States*. New York/London: Guilford Press, 1995.

Dies, Martin. *The Trojan Horse in America*. New York: Dodd, Mead, 1940.

Dietrich, John W., ed. *The George W. Bush Foreign Policy Reader: Presidential Speeches with Commentary*. Armonk, NY/London: M. E. Sharpe, 2005.

Diggins, John P. *Up from Communism: Conservative Odysseys in American Intellectual History*. New York: Harper and Row, 1975.

Dilling, Elizabeth. *The Red Network: A "Who's Who" and Handbook of Radicalism for Patriots*. Kenilworth, IL: Author, 1935.

Dilling, Elizabeth. *The Roosevelt Red Record and Its Background*. Kenilworth, IL: Author, 1936.

Dochuk, Darren. *From Bible to Sunbelt: Plain-Folk Religion, Grassroots Politics, and the Rise of Evangelical Conservatism*. New York/London: Norton, 2011.

Doherty, Brian. *Radicals for Capitalism: A Freewheeling History of the Modern American Liberation Movement*. New York: Public Affairs, 2007.

Doherty, Thomas. *Cold War, Cool Medium: Television, McCarthyism, and American Culture* (New York: Columbia University Press, 2003).

Donner, Frank. *Protectors of Privilege: Red Squads and Police Repression in Urban America*. Berkeley/Los Angeles, CA: University of California Press, 1990.

Donovan, John T. *Crusader in the Cold War: A Biography of Fr. John F. Cronin, S.S. (1908–1994)*. New York: Peter Lang, 2005.

Donovan, Robert J. *Conflict and Crisis: The Presidency of Harry Truman, 1945–1948*. New York: Norton, 1977

Donovan, Robert J. *Eisenhower: The Inside Story*. New York: Harper and Brothers, 1956.

Donovan, Robert J. *Tumultuous Years: The Presidency of Harry S. Truman, 1949–1953*. New York: Norton, 1982.

Donovan, William J., and Mary Gardiner Jones. "Program for a Counter Attack to Communist Penetration of Government Service." *Yale Law Journal* 58, no. 8 (July 1949): 1211–41.

Dorrien, Gary. *The Neoconservative Mind: Politics, Culture, and the War of Ideology*. Philadelphia, PA: Temple University Press, 1993.

Douglas, Paul H. *In the Fullness of Time: The Memoirs of Paul H. Douglas*. New York: Harcourt Brace Jovanovich, 1972.

Dower, John W. *Cultures of War: Pearl Harbor/Hiroshima/9-11/Iraq*. New York/ London: Norton/The New Press, 2010.

Draper, Theodore. *American Communism and Soviet Russia: The Formative Period*. New York: Viking Press, 1960.

Draper, Theodore. "The Ghost of Social Fascism." *Commentary* (February 1969): 29–42.

Draper, Theodore. "The Specter of Weimar." *Commentary* (December 1971): 43–49.

Drucker, Peter F. *The End of Economic Man: A Study of the New Totalitarianism*. London: William Heinemann, 1939.

D'Souza, Dinesh. *The Enemy at Home: The Cultural Left and Its Responsibility for 9/11*. New York/London: Doubleday, 2007.

Dubinsky, David and A. H. Raskin, *David Dubinsky: In Life with Labor*. New York: Simon and Schuster, 1977.

Dulles, John Foster. "A Policy of Boldness, *Life* (May 19, 1952): 146–54.

Dulles, John Foster. "Thoughts on Soviet Foreign Policy and What to Do About It." *Life* (June 3, 1946): 112–26; (June 10, 1946): 118–30.

Dulles, John Foster. *War or Peace*. New York: Macmillan, 1950.

Dunne, Philip. *Take Two*. New York: McGraw-Hill, 1980.

Eastman, Max. "Facts and Logic re McCarthy." *The Freeman* (April 19, 1954): 532–34.

Editors of *National Review*. "The John Birch Society and the Conservative Movement." *National Review* (October 19, 1956): 914–29.

Ehrman, John. *The Rise of Neoconservatism: Intellectuals and Foreign Affairs, 1945–1994*. New Haven, CT/London: Yale University Press, 1995.

Einstein, Albert. "The Military Mentality." *American Scholar* 16, no. 3 (Summer 1947): 353–54.

Eisele, Albert. *Almost to the Presidency: A Biography of Two American Politicians*. Blue Earth, MN/San Francisco: Piper, 1972.

Eisenhower, Dwight D. *Mandate for Change, 1953–1956*. Garden City, NY: Doubleday, 1963.

Ekirch, Arthur A., Jr. *The Decline of American Liberalism*. New York/London: Longmans, Green, 1955.

Emerson, Steven. *American Jihad: The Terrorists Living Among Us*. New York: Free Press, 2002.

Emerson, Steven. *Jihad Incorporated: A Guide to Militant Islam in the United States*. Amherst, NY: Prometheus Books, 2006.

Emerson, Thomas J., and David Haber. *Political and Civil Rights in the United States: A Collection of Legal and Related Materials*. Buffalo, NY: Dennis, 1952.

Emerson, Thomas J., and David M. Helfeld. "Loyalty Among Government Employees." *Yale Law Journal* 58, no. 1 (December 1948): 1–143.

Emspak, Frank. *The Break-up of the Congress of Industrial Organizations (CIO): 1945–1950* [Ph.D. dissertation]. Los Angeles, CA: University of California at Los Angeles, 1972.

English, Raymond. "Conservatism: The Forbidden Faith." *American Scholar* 21, no. 4 (Autumn 1952): 393–95.

Epstein, Benjamin R., and Arnold Forster. *The Radical Right: Report on the John Birch Society and Its Allies*. New York: Random House, 1967.

Epstein, Melech. *The Jew and Communism: The Story of Early Communist Victories and Ultimate Defeats in the Jewish Community, U.S.A., 1919–1941*. New York: Trade Union Sponsoring Committee, 1959.

Ernst, Morris. *The First Freedom*. New York: Macmillan, 1946.

Ernst, Morris. *Report on the American Communist*. New York: Henry Holt, 1952.

Evanier, David, and Harvey Klehr. "Anticommunism and Mental Health." *American Spectator* 22, no. 2 (February 1989): 28–30.

Evans, Medford. *The Assassination of Joe McCarthy*. Belmont, MA: Western Islands, 1970.

Evans, M. Stanton. *Blacklisted by History: The Untold Story of Joe McCarthy and His Fight Against America's Enemies*. New York: Crown Forum, 2007.

Everitt, David. *A Shadow of Red: Communism and the Blacklist in Radio and Television*. Chicago: Ivan R. Dee, 2007.

Ewald, William Bragg, Jr. *Who Killed Joe McCarthy?* New York: Simon and Schuster, 1984.

Fainsod, Merle. *How Russia Is Ruled*. Cambridge, MA: Harvard University Press, 1954.

Fariello, Griffen. *Red Scare: Memories of the American Inquisition: An Oral History*. New York: Norton, 1995.

Fenton, John M. *In Your Opinion . . . : The Managing Editor of the Gallup Poll Looks at Polls, Politics, and the People from 1945 to 1960*. Boston/Toronto: Little, Brown, 1960.

Fielder, Leslie A. "Hiss, Chambers, and the Age of Innocence." *Commentary* (August 1951). Reprinted in Swan, *Alger Hiss*, 1–26.

Filene, Peter G. *Americans and the Soviet Experiment, 1917–1933*. Cambridge, MA: Harvard University Press, 1967.

Fischer, Nick. "The Founders of American Anti-Communism." *American Communist History* 5, no. 1 (June 2006): 72–80.

Fischer, Ruth. *Stalin and German Communism: A Study in the Origins of the State Party*. Cambridge, MA: Harvard University Press, 1948.

Fish, Hamilton. *The Challenge of World Communism*. Milwaukee, WI: Bruce, 1946.

Fleming, D. F. *The Cold War and its Origins, 1917–1960*. Garden City, NY: Doubleday, 1961.

Fleming, John V. *The Anti-Communist Manifestos: Four Books That Shaped the Cold War*. New York: Norton, 2009.

Foner, Philip S. *The Fur and Leather Workers Union: A Story of Dramatic Struggles and Achievements*. Newark, NJ: Nordan Press, 1950.

Fordham, Benjamin O. *Building the Cold War Consensus: The Political Economy of United States National Security, 1949–1951*. Ann Arbor, MI: University of Michigan Press, 1998.

Forster, Arnold. *Square One*. New York: Donald I. Fine, 1988.

Foster, William Z. *History of the Communist Party of the United States*. New York: International Publishers, 1952.

Foster, William Z. *Toward Soviet America*. New York: Coward-McCann, 1932.

Fox, Richard Wightman. *Reinhold Niebuhr: A Biography*. New York: Pantheon, 1985.

Fraser, Steven. *Labor Will Rule: Sidney Hillman and the Rise of American Labor.* New York: Free Press, 1991.

Freeberg, Ernest. *Democracy's Prisoner: Eugene V. Debs, the Great War, and the Right to Dissent.* Cambridge, MA/London: Harvard University Press, 2008.

Freeman, Joshua B., and Steve Rosswurm. "The Education of an Anti-Communist: Father John F. Cronin and the Baltimore Labor Movement." *Labor History* 33, no. 2 (Spring 1992): 217–47.

Freud, Sigmund. *The Standard Edition of the Complete Psychological Works of Sigmund Freud, Vol. 21.* Translated and edited by James Strachey. London: Hogarth Press, 1961.

Fried, Richard M. "Electoral Politics and McCarthyism: The 1950 Campaign." In Griffith and Theoharis, *The Specter,* 190–222.

Fried, Richard M. *The Russians Are Coming! The Russians Are Coming!* New York/Oxford, UK: Oxford University Press, 1998.

Friedberg, Aaron L. *In the Shadow of the Garrison State: America's Anti-Stalinism and Its Cold War Grand Strategy.* Princeton, NJ: Princeton University Press, 2000.

Friedheim, Robert L. *The Seattle General Strike.* Seattle, WA: University of Washington Press, 1964.

Friedman, Murray. *The Neoconservative Revolution: Jewish Intellectuals and the Shaping of Public Policy.* Cambridge, UK: Cambridge University Press, 2005.

Friedrich, Carl J. "The Problem of Totalitarianism: An Introduction" In *Totalitarianism: Proceedings of a Conference Held at the American Academy of Arts and Sciences, March 1953,* edited by Carl. J. Friedrich. Cambridge, MA: Harvard University Press, 1954.

Frum, David, and Richard Perle. *An End to Evil: How to Win the War on Terror.* New York: Random House, 2003.

Fryer, Russell G. *Recent Conservative Political Thought: American Perspectives.* Washington, DC: University Press of America, 1986.

Gabler, Neal. *Winchell: Gossip, Power and the Culture of Celebrity.* New York: Knopf, 1994.

Gaddis, John Lewis. *The Cold War: A New History.* New York: Penguin, 2005.

Gaddis, John Lewis. "The Insecurities of Victory: The United States and the Perception of the Soviet Threat after World War II." In *The Truman Presidency,* edited by Mitchell J. Lacey, 235–72. Cambridge, UK: Cambridge University Press, 1989.

Gaddis, John Lewis. *Strategies of Containment: A Critical Appraisal of Postwar American National Security Policy.* New York/Oxford, UK: Oxford University Press, 1982.

Gaddis, John Lewis. "The Unexpected John Foster Dulles." In *John Foster Dulles and the Diplomacy of the Cold War,* edited by Richard H. Immerman, 47–78. Princeton, NJ: Princeton University Press, 1990.

Gallup, George H. *The Gallup Poll: Public Opinion, 1953–1971.* New York: Random House, 1972.

Gardiner, A. G. *Portraits and Portents.* New York/London: Harper and Brothers, 1926.

Garrow, David J. *The FBI and Martin Luther King, Jr.* New York: Penguin Books, 1981.

Gary, Brett. "Morris Ernst's Troubled Legacy." *Reconstruction: Studies in Contemporary Culture* 8, no. 1 (2008). creconstruction.eserver.org/081/gary.SHTML#11.

Gearty, Patrick W. *The Economic Thought of Monsignor John A. Ryan.* Washington, DC: Catholic University of America Press, 1953.

Gellerman, William B. *Martin Dies.* New York: John Day, 1944.

Gellhorn, Walter. "Report on a Report of the House Committee on Un-American Activities." *Harvard Law Review* 60, no. 8 (October 1947): 1192–234.

Gellman, Irwin F. *The Contender: Richard Nixon—The Congress Years, 1946–1952.* New York: Free Press, 1999.

Gerson, Mark. *The Neoconservative Version: From the Cold War to the Culture Wars.* Lanham, MD/New York: Madison Books, 1996.

Ghosh, Bobby. "Does America Have a Muslim Problem." *Time* (August 19, 2010). www.time.com/time/national/0,8599,2011798-2,00.html.

Gibney, Frank. "After the Ball." *Commonweal* 60 (September 3, 1954): 531–34.

Gilbert, Brian. "New Light on the Lattimore Case." *New Republic* (December 27, 1954): 7–12.

Gilbert, James B. *Writers and Partisans: A History of Literary Radicalism in America.* New York: Wiley, 1968.

Gillmor, Dan. *Fear, the Accuser.* New York: Abelard-Schuman, 1954.

Gillon, Steven M. *Politics and Vision: The ADA and American Liberalism, 1947–1985.* New York/Oxford, UK: Oxford University Press, 1987.

Gitlow, Benjamin. *I Confess: The Truth About American Communism.* New York: Dutton, 1940.

Givertz, Harry K. *From Wealth to Welfare: The Evolution of Liberalism.* Stanford, CA: Stanford University Press, 1950.

Glazer, Nathan. "An Excerpt from *From Socialism to Sociology.*" www.pbs.org/arguing/nyintellectuals_glazer_2.html.

Glazer, Nathan. "*Commentary*: The Early Years." In *Commentary in American Life,* edited by Murray Freedman, 46–47. Philadelphia, PA: Temple University Press, 2005.

Glazer, Nathan. "On Being Deradicalized." *Commentary* (October 1970): 74–80.

Glazov, Jamie. "An Interview with John Earl Haynes and Harvey Klehr." *History News Network* (December 1, 2003). hnn.us/articles/1832.html.

Goldbloom, Maurice J. "The American Communists Today." *Commentary* (February 1957): 134.

Goldman, Emma. *My Disillusionment in Russia.* New York: Crowell, 1970.

Goldman, Emma. *My Further Disillusionment in Russia.* Garden City, NY: Doubleday, Page, 1924.

Goldman, Emma. "The Tragedy of the Political Exiles." *The Nation* (October 10, 1934): 401–2.

Goldman, Eric F. *The Crucial Decade—and After: America, 1945–1960.* New York: Vintage, 1960.

Goldstein, Robert Justin. *American Blacklist: The Attorney General's List of Subversive Organizations.* Lawrence, KS: University Press of Kansas, 2008.

Goldstein, Robert Justin. *Political Repression in Modern America: From 1870 to the Present.* Cambridge, MA: Schenckman, 1978.

Gompers, Samuel. *Out of Their Own Mouths: A Revelation and Indictment of Sovietism.* New York: Dutton, 1921.

Goodman, Walter. *The Committee: The Extraordinary Career of the House Committee on Un-American Activities.* Baltimore, MD: Penguin Books, 1969.

Goodwin, Doris Kearns. *Wait Till Next Year: A Memoir.* New York: Simon and Schuster, 1997.

Green, David. *Shaping Political Consciousness: The Language of Politics in America from McKinley to Reagan.* Ithaca, NY/London: Cornell University Press, 1987.

Greenberg, David. *Nixon's Shadow: The History of an Image.* Norton, 2003.

Griffin, Robert. "The Selling of America: The Advertising Council and American Politics, 1942–1960." *Business History Review* 57, no. 3 (Autumn 1983): 388–412.

Griffith, Robert. *The Politics of Fear: Joseph R. McCarthy and the Senate,* 2nd ed. Amherst, MA: University of Massachusetts Press, 1987.

Griffith, Robert. "Ralph Flanders and the Censure of Senator Joseph R. McCarthy." *Vermont History* 39, no. 1 (Winter 1971): 5–20.

Griffith, Robert, and Athan Theoharis, eds. *The Specter: Original Essays on the Cold War and the Origins of McCarthyism.* New York: New Viewpoints, 1974.

Grose, Peter. *Gentleman Spy: The Life of Allen Dulles.* Boston/New York: Houghton Mifflin, 1994.

Grupp, Fred W., Jr. "The Political Perspectives of Birch Society Members." In *The American Right Wing,* edited by Robert A. Schoenberger, 91. New York: Holt, Rinehart and Winston, 1969.

Guttenplan, D. D. *American Radical: The Life and Times of I. F. Stone.* New York: Farrar, Straus and Giroux, 2009.

Gurtov, Mel Gurtov. *Superpower on Crusade: The Bush Doctrine in US Foreign Policy.* Boulder, CO/London: Lynne Rienner, 2006.

Hackett, Alice Payne. *70 Years of Best Sellers, 1895–1965.* New York/London: Bowker, 1967.

Hagedon, Ann. *Savage Peace: Hope and Fear in America, 1919.* New York: Simon and Schuster, 2007.

Hamby, Alonzo L. *Beyond the New Deal: Harry S Truman and American Liberalism.* New York/London: Columbia University Press, 1973.

Hamby, Alonzo L. *Liberalism and its Challenges: FDR to Reagan.* New York/Oxford, UK: Oxford University Press, 1985.

Handicapper. "Those Liberal Journalists." *Human Events* (December 22, 1954): np.

Hanson, Ole. *Americanism versus Bolshevism.* Garden City, NY/London: Doubleday, Page, 1920.

Hapgood, Norman, ed. *Professional Patriots: An Exposure of the Personalities, Methods and Objectives Involved in the Organized Effort to Exploit Patriotic Impulses in These United States During and After the Late War.* New York: Albert and Charles Boni, 1927.

Harrington, Michael. "The Committee for Cultural Freedom." *Dissent* 2, no. 2 (Spring 1955): 113–22.

Harrington, Michael. *Fragments of the Century: A Serial Autobiography.* New York: Saturday Review Press/E. P. Dutton, 1973.

Harrington, Michael. "In the United States: Communism After Hungary." *Commonweal* (February 1, 1957): 455–57.

Harrington, Michael. "Myths of U.S. Liberalism." *Commonweal* (December 17, 1954): 303–6.

Harrington, Michael. "New Communist Line." *Commonweal* (July 13, 1956): 363–65.

Harrington, Michael. "Politics in a New World." *Commonweal* (August 26, 1955): 511–13.

Harrington, Michael. "The Post-McCarthy Atmosphere." *Dissent* 2, no. 4 (Autumn 1955): 291–94.

Harrington, Michael. "Rights of the Guilty." *Commonweal* (August 7, 1953): 435–37.

Harrington, Michael. "Silence on the Left." *Commonweal* (October 2, 1953): 627–30.

Harrington, Michael. *Taking Sides: The Education of a Militant Mind.* New York: Holt, Rinehart and Winston, 1985.

Harris, Louis. *Is There a Republican Majority?: Political Trends, 1952–1956.* New York: Harper and Brothers, 1954.

Harris, Ruth. *Dreyfus: Politics, Emotion, and the Scandal of the Century.* New York: Metropolitan Books, 2010.

Hartz, Louis. *The Liberal Tradition in America: An Interpretation of American Political Thought Since the Revolution.* New York/London: Harcourt Brace Jovanovich, 1955.

Hayek, Friedrich A. *The Constitution of Liberty.* Chicago: University of Chicago Press, 1960.

Hayek, Friedrich A. *The Road to Serfdom.* Chicago: University of Chicago Press, 1944.

Haynes, C. Groves, ed. *The Threat of Soviet Imperialism.* Baltimore, MD: Johns Hopkins University Press, 1954.

Haynes, John Earl. "An Essay on Historical Writing on Domestic Communism and Anti-Communism." A fuller version of "The Cold War Debate Continues: A Traditionalist Looks at Historical Writing on Domestic Communism and Anti-Communism." *Journal of Cold War Studies* 2, no. 1 (Winter 2000). www.johnearlhaynes.org/pag367.html.

Haynes, John Earl. *Red Scare or Red Menace?: American Communism and Anticommunism in the Cold War Era.* Chicago: Ivan R. Dee, 1996.

Haynes, John Earl. Response to Ellen Schrecker comments on "The Cold War Debate Continues." www.people.fas.harvard.edu/~hpcws/comment.16.htm.

Haynes, John Earl, and Harvey Klehr. *Early Cold War Spies: The Espionage Trials That Shaped American Politics.* Cambridge, UK: Cambridge University Press, 2006.

Haynes, John Earl,and Harvey Klehr. *Venona: Decoding Soviet Espionage in America*. New Haven, CT/London: Yale University Press, 1999.

Haynes, John Earl, Harvey Klehr, and Alexander Vassiliev. *Spies: The Rise and Fall of the KGB in America*. New Haven, CT/London: Yale University Press, 2009.

Hays, Paul R. "Congress's Right to Investigate: Two Books Examined." *Commentary* (November 1955): 440–46.

Heale, M. J. *American Anticommunism: Combating the Enemy Within, 1830–1970.* Baltimore, MD: Johns Hopkins University Press, 1990.

Heller, Anne C. *Ayn Rand and the World She Made*. New York: Doubleday, 2009.

Hellman, Lillian. *Scoundrel Time*. Boston: Little, Brown, 1976.

Herken, Gregg. *Brotherhood of the Bomb: The Troubled Lives and Loyalties of Robert Oppenheimer, Ernest Lawrence, and Edward Teller*. New York: Henry Holt, 2002.

Herring, George C., Jr. *Aid to Russia: Strategy, Diplomacy, the Origins of the Cold War*. New York/London: Columbia University Press, 1973.

Hersh, Burton. *The Old Boys: The American Elite and the Origins of the CIA*. New York: Scribner's and Maxwell Macmillan, 1992.

Hewison, Robert. *In Anger: Culture in the Cold War, 1945–60*. London: Weidenfeld and Nicolson, 1981.

Hicks, Granville. *Part of the Truth*. New York: Harcourt, Brace and World, 1965.

Hinds, Lynn Boyd, and Theodor Otto Windt, Jr. *The Cold War as Rhetoric: The Beginnings, 1945–1950*. New York/Westport, CT: Praeger, 1991.

Hodgson, Geoffrey. *The Gentleman from New York: Daniel Patrick Moynihan: A Biography*. Boston/New York: Houghton Mifflin, 2000.

Hoeveler, J. David, Jr. *The New Humanism: A Critique of Modern America, 1900–1940*. Charlottesville, VA: University Press of Virginia, 1977.

Hofstadter, Richard. *The Age of Reform*. New York: Knopf, 1956.

Hofstadter, Richard. *The Paranoid Style in American Politics and Other Essays*. New York: Knopf, 1965.

Hofstadter, Richard. "The Pseudo-Conservative Revolt." In Bell, *The New American Right,*— 33–55.

Hofstadter, Richard. "The Pseudo-Conservative Revolt Revisited: A Postscript—1962." In Bell, *The New American Right*, 81–86.

Hofstadter, Richard, and Beatrice Hofstadter, eds. *Great Issues in American History: From Reconstruction to the Present Day, 1864–1981*, rev. ed. New York: Vintage, 1982.

Hogan, Michael J. *A Cross of Iron: Harry S. Truman and the Origins of the National Security State, 1945–1954*. Cambridge, UK: Cambridge University Press, 1998.

Hollander, Paul. *Anti-Americanism: Critiques at Home and Abroad, 1965–1990*. New York/Oxford, UK: Oxford University Press, 1992.

Hook, Sidney. *Convictions*. Buffalo, NY: Prometheus Books, 1990.

Hook, Sidney. *Heresy, Yes—Conspiracy, No!* New York: ACCF, 1951.

Hook, Sidney. *Letters of Sidney Hook: Democracy, Communism, and the Cold War*. Edited by Edward S. Shapiro. Armonk, NY/London: M. E. Sharpe, 1995.

Hook, Sidney. *Out of Step: An Unquiet Life in the 20th Century.* New York: Harper and Row, 1987.

Hook, Sidney. "Unpragmatic Liberalism." *New Republic* (May 24, 1954): 18–21.

Hook, Sidney. "Wanted: An Ethics of Employment for Our Time." *New York Times Book Review* (July 22, 1956): 6, 14.

Hoopes, Townsend. *The Devil and John Foster Dulles.* Boston/Toronto: Little, Brown, 1973.

Hoover, J. Edgar. *Masters of Deceit: The Story of Communism in America and How to Fight It.* New York: Henry Holt, 1958.

Hoover, J. Edgar. *On Communism.* New York: Random House, 1969.

Hoover, J. Edgar. *One Nation's Response to Communism.* Washington, DC: Federal Bureau of Investigation, 1960.

Hoover, J. Edgar. *A Study of Communism.* New York: Holt, Rinehart and Winston, 1962.

Hopper, Hedda. *The Whole Truth and Nothing But.* Garden City, NY: Doubleday, 1963.

Horton, Philip. "The China Lobby: Part II." *The Reporter* (April 15–29, 1952): 5–18.

Houseman, John. "Today's Hero: A Review." *Hollywood Quarterly* 2, no. 2, (January 1947): 161–63.

Howe, Irving. "The ADA: Vision and Myopia." *Dissent* 2, no. 2 (Spring 1955): 107–13.

Howe, Irving. "The New York Intellectuals: A Chronicle and a Critique." *Commentary* (October 1968): 329–51.

Howe, Irving. *Steady Work: Essays in the Politics of Democratic Radicalism, 1953–1966.* New York: Harcourt, Brace and World, 1966.

Howe, Irving, and Lewis Coser, *The American Communist Party: A Critical History.* Boston: Beacon Press, 1957; New York: Praeger, 1962.

Humphrey, Hubert H. *The Education of a Public Man: My Life and Politics.* Garden City, NY: Doubleday, 1976.

Hunt, Marsha. *The Way We Wore: Styles of the 1930s and 1940s and Our World Since Then, Shown and Recalled by Marsha Hunt.* Fallbrook, CA: Fallbrook, 1993.

Huntington, Samuel P. *American Politics: The Promise of Disharmony.* Cambridge, MA/London: Belknap, 1981.

Huntington, Samuel P. *The Clash of Civilizations and the Remaking of World Order* (New York: Simon and Schuster, 1996).

Hyman, Herbert H. "England and America: Climates of Tolerance and Intolerance—1962." In Bell, *The Radical Right,* 227–57.

Hyman, Herbert H., and Paul B. Sheatsley. "Trends in Public Opinion on Civil Liberties." *Journal of Public Issues* 9, no. 3 (1953): 6–16.

Hyman, Sidney. *The Lives of William Benton.* Chicago: University of Chicago Press, 1969.

International Committee for Political Prisoners. *Letters from Russian Prisons, Consisting of Documents by Political Prisoners in Soviet Prisons, Prison Camp and Exile, and Reprints of Affidavits Concerning Political Persecution in Soviet Russia, Official Statements by Soviet Authorities, Excerpts from Soviet Laws*

Pertaining to Civil Liberties and Other Documents. New York: A. and C. Boni, 1925.

Irons, Peter H. "The Cold War Crusade of the United States Chamber of Commerce." In Griffith and Theoharis, *The Specter*, 72–89.

Irons, Peter H. " 'Fighting Fair': Zechariah Chafee, Jr., the Department of Justice, and the 'Trial at the Harvard Club,' " *Harvard Law Review* 94, no. 6 (April 1981): 1205–36.

Isaacson, Walter, and Evan Thomas. *The Wise Men: Six Friends and the World They Made—Acheson, Bohlen, Harriman, Kennan, Lovett, McCloy.* New York: Simon and Schuster, 1986.

Isms: A Review of Alien Isms, Revolutionary Communism and Their Active Sympathizers in the United States. Indianapolis, IN: American Legion, 1936.

Isserman, Maurice. *The Other American: The Life of Michael Harrington.* New York: Public Affairs, 2000.

Jacobs, Paul. *Is Curly Jewish?: A Political Self-Portrait Illuminating Three Turbulent Decades of Social Revolt, 1955–1965.* New York: Atheneum, 1965.

Jacoby, Susan. *Alger Hiss and the Battle for History.* New Haven, CT/London: Yale University Press, 2009.

Jacoby, Susan. *Freethinkers: A History of American Secularism.* New York: Metropolitan Books, 2004.

Jeansonne, Glen. *Women of the Far Right: The Mother's Movement and World War II.* Chicago/London: University of Chicago Press, 1996.

Jeffers, Thomas L. *Norman Podhoretz: A Biography.* Cambridge, UK: Cambridge University Press, 2010.

Jerome, Fred. *The Einstein File: J. Edgar Hoover's Secret War Against the World's Most Famous Scientist.* New York: St. Martin's Press, 2002.

Jones, Howard Mumford, ed. *Primer of Intellectual Freedom.* Cambridge, MA: Harvard University Press, 1949.

Judis, John B. *William F. Buckley: Patron Saint of the Conservatives.* New York: Simon and Schuster, 1988.

Jumonville, Neil. *Henry Steele Commager: Midcentury Liberalism and the History of the Present.* Chapel Hill, NC/London: University of North Carolina Press, 1999.

Kahn, Albert E. *The Matusow Affair: Memoir of a National Scandal.* Mt. Kisco, NY: Moyer Bell, 1987.

Kalman, Laura. *Abe Fortas: A Biography.* New Haven, CT/London: Yale University Press, 1990.

Kalven, Harry, Jr. *A Worthy Tradition: Freedom of Speech in America.* New York: Harper and Row, 1988.

Katznelson, Ira, Kim Geiger, and Daniel Kryder. "Limiting Liberalism: The Southern Veto in Congress, 1933–1950." *Political Science Quarterly* 108, no. 2 (Summer 1993): 283–306.

Kauffman, Christopher J. *Faith and Fraternalism: The History of the Knights of Columbus, 1882–1982.* New York: Harper and Row, 1982.

Keeley, Joseph. *The China Lobby Man: The Story of Alfred Kohlberg.* New Rochelle, NY: Arlington House, 1969.

Kegley, Charles W., and Robert W. Bretall, eds. *Reinhold Niebuhr: His Religious, Social, and Political Thought.* New York: Macmillan, 1956.

Keith, Caroline H. *"For Hell and a Brown Mule": The Biography of Senator Millard E. Tydings.* Lanham, MD: Madison Books, 1991.

Keller, William W. *The Liberals and J. Edgar Hoover: Rise and Fall of a Domestic Intelligence State.* Princeton, NJ: Princeton University Press, 1989.

Kempton, Murray. *Part of Our Time: Some Ruins and Monuments of the Thirties.* New York: Simon and Schuster, 1955.

Kendall, Willmoore. *The Conservative Affirmation.* Chicago: Henry Regnery, 1963.

Kennan, George F. *Soviet-American Relations, 1917–1920: The Decision to Intervene.* Princeton, NJ: Princeton University Press, 1958.

Kerby, Phil. "Hollywood Blacklist." *Frontier* (July 1952): 5–7.

Kerby, Phil. "The Legion Blacklist." *New Republic* (June 16, 1952): 14–15.

Kessler, Lauren. *Clever Girl: Elizabeth Bentley, the Spy Who Ushered in the McCarthy Era.* New York: HarperCollins, 2003.

Kimball, Penn. *The File.* San Diego, CA/New York: Harcourt Brace Jovanovich, 1983.

Kirk, Russell. *A Program for Conservatives.* Chicago: Henry Regnery, 1954.

Klehr, Harvey. *Communist Cadre: The Social Background of the American Communist Party Elite.* Stanford, CA: Hoover Institute Press, 1978.

Klehr, Harvey. *Far Left of Center: The American Radical Left Today.* New Brunswick, NJ/Oxford, UK: Transaction Books, 1988.

Klehr, Harvey. *The Heyday of American Communism: The Depression Decade.* New York: Basic Books, 1984.

Klehr, Harvey. "Redfest '85.' " *New Republic* (August 12–19, 1985): 16–17.

Klehr, Harvey, and John Earl Haynes. *In Denial: Historians, Communism and Espionage.* San Francisco, CA: Encounter Books, 2003.

Klehr, Harvey, John Earl Haynes, and Kyrill M. Anderson. *The Soviet World of American Communism.* New Haven, CT/London: Yale University Press, 1998.

Klehr, Harvey, John Earl Haynes, and Fridrikh Igorevitch Firsov. *The Secret World of American Communism.* New Haven, CT/London: Yale University Press, 1995.

Klehr, Harvey, and Ronald Radosh. *The Amerasia Spy Case: Prelude to McCarthyism.* Chapel Hill, NC/London: University of North Carolina Press, 1996.

Knight, Amy. *How the Cold War Began: The Gouzenko Affair and the Hunt for Soviet Spies.* Toronto: McClelland and Stewart, 2005.

Koen, Ross Y. *The China Lobby in American Politics.* New York: Octagon Books, 1974.

Koestler, Arthur. "The Complex Issue of the Ex-Communists." *New York Times Magazine* (February 19, 1950). Reprinted in Swan, *Alger Hiss*, 49–56.

Koestler, Arthur. *The Trail of the Dinosaur and Other Essays.* New York: Macmillan, 1955.

Koestler, Arthur, et al. *The God That Failed.* Edited by Richard Crossman. New York/Evanston, IL: HarperColophon, 1963 [1949].

Kovel, Joel. *Red Hunting in the Promised Land: Anticommunism and the Making of America.* New York: Basic Books, 1994.

Kramer, Hilton. *The Twilight of the Intellectuals: Culture and Politics in the Era of the Cold War.* Chicago: Ivan R. Dee, 1999.

Kravchenko, Victor. *I Chose Freedom: The Personal and Political Life of a Soviet Official*. New York: Scribner's, 1946.

Kristol, Irving. " 'Civil Liberties,' 1952—A Study in Confusion: Do We Defend Our Rights by Protecting Communists?" *Commentary* (March 1952): 228–36.

Kristol, Irving. "Memoirs of a 'Cold Warrior.' " *New York Times Magazine* (February 11, 1968): 25, 90–98.

Kristol, Irving. *Neoconservatism: The Autobiography of an Idea*. New York/London: Free Press, 1995.

Kristol, Irving. *The Neoconservative Persuasion: Selected Essays, 1942–2009*. Edited by Gertrude Himmelfarb. New York: Basic Books, 2011.

Kristol, Irving. *Reflections of a Neoconservative: Looking Back, Looking Ahead*. New York: Basic Books, 1983.

Krivitsky, Walter. *In Stalin's Secret Service: An Exposé of Russian Secret Policies by the Chief of the Soviet Intelligence in Western Europe*. New York/London: Harper and Brothers, 1939.

Kutler, Stanley I. *The American Inquisition: Justice and Injustice in the Cold War*. New York: Hill and Wang, 1982.

Kyniston, David. *Austerity Britain, 1945–51*. New York: Walker, 2008.

Lansing, Robert. "Some Legal Questions on the Peace Conference" [Address to the American Bar Association, Boston, September 5, 1919]. *American Journal of International Law* 13, no. 4 (October 1919): 632–50.

Larson, Arthur. *A Republican Looks at His Party*. New York: Harper and Brothers, 1956.

Lasch, Christopher. *The Agony of the American Left*. New York: Knopf, 1969.

Latham, Earl. *The Communist Controversy in Washington: From the New Deal to McCarthy*. Cambridge, MA: Harvard University Press, 1966.

Leab, Daniel J. *I Was a Communist for the FBI: The Unhappy Life and Times of Matt Cvetic*. University Park, PA: Pennsylvania State University Press, 2000.

Leab, Daniel J. " 'The Iron Curtain' (1948): Hollywood's First Cold War Movie." *Historical Journal of Film, Radio and Television* 8, no. 2 (1988):153–88.

Lee, Albert. *Henry Ford and the Jews*. New York: Stein and Day, 1980.

Leffler, Melvin P. *A Preponderance of Power: National Security, the Truman Administration, and the Cold War*. Stanford, CA: Stanford University Press, 1992.

Levenstein, Aaron, in collaboration with William Agar. *Freedom's Advocate: A Twenty-Five Year Chronicle*. New York: Viking, 1965.

Levenstein, Harvey A. *Communism, Anticommunism, and the CIO*. Westport, CT: Greenwood Press, 1981.

Levin, Murray B. *Political Hysteria in America: The Democratic Capacity of Repression*. New York/London: Basic Books, 1971.

Levine, Isaac Don. *Eyewitness to History: Memoirs and Reflections of a Foreign Correspondent for Half a Century*. New York: Hawthorn Books, 1973.

Lewy, Guenter. *The Cause That Failed: Communism in American Political Life*. New York/Oxford, UK: Oxford University Press, 1990.

"Liberal Anti-Communism Revisited: A Symposium." *Commentary* 44 (September 1967): 31–80.

Lichtman, Robert M. "J. B. Matthews and the 'Counter-Subversives': Names as a Political and Financial Resource in the McCarthy Era." *American Communist History* 5, no. 1 (June 2006): 1–36.

Lichtman, Robert M., and Ronald D. Cohen. *Deadly Farce: Harvey Matusow and the Informer System in the McCarthy Era.* Urbana/Chicago, IL: University of Illinois Press, 2005.

Liebman, Marvin. *Coming Out Conservative.* San Francisco: Chronicle Books, 1992.

Liebowitz, Nathan. *Daniel Bell and the Agony of Modern Liberalism.* Westport, CT: Greenwood Press, 1985.

Lipset, Seymour Martin. "The Sources of the 'Radical Right.'" In Bell, *The New American Right,* 166–234.

Lipset, Seymour Martin, and Gary Marks. *It Didn't Happen Here: Why Socialism Failed in the United States.* New York/London: Norton, 2000.

Lipset, Seymour Martin, and Earl Raab. *The Politics of Unreason: Right-Wing Extremism in America, 1790–1970.* New York: Harper and Row, 1970.

Lora, Ronald. "Conservative Intellectuals, the Cold War, and McCarthy." In Griffith and Theoharis, *The Specter,* 40–71.

Lowenthal, Max. *The Federal Bureau of Investigation.* New York: Harcourt, Brace, 1950.

Lubell, Samuel. *Revolt of the Moderates.* New York: Harper and Brothers, 1956.

Lyons, Eugene. Assignment in Utopia. New York: Harcourt, Brace, 1937.

Lyons, Eugene. *Moscow Carrousel.* New York: Knopf, 1935.

Lyons, Eugene. *Our Secret Allies: The Peoples of Russia.* New York: Duell, Sloan and Pearce; Boston: Little, Brown, 1953.

Lyons, Eugene. *The Red Decade.* Indianapolis, IN: Bobbs-Merrill, 1941.

Macdonald, Dwight. "Scrambled Eggheads on the Right: Mr. Buckley's New Weekly." *Commentary* (April 1956): 367–73.

MacPherson, Myra. *All Governments Lie!: The Life and Times of Rebel Journalist I. F. Stone.* New York: Scribner, 2006.

Maddox, Robert James. *The New Left and the Origins of the Cold War.* Princeton, NJ: Princeton University Press, 1973.

Maeder, Jay. "Turncoat: The Estrangements of Howard Rushmore, January 1958, Chapter 282." *New York Daily News,* February 26, 2001. Posted on www.nydailynews.com/archives/news/2001/02/26/200i_o2_26 _turncoat_the-estrangements_o.html.

Malsberger, John W. *From Obstructionism to Moderation: The Transformation of Senate Conservatism, 1938–1952.* Susquehanna, PA: Susquehanna University Press; London: Associated Universities Presses, 2000.

Mandel, Bernard. *Samuel Gompers: A Biography.* Yellow Springs, OH: Antioch Press, 1963.

Markowitz, Norman. "From the Popular Front to Cold War Liberalism." In Griffith and Theoharis, *The Specter,* 90–115.

Martin, James J. *American Liberalism and World Politics, 1931–1941: Liberalism's Press and Spokesmen on the Road Back to War Between Mukden and Pearl Harbor.* New York: Devin-Adair, 1964.

Martin, William. *With God on Our Side: The Rise of the Religious Right in America.* New York: Broadway Books, 1996.

Marx, Frist Morstein. "Totalitarian Politics." *Symposium on the Totalitarian State: From the Standpoint of History, Political Science, Economics and Sociology, Proceedings of the American Philosophical Society* 82, no. 1 (February 23, 1940): 1–38.

Matthews, J. B. "Did the Movies Really Clean House?" *American Legion Magazine* (December 1951): 12–13, 49–56.

Mattson, Kevin. *Intellectuals in Action: The Origins of the New Left and Radical Liberalism, 1945–1970.* University Park, PA: Pennsylvania State University Press, 2002.

Maximoff, G. P. *The Guillotine at Work: Twenty Years of Terror in Russia (Data and Documents).* Chicago: Chicago Section of the Alexander Berkman Fund, 1940.

May, Ernest R., ed. *American Cold War Strategy: Interpreting NSC 68.* Boston/New York: Bedford Books, 1993.

May, Gary. *Un-American Activities: The Trials of William Remington.* New York/Oxford, UK: Oxford University Press, 1994.

Mayer, Arno J. *Politics and Diplomacy of Peacemaking: Containment and Counterrevolution at Versailles, 1918–1919.* New York: Knopf, 1967.

Mayer, Arno J. *Wilson v. Lenin: Political Origins of the New Diplomacy, 1917–1918.* Cleveland, OH/New York: Meridian Books, 1964.

Mayer, Milton. *Robert Maynard Hutchins: A Memoir.* Berkeley/Los Angeles, CA: University of California Press, 1993.

Mayhew, Robert. *Ayn Rand and* Song of Russia: *Communism and Anti-Communism in 1940s Hollywood.* Lanham, MD: Scarecrow Press, 2005.

Mayhew, Robert. "MGM's Potemkin Church: Religion in *Song of Russia.*" *American Communist History* 1, no. 1 (June 2002): 91–103.

Mazo, Earl. *Richard Nixon: A Political and Personal Portrait.* New York: Harper and Brothers, 1959.

McAuliffe, Mary Sperling. "The ACLU During the McCarthy Years." In Griffith and Theoharis, *The Specter,* 152–71.

McAuliffe, Mary Sperling. *Crisis on the Left: Cold War Politics and American Liberals.* Amherst, MA: University of Massachusetts Press, 1978.

McAuliffe, Mary Sperling. "Liberals and the Communist Control Act of 1954." *Journal of American History* 63 (September 1976): 352–60.

McCallester, Charles, J., ed. *Fighter with a Heart: Writings of Charles Owen Rice, Pittsburgh's Labor Priest.* Pittsburgh, PA: University of Pittsburgh Press, 1996.

McCarthy, Joseph. *McCarthyism: The Fight for America, Documented Answers to Questions Asked by Friend and Foe.* New York: Devin-Adair, 1952.

McConnell, Scott, ed. *100 Voices: An Oral History of Ayn Rand.* New York: NAL, 2010.

McCulloch, Mark. "The Shop-Floor Dimension of Union Rivalry: The Case of Westinghouse in the 1950s." In Rosswurm, *The CIO's Left-Led Unions,* 183–200.

McFadden, Charles J. *The Philosophy of Communism.* New York: Benziger Brothers, 1939.

McGirr, Lisa. *Suburban Warriors: The Origins of the New American Right.* Princeton, NJ/Oxford, UK: Princeton University Press, 2001.

McNamara, Patrick. *A Catholic Cold War: Edmund A. Walsh, S.J., and the Politics of American Anticommunism*. New York: Fordham University Press, 2005.

McWilliams, Carey. *The Education of Carey McWilliams*. New York: Simon and Schuster, 1979.

Merry, Robert W. *Taking on the World: Joseph and Stewart Alsop—Guardians of the America Century*. New York: Viking, 1996.

Messer, Robert L. *The End of an Alliance: James F. Byrnes, Roosevelt, Truman, and the Origins of the Cold War*. Chapel Hill, NC: University of North Carolina Press, 1982.

Methvin, Eugene H. "Isaac Don Levine: Herald of Free Russia." www.mmisi.org/ma/37_03/methvin.pdf. Accessed December 19, 2010.

Michels, Tony. *A Fire in Their Hearts: Yiddish Socialists in New York*. Cambridge, MA/London: Harvard University Press, 2005.

Miles, Michael. *The Odyssey of the American Right*. New York/Oxford, UK: Oxford University Press, 1980.

Miller, James A. *Examined Lives: From Socrates to Nietzsche*. New York: Farrar, Straus and Giroux, 2011.

Miller, William D. *Dorothy Day: A Biography*. New York: Harper and Row, 1982.

Minott, Rodney G. *Peerless Patriots: Organized Veterans and the Spirit of Americanism*. Washington, DC: Public Affairs Press, 1962.

Mitchell, Greg. *Tricky Dick and the Pink Lady: Richard Nixon Versus Helen Gahagan Douglas—Sexual Politics and the Red Scare, 1950*. New York: Random House, 1998.

Montgomery, Gayle B., and James W. Johnson. *One Step from the White House: The Rise and Fall of Senator William F. Knowland*. Berkeley/Los Angeles, CA: University of California Press, 1998.

Moore, Barrington, Jr. "The Communist Party of the USA: An Analysis of a Political Movement." *American Political Science Review* 39, no. 1 (February 1945): 31–41.

Morgan, Ted. *A Covert Life: Jay Lovestone, Communist, Anti-Communist, and Spymaster*. New York: Random House, 1999.

Moynihan, Daniel Patrick. *Daniel Patrick Moynihan: A Portrait in Letters of an American Visionary*. Edited by Steven R. Weissman. New York: Public Affairs, 2010.

Muravchik, Joshua. "The Bush Manifesto." *Commentary* (December 2002): 23–30.

Muravchik, Joshua. "The Neoconservative Cabal." *Commentary* (September 2003): 26–33.

Muravchik, Joshua. "Renegades." *Commentary* (October 2002): 85–88.

Murphy, Bruce Allen. *Fortas: The Rise and Ruin of a Supreme Court Justice*. New York: William Morrow, 1988.

Murphy, Paul L. *The Constitution in Crisis Times, 1918–1969*. New York: Harper and Row, 1972.

Murphy, Paul L. *The Meaning of Freedom of Speech: First Amendment Freedoms from Wilson to FDR*. Westport, CT: Greenwood, 1972.

Murphy, Paul L. "Sources and Nature of Intolerance in the 1920s." *Journal of American History* 51, no. 1 (June 1964): 60–76.

Murphy, Paul L. *World War I and the Origins of Civil Liberties in the United States*. New York/London: Norton, 1979.

Murray, Robert K. "Communism and the Great Steel Strike of 1919." *Mississippi Valley Historical Review* 38, no. 3 (December 1951): 445–66.

Murray, Robert K. *Red Scare: A Study in National Hysteria, 1919–1920*. Minneapolis, MN: University of Minnesota Press, 1956.

Myers, Constance Ashton. *The Prophet's Army: Trotskyists in America, 1928–1941*. Westport, CT: Greenwood Press, 1977.

Nash, George H. *The Conservative Intellectual Movement in America Since 1945*. New York: Basic Books, 1976.

National Community Relations Advisory Council. *Guide to Program Planning* 19. www.Jewishpublicaffairs.org/www.e-guana.net/organizations/org/JointProgramPlan1956-1.pdf.

National Community Relations Advisory Council. *Joint Program Plan for Jewish Community Relations in 1953*. New York: 1953, 19. www.Jewishpublicaffairs.org/www.e-guana.net/organizations/org/JointProgramPlan1953-1.pdf.

Navasky, Victor S. *Naming Names*. New York: Viking, 1980.

N. E. L. "Restraints on American Communist Activities." *University of Pennsylvania Law Review* 96, no. 3 (February 1948): 381–401. [Those are the initials of the author, probably a law student, printed in the review.]

Nevins, Allen. *Herbert H. Lehman and His Era*. New York: Scribner's, 1963.

Newman, Robert P. *Owen Lattimore and the "Loss" of China*. Berkeley/Los Angeles, CA: University of California Press, 1992.

Niebuhr, Reinhold. "The Cause and Cure of the American Psychosis." *American Scholar* 25, no. 1 (Winter 1955–1956): 11–19.

Niebuhr, Reinhold. *The Children of Light and the Children of Darkness: A Vindication of Democracy and a Critique of Its Traditional Defense*. New York: Scribner's, 1944.

Niebuhr, Reinhold. *Christian Realism and Political Problems*. London: Faber and Faber, 1954.

Niebuhr, Reinhold. *Faith and History: A Comparison of Christian and Modern Views of History*. New York: Scribner's, 1949.

Niebuhr, Reinhold. *Faith and Politics: A Commentary on Religious, Social and Political Thought in a Technological Age*. Edited by Ronald H. Stone. New York: George Braziller, 1968.

Niebuhr, Reinhold. *The Irony of American History*. New York: Scribner's, 1962.

Niebuhr, Reinhold. "Liberals and the Marxist Heresy." *New Republic* 129 (October 12, 1953): 13–15.

Niebuhr, Reinhold. *Moral Man and Immoral Society: A Study in Ethics and Politics*. New York: Scribner's, 1960 [1932].

Niebuhr, Reinhold. *Reflections on the End of an Era*. New York/London: Scribner's, 1934.

Nisbet, Robert A., Roger Starr, and David L. Bromwich. "The Counter-Culture and Its Apologists." *Commentary* (December 1970): 40–59.

Noonan, D. P. *The Passion of Fulton Sheen*. New York: Dodd, Mead, 1972.

Not Guilty: Report of the Commission of Inquiry into the Charges Made Against Leon Trotsky in the Moscow Trials. New York/London: Harper and Brothers, 1938.

O'Brian, John Lord. "Loyalty Tests and Guilt by Association." *Harvard Law Review* 61, no. 4 (April 1948): 592–611.

O'Brien, David. "American Catholics and Organized Labor in the 1930's." *Catholic Historical Review* 51, no. 3 (October 1966): 323–49.

O'Brien, David. *American Catholics and Social Reform: The New Deal Years.* New York: Oxford University Press, 1968.

Ogden, August Raymond. *The Dies Committee: A Study of the Special House Committee for the Investigation of Un-American Activities, 1938–1944.* Washington, DC: Catholic University of America Press, 1945.

Olmstead, Kathryn S. *Red Spy Queen: A Biography of Elizabeth Bentley.* Chapel Hill, NC: University of North Carolina Press, 2002.

O'Neill, William L. *American High: The Years of Confidence, 1945–1960.* New York: Free Press, 1986.

O'Neill, William L. *A Better World: The Great Schism: Stalinism and the American Intellectuals.* New York: Simon and Schuster, 1982.

O'Neill, William L. *The Last Romantic: A Life of Max Eastman.* New York: Oxford University Press, 1978.

O'Reilly, Kenneth. *Hoover and the Un-Americans: The FBI, HUAC, and the Red Menace.* Philadelphia, PA: Temple University Press, 1983.

O'Reilly, Kenneth. "Liberals Values, the Cold War, and American Intellectuals." In *Beyond the Hiss Case: The FBI, Congress, and the Cold War,* edited by Athan G. Theoharis, 309–40. Philadelphia: Temple University Press, 1982.

Ornstein, Norman, Andrew Kohut, and Larry McCarthy. *The People, the Press, and Politics: The* Times Mirror *Study of the American Electorate.* Reading, MA: Addison-Wesley, 1988.

Oshinsky, David M. *A Conspiracy so Immense: The World of Joe McCarthy.* New York: Free Press, 1983.

Oshinsky, David M. *Senator Joseph McCarthy and the American Labor Movement.* Columbus, MO: University of Missouri Press, 1976.

Ottanelli, Fraser M. *The Communist Party of the United States: From Depression to World War II.* New Brunswick, NJ: Rutgers University Press, 1991.

Overstreet, Harry, and Bonaro Overstreet. *What We Must Know About Communism.* New York: Norton, 1958.

Packer, Herbert L. *Ex-Communist Witnesses: Four Studies in Fact Finding.* Stanford, CA: Stanford University Press, 1962.

Pangle, Thomas L. *The Spirit of Modern Republicanism: The Moral Vision of the American Founders and the Philosophy of Locke.* Chicago/London: University of Chicago Press, 1988.

Parmet, Herbert S. *Richard Nixon and His America.* Boston: Little, Brown, 1990.

Parrish, Michael E. *Citizen Rauh: An American Liberal's Life in Law and Politics.* Ann Arbor, MI: University of Michigan Press, 2010.

Parrish, Michael E. "The Supreme Court and the Rosenbergs." *American Historical Review* 82, no. 4 (October 1977): 805–42.

Parsons, Steve. "British 'McCarthyism' and the Intellectuals." In *Labour's Promised Land? Culture and Society in Labour Britain, 1945–51*, edited by Jim Fyrth. London: Lawrence and Wishart, 1995.

Parsons, Talcott. "Social Strains in America." In Bell, *The New American Right*, 117–40.

Paterson, Thomas G. *Meeting the Communist Threat: From Truman to Reagan*. New York/Oxford, UK: Oxford University Press, 1988.

Patterson, James T. *Mr. Republican: A Biography of Robert A. Taft*. Boston: Houghton Mifflin, 1972.

Pencak, William. *For God and Country: The American Legion, 1919–1941*. Boston: Northeastern University Press, 1989.

Perret, Geoffrey. *Eisenhower*. New York: Random House, 1999.

Pfannstiel, Todd J. *Rethinking the Red Scare: The Lusk Committee and New York's Crusade Against Radicalism, 1919–1923*. New York: Routledge, 2003.

Phelan, Towner. "Modern School for Scandal." *The Freeman* (September 24, 1951): 813–17.

Phelan, Towner. "Rebirth of the Popular Front?" *National Review* (February 23, 1957): 183–84.

Phelan, Towner, and Joseph McCarthy. "Is McCarthy Guilty of McCarthyism?" *The Freeman* (February 11, 1952): 297–301.

Phelps, Christopher. *Young Sidney Hook: Marxist and Pragmatist*. Ithaca, NY: Cornell University Press, 1997.

Phillips, William. "In and Out of the Underground: The Confessions of Whittaker Chambers." *American Mercury* (June 1952): 92–99.

Pichel, Irving. "Areas of Silence." *Hollywood Quarterly* 3, no. 1 (Autumn 1947): 51–55.

Piehl, Mel. *Breaking Bread: The Catholic Worker and the Origin of Catholic Radicalism in America*. Philadelphia: Temple University Press, 1982.

Pipes, Daniel. "Americans Wake Up to Islamism." *National Review* (September 7, 2010). www.nationalreview.com/articles/245737/americans -wake-islamism-daniel-pipes.

Pipes, Daniel. "The Danger Within: Militant Islam in America." *Commentary* (November 2001): 19–24.

Pipes, Daniel. "Who Is the Enemy?" *Commentary* (January 2002): 21–27.

Pitkin, Robert P. "The Movies and the American Legion." *American Legion Magazine* (May 1953): 39.

Pizzitola, Louis. *Hearst Over Hollywood: Power, Passion, and Propaganda in the Movies*. New York: Columbia University Press, 2002.

Plotke, David. *Building a Democratic Political Order: Reshaping American Liberalism in the 1930s and 1940s*. Cambridge, UK: Cambridge University Press, 1996.

Pocock, J. G. A., and Richard Ashcraft. *John Locke: Papers Read at a Clark Library Seminar, 10 December 1977*. Los Angeles, CA: William Andrews Clark Memorial Library, University of California at Los Angeles, 1980.

Podhoretz, Norman. "How to Win World War IV." *Commentary* (February 2002): 27–29.

Podhoretz, Norman. "Laws, Kings, and Cures." *Commentary* (October 1970): 30–31.

Podhoretz, Norman. *Making It.* New York: Random House, 1967.

Podhoretz, Norman. "The New Hypocrisy." *Commentary* (December 1970): 5–6.

Podhoretz, Norman. *World War IV: The Long Struggle Against Islamofascism.* New York/London: Doubleday, 2007.

Poe, Elizabeth. "The Hollywood Story." *Frontier* (May 1954): 6–25.

Polner, Murray. "James Wechsler: The Editor Who Challenged McCarthy." *History News Network* (January 5, 2004). hnn.us/articles/2869.html.

Porter, Kirk H., and Donald Bruce Johnson, eds. *National Party Platforms, 1840–1964.* Urbana, IL/London: University of Illinois Press, 1966.

Powers, Richard Gid. *Not Without Honor: The History of American Anticommunism.* New York: Free Press, 1995.

Preis, Art. *Labor's Giant Step.* New York: Pioneer, 1964.

Preussen, Ronald W. *John Foster Dulles: The Road to Power.* New York: Free Press, 1982.

Project for the New American Century. "Statement of Principles" (June 3, 1997). www.newamericancentury.org/statementofprinciples.

Public Papers of the Presidents of the United States, Dwight D. Eisenhower. Washington, DC: U.S. Government Printing Office, 1960.

Public Papers of the Presidents of the United States, Harry S Truman. Washington, DC: U.S. Government Printing Office, 1965.

Puddington, Arch. *Broadcasting Freedom: The Cold War Triumph of Radio Free Europe and Radio Liberty.* Lexington, KY: University Press of Kentucky, 2000.

Purifoy, Lewis McCarroll. *Harry Truman's China Policy: McCarthyism and the Diplomacy of Hysteria.* New York/London: New Viewpoints, 1976.

Quine, W. V., and J. S. Ullian. *The Web of Belief*, 2nd ed. New York: Random House, 1978.

Radosh, Ronald. *American Labor and United States Foreign Policy.* New York: Random House, 1969.

Radosh, Ronald. *Commies: A Journey Through the Old Left, the New Left and the Leftover Left.* San Francisco: Encounter Books, 2001.

Radosh, Ronald. *Prophets on the Right: Profiles of Conservative Critics of American Globalism.* New York: Simon and Schuster, 1975.

Radosh, Ronald, Mary R. Habeck, and Grigory Sevostianov. *Spain Betrayed: The Soviet Union in the Spanish Civil War.* New Haven, CT/London: Yale University Press, 2001.

Radosh, Ronald, and Joyce Milton. *The Rosenberg File: A Search for the Truth.* New York: Holt, Rinehart and Winston, 1983.

Radosh, Ronald, and Allis Radosh. *Red Star Over Hollywood: The Film Colony's Long Romance with the Left.* San Francisco: Encounter Books, 2005.

Rahv, Philip. "The Sense and Nonsense of Whittaker Chambers." *Partisan Review* (July–August 1952): 472–82.

Rand, Ayn. *Journals of Ayn Rand.* Edited by David Harriman. New York: Dutton, 1997.

Rand, Ayn. *Letters of Ayn Rand.* Edited by Michael S. Berliner. New York: Dutton, 1995.

Rauh, Joseph L., Jr. "Informers, G-Men, and Free Men," *The Progressive*, May 1950, 9–11.

Rauh, Joseph L., Jr. "The McCarthy Era Is Over." *U.S. News and World Report* (August 26, 1955): 68–70.

Rauh, Joseph L., Jr. Oral History Interview, Harry S. Truman Memorial Library and Museum, 1989. www.trumanlibrary.org/oralhist/rauh.htm.

Rauh, Joseph L., Jr. "An Unabashed Liberal Looks at a Half-Century of the Supreme Court." *North Carolina Law Review* 69, no. 1 (December 1969): 223–24.

Reinhard, David W. *The Republican Right Since 1945.* Lexington, KY: University Press of Kentucky, 1983.

Report of the Commission on Government Security. Washington, DC: U.S. Government Printing Office, 1957, xiii, xvi, xvii. www.archives.org/details/reportofcommisi1957unit.

Rice, Charles Owen Rice. "Confessions of an Anti-Communist." *Labor History* 30, no. 3 (Summer 1989).

Rice, Daniel F. *Reinhold Niebuhr and John Dewey: An American Odyssey.* Albany, NY: State University of New York Press, 1993.

Richardson, James D., ed. *A Compilation of the Messages and Papers of the Presidents, Vol. 16.* New York: Bureau of National Literature, 1917.

Richardson, Peter. *American Prophet: The Life and Work of Carey McWilliams.* Ann Arbor, MI: University of Michigan Press, 2005.

Riesman, David, and Nathan Glazer. "The Intellectuals and the Discontented Classes." In Bell, *The New American Right,*—56–90.

Rigoulot, Pierre. *Les Paupières Lourdes: Les Français face au goulag—aveugelements et indignations.* Paris: Editions Universitaires, 1991.

Robins, Natalie. *Alien Ink: The FBI's War on Freedom of Expression.* New York: William Morrow, 1992.

Robinson, Greg. *By Order of the President: FDR and the Internment of Japanese Americans.* Cambridge, MA/London: Harvard University Press, 2001.

Rogin, Michael Paul. *The Intellectuals and McCarthy: The Radical Specter.* Cambridge, MA/London: MIT Press, 1967.

Romerstein, Herbert, and Eric Breindel. *The Venona Secrets: Exposing Soviet Espionage and America's Traitors.* Washington, DC: Regnery, 2000.

Rorty, James, and Moshe Decter. *McCarthy and the Communists.* Boston: Beacon Press, 1954.

Rosenof, Theodore. "Freedom, Planning, and Totalitarianism: The Reception of F. A. Hayek's *Road to Serfdom.*" *Canadian Review of American Studies* 5, no. 2 (Fall 1974): 148–65.

Rosswurm, Steve. "The Catholic Church and the Left-Led Unions: Labor Priests, Labor Schools, and the ACTU." In *The CIO's Left-Led Unions,* edited by Steve Rosswurm, 119–38. New Brunswick, NJ: Rutgers University Press, 1992.

Rosswurm, Steve. *The FBI and the Catholic Church, 1935–1962.* Amherst, MA: University of Massachusetts Press, 2009.

Rothschild, Sylvia. *A Special Legacy: An Oral History of Soviet Jewish Émigrés in the United States.* New York: Simon and Schuster, 1985.

Rovere, Richard H. "The Adventures of Cohn and Schine." *The Reporter* (July 21, 1953): 9–16.

Rovere, Richard H. *The American Establishment and Other Reports, Opinions, and Speculations*. New York: Harcourt, Brace and World, 1962.

Rovere, Richard H. "Communists in a Free Society." *Partisan Review* 19, no. 3 (May–June 1952): 339–46.

Rovere, Richard H. "Factions on the Far Left." *New Republic* (April 8, 1940): 468–70.

Rovere, Richard H. *Final Reports: Personal Reflections on Politics and History in Our Time*. Garden City, NY: Doubleday, 1984.

Rovere, Richard H. "J. B. Matthews—The Informer." *The Nation* (October 3, 1942): 314–17.

Rovere, Richard H. "The Kept Witnesses." *Harper's* (May 1955): 25–34.

Rovere, Richard H. "Labor's Catholic Bloc." *The Nation* (January 4, 1941): 11–14.

Rovere, Richard H. *Senator Joe McCarthy*. Berkeley/Los Angeles, CA: University of California Press, 1996 [1959].

Rovere, Richard H., and Arthur Schlesinger, Jr. *The General and the Press, and the Failure of American Foreign Policy*. New York: Farrar, Straus and Giroux, 1951.

Rowe, David E., and Robert Schulmann, eds. *Einstein on Politics: His Private Thoughts and Public Stands on Nationalism, Zionism, War, Peace, and the Bomb*. Princeton, NJ/Oxford, UK: Princeton University Press, 2009.

Roy, Ralph Lord. *Communism and the Churches*. New York: Harper and Brothers, 1960.

Rudolph, Frederick. "The American Liberty League, 1934–1940." *American Historical Review* 56, no. 1 (October 1950): 19–33.

Reuther, Victor G. *The Brothers Reuther and the Story of the UAW: A Memoir*. Boston: Houghton Mifflin, 1976.

Salisbury, Harrison E. "The Strange Correspondence of Morris Ernst and J. Edgar Hoover, 1939–1964." *The Nation* 239 (December 1, 1984): 575–89.

Salzman, Jack. *Albert Maltz*. Boston: Twayne, 1978.

Sandbrook, Dominic. *Never Had It So Good: A History of Britain from Suez to the Beatles*. Boston: Little, Brown, 2005.

Sanua, Marianne R. *Let Us Prove Strong: The American Jewish Committee, 1945–2006*. Waltham, MA: Brandeis University Press, 2007.

Sartre, Jean-Paul. "The Chances of Peace." *The Nation* (December 30, 1950): 696–700.

Scammell, Michael. *Koestler: The Life and Political Odyssey of a Twentieth-Century Skeptic*. New York: Random House, 2009.

Schary, Dore. *Heyday*. Boston: Little, Brown, 1979.

Schatz, Ronald W. *The Electrical Workers: A History of Labor at General Electric and Westinghouse, 1923–60*. Urbana/Chicago, IL: University of Illinois Press, 1983.

Schickel, Richard. "Still Seeing Red." *Los Angeles Times*, September 16, 2007, M4

chlamm S, William S. "Apropos Apostasy." *The Freeman* (March 26, 1951): 400–2.

Schlesinger, Arthur, Jr. "Democracy in Wartime." *New York Times*, October 3, 2001, A23.

Schlesinger, Arthur, Jr. *The Disuniting of America* (New York: Norton, 1992).

Schlesinger, Arthur, Jr. "Espionage or Frame-Up?" *Saturday Review of Literature* (April 15, 1950): 21–23.

Schlesinger, Arthur, Jr. "Faith, Fear and Freedom." *Saturday Review of Literature* (February 3, 1951): 10–11.

Schlesinger, Arthur, Jr. Letter to the editor. *New York Review of Books* (October 20, 1966): 37.

Schlesinger, Arthur, Jr. *A Life in the Twentieth Century: Innocent Beginnings, 1917–1950.* Boston/New York: Houghton Mifflin, 2000.

Schlesinger, Arthur, Jr. "The Life of the Party: What It Means to Be a Communist." *Saturday Review of Literature* (July 16, 1949): 6–7, 34–36.

Schlesinger, Arthur, Jr. "Not Left, Not Right, But a Vital Center." *New York Times Magazine* (April 4, 1948): 7, 44–47.

Schlesinger, Arthur, Jr. "Origins of the Cold War." *Foreign Affairs* 46, no. 1 (October 1967): 22–52.

Schlesinger, Arthur, Jr. "Our Country and Our Culture: A Symposium." *Partisan Review* (September–October, 1952): 590–93.

Schlesinger, Arthur, Jr. *The Politics of Upheaval.* Boston: Houghton Mifflin, 1960.

Schlesinger, Arthur, Jr. "Reinhold Niebuhr's Role in American Political Thought and Life." In Kegley and Bretall, *Reinhold Niebuhr*, 125–50.

Schlesinger, Arthur, Jr. "A Reply to Carroll Engelhardt, 'Man in the Middle: Arthur Schlesinger, Jr. and Postwar American Liberalism.' " *South Atlantic Quarterly* 80, no. 2 (Spring 1981): 119–42.

Schlesinger, Arthur, Jr. "The Right to Loathsome Ideas." *Saturday Review of Literature* (May 14, 1949): 17–18, 47.

Schlesinger, Arthur, Jr. *A Thousand Days: John F. Kennedy in the White House.* Boston: Houghton Mifflin, 1965.

Schlesinger, Arthur, Jr. "The U.S. Communist Party." *Life* (July 29, 1946): 84–98.

Schlesinger, Arthur, Jr. *The Vital Center: The Politics of Freedom.* Boston: Houghton Mifflin, 1949.

Schlesinger, Arthur, Jr. *Wartime and the American Presidency.* New York/London: Norton, 2004.

Schlesinger, Arthur, Jr. "What Is Loyalty? A Difficult Question." *New York Times Magazine* (November 2, 1947): 7, 48–51.

Schlesinger, Arthur, Jr., and Roger Bruns, *Congress Investigates: A Documented History, 1792–1974.* New York: Chelsea House, 1975.

Schmidt, Regin. *Red Scare: FBI and the Origins of Anticommunism in the United States, 1919–1943.* Copenhagen: Museum Tusculanum Press, 2000.

Schrecker, Ellen. *Many Are the Crimes: McCarthyism in America.* Boston: Little, Brown, 1998.

Schrecker, Ellen. "McCarthyism and the Labor Movement: The Role of the State." In Rosswurm, *The CIO's Left-Led Unions*, 139–58.

Schuessler, Jennifer. "Hayek: The Back Story." *New York Times Book Review* (July 11, 2010): 27.

Schultz, Bud, and Ruth Schultz. *It Did Happen Here: Recollections of Political Repression in America.* Berkeley/Los Angeles, CA: University of California Press, 1989.

Schultz, Bud, and Ruth Schultz. *The Price of Dissent: Testimonies to Political Repression in America.* Berkeley/Los Angeles, CA: University of California Press, 2001.

Schuman, Frederick L. *Soviet Politics: At Home and Abroad.* New York: Knopf, 1946.

Schwarz, Fred. *You Can Trust the Communists (. . . to do exactly as they say!).* Englewood Cliffs, NJ: Prentice-Hall, 1960.

Schwarz, Jordan A. *Liberal: Adolf A. Berle and the Vision of an American Era.* New York: Free Press, 1987.

Scott-Smith, Giles. *The Politics of Apolitical Culture: The Congress for Cultural Freedom, the CIA and Post-War American Hegemony.* London and New York: Routledge, 2002.

Scott-Smith, Giles. " 'A Radical Democratic Political Offensive': Melvin J. Lasky, *Der Monat,* and the Congress for Cultural Freedom." *Journal of Contemporary History* 35, no. 2 (April 2000): 263–80.

Seaton, Douglas P. *Catholics and Radicals: The Association of Catholic Trade Unionists and the American Labor Movement, from Depression to Cold War.* Lewisburg, PA: Bucknell University Press; London/Toronto: Associated University Presses, 1981.

Sharlitt, Joseph H. *Fatal Error: The Miscarriage of Justice That Sealed the Rosenberg's Fate.* New York: Scribner's, 1989.

Sheen, Fulton J. *Communism and the Conscience of the West.* Indianapolis, IN/New York: Bobbs-Merrill, 1948.

Sheen, Fulton J. "The Thing We Are Fighting Against." www.fultonsheen.com/Fulton-Sheen-articles/The-Thing-We-Are-Fighting-Against.cfm?articl=2.

Sheen, Fulton J. *Treasure in Clay: The Autobiography of Fulton J. Sheen.* Garden City, NY: Doubleday, 1980.

Sheen, Fulton J. "War and Revolution." January 3, 1943. www.fultonsheen.com/Fulton-Sheen-articles/War-and-Revolution.cfm?articl=2.

Sherman, Janann. *No Place for a Woman: A Life of Senator Margaret Chase Smith.* New Brunswick, NJ/London: Rutgers University Press, 2000.

Sherrill, Robert. *First Amendment Felon: The Story of Frank Wilkinson, His 132,000-Page FBI File, and His Epic Fight for Civil Rights and Liberties.* New York: Nation Books, 2005.

Sherrill, Robert, and Harry W. Ernst. *The Drugstore Liberal.* New York: Grossman, 1968.

Sherry, Michael S. *In the Shadow of War: The United States Since the 1930s.* New Haven, CT/London: Yale University Press, 1995.

Shils, Edward A. *The Torment of Secrecy: The Background and Consequences of American Security Policies.* Glencoe, IL: Free Press, 1956.

Silverman, Sheldon Arnold. *At the Water's Edge: Arthur Vandenberg and the Foundation of American Bipartisan Foreign Policy* [Ph.D. dissertation]. Los Angeles, CA: University of California at Los Angeles, 1967.

Sirgiovanni, George. *An Undercurrent of Suspicion: Anti-Communism During World War II.* New Brunswick, NJ/London: Transaction, 1990.

Skotheim, Robert Allen. *Totalitarianism and American Social Thought.* New York: Holt, Rinehart and Winston, 1971.

Smant, Kevin J. *Principles and Heresies: Frank S. Meyer and the Shaping of the American Conservative Movement*. Wilmington, DE: ISI Books, 2002.

Smith, Donald L. *Zechariah Chafee, Jr.: Defender of Law and Liberty*. Cambridge, MA/London: Harvard University Press, 1986.

Smith, Margaret Chase. *Declaration of Conscience*. Edited by William C. Lewis. Garden City, NY: Doubleday, 1972.

Sokolsky, George. "The Conservative's Plight." *The Freeman* (September 8, 1952): 839–40.

Solberg, Carl. *Hubert Humphrey: A Biography*. New York/London: Norton, 1984.

Spargo, John. *Bolshevism: The Enemy of Political and Industrial Democracy*. New York: Harper and Brothers, 1919.

Steel, Ronald. *Walter Lippmann and the American Century*. Boston/Toronto: Little, Brown, 1980.

Steele, Richard W. *Free Speech in the Good War*. New York: St. Martin's Press, 1994.

Steinberg, Julien, ed. *Verdict of Three Decades: From the Literature of the Individual Revolt Against Soviet Communism*. New York: Duell, Sloan and Pearce, 1950.

Steinberg, Peter L. *The Great "Red Menace": United States Prosecution of American Communists, 1947–1952*. Westport, CT/London: Greenwood Press, 1984.

Steinfels, Peter. *The Neoconservatives: The Men Who Are Changing America's Politics*. New York: Simon and Schuster, 1979.

Stephan, Alexander. *"Communazis": FBI Surveillance of German Émigré Writers*. Translated by Jan Ven Heurck. New Haven, CT/London: Yale University Press, 2000.

Stolberg, Benjamin. *The Story of the CIO*. New York: Viking Press, 1938.

Stone, Geoffrey R. *Perilous Times: Free Speech in Wartime, from the Sedition Act of 1798 to the War on Terrorism*. New York: Norton, 2004.

Stone, I. F. *The Haunted Fifties*. New York: Random House, 1963.

Stone, I. F. *The Truman Era*. New York: Monthly Review Press, 1953.

Stone, Ronald H. *Reinhold Niebuhr: Prophet to Politicians*. Nashville, TN/New York: Abingdon Press, 1972.

Stouffer, Samuel A. *Communism, Conformity, and Civil Liberties: A Cross Section of the Nation Speaks Its Mind*. Garden City, NY: Doubleday, 1955.

Stripling, Robert E. *The Red Plot Against America*. Drexel Hill, PA: Bell Publishing, 1949.

Suber, Howard. *The Anti-Communist Blacklist in the Hollywood Motion Picture Industry*. Ph. D. Dissertation. Los Angeles, CA: University of California, Los Angeles, 1968.

Sullivan, William C. *The Bureau: My Thirty Years in Hoover's FBI*. New York/London: Norton, 1979.

Swan, Patrick, ed. *Alger Hiss, Whittaker Chambers, and the Schism in the American Soul*. Wilmington, DE: Intercollegiate Studies Institute, 2003.

Swanberg, W. A. *Norman Thomas: The Last Idealist*. New York: Scribner's, 1976.

Taft, Philip. *The A. F. of L. from the Death of Gompers to the Merger*. New York: Harper and Brothers, 1959

Taft, Philip. "The Association of Catholic Trade Unions." *Industrial and Labor Relations Review* 2, no. 2 (January 1949): 210–18.

Taft, Philip. *Organized Labor in American History.* New York: Harper and Row, 1964.

Taft, Robert A. *A Foreign Policy for Americans.* Garden City, NY: Doubleday, 1951, 19, 114–21.

Tanenhaus, Sam. *The Death of Conservatism.* New York: Random House, 2009.

Tanenhaus, Sam. *Whittaker Chambers: A Biography.* New York: Modern Library, 1998.

Tanner, William R., and Robert Griffith. "The Internal Security Act of 1950." In Griffith and Theoharis, *The Specter,* 172–89.

Taracouzio, T. A. *War and Peace in Soviet Diplomacy.* New York: Macmillan, 1940.

Taylor, Harold. *On Education and Freedom.* New York: Abelard-Schuman, 1954.

Taylor, Jay. *The Generalissimo: Chiang Kai-shek and the Struggle for Modern China.* Cambridge, MA/London: Belknap Press, 2009.

Taylor, Telford. *Grand Inquest: The Story of Congressional Investigations.* New York: Simon and Schuster, 1955.

Teigrob, Robert. *Warming Up to the Cold War: Canada and the United States' Coalition of the Willing, from Hiroshima to Korea.* Toronto/Buffalo, NY: University of Toronto Press, 2009.

Theoharis, Athan G. *Chasing Spies: How the FBI Failed in Counterintelligence But Promoted the Politics of McCarthyism in the Cold War Years.* Chicago: Ivan R. Dee, 2002.

Theoharis, Athan G. *The FBI and American Democracy: A Brief Critical History.* Lawrence, KA: University Press of Kansas, 2004.

Theoharis, Athan G. "The Politics of Scholarship: Liberals, Anti-Communists, and McCarthyism." In Griffith and Theoharis, *The Specter,* 262–81.

Theoharis, Athan G. *The Truman Presidency: The Origins of the Imperial Presidency and the National Security State.* Stanfordsville, NY: Earl M. Coleman, 1979.

Theoharis, Athan G. *The Yalta Myths: An Issue in U.S. Politics, 1945–1955.* Columbia, MO: University of Missouri Press, 1970.

Theoharis, Athan G., and John Stuart Cox. *The Boss: J. Edgar Hoover and the Great American Inquisition.* Philadelphia, PA: Temple University Press, 1988.

Thernstrom, Stephen, ed. *The Harvard Encyclopedia of American Ethnic Groups.* Cambridge, MA/London: Belknap Press, 1980.

Thomas, John N. *The Institute of Pacific Relations: Asian Scholars and American Politics.* Seattle, WA/London: University of Washington Press, 1974.

Thompson, Kenneth W. *Political Realism and the Crisis of World Politics: An American Approach to Foreign Policy.* Princeton, NJ: Princeton University Press, 1960.

Thompson, Nicholas. *The Hawk and the Dove: Paul Nitze, George Kennan and the History of the Cold War.* New York: Henry Holt, 2009.

Thurlow, Richard. *The Secret State: British Internal Security in the Twentieth Century.* Oxford, UK/Cambridge, MA: Blackwell, 1994.

To Secure These Rights: The Report of the President's Committee on Civil Rights. Washington, DC: U.S. Government Printing Office, 1947.

Tomlins, Christopher L. *The State and the Unions: Labor Relations, Law, and the Organized Labor Movement in America, 1880–1960*. Cambridge, UK: Cambridge University Press, 1985.

Trilling, Diana. "A Memorandum on the Hiss Case." *Partisan Review* (May–June 1950). Reprinted in Swan, *Alger Hiss*, 27–48.

Trilling, Lionel. *The Liberal Imagination: Essays on Literature and Society*. New York: Viking, 1950.

Trumbo, Dalton. *The Time of the Toad: A Study of Inquisition in America*. Reprinted in *The Time of the Toad: A Study of Inquisition in America, and Two Related Pamphlets*. New York: Harper and Row, 1972.

Tsou, Teng. *America's Failure in China, 1941–1950*. Chicago: University of Chicago Press, 1963.

Tull, Charles J. *Father Coughlin and the New Deal*. Syracuse, NY: Syracuse University Press, 1965.

Unger, Irwin. "The 'New Left' and American History: Some Recent Trends in United States Historiography." *American Historical Review* 72, no. 4 (July 1967): 1237–63.

Unger, Irwin, and Robert R. Tomes, eds. *American Issues: A Primary Source Reader in United States History*, 2nd ed. Upper Saddle River, NJ: Prentice Hall, 1999.

Urofsky, Melvin I. *Felix Frankfurter: Judicial Restraint and Individual Liberties*. Boston: Twayne, 1991.

Urofsky, Melvin I. *Louis D. Brandeis: A Life*. New York: Pantheon Books, 2009.

United States, Congress, House of Representatives, Committee on Post Office and Civil Service, *Federal Employees Security Program*, 86th Congress, 1st Session, April-June 1959. Washington, D. C.: U. S. Government Printing Office, 1960.

U.S. Congress, House of Representatives, Committee on Un-American Activities. *The Ideological Fallacies of Communism*. Staff Consultations with Rabbi Andhil Fineberg, Bishop Fulton J. Sheen, Doctor Daniel A. Poling, 85th Congress, 1st Session, September 4, September 25, and October 18, 1957. Washington, DC: U.S. Government Printing Office, 1958.

U.S. Congress, House of Representatives, Special Committee on Un-American Activities. *Investigation of Nazi Propaganda and Investigation of Certain Other Propaganda Activities*. 73d Congress, 2d Session, November–December 1934. Washington, DC: U.S. Government Printing Office, 1935.

U.S. Congress, House of Representatives, Special Committee on Un-American Activities. *Investigation of So-Called "Blacklisting" in Entertainment Industry: Report of the Fund for the Republic, Inc*. 84th Congress, 2nd Session, Part I, July 10 and 11, 1956. Washington, DC: U.S. Government Printing Office, 1956.

U.S. Congress, House of Representatives, Special Committee on Un-American Activities. *Investigation of Un-American Propaganda Activities in the United States*. 75th Congress, 3rd Session, August 1938. Washington, DC: U.S. Government Printing Office, 1938.

U.S. Congress, House of Representatives, Special Committee on Un-American Activities. *Investigation of Un-American Propaganda Activities in the United States*. 78th Congress, 2d Session, September and October 1944.

Appendix—Part IX, *Communist Front Organizations*. Washington, DC: U.S. Government Printing Office, 1944.

U.S. Congress, House of Representatives, Special Committee on Un-American Activities. *Investigation of Un-American Propaganda Activities in the United States*. 79th Congress, 2d Session, November 22, 1946. Washington, DC: U.S. Government Printing Office, 1946.

U.S. Congress, House of Representatives, Special Committee on Un-American Activities. *Investigation of Un-American Propaganda Activities in the United States*, 80th Congress, 1st Session, March 24, 1947. Washington, DC: U.S. Government Printing Office, 1947.

U.S. Congress, House of Representatives, Special Committee on Un-American Activities. *Investigation of Un-American Propaganda Activities in the United States: Hearings Before the Committee on Un-American Activities, on HR 1884 and HR2122, Bills to Curb or Outlaw the Communist Party of the United States*. 80th Congress, 1st Session, March 24–27, 1947. Washington, DC: U.S. Government Printing Office, 1947.

U.S. Congress, House of Representatives, Special Committee on Un-American Activities. *Review of the Scientific and Cultural Conference for World Peace, Arranged by the National Council of the Arts, Sciences and Professions, and Held at New York City, March 25, 26, and 27, 1949*, April 19, 1949. Washington, DC: U.S. Government Printing Office, 1949.

U.S. Congress, Senate. Hearings Before the Permanent Subcommittee on Investigations of the Committee on Government Operations, *State Department Information Program—Information Centers*. 83rd Congress, 1st Session, Part 4, April 24, 1953. Washington, DC: U.S. Government Printing Office, 1953.

U.S. Congress, Senate. Hearings Before the Subcommittee on Immigration and Naturalization of the Committee of the Judiciary. *Communist Activities Among Aliens and National Groups*. 81st Congress, 1st Session, Part 1, May–August 1949. Washington, DC: U.S. Government Printing Office, 1950.

U.S. Congress, Senate. *Strategy and Tactics of World Communism (Significance of the Matusow Case): Report of the Subcommittee to Investigate the Administration of the Internal Security Act and other Internal Security Laws, to the Committee on the Judiciary, United States Senate*. 84th Congress, 1st Session, April 6, 1955. Washington, DC: U.S. Government Printing Office, 1955.

U.S. Congress, Senate, Subcommittee to Investigate the Administration of the Internal Security Act and Other Internal Security Laws of the Committee on the Judiciary. *Communist Party, U.S A.—Soviet Pawn*. 90th Congress, 1st Session. Washington, DC: U.S. Government Printing Office, 1967.

U.S. Congress, Senate, Subcommittee to Investigate the Administration of the Internal Security Act and Other Internal Security Laws of the Committee on the Judiciary. *The 16th Convention of the Communist Party, U.S.A.: Interim Report*. 85th Congress, 1st Session, June 13, 1957. Washington, DC: U.S. Government Printing Office, 1957.

U.S. Department of Homeland. "The Department of Homeland Security" June 2002, 8. www.DHS.gov/xlibrary/assets/book.pdf.

U.S. National Labor Relations Board. *Legislative History of the Labor Management Relations Act, 1947*. Washington, DC: U.S. Government Printing Office, 1959.

Viereck, Peter. *Conservatism Revisited: The Revolt Against Revolt, 1815–1949*. New York: Scribner's, 1949.

Viereck, Peter. "The Revolt Against the Elite." In Bell, *The New American Right*, 91–116.

Viereck, Peter. *Shame and Glory of the Intellectuals: Babbitt, Jr. vs. the Rediscovery of American Values*. Boston: Beacon Press, 1953.

Von Hoffman, Nicholas. *Citizen Cohn*. New York: Doubleday, 1988.

W. H. D. R. "Communism in America Under Attack." *Virginia Law Review* 34, no. 4 (May 1948): 439–50.

Wald, Alan M. *The New York Intellectuals: The Rise and Decline of the Anti-Stalinist Left from the 1930s to the 1980s*. Chapel Hill, NC: University of North Carolina Press, 1987.

Walker, Samuel. *In Defense of American Liberties: A History of the ACLU*, 2nd ed. Carbondale/Edwardsville, IL: Southern Illinois University Press, 1999.

Walsh, Edmund J. *The Fall of the Russian Empire: The Story of the Last Romanovs and the Coming of the Bolsheviki*. Boston: Little, Brown, 1928.

Walsh, Edmund J. *The Last Stand: An Interpretation of the Soviet Five-Year Plan*. Boston: Little, Brown, 1931.

Walsh, Edmund J. *Total Empire: The Roots and Progress of World Communism*. Milwaukee, WI: Bruce, 1951.

Ward, Richard J. "The Role of the Association of Catholic Trade Unionists in the Labor Movement." *Review of Social Economy* 14, no. 2 (September 1956): 79–100.

Ward, Robert D. "The Origins and Activities of the National Security League, 1914–1919." *Mississippi Valley Historical Review* 47, no. 1 (June 1960): 51–65.

Warren, Donald. *Radio Priest: Charles Coughlin, the Father of Hate Radio*. New York: Free Press, 1996.

Warren, Frank A. *An Alternative Vision: The Socialist Party in the 1930's*. Bloomington, IN: Indiana University Press, 1974.

Wechsler, James A. *The Age of Suspicion*. New York: Random House, 1953.

Wechsler, James A. "Carey and the Communists." *The Nation* (September 13, 1941): 224–25.

Wechsler, James A. "How to Rid the Government of Communists." *Harper's* (November 1947): 438–43.

Wechsler, James A. *Labor Baron: A Portrait of John L. Lewis*. New York: Morrow, 1944.

Wechsler, James A. *Reflections of an Angry Middle-Aged Editor*. New York: Random House, 1960.

Wechsler, James A. "The Remington Loyalty Case." *New Republic* (February 28, 1949): 18–20.

Wechsler, James A. *Revolt on the Campus*. New York: Covici, Friede, 1935

Wechsler, James A. "Stalin and Union Square." *The Nation* (September 30, 1939): 342–45.

Wechsler, James A. "The Trial of Our Times (Cont'd)." *The Progressive*, March 1950, 5–6.

Wechsler, James A., and Joseph P. Lash. *War: Our Heritage*. New York: International Publishers, 1936.

Wechsler, James A., and Harold Lavine. *War Propaganda and the United States*. New Haven, CT: Yale University Press, 1940.

Weiner, Tim. *Legacy of Ashes: The History of the CIA*. New York: Doubleday, 2007.

Weinstein, Allen. *Perjury: The Hiss-Chambers Case*. New York: Knopf, 1978.

Weinstein, Allen, and Vassiliev, *The Haunted Wood: Soviet Espionage in America— The Stalin Era*. New York: Random House, 1999.

Weisbord, Merrily. *The Strangest Dream: Canadian Communists, the Spy Trials, and the Cold War*. Toronto: Lester and Orpen Dennys, 1983.

Wertenbaker, Charles. "The China Lobby." *The Reporter* (April 15, 1952): 4–24.

Westbrook, Robert B. *John Dewey and American Democracy*. Ithaca, NY/ London: Cornell University Press, 1991.

Westin, Alan F. "Anti-Communism and the Corporations." *Commentary* (December 1963): 479–87.

Westin, Alan F. "The John Birch Society: Fundamentalism on the Right." *Commentary* (August 1961): 93–104.

Westin, Alan F. "Our Freedom—and the Rights of Communists: A Reply to Irving Kristol." *Commentary* 14, no. 1 (July 1952): 33–40.

Whitaker, Reg, and Gary Marcuse. *Cold War Canada: The Making of a National Insecurity State, 1945–1957*. Toronto/Buffalo, NY: University of Toronto Press, 1994.

White, W. L. *Report on the Russians*. New York: Harcourt, Brace, 1944.

Whitfield, Stephen J. *Into the Dark: Hannah Arendt and Totalitarianism*. Philadelphia, PA: Temple University Press, 1980.

Wiener, Jonathan M. "Radical Historians and the Crisis in American History, 1959–1980." *Journal of American History* 76, no. 2 (September 1989): 399–434.

Wilcox, Leonard. *V. F. Calverton: Radical in the American Grain*. Philadelphia, PA: Temple University Press, 1992.

Wilford, Hugh. *The New York Intellectuals: From Vanguard to Institution*. Manchester, UK/New York: Manchester University Press, 1995.

Williams, Daniel D. "Niebuhr and Liberalism." In Kegley and Bretall, *Reinhold Niebuhr*, 193–214.

Williams, Daniel K. *God's Own Party: The Making of the Christian Right*. Oxford, UK/New York: Oxford University Press, 2010.

Williams, David. "The Bureau of Investigation and Its Critics, 1919–1921: The Origins of Federal Police Surveillance." *Journal of American History* 68, no. 3 (December 1983): 560–79.

Wills, Garry. *Confessions of a Conservative*. Garden City, NY: Doubleday, 1979.

Wilson, Edmund. "First Days in Moscow." *New Republic* (March 25, 1936): 184–86.

Wilson, Edmund. "Letters in the Soviet Union." *New Republic* (April 1, 1936): 212–14.

Wilson, Edmund. "Russian Idyls." *New Republic* (April 29, 1936): 339–42.

Wilson, Edmund. "Stalin as Icon." *New Republic* (April 15, 1936): 271–73.

Wilson, Edmund. *Travels in Two Democracies*. New York: Harcourt, Brace, 1936.

Wilson, H. H., and Harvey Glickman. *The Problem of Internal Security in Great Britain, 1948–1953*. Garden City, NY: Doubleday, 1954.

Wilson, Woodrow, and Albert Fried. *A Day of Dedication*. New York: Macmillan, 1965.

Winston, Francis Graham. *The Case for Conservatism: Three Lectures Delivered at the University of Washington*. Seattle, WA: University of Washington Press, 1951.

Wolfinger, Raymond E., Barbara Kaye Wolfinger, Kenneth Prewitt, and Sheila Rosenhack. "America's Radical Right: Politics and Ideology." In *Ideology and Discontent*, edited by David E. Apter, 263–88. New York: Free Press of Glencoe, 1964.

Wolfskill, George. *The Revolt of the Conservatives: The American Liberty League, 1934–1940*. Boston: Houghton Mifflin, 1962.

Wrezsin, Michael. "Arthur Schlesinger, Jr., Scholar-Activist in Cold War America: 1946–1956." *Salmagundi* 63–64 (Spring–Summer 1984): 255–85.

Wrezsin, Michael. *A Rebel in Defense of Tradition: The Life and Politics of Dwight Macdonald*. New York: Basic Books, 1994.

Yarnell, Allen. *Democrats and Progressives: The 1948 Presidential Election as a Test of Postwar Liberalism*. Berkeley/Los Angeles, CA: University of California Press, 1974.

Ybarra, Michael J. *Washington Gone Crazy: Senator Pat McCarran and the Great American Communist Hunt*. Hanover, NH: Steerforth Press, 2004.

Young, James R. *The Politics of Affluence: Ideology in the United States since World War I*. San Francisco: Chandler, 1968.

Zelizer, Julian C. *Arsenal of Democracy: The Politics of National Security—From World War II to the War on Terrorism*. New York: Basic Books, 2010.

Zion, Sidney. *The Autobiography of Roy Cohn*. Secaucus, NJ: Lyle Stuart, 1988.

Index

Note: The terms "anti-Communist," "Cold War," "communism," "Communist," "Communist Party," "Soviet Union," and "United States" are not included in this index.

Abel, Lionel, 131
Abrams, Elliott, 311 n.2
Academic anti-communism, 63, 127–29, 204–9
Academy Awards, 198
Academy of Motion Picture Arts and Sciences, 198, 304 n.27
Acheson, Dean, 143, 148, 156
Adams, John, 283 n.62
Adams, Sherman, 283 n.62
Adamson, Ernie, 80
Ad Hoc Committee for Cultural Freedom, 167
Advertising Council, 78
Aiken, George, 94
Alaska
Albertson v. Subversive Activities Control Board, 198
Alert, 121
Alger, Horatio, 9
Alien Act, 12
Alien and Sedition Acts, 11
Alien Registration Act, 6, 56, 57–58, 63, 66, 73, 88, 91, 107, 109, 110, 161, 174, 181, 193, 197, 244 n.52, 247–48 n.14, 248 n.16, 263 n.24

Ali, Muhammad, 100
All-American Conferences, 119, 121
Allis-Chalmers, 57
Allit, Patrick, 43
Allport, Gordon W., 7, 10, 15, 233 n.43
Almond, Gabriel A., 233–34 n.48, 242 n.30
Alperovitz, Gar, 202
Al Qaeda, 222
Alsop, Joseph, 132, 154
Alsop, Stewart, 154
Amalgamated Clothing Workers of America, 59
Amerasia, 205
American Bar Association, 70, 125–26, 172
American Business Consultants, 84–85
American China Policy Association, 127
American Civil Liberties Union, 25, 38, 46, 62, 154, 161, 177, 195, 201, 241 n.19, 250 n.34, 290 nn.49, 51, 302 n.5, 311 n.1
American Coalition, 25
American Committee for Cultural Freedom, 134, 146, 159, 167–69, 178,

187, 294 n.82, 294–95 n.86, 295 n.87,
301 n.86
American Committee for the
Protection of the Foreign Born,
263–64 n.25
*American Communications Association v.
Douds*, 106
American Council of Christian
Churches, 117
American Defense Committee for
Leon Trotsky, 46, 52, 73, 246 n.84
American Federation of Labor, 6, 13,
17, 21, 25, 26, 27, 33, 34, 39–40, 55, 70,
72, 78, 81, 85, 115, 123–25, 167, 236
n.10, 238 n.29, 241 nn.21, 22, 278
n.15, 293 n.75
American Federation of Teachers, 60
American Forum on the Air, 182
American Heritage Foundation, 80
Americanism, 100, 232 n.29, 236 n.11
Americanization, 12
American Jewish Committee, 3, 118,
119, 120, 269–70 n.8
American Jewish League Against
Communism, 119
American Labor Party, 60, 72
American League Against War and
Fascism, 25
American League for Peace and
Democracy, 54
American Legion, 13, 17, 28, 33, 37–38,
59, 70, 81, 119, 120–23, 192, 198–99,
219, 241 nn.19, 21, 243 n.46, 260 n.47,
278 n.15, 304 n.24
American Legion Magazine, 122, 123
American Legion Weekly, 38
American Mercury, 44, 264 n.32,
278 n.10
American Newspaper Guild, 60,
105, 177, 249 n.21
American Opinion, 199
American Philosophical Society, 63
American Protective League, 13
American Security Council,
259 n.44
Americans for Democratic Action,
124, 155–56, 159–60, 178, 180–83
passim, 256 n.14, 228 n.29, 291 n.55

Americans for Intellectual
Freedom, 167
American Society of Newspaper
Editors, 180
American Student Union, 177
American Workers Party, 51, 244 n.52
Anarchism, anarchists, 11, 21, 38, 49,
246 n.82
Anglo-American Trade Union
Committee, 124
Anti-communism: Catholic, 33–37,
70–71, 113–17; civil-libertarian,
171–90; conservative, 42–45, 134,
135–38, 200–201, 219; critique of,
209–13; ex-Communist, 40–42,
132–35; Jewish, 118–20; left-of-
liberal, 49–52, 62–63, 164–69, 203;
liberal, 45–49, 61–62, 72–73, 134,
153–64, 178, 201, 285 n.7, 286 n.12;
Protestant, 37, 117–18, 200; "soft"
versus "hard," 289 n.36
"Anti-Communism and the U.S:
History and Consequences," 205–6
Anti-Communist Crusade, 200
Anti-Communist Leadership
School, 117
Anti-Defamation League, 126,
205, 308 n.61
Anti-fascism, 183
Anti-McCarthy, 292 n.64
Anti-radicalism, 10–13
Anti-Semitism, 17, 36, 37, 118, 119, 164,
184, 235 n.58, 257 n.20, 285–86 n.11
Anti-Stalinism/anti-Stalinist, 49–52,
73, 118, 166, 169, 186, 188, 244 n.54,
246 n.84
Anti-terrorism, 222–25
Anvil, 186
Archangel, 20
Arendt, Hannah, 42, 73, 128, 169,
295 n.90
Arens, Richard, 114, 188
Arkansas, 238 n.24
Army-McCarthy Hearings, 104, 147, 163
Army Signal Corps, 99
Arnold, Fortas and Porter, 180
Arnold, Thurman, 180
Assignment in Utopia, 44, 177

Association of the Bar of the City of New York, 274–75 n.55
Association of Catholic Trade Unionists, 37, 59, 70, 71, 116–17, 124, 249 n.21, 270 nn.11, 12
Association of Motion Picture Producers, 198
Atomic bomb, 107
Atomic Diplomacy, 202
Atomic Energy Commission, 91
Attorney General (U.S.), 29, 56–57, 66, 86–87, 95, 98, 101, 105, 107, 109, 122, 188, 265 n.33, 268 n.80
Attorney General's List of Subversive Organizations, 87, 121, 161, 194, 247 n.15, 260 n.55
Austin, Warren R., 250 n.28
Avukah, 118
Aware, Inc., 85
Axis, 64, 72

Baarslag, Karl, 85, 120, 260 n.47
Baldwin, Roger, 46
Baltimore, Maryland, 71
Bar Association of the City of Chicago, 274–75 n.55
Barenblatt v. United States
Barrett, William, 165, 292 n.67
Barrows, David B., 59
Barsky, et al. v. United States, 106
Barth, Alan, 16, 40, 157, 172, 175–77, 189, 265 n.33
Bean, Louis, 162
Beard, Charles, 251 n.43
Becker, Jean-Jacques, 229 n.1
Belfrage, Cedric, 298 n.43
Bell, Daniel, 7, 168, 203
Bell, Jonathan, 81
Bendiner, Robert, 154, 286 n.16
Bennett, William J., 223
Bentley, Elizabeth, 88, 181, 216, 217, 281 n.54
Benton, William, 163, 175, 286–87 n.18
Bercovici, Leonardo, 299 n.57
Berkman, Alexander, 40, 49, 276 n.68
Berle, Adolf, Jr., 60, 243 n.47, 250 n.28
Berlin, 166, 300 n.68
Berman, Paul, 245–46 n.73, 312 n.11

Bernstein, Serge, 229 n.1
Biddle, Francis, 57, 247–48 n.14
Bin Laden, Osama, 222, 224
Black, Hugo, 108, 268 n.75
Blacklist, 2 n.†, 187–88, 191, 198–99, 206–07, 272 n.30, 275 n.60, 304 n.27
Black Panther Party, 204
Blankfort, Michael, 121–22, 273 n.39
Blessings of Liberty, 174
The Blue Book, 199
B'nai Brith, 58, 70, 205
Board of Economic Warfare, 65
Bohlen, Charles, 156, 266 n.44, 283 n.65
The Bolshevik Myth, 49
Bolsheviks/Bolshevism, 19, 20, 21, 22, 29, 34, 38, 39, 43, 44, 50, 71, 118, 209, 211, 237 n.16
Bontecou, Eleanor, 4
Bonus Army, 30
Boston police strike, 21
Bourdet, Claude, 7, 9
Bouscaren, Anthony T., 129
Bowles, Chester, 155, 286–87 n.18
Boyer, Paul, 255 n.2
Boy Scouts of America, 70
Bozell, L. Brent, 146
Braden, Thomas W., 274 n.48
Braden v. United States, 197 n.20
Brandeis, Louis D., 20, 87, 296 n.10
Brands, H. W., Jr., 148
Brecht, Bertolt, 258 n.26
Breindel, Eric, 207–08
Brennan, William, 109, 110
Brest-Litovsk, Treaty of, 19, 20
Brewer, Roy, 16, 84, 235 n.58, 284 n.75
Bricker, John, 69
Bridges, Harry, 57, 59, 67, 95, 238 n.27, 241 n.21, 247–48 n.14
Bridges v. United States, 247–48 n.14
Bridges v. Wixon, 66–67, 247–48 n.14
Brinkley, Alan, 276 n.65
Brock, Clifton, 288 n.29
Brooklyn College, 109
Brooklyn Tablet, 36
Brophy, John, 59
Browder, Earl, 25, 44, 54, 55, 240 n.46, 247 n.7, 248 n.19
Browder, Raissa, 247 n.7

Brown, Irving, 72, 124, 254 n.31,
    293 n.75
Brown, Ralph S., Jr., 14, 301 n.1
Brownell, Herbert, Jr., 102–3,
    266–67 n.55, 281 n.54, 283 n.62
Broyles Commission. *See* Seditious
    Activities Investigating
    Commission
Buckley, William F., Jr., 134, 136, 139,
    146, 151, 201, 279 n.17, 280–81 n.34,
    282 n.55, 299 n.59
Budenz, Louis, 40, 41, 80, 132, 269 n.7,
    276 n.68, 277 nn.3, 4, 6
Bullitt, William C., 69–70, 135,
    250 n.28, 253 n.19
Burdett, Winston, 105
Bureau of Immigration, 12
Bureau of Investigation, 29, 239 n.39
Burnham, James, 61, 135–36, 146, 171,
    218, 279 n.17
Burns, William, 44
Burton, Harold, 106
Bush, George W., 222, 223, 311 n.1
Butterworth, Benjamin, 11

Cahan, Abraham, 118
California, 58, 97, 123, 192, 198, 199,
    263 n.24, 301 n.87
California Fact-Finding Committee
    on Un-American Activities, 121–22
Calvary Cemetery, 117
Calverton, V. F., 45, 244 n.54
Cameron, Angus, 133
Cameron and Kahn, 133
Canada, 4–6, 83
Cantwell, John J., 58
Carey, James B., 115–16, 124, 270 n.11,
    297 n.30
Carmody, Martin, 34
Carnegie Endowment for Peace,
    283 n.60
Carr, Frank P. 264 n.32
Catholic anti-communism, 33–37,
    70–71, 113–17
Catholic Church, 17, 26, 33, 220,
    269 n.7, 270–71 n.13, 278 n.15
"Catholic Hour," 35, 71
Catholic Information Society, 114

Catholic Labor Defense, 117
Catholic Radical Alliance, 241 n.15
Catholics, 11, 14, 15–16, 58, 171, 186,
    239 n.1, 277 n.4
Catholic Trade Union Associations.
    See Association of Catholic Trade
    Unions
Catholic University, 35
Catholic War Veterans, 114, 199
Catholic Worker, 36, 186
Catholic Worker Movement, 36–37,
    186, 240 n.1, 239–40 n.1, 271 n.18
CBS, 105
Celler, Emanuel, 292 n.63
Censorship Office (U.S.), 13
Centralia, Washington, 241 n.19
Central Intelligence Agency, 14, 16, 85,
    124, 167, 225, 279 n.17, 281 n.39, 293
    n.75, 303 n.10,
Chafe, William H., 76
Chafee, Zechariah, Jr., 171, 172–75,
    176, 189, 295 n.21
Chaillaux, H. L., 28, 38
Chamberlain, John, 43, 138
Chamberlin, William Henry, 69,
    251 n.43, 276 n.68
Chamber of Commerce, 25, 77–78, 81,
    114, 278 n.15
Chambers, Whittaker, 41, 60, 68, 88,
    134, 138, 144, 157, 165, 217, 242 n.34,
    243 n.47, 250 n.28, 276 n.61, 278 n.12,
    281 n.54
Chavez, Dennis, 132, 163, 277 n.4
Cheney, Dick, 311–12 n.2
Cheyenne, Wyoming, 89
Chiang Kai-shek, 3, 97, 108, 126,
    127, 164
Chiaramonte, Nicola, 164
Chicago, Illinois, 161
Chicago Tribune, 43
The Children of Light, 285 n.4
China, 3, 69, 126–27, 157, 218
"China Lobby," 108, 126–27, 201,
    276 n.65, 306 n.38
The China Lobby in American Politics,
    306 n.38
Chinese Americans, 11
Chodorov, Frank, 280 n.29

Christian Crusade, 117
Christian Front of Social Justice
  Platoons, 36
Christian Herald, 269–70 n.8
Churchill, Winston, 3
Church League of America, 117
CIO-PAC, 65, 80, 81, 135, 140,
  144, 254 n.32
City College of New York, 118
Civil-libertarian anti-communism,
  171–90
Civil Rights Defense Committee, 73
Civil Service Commission, 216,
  260 n.53
Clark, Bennet C., 106
Clark, Tom, 78, 81, 86–87, 106, 260–61
  n.54, 261 n.55
Clay, Lucius, 14
Clearing House, 162
Cleveland, Grover, 12
Clifford, Clark, 86, 87, 288 n.29
Coast Guard, 85
Coben, Stanley, 232–33 n.42
Cogley, John, 187–88, 275 n.60,
  301 n.87
Cohen, Naomi, 120
Cohn, Roy, 15, 16, 100, 151–52, 178,
  182, 275 n.57
COINTELPRO-Communist Party,
  106, 196
The Cold War and Its Origins, 202
Cole v. Young, 109
Colorado, 58
Columbia Law School, 177
Columbia Pictures, 198
Columbia University, 45, 177
The Coming Defeat of Communism,
  279 n.19
Comintern. *See* Communist
  International
Commager, Henry Steele, 45
Commentary, 119, 189,
  201, 204
Commission of Inquiry into the
  Charges Made Against Leon
  Trotsky in the Moscow Trials, 52,
  242 n.29
Commission on Communism, 119

Commission on Government
  Security, 163
Commission on Internal Security and
  Individual Rights, 97
Committee for Cultural Freedom, 46,
  47, 52, 62, 73, 167, 244 n.57
Committee for Democratic Trade
  Unionism, 124
Committee for Industrial
  Organization, 36
Committee for the First Amendment,
  154, 286 n.12
Committee of One Million, 201
Committee on Appropriations (House
  of Representatives), 55, 66
Committee on Appropriations
  (Senate), 92, 93
Committee on Education and Labor
  (House of Representatives), 21, 144
Committee on Foreign Relations
  (Senate), 93,
Committee on Government
  Operations (Senate), 99, 104, 163
Committee on Homeland Security
  (House of Representatives), 225
Committee on Internal Security
  (House of Representatives), 192
Committee on the Judiciary
  (Senate), 22
Committee on Rules and
  Administration (Senate), 104
Committee on Un-American Activ-
  ities (House of Representatives),
  14, 33, 38, 78–85, 86, 88, 92, 98, 105,
  115–19 passim, 122, 124, 125, 135,
  144, 145, 150, 154, 159, 163, 176, 179,
  182, 185, 188, 191–93, 195–96, 197,
  207, 217, 219, 225, 260 nn.47, 54,
  269–70 n.8, 273 n.39, 275 n.57, 276
  n.61, 281 n.54, 290 n.51, 292 n.63,
  293 n.77, 304 n.27
Committee to Secure Justice for the
  Rosenbergs, 119
The Common Enemy, 44
Common Sense, 48
Commonweal, 117, 186, 187
*Communism and the Conscience of the
  West*, 114

Communism and the Negro Movement, 196

Communism Within the Labor Movement, 78

Communist, 127

Communist Control Act, 103–04, 159, 163, 164, 187

Communist Infiltration in the United States, 78

Communist International, 25, 54

Communist League of America, 50

Communist (Opposition) Party, 50

Communist Party, China, 3, 77, 91

Communist Target—Youth, 196

Community Relations Committee, 119

COMPIC (FBI), 66

Condon, Edward U., 181

Congress for Cultural Freedom, 166–67, 169, 259 n.45, 293 n.75, 297 n.17

Congress of Industrial Organizations (CIO), 27, 36, 59, 60, 65, 71–72, 76, 95, 115–16, 123–25, 140, 144, 241 n.21, 242 n.29, 257 n.18, 269 n.11, 272 n.30, 274 n.50, 285 n.7, 301 n.87

Connecticut, 155, 286–87 n.18

Consensus theories, 9

Conservative anti-communism, 42–45, 134, 135–38, 200–201, 219

Conspiracy theories, 232 n.34

Conspirator, 83

Cook, Fred C., 305 n.33

Coolidge, Calvin, 21

Cooper, John Sherman, 104

Coplon, Judith, 91

Coser, Lewis, 50, 311 n.15

Coughlin, Charles E., 17, 35–36, 37, 44, 45

Counterattack, 114

Counterculture, 203, 204

Counts, George S., 293 n.77

Cowley, Malcolm, 251 n.34

Criminal syndicalist laws, 23, 31, 109

Cronin, John F., 71, 78, 114, 117, 127, 144

Crusade for Christian Democracy, 34–35

Crusade for the Preservation and Promotion of American Ideals, 114

Cultural and Scientific Congress for World Peace, 167, 184, 293 n.77

Cutler, Robert, 283 n.62

Cvetic, Matt, 235 n.58

Daily Worker, 40, 127, 179

Dallin, David, 73

Daughters of the American Revolution, 44, 81, 85

David, Henry, 11

Davies, John Paton, Jr., 148

Davis, Elmer, 251 n.43

Davis, Forrest, 201, 306 n.38

Day, Dorothy, 36–37, 239–40 n.1, 271 n.18

Dearborn Independent, 44

Debs, Eugene V., 21, 236 n.14

Decalogue Society of American Lawyers, 186

De Caux, Len, 60

Decter, Midge, 311 n.2

Decter, Moshe, 159

The Defiant Ones, 304 n.27

Delaware, 238 n.24

Democratic Digest, 182

Democratic party, 25, 44, 55, 81, 88, 89, 92–96 passim, 135, 151, 155, 162–63, 183, 191, 194, 220, 250 n.32, 311 n.1

Denicke, George, 277 n.72

Dennis case defendants, 311 n.15

Dennis v. United States, 107, 110, 160, 182

Department of Commerce (U.S.), 95, 181

Department of Justice (U.S.), 12, 14, 29, 44, 55, 56, 57, 66–67, 81, 85, 86, 88, 91, 103, 108, 132, 182, 195, 225, 232–33 n.42, 260–61 n.55, 263 n.24, 277 n.2

Department of Labor (U.S.), 25, 95

Department of Navy (U.S.), 25

Department of Post Office (U.S.), 99

Department of State (U.S.), 25, 92, 93, 110, 111, 143, 148, 178, 187, 201, 259 n.45, 266 n.50, 279 n.17, 282 n.55

Department of Treasury (U.S.),
281 n.54
Department of War (U.S.), 25
Der Monat, 166
Despol, John, 301 n.87
de Tocqueville, Alexis, 9, 10
Detroit, MI, 115, 263 n.24
Deutscher, Isaac, 41, 42
Dewey, John, 46–47, 48, 73, 244 n.58,
245 n.66, 246 n.82, 251 n.45, 287
nn.19, 21
Dewey, Thomas E., 69, 89, 143,
228 n.26
Dickstein, Samuel, 23–24, 192
Dies, Martin, 26–29, 54, 63, 65, 66, 67,
71, 79, 80, 103, 238 nn.27, 28, 250
n.34, 278–79 n.15
Dilling, Elizabeth, 45, 244 n.52
Dissent, 187, 289 n.41
Divini Redemptoris, 34
Division of Internal Security
(Department of Justice), 104
Douglas, Helen Gahagan, 145
Douglas, Kirk, 199
Douglas, Melvyn, 154
Douglas, Paul H., 162, 163, 182
Douglas, William O., 67, 108, 268 n.75
Dower, John W., 312 n.12
Draper, Theodore, 204
Drucker, Peter F., 63
D'Souza, Dinesh, 311 n.1
Dubinsky, David, 39, 44, 72, 250 n.28
DuBois, W. E. B., 184
Dulles, Allen, 14, 202, 281 n.39
Dulles, John Foster, 136, 141–44, 148,
266 n.50, 283 nn.65, 66
Dunne, Philip, 154

Earle, George H., 86
Easley, Ralph, 24
Eastland, James, 105
Eastman, Max, 10, 61, 69, 146,
276 n.68
Economic Cooperation Act, 157
Ehardt, George, C., 117
Ehrman, John, 154
Einstein, Albert, 4, 153, 169, 183–86,
294 n.82, 299 n.62, 300 nn.68, 70

Eisenhower administration, 86,
101–5, 111, 125, 139, 144, 145, 148,
268–69 n.80
Eisenhower, Dwight D., 14, 42, 99–111
passim, 139, 143, 147, 151, 159, 191,
264 nn.30, 31, 266 nn.44, 53, 266–67
n.55, 267 n.59, 268–69 n.80, 283 n.62
Eisler, Gerhart, 80
Eisler, Hanns, 80, 84, 258 n.26
Ekirch, Arthur A., Jr., 153
Ellender, Allen, 163
Emergency Civil Liberties Committee,
159, 161, 168, 185, 290 n.51, 294 n.82
Emerson, Thomas I., 298 n.45
Emery, DeWitt, 150
Emmons. Delos, 216
Encounter, 167, 189
The End of Economic Man, 63
English, Raymond, 153
Englund, Steven, 235 n.57
Ernst, Morris, 161, 250 n.34, 290 n.46
Espionage Act, 12, 21, 55, 173
Estonia, 62
Europe-American Groups, 164, 167
European Recovery Program, 140, 156
Ex-Communists, 40–42, 132–35, 219,
242 n.30
The Execution of Private Slovik, 196, 199
Executive orders, 57, 65, 86, 95,
101, 194
Exodus, 191, 196, 199

Fagan, Myron C., 304 n.24
Fainsod, Merle, 129
Fair Deal, 146
Fair Play for Cuba Committee, 196
Farrell, James T., 73
Far Left of Center, 205
Fascism/fascists, 26, 29, 36, 38, 45, 46,
48, 57, 58, 59, 62, 87, 136, 155, 164,
171, 189, 194, 212, 213, 239–40 n.1,
248 n.16, 289 n.41
Federal Bar Association, 92
Federal Bureau of Investigation (FBI),
30–31, 33, 38, 57, 58, 63, 66, 68, 70, 71,
78, 79, 80, 85, 92, 95, 102, 103, 105,
114, 122, 125, 127, 132, 134, 145, 151,
176, 179, 181, 182, 188, 192, 194,

195–97, 215, 216, 218, 219, 250 nn.28,
34, 261 n.59, 264 n.32, 266 n.50,
266–67 n.55, 268 n.80, 270 n.9,
281 n.54, 290 n.51, 299 n.62, 305 n.35
Federal Communications
Commission, 65
Federal Internal Security Board, 195
Federalists, 10
Federal Theater Project, 28
Fenton, John M., 76
Fiedler, Leslie A., 158
Fifth Amendment, 105, 109, 111, 116,
125, 176, 197, 198, 298 n.43, 299 n.57
Fineberg, Andhil, 269–70 n.8
Finland, 54, 62
Finn, Aubrey, 263–64 n.25
First Amendment, 95, 106–9, 116, 161,
173, 185, 197, 304 n.23
Fischer, Louis, 40
Fischer, Ruth, 80, 258 n.26
Fish, Hamilton, 23, 135, 278 n.15
Fiske v. Kansas, 31
Fitzpatrick, Thomas J., 116, 271 n.14
Flanders, Ralph, 104, 162
Fleeson, Doris, 94
Fleming, D. F., 202
Flynn, Elizabeth Gurley, 62, 201
Ford, Henry, 44
Ford, James, 51
Fordham, Benjamin O., 157
Foreign Affairs, 202
Foreign Agents Registration Act, 184,
250 n.28
Foreign Economic Administration,
254 n.31
Foreign Policy for Americans, 140–41
Foreman, Carl, 299 n.57, 304 n.27
Forster, Arnold, 126
Fortas, Abe, 180–81
Fort Monmouth, 182
Foster, William Z., 51, 54, 58
Foundation for Economic
Freedom, 150
The Fountainhead, 150
France, 4, 6, 7, 124, 166, 229 n.1,
309 n.76
Franco, Francisco, 164
Frankfurter, Felix, 108, 253 n.12, 268 n.75

Frauenglass, William, 185
Freedom Foundation, 114
Freedom from Victory, 78
Freedom House, 72, 161–62
Freedom of Speech, 173–74
The Freeman, 138, 276 n.54, 278 n.10,
280 n.29, 282 n.55
Free Speech in the United States, 174
Free Trade Union Committee
(AFL), 72
Freud, Sigmund, 231 n.25
Frey, John P., 27–28, 78, 238 n.29
Fried, Emmanuel, 185
Fried, Richard, 97, 191
Friedman, Morton, 180
Friedrich, Carl J., 128
Friends of Russian Freedom, 167
Friends of Soviet Russia, 44
Fritchey, Clayton, 182
Frontier, 301 n.87
Frum, David, 223
Fryer, Russell G., 43
Fuchs, Klaus, 91
Fulbright, J. William, 163
Fund for the Republic, 102, 187, 188,
272 n.30, 294 n.86

Gaddis, John Lewis, 76, 156
Gallup Poll, 28, 76, 97, 217, 264 n.26
Gandhi, Mohandas, 185
Garrisonians, 11
Gellhorn, Walter, 298 n.45
General Intelligence Division
(Department of Justice), 14, 29
General Motors, 253 n.7
Gentile, Giovanni, 241 n.43
Georgetown University, 35
German-American Bund, 27, 56
German-Soviet Nonaggression Treaty,
5, 31, 37, 40, 45, 46, 47, 53–54, 57–63,
167, 177, 183, 247 n.7
German Writers Congress, 166
Germany, 19, 20, 46, 53, 54, 59, 61, 63,
64, 69, 70, 72, 204, 239–40 n.1
Gibbons, Edward, 273 n.38
Gibney, Frank, 15–16
Gillmor, Dan, 101
Gillon, Steven, 160

Ginsberg, Henry, 84
Gitlow, Benjamin, 42, 54, 119, 121
Givertz, Harry K., 153
Glazer, Nathan, 7, 118, 119, 292 n.64, 307 n.56
Glickman, Harvey, 4, 5
God and Man at Yale, 139
The God That Failed, 41
Gold, Harry, 92
Goldman, Emma, 40, 49, 276 n.68
Goldman, Eric F., 76
Goldstein, Robert Justin, 58, 260 n.55
Gompers, Samuel, 39
Goodman, Walter, 193, 257 n.20
Goodwin, Doris Kearns, 75
Gouzenko, Igor, 5, 83, 216
Government by Investigation, 177
Graham, Billy, 117–18
Graham, Philip, 182
Grand Alliance, 64, 65, 73
Grazia, Alfred de, 264 n.31
Great Britain (and all things British). *See* United Kingdom
The Great Globe Itself, 70
Greece, 141, 156, 164
Green, William, 39
Gregory, Thomas, 13, 29
Griffith, Robert, 162
Gropper, William, 258 n.22
The Guillotine at Work, 245–46 n.73

Halls of Montezuma, 121
Hamby, Alonzo L., 157
Hammond, Paul Y., 156
Hand, Learned, 267–68 n.67
Hansen, Ole, 20, 236 n.11
Hapgood, Norman, 44
Harding, Warren G., 22, 236 n.14
Hardwick, Thomas W., 25
Hargis, Billy Ray, 117, 118, 305 n.33
Harisiades v. Shaughnessy, 239 n.44
Harlan, John M., II, 107, 110, 197
Harriman, Averill, 156
Harrington, Michael, 172, 186–89, 301 n.87
Harris, Louis, 264 n.31
Hart, Ed, 94
Hartnett, Robert, S. J., 117

Hartz, Louis, 9, 10, 153
Harvard Crimson, 118
Harvard Law School, 172
Harvard University, 247 n.7, 287 n.19
Hatch Act, 55
Hawaii, 216, 263 n.24
Hayek, Friedrich, 43, 69, 253 n.17
Haymarket Square, 11
Haynes, John Earl, 207–9, 210, 215–16, 217, 277 n.6, 309 n.76
Hays, Arthur Garfield, 161, 251 n.43, 290 n.49
Hays, Paul R., 171
Hays, Will, 79, 82
Haywood, Allen, 59
Hazlitt, Henry, 138
Hearst, William Randolph: 43; newspapers, 74, 126, 199, 243 n.46, 275 n.60, 276 n.61, 278–79 n.15
Hellman, Lillian, 180, 181, 182, 299 n.57
Henderson, Loy, 250 n.28
Hendrickson, Robert C., 262 n.11
Herndon, Angelo, 31
Hess, Karl, 85
Hicks, Granville, 251 n.41, 289 n.36
Hillman, Sidney, 59, 71, 249 n.22
Hinds, Lynn Boyd, 229 n.22
Hiroshima, 75
Hiss, Alger, 88, 91, 114, 134, 138, 144–46, 148, 151, 157, 158, 164, 165–66, 202, 255 n.4, 280 n.24, 283 n.66, 287 n.19, 289 n.36
Hitler, Adolf, 59, 63
Hoffman, Paul G., 162
Hofstadter, Richard, 7, 9, 10, 42
Hogan, Michael J., 157
Hollander, Paul, 203, 206
Hollywood Anti-Nazi League, 27
Hollywood motion picture industry, 27, 65, 78, 79–85, 98, 121–26, 150–51, 196, 198–99, 206–7, 238 nn.27, 28, 258 n.22
Hollywood Nineteen, 273 n.39, 286 n.1
Hollywood Ten, 106
Hollywood Writers' Mobilization, 252 n.7, 254 n.32, 257 n.20
Holmes, Oliver Wendell, Jr., 173

Holmgren, Christine, 309 nn.75, 77
Holy Cross College, 186
Hook, Sidney, 41, 45, 51–52, 62, 164,
  166–68, 169, 187, 189, 244 n.57, 245
  n.59, 246 n.82, 276 n.68, 287 n.21, 293
  nn.77, 80, 294 n.83, 294–95 n.86, 295
  n.90, 300 n.68, 309 n.73
Hoopes, Townsend, 143, 279 n.17
Hoover, Herbert, 43, 68, 135, 136, 215,
  251 n.43
Hoover, J. Edgar, 6, 14, 17–18, 29–30,
  57, 63, 66, 79, 81–82, 83, 85, 86, 92,
  105, 108, 145, 173, 181, 195–97, 218,
  247–48 n.14, 250 n.34, 253 n.19, 266
  n.50, 281 n.54, 290 n.51, 305 n.35
Hopper, Hedda, 264 n.30
Houseman, John, 75
Howard, John, 304 n.24
Howe, Irving, 50, 159, 204, 289 n.41,
  311 n.15
How to Decontrol Your Union of
  Communists, 116
Huberman, Leo, 251 n.34
Hughes, Howard, 123
Hughes, Paul, 182–83
Human Events, 146
Human Rights Watch, 311 n.1
Humphrey, Hubert H., 103,
  159–60, 162, 163, 182, 187, 194,
  291 nn.59, 61
Hungary, 189
Hunter Robert, 306 n.38
Huntington, Samuel, 307 n.57
Hussein, Saddam, 222, 224, 312 n.12
Hutchins, Robert, 188, 294–95 n.86,
  301 n.87
Hyman, Herbert H., 5
Hyper-individualists, 148–51

I Chose Freedom, 68
I Confess, 42
Illinois, 120
I Married a Communist, 83
Immigration and Naturalization
  Service, 58, 98
Immigration Bureau, 29
Immigration laws, 11, 12, 23,
  31, 98

Independent Citizens Committee for
  the Arts, Sciences and Professions,
  257 n.20
Independent Labor League of
  America, 50
Independent Progressive Party, 87,
  261 n.58
Independent Socialist League, 186
Independent Voters Committee of
  Artists, Writers and Scientists for
  the Re-election of President
  Roosevelt, 254 n.32
Indiana, 238 n.24
Industrial Union of Marine and
  Shipbuilding Workers, 71
Industrial Workers of the World, 13,
  20, 21, 236 n.10, 237 n.16, 241 n.18
Ingersoll, Ralph, 177
In Stalin's Secret Service, 42
Institute for American Strategy,
  259 n.44
Institute for Policy Studies, 205
Institute of Pacific Relations, 127
Internal Revenue Service, 250–51 n.34
Internal Security Act, 6, 96–97, 99, 107,
  109, 111, 115, 160, 163, 256 n.14,
  274–75 n.55, 291 n.55, 303 n.12
International Alliance of Theatrical
  Stage Employees, 235 n.58
International Brotherhood of
  Teamsters, 57
International Conference of Free Trade
  Unions, 124
International Federation of Trade
  Unions, 39, 124
International Fur Workers, 39
International Labor Defense, 50,
  300 n.79
International Labor Organization, 123
International Labor Relations
  Commission (AFL), 72
International Ladies Garment Workers
  Union, 39, 44, 50
International Longshoremen's and
  Warehousemen's Union, 95,
  272 n.30
International Monetary Fund,
  281 n.54

International Union of Electrical, Radio and Machine Workers, 116–17
International Woodworkers of America, 59
Interstate Legislative Conference on Un-American Activities, 120
Iron Curtain, 83
Islam, 222–24, 311 n.1
"Islamism," 225, 312 n.11
"Islamofascism," 223, 224, 312 n.11
"Islamophobia," 224–25
ISMS: A Review of Alien Isms, 38
Italy, 4, 6, 7, 46, 54, 59, 63, 70, 124, 166
Ives, Irving M., 262 n.11

Jackson, C. D., 283 n.62
Jackson, Robert, 56–57, 63, 247–48 n.14, 267 n.67, 268 n.71
Jacobs, Paul, 3, 119, 247 n.16, 272 n.30
Jacoby, Norman, 273 n.38
Jains, 309 n.77
Japan, 54, 59, 64
Japanese Americans, 57, 216
Jeffersonians, 11
Jencks, Clinton, 110, 133, 268 n.80
Jencks v. United States, 110
Jenner, William, 101, 264 n.31
Jesuits, 37
Jewish anti-communism, 118–20
Jewish Federation Council, 119
Jewish Labor Committee, 118, 301 n.87
Jews, 205, 257 n.20, 308 n.61
John Birch Society, 14, 192, 199–200, 267 n.59, 305 n.35
John Reed Club, 51
Johns Hopkins University, 129
Johnson, Lyndon B., 194, 220, 303 n.18
Johnston, Eric, 78, 82–83, 122–23
Joint Anti-Fascist Refugee Committee v. McGrath, 108 n.73
Joint Fact-Finding Committee on Un-American Activities, in California, 249 n.18, 252 n.7, 301 n.91
Joint Legislative Committee to Investigate Un-American Activities (NY), 249 n.18
Josselson, Michael, 169, 295 n.87

Jozef Cardinal Mindzenty Circles, 114
Judis, John, 282 n.55

Kahane, B. B., 198, 304 n.24
Kahn, Albert, 133
Kalven, Harry, Jr., 107, 197
Kampelman, Max, 291 n.59
Kaufman, Irving R., 107
Kecskemeti, Paul, 129
Kempton, Murray, 178
Kendall, Willmoore, 43
Kennan, George, 128–29, 156, 223
Kennedy administration, 193
Kennedy, John F., 191, 199
Kennedy, Robert F., 193, 194, 199, 303 n.18
Kerby, Elizabeth Poe, 188, 301 n.87, 304 n.24
Kessler v. Strecker, 31–32
Kheifets, Gregory, 258 n.26
Kilgore, Harley, 162
Kimball, Penn, 155, 286–87 n.18
King Features, 126
King, Martin Luther, Jr., 196
King, Peter, 225
Kirk, Russell, 138–39, 151, 187
Klehr, Harvey, 204–6, 207–9, 210, 215–16, 277 n.6, 308 n.61, 309 nn.74, 76
Knights of Columbus, 34, 70, 78, 114, 117
Knowland, William F., 283 n.61
Koen, Ross Y., 306 n.38
Koestler, Arthur, 40, 41, 166, 242 n.34, 308 n.61
Kohlberg, Alfred, 119, 126–27
Korean War, 77, 92, 95, 97, 99, 107, 124, 140, 143, 157, 186, 280 n.24
Kornfeder, Joseph, 121
Kramer, Hilton, 309 n.73
Kramer, Stanley, 199, 304 n.27
Kravchenko, Victor, 68, 92
Krebs, Richard J. H. *See* Valtin, Jan
Kristol, Irving, 16, 168, 189–90, 203–4, 302 n.95
Kristol, William, 311 n.2
Krivitsky, Walter G., 42, 54, 243 n.47, 276 n.68

Kronstadt, 40
Ku Klux Klan, 38, 45, 192
Kulaks, 211
Kutler, Stanley I., 219

Labor Leader, 37
Ladd, D. Milton, 85
Laffin, William P., 121–22
La Follette, Suzanne, 73, 246 n.82
Lamont, Corliss, 185
Lansing, Robert, 19, 20
Larson, Charles L., 121
Lasch, Christopher, 168
Lasky, Melvin, 166–67
Lasky, Victor, 126, 257 n.59
Lasswell, Harold D., 175–76
Lattimore, Owen, 97, 108–9, 169, 181
Latvia, 62
Lautner, John, 132
Lawson v. United States, 106
League Against Totalitarianism, 52
League Against War and Fascism, 16
League for Cultural Freedom and
    Socialism, 52, 62
League of American Writers, 51
League of Professional Groups, 51
Left-of-liberal anti-communism,
    49–52, 62–63, 164–69, 203
Lehman, Herbert, 104, 143,
    163, 178
Lemke, William, 44
Lend-lease aid, 64, 68
Leninist, 210
Lenin, V. I., 50, 62
Lerner, Max, 178, 251 n.41
Letters from Russian Prisons, 44
Levin, Murray B., 9, 10
Levine, Isaac Don, 43–44, 60, 119, 127,
    145, 250 n.28
Lewis, Anthony, 151
Lewis, Fulton, Jr., 100
Lewis, John L., 59
Lewy, Guenter, 206
Libby, I. Lewis, 311–12 n.2
Liberal anti-communism, 45–49,
    61–62, 72–73, 134, 153–64, 178, 201,
    285 n.7, 286 n.12
Liberal fascism, 204

Liberalism and Social Action, 48,
    244 n.58
Liberal Party (N.Y.), 72
Liberals, 137, 138, 139, 165–66, 169,
    181, 187, 189, 203, 220, 254 n.32, 285
    n.5, 286 n.16, 228 n.26, 291 nn.59, 61,
    292 n.67, 29–94 n.80
Liberty League, 43
Libya, 226
Liebman, Marvin, 201
Life, 69, 142, 143
Lippmann, Walter, 251 n.43
Lipset, Seymour Martin, 7, 76, 232 n.29
Lithuania, 62
Living My Life, 49
Locke, John, 9, 10, 232 n.30
Lodge, Henry Cabot, 266 n.50,
    283 n.62
Loeb, James, Jr., 61, 155
Look, 253 n.7
Los Alamos, New Mexico, 91
Los Angeles, California, 301 n.87
Los Angeles Conference of Civic
    Organizations to Fight
    Communism, 273 n.38
Losey, Joseph, 255 n.4
Lovestone, Jay, 50, 62, 72, 124
The Loyalty of Free Men, 175, 176
Loyalty programs, 5, 86–87, 161, 178,
    180–81, 216, 218, 260 n.53, 263 n.13,
    266 n.50, 274–75 n.55, 291 n.62,
    298 n.53
Lubell, Samuel, 264 n.31, 283 n.63
Luce, Henry, 43, 127, 276 nn.61, 65
Lusk, Clayton R., 14, 18, 237 n.16
Lyons, Eugene, 43–44, 119, 177,
    276 n.68

Macdonald, Dwight, 73, 164–65, 167,
    168, 246 n.84, 280 n.34, 292 n.66
MacLeish, Archibald, 251 n.43
Maddox, Robert James, 202
Malsberger, John W., 136
Maltz, Albert, 196, 199
Mandel, Benjamin, 85, 124, 127,
    260 n.47
Manifesto of the Communist Party, 33
Marcuse, Herbert, 204

Marine Cooks and Stewards, 95
Marks, Gary, 232 n.29
Marshall, George, C., 99, 147, 156
Marshall Plan. *See* European Recovery
  Program
Martin, Homer, 50
Martin, James J., 137
Martin, Joseph, 100
Marxism/Marxists, 47–48, 49, 51, 62,
  100, 125, 158, 164, 188, 205, 263 n.24,
  286 n.16
Maryland, 97
Massachusetts Institute of Technology,
  247 n.7
Masters of Deceit, 303 n.14
Matthews, Francis P., 78
Matthews, J. B., 14–15, 28, 43, 66, 71,
  118, 122, 151, 162, 238 n.30, 243 n.46,
  264 n.32, 273 n.34
Matusow, Harvey, 132–33
Maurin, Peter, 36
Maximoff, G. P., 245–46 n.73
McAuliffe, Mary, 160, 161, 289 n.36
McCarran, Pat, 66, 95–96, 98, 100, 108,
  127, 160, 162, 163, 218, 252 n.6,
  260–61 n.55, 275 n.60
McCarran-Walter Act, 98, 111, 164
McCarthy, Eugene, 117, 194
McCarthyism, 7, 41, 138, 151, 158, 159,
  168, 183, 272 n.32
McCarthy, Joseph, 6, 16, 28, 86, 92–94,
  97, 99–101, 104, 108, 114, 117, 118,
  124, 125, 126, 127, 133–36 passim,
  145–48, 151, 160, 161–62, 163, 165,
  168, 169, 171, 175, 177, 178–80,
  182–83, 185, 187, 188, 189, 201, 206,
  218, 219, 234 n.50, 243 n.46, 244 n.52,
  260 n.47, 262 n.11, 264 nn.31, 32, 265
  nn.33, 36, 38, 267 n.59, 275 nn.57, 58,
  276 n.61, 278 n.14, 280 n.34, 282 n.55,
  283 nn.61, 63, 65, 289 n.36, 290 n.53,
  294 n.83, 295 n.90, 298 n.43, 302 n.95
McCarthy, Mary, 164, 295 n.90
McClellan, John, 193
McCleod, Scott, 148, 283 n.65
McCormack, John, 24, 78
McCormick-Patterson newspapers,
  126, 276 n.61, 278–79 n.15

McCormick, Robert, 43, 74
McDowell, John, 84
McFadden, Charles J., 35
McGranery, James R., 108
McIntire, Carl, 117, 118
McIntyre, Marvin, 60
McKneally, Martin, 199
McWilliams, Carey, 6, 9
Meiklejohn, Alexander, 298 n.45
Methodist League Against
  Communism, Fascism and
  Unpatriotic Pacifism, 37
Meyer, Frank S., 134, 137, 278 n.10
M-G-M, 83
Mid-Western Research Library,
  259 n.44
Milestone, Lewis, 121, 273 n.39
Military-industrial complex, 191
Military Intelligence Division (U.S.),
  13, 23, 58
Militia of Christ for Social Service, 34
Miliukov, Paul, 19
Miller, Arthur, 182
Miller, James A., 213
Million League, 36
Milton, Joyce, 203
Mindszenty, Josef Cardinal, 269 n.3
Minneapolis Local 544 (Teamsters), 57
Minton, Sherman, 106
Mission to Moscow, 73
Modern Monthly, 244 n.54
Modern Quarterly, 244 n.54
Monskey, Henry, 58
Mont, Max, 301 n.87
Montgomery, Ed, 85
Moore, Barrington, Jr., 74
Moral Man and Immoral Society, 47
Morgan, Jerry, 283 n.62
Morse, Wayne L., 262 n.11
Moscow Carrousel, 44
Mosinee, WI, 121
Motion Picture Alliance for the
  Preservation of American Ideals, 84,
  150, 284 n.75
Motion Picture Producers and
  Distributors of America, 82,
Motion Picture Producers
  Association, 79, 82

Moveon.org, 311 n.1
Moynihan, Daniel Patrick, 310 n.2
Multiculturalism, 307 n.57
Mundt, Karl, 80, 83, 144
Mundt-Nixon Bill, 95–96, 114, 143, 144, 161, 162, 182, 274–75 n.55, 290 n.49
Muravchik, Joshua, 222
Murmansk, 20
Murphy, Frank, 67–68
Murphy, Paul L., 31, 32, 44
Murray, Philip, 71, 115, 124, 270 n.11
Murray, Robert K., 20
Murrow, Edward R., 100, 162
Mussolini, Benito, 38, 164
Muste, A. J., 51
My Disillusionment in Russia, 49
My Further Disillusionment in Russia, 49

Nagasaki, 76
The Nation, 137, 165, 177
National Association of Evangelicals, 117
National Association of Manufacturers, 77–78, 285–86 n.11
National Catholic Educational ⁄ Association, 35
National Catholic Welfare Conference, 114, 119
National Citizens Political Action Committee, 81, 254 n.32
National Civic Federation, 24, 25
National Committee for a Free Europe, 14
National Committee for an Effective Congress, 162, 183
National Committee for Civilian Control of Atomic Energy, 181
National Committee for Organizing Iron and Steel Workers, 21
National Committee for the Defense of Political Prisoners, 56
National Committee to Abolish the House Un-American Activities Committee, 196
National Committee to Defeat the Mundt Bill, 175

National Community Relations Advisory Council, 119
National Council of Churches for Christ, 119
National Guardian, 298 n.43
Nationality Act, 56
National Labor Relations Act, 78
National Labor Relations Board, 55, 257 n.18
National Lawyers Guild, 126, 168, 180
National Maritime Union, 28, 263 n.12, 275 n.6
National Republic Magazine, 25
National Review, 61, 134, 139, 201, 278 n.10, 279 n.17, 305 n.31
National Security and Individual Freedom, 175
National Security Council, 87
National Small Business Men's Association, 150
National Theater Owners of America, 122
National Union for Social Justice, 36
National Union Party, 36, 44, 244 n.30
National Welfare Conference, 71
Nativism, 10, 11–12, 118, 232–33 n.42
Naturalization Act, 67
Navasky, Victor S., 180
Nazis/Nazism, 24, 26, 30, 58, 59, 82, 138, 150, 189, 212, 213, 250 n.30, 285–86 n.11
Nazi-Soviet Pact. *See* German-Soviet Nonaggression Treaty
Near v. Minnesota, 239 n.42
Nelson, Reuben, 271 n.21
Neoconservatism, 203–4, 311 n.2
New American Movement, 2 n
New Beginnings, 63
New Deal, 26, 27, 43, 46, 78, 125, 137, 250 n.30, 252 n.6, 257 n.18
New International, 186
New Leader, 40, 48, 166
New Left, 196, 204, 206, 209
New Masses, 258 n.22
New Republic, 137, 155, 165, 173, 286–87 n.18
New York, 58, 121, 166, 263 n.24

New York Board of Higher Education, 58
New York City, 60, 167, 185
New York Post, 134, 157, 177–79, 298 n.43
New York Review of Books, 202
New York Times, 29, 105, 167
Niebuhr, Reinhold, 7–8, 9, 41, 47–48, 61–62, 72, 154, 155, 158–59, 245 n.66, 246 n.82, 285 n.4, 287 nn.19, 21
Nitze, Paul, 156
Nixon, Richard M., 81, 83, 114, 136, 144–45, 146, 147–48, 194, 234 n.49, 262 n.11, 273 n.35, 281 n.47, 283 n.63, 290 n.49, 303 n.12
Nock, Albert J., 43
Non-Partisan Legal Defense, 51
North American Aviation strike, 57, 249 n.22
North Atlantic Treaty Organization, 140, 156, 157, 221
Novack, George, 246 n.82
NOW (National Organization for Women), 311 n.1
Nugent v. United States, 108

Obama, Barack, 225
Odyssey of a Fellow Traveler, 14
Office of Censorship, 58
Office of Civil Defense, 65
Office of Naval Intelligence, 13, 58, 85, 95
Office of Policy Coordination, 85, 259 n.45
Office of Price Administration, 65, 78
Office of Strategic Services, 58
Ohio, 241 n.15
Oklahoma, 58
Oklahoma City, Oklahoma, 88
O'Neil, James, 122
Operation Abolition, 192
Operation Correction, 302 n.5
Organization of Secret Services
Origins of Totalitarianism, 128, 169
Oshinsky, David M., 125
Out of Their Own Mouths, 39
Out of the Night, 68

Overstreet, Harry and Bonaro, 200
Owsley, Alvin, 38

Packer, Herbert L., 132
Palestine, 118
Palmer, A. Mitchell, 17, 22, 29
Panzino, Frank, 116, 271 n.14
Paris, 166, 167
Parrish, Michael E., 276 n.64
Parsons, Steve, 4
Parsons, Talcott, 7
Partisan Review, 51–52, 62, 165–66, 294 n.83
Passport Office, 13
Patterson newspapers, 74
Paul Reveres, 45
Pearl Harbor, 64, 69, 216, 312 n.12
Pegler, Westbrook, 126, 243 n.46
Peirce, C. S., 309 n.75
Pelley, William Dudley, 235 n.58
Pennsylvania, 263 n.24
Pennsylvania v. Nelson, 109
People for the American Way, 311 n.11
People's Republic of China, 92, 143, 169, 201
Perkins, Frances, 247–48 n.14
Perle, Richard, 223
Permanent Subcommittee on Investigations (Senate), 15, 99, 151, 178–80, 181, 193, 262 n.11
Philadelphia, Pennsylvania, 60
Philbrick, Herbert, 235 n.58
Phillips, William, 165–66
Pichel, Irving, 255 n.4
Pike, James, 271 n.21
Pipes, Daniel, 222, 223, 224–25
Pittsburgh Catholic, 116
Pittsburgh, Pennsylvania, 115–16
Pius XI, 34
Pizzitola, Louis, 43
Plain Talk, 114, 127, 150, 276 n.64
Planned Parenthood, 311 n.1
Plato, 213
Plotke, David, 156, 160–61
PM, 165, 167, 286–87 n.18
Podhoretz, Norman, 168, 204, 222–24, 311 n.2
Poland, 114

Poling, David A., 269–70 n.18
Polish-American Congress, 114
politics (magazine), 73
Popular Front, 14, 28, 45, 51, 52, 59, 62,
    157, 165
Porter, Paul A., 180
Post, Louis F., 29
Potsdam, 114
Powers, Richard Gid, 17–18, 156
Preminger, Otto, 191, 196, 199, 304 n.27
President's Committee on Civil
    Rights, 87
Prettyman, E. Barrett, 106
Preuves, 167
Princeton University, 247 n.17
*The Problem of American Communism
    in 1945*, 114
Project for the New American
    Century, 221
Protestant anti-communism, 37,
    117–18, 200
Protestants, 15, 26, 159, 192, 219, 264
    n.32, 271 n.20
Protocols of the Elders of Zion, 44
Provisional Government (Russia), 19
Proxmire, William, 195
The Public Interest, 203
Purge trials, Soviet Union, 40, 45, 46,
    51, 177, 183, 246 n.84

Quinn, Tom, 116, 271 n.14
Quinn v. United States, 109

Raab, Earl, 76
Radosh, Ronald, 203, 204–5, 306 n.47
Rahv, Philip, 165
Rainbow Coalition, 205–6
Rand, Ayn, 149–51, 284 nn.74, 75
Rand School, 137 n.16
Rankin, John, 66, 78, 79, 80, 83, 257
    n.20, 258 n.22
Rapp-Coudert Committee. *See* Joint
    Legislative Committee to Investi-
    gate Un-American Activities (N.Y.)
Rauh, Joseph L., Jr., 181–83,
    299 nn.57, 59
Reader's Digest, 43, 44, 69,
    250–51 n.34, 253 n.7

Red China Lobby, 201, 306 n.38
The Red Decade, 44
Red-flag laws, 23, 31
The Red Menace, 83
Red Network, 244 n.52
Red Pawn, 149
The Red Revolution, 45
Red scares, explained, 13–14
Red Smoke, 44
Red squads, 237 n.19
Reece, B. Carroll, 80
Reed, John, 19
Reisel, Victor, 126, 275 n.60
Remington, William, 151, 181, 298 n.53
Report on Blacklisting, 188
Republican party, 8, 21, 22, 25, 55, 69,
    80, 87, 88, 89, 92, 93, 94–106, 110, 191,
    216, 218, 264 n.26, 265 n.35, 280 n.23
Republic Pictures, 83
Reuben, Nelson, 271 n.21
Reuther brothers, 115, 124, 274 n.48
Reuther, Walter, 59
Revisionism, 127, 202–3
Revolutionary Radicalism, 237 n.16
Rice, Charles, 3, 16, 37, 70, 115–16, 241
    n.15, 270 n.13
Riesman, David, 7, 169, 292 n.64
Rigoulot, Pierre, 309 n.76
RKO Pictures, 83, 123
The Road to Serfdom, 69
Roberts, Owen, 32, 253 n.12
Robertson, Joseph, 270 n.12
Robins, Natalie, 244 n.52
Rogers, Lela, 84
Rogers, William P., 283 n.62
Rogin, Michael Paul, 43, 265 n.35
Roman Holiday, 199
Romerstein, Herbert, 207–08
Roosevelt administration, 53, 55, 59,
    63, 68–69, 91, 137, 144, 216,
    238 n.27, 254 n.58
Roosevelt, Eleanor, 65, 290 n.53
Roosevelt, Franklin D., 3, 30, 57, 60, 65,
    70, 74, 76, 137, 138, 247–48 n.14, 249
    n.22, 250 n.28
The Roosevelt Red Record, 45
Rorty, James, 159
Rose, Alex, 72

Rosenberg, Ethel and Julius, 92, 107, 120, 151, 159, 184, 203, 268 n.75, 306 n.47
Rosenblatt, Maurice, 162
Rovere, Richard, 41, 49, 63, 132, 147, 151, 169, 249 n.21, 251 n.34, 265 n.33
Rushmore, Howard, 126, 135, 275 n.57, 278 n.14
Russell, Louis, 80, 84
Russia, 19, 20
The Russian Enigma, 69
Russian Institute, 167
Russian Orthodox Church, 34
Ryan, John, 36
Ryan, Sylvester J., 107

Saint Joseph's College, 37
Salt of the Earth, 123
San Francisco, California, 191, 192, 196, 258 n.26
Sarah Lawrence College, 219
Sartre, Jean-Paul, 7, 9, 169
Sawyer, William C., 121
Sayre, Francis B., Jr., 271 n.21
Scales, Junius, 193, 197
Scales v. United States, 197
Scanlan, Patrick, 17, 36, 37
Schaefer v. United States, 87
Schenck v. United States, 173
Schenectady, Pennsylvania, 115
Schlamm, William A., 42, 139, 146
Schlesinger, Arthur, Jr., 61, 154, 155–56, 158, 168, 169, 171, 175, 178, 189, 202, 215, 285 n.4, 285–86 n.11, 286 n.14, 286–87 n.16, 287 nn.19–21, 307 n.57, 313 n.15
Schmidt, Regin, 44
Schneiderman v. United States, 67–68
Schneiderman, William, 55, 67
School of Social Action, 71
School of Social Sciences, 37
Schwarz, Fred C., 200, 305 n.33
Scoundrel Time, 180
Screen Cartoonists Guild, 258 n.22
"Screen Guide for Americans," 150, 284 n.75
Scripps-Howard, 126
Seattle, Washington, 20–21, 263 n.24

The Secret Surrender, 202
Sedition laws, 12, 23, 109, 244 n.52
Seditious Activities Investigation Commission, 120
See It Now, 100
Selective Service Act, 56
Senate Internal Security Subcommittee. *See* Subcommittee on Internal Security
Serge, Victor, 164
Service v. Dulles, 110
Shachtman, Max, 186
Shadowitz, Albert, 185
Sharon Statement, 201
Sheen, Fulton J., 35, 71, 85, 114–15, 269–70 n.8
Shiel, Bernard J., 117
Shils, Edward A., 7–8, 10
Sinatra, Frank, 196, 199
Sinclair, Upton, 50
Slochower v. Board of Education of New York City, 109
Smith Act. *See* Alien Registration Act
Smith, Adam, 9
Smith, Gerald L. K., 44, 235 n.58
Smith, Harold, 304 n.27
Smith, Howard, 55
Smith, Margaret Chase, 94, 262 n.11
Smoot-Hawley Tariff Act, 237 n.20
Sobell, Morton, 92
Social Action Department, 71
Social fascism, 204
Socialism/socialists, 33, 44, 46, 47, 62, 118, 136. 171, 173, 183
Socialist Party of America, 49–50, 51, 61, 204, 248 n.16
Socialist Workers Party, 50, 57–58, 62, 73, 246 n.84, 247–48 n.16
Sokolsky, George, 85, 99, 119, 126, 151, 243 n.46, 264 n.30, 275 n.60
Song of Russia, 150
Southern Baptist Convention, 37
Southern Christian Leadership Conference, 196
Southern Democrat/Republican bloc, 78, 256 n.14
Soviet Bureau, 237 n.16
Soviet Purchasing Committee, 68

Soviet Russia Pictorial, 44
Spanish Civil War, 34, 36, 45, 49, 177, 239–40 n.1
Spargo, John, 50
Spartacus, 199
Special Committee on Communist Activities (House of Representatives), 23
Special Committee on Un-American Activities (House of Representatives), 24, 26–29, 35, 42, 54–55, 58, 63, 65–66, 78, 135
Special War Policies Unit, 66
Spellman, Francis Cardinal, 117, 271 n.18
Spies, 215–16
Staff Committee on Communism, 119
Stalinism/Stalinist, 41, 70, 138, 145, 164, 165, 167, 169, 171, 187, 188, 207, 211, 242 n.29, 250 n.30, 289 n.41, 295 n.90, 309 n.73
Stalin, Josef, 3, 44, 59, 62, 151, 210, 211, 224, 256 n.11, 287 n.19
Stalinoids, 292 n.66
Status-anxiety theories, 8–9
Steele, Walter S., 25, 28, 85, 237 n.22, 278–79 n.15
Steel Workers Organizing Committee, 28
Stein, Sol, 168–69, 294 n.82
Stennis, John, 163
Stevenson, Adlai E., 99, 145
Stevenson, Archibald E., 22, 237 n.16
St. Louis, Missouri, 186, 263 n.24
Stolberg, Benjamin, 242 n.29
Stone, Harlan Fiske, 253 n.12
Stone, I. F., 233–34 n.48, 248 n.16, 251 n.34, 256 n.15, 290 n.51
Strauss, Leo, 43
Stripling, Robert, 84
Studies on the Left, 202
Subcommittee on Internal Security (Senate), 97, 105, 108, 147, 159, 168, 185, 192, 193, 260 n.47
Subversive Activities Control Board, 96–97, 99, 102, 103, 132–33, 194, 198, 263 n.17, 304 n.23
Sullivan, Edward E., 238 n.27

Sullivan, William, 85
Sulzberger, Arthur Hays, 154
Sulzberger, Arthur Ochs, 105
Supreme Court. *See* United States Supreme Court
Swarthmore College, 174
Sweezy, Paul, 251 n.34
Sweezy v. New Hampshire, 110

Taft-Hartley Act, 66, 106, 110, 140, 257 n.18
Taft, Robert A., 99, 136, 140–41, 147, 264 n.30, 266 n.44, 283 n.61
Taiwan, 201
Tass, 44
Taylor, Harold, 219
Temporary Commission on Employee Loyalty, 86
Ten Days That Shook the World, 19
Tennessee, 238 n.24
Tenney committee. *See* Joint Fact-Finding Committee on Un-American Activities, in California
Tenney, Jack, 81, 120, 248 n.18
Terrorism, 222–23
Theoharis, Athan G., 137
Thomas, John, 27
Thomas, J. Parnell, 55, 81, 84
Thomas, Norman, 161, 186, 246 n.82, 300 n.79
Thurlow, Richard, 4
Thye, Edward J. 262 n.11
Tiananmen Square, 206
Time, 60, 75, 286–87 n.18
Time-Abt SRI Poll, 224
Time Life publications, 43
Tobey, Charles W., 262 n.11
Tobin, Daniel, 57
Toledano, Ralph de, 48, 85, 138, 146, 148, 257 n.59
Tomlins, Christopher L., 257 n.18
Total Empire, 115
Totalitarianism, 61, 63, 69, 128–29, 138, 139, 149, 172, 251 n.43, 277 n.72, 312 n.11
Toward Soviet America, 51
Townsend, Francis, 44

Trade Union Congress, 124
Trading with the Enemies Act, 12
Tragedy of American Diplomacy, 202
Transport Workers Union, 59
Tresca, Carlo, 49, 73
Trilling, Diana, 158
Trilling, Lionel, 153
Trohan, Walter, 85
Trotskyism, 41, 50, 118, 186, 248 n.16, 292 n.66
Trotsky, Leon, 46, 51, 61, 62, 246 n.82, 249 n.59, 276 n.68
Truman administration, 86–89, 91–98, 136, 137, 144, 156, 165, 181, 216, 218, 254 n.58, 292 n.66
Truman, Harry S, 3, 85, 86, 88–98, 101, 137, 139, 143, 155, 162, 164, 174, 175, 178, 180, 215, 218, 222, 257 n.18, 260 n.53, 281 n.54, 288 nn.26, 29
Trumbo, Dalton, 191, 196, 199, 286 n.12, 304 n.27
Trumbo v. United States, 106
Turkey, 141, 156
Twentieth Century-Fox, 83, 121
Tydings Committee, 93–94, 96, 146, 147
Tydings, Millard, 262 n.8

Ukraine, 211
Unger, Irwin, 306 n.44
Union for Democratic Action, 61–62, 65, 72, 155, 250 n.32
United Automobile Workers, 28, 50, 59, 72, 124, 247 n.50
United Cemetery Workers, 117
United Electrical, Radio and Machine Workers of America, 59, 70, 115–16, 124, 270 n.11, 274 n.50
United Electrical Workers for Democratic Action, 270 n.11
United Farm Equipment Workers, 274 n.50
United Kingdom, 4, 5, 41, 53, 54, 64, 65, 70, 91, 123, 166, 216, 230 n.11, 278 n.10
United Nations, 141, 142, 151, 201, 266 n.50

United Office and Professional Workers of America, 272 n.30
United Press International, 44
United States Army, 99, 185, 282 n.55
United States Information Service, 99
United States Steel Corporation strike, 21
United States Supreme Court, 31–32, 58, 66–68, 106–11, 133, 173, 181, 197–98, 247–48 n.14, 252 n.4, 267 n.64, 269 n.82
United States v. Abrams, 173, 295–96 n.7
United States v. Elizabeth Gurley Finn, 133
United States v. Rumely, 108
University of California, 58, 252 n.7
University of Chicago, 186
University of San Francisco, 129
University of Wisconsin, 202
USA Patriot Act, 225, 13 n.15
Utah, 97

Valtin, Jan, 68, 243 n.47
Vandenberg, Arthur, 156
Variety, 83
Vassiliev, Alexander, 216
Vatican, 35
Venona cables, 207–8, 215, 216, 277 n.6
Versailles peace conference (1919), 20
Veterans of Foreign Wars, 70, 81, 278 n.15
Viereck, Peter, 136, 138, 145–46
Vietnam, 194, 220
Vigil, 150
Vincent, John Carter, 148
Vinson, Fred, 106
The Vital Center, 155–57, 285 n.4, 287 n.23
Voice of America, 99
Voorhis Act, 56
Voorhis, Jerry, 144
Vultee Aircraft strike, 57

Walker, Samuel, 161
Wallace, De Witt, 43
Wallace, Henry, 87–88, 144, 155, 184
Wall Street Journal, 307 n.57
Walsh, Edmund, A., S. J., 35, 71, 85, 115

Walter, Francis, 116, 188, 195, 263 n.23,
    268 n.80, 269 n.82, 290 n.51, 304 n.27
Wanger, Walter, 79
War Manpower Commission, 180
Warner, Jack L., 84
War or Peace, 143
Warren, Earl, 109
Warsaw Bloc, 143
Washington, D.C., 71, 125, 139, 218,
    253 n.19, 281 n.54
Washington Post, 175, 182
Watkins v. United States, 110, 269 n.82
Wechsler, James, 62–63, 75, 134–35,
    157, 177–80, 182, 278 n.14, 288 n.26,
    297 n.36, 298 nn.41, 43, 298 n.53
Weiner, Tim, 259 n.45
Weinstein, Allen, 203, 216
Welch, Robert, Jr., 199, 267 n.59,
    305 n.31
Westin, Alan F., 200
Westinghouse Local 601 (U.E.), 70, 116
We the Living, 149
*What We Must Know About
    Communism*, 200
Wheeling, West Virginia, 92, 147
White, Harry Dexter, 146, 282 n.54
White, W. L., 255 n.39
Whitfield, Stephen J., 128
Whitney v. California, 296 n.10
Wiener, Jonathan M., 202
Wilkinson v. United States, 197
William Allen White Committee to
    Defend America by Aiding the
    Allies, 61
William, Maurice, 126
Williams, William Appleman, 202
Wills, Gary, 139
Wilson, Donald, 122–23
Wilson, Edmund, 40
Wilson, H. H., 4, 5
Wilson, Michael, 304 n.27
Wilson, Woodrow, 12, 19, 173,
    295–96 n.7
Winchell, Walter, 250 n.28, 278 n.14
Windt, Theodore Otto, Jr., 229 n.2
Wirin, A. L., 298 n.45
Wisner, Frank, 259 n.45, 279 n.17

Witness, 41, 60, 165
Wolfowitz, Paul, 311–12 n.2
Wolfson, Mitchell W., 122
Woll, Matthew, 238 n.29
Woltman, Frederick, 80, 126, 188, 275
    nn.58, 59, 310 n.91
Wood, John, 80, 84
Wood, Leonard, 21, 22
Workers Alliance, 28
Workers Party, 62
Workers Party of the United States,
    50, 51
Works Project Administration, 28
World Federation of Democratic
    Youth, 205
World Federation of Trade Unions, 124
World Trade Union Conference, 124
World War I, 12–13, 212
World War II, 3, 5, 7, 65–74, 137, 181,
    183, 215
Writers' Congress (1943), 252 n.7
Wrocslaw, 166
Wucinich, George, 185
Wyler, William, 154

Yale Daily News, 139
Yale University, 139, 186, 247 n.7
Yalta, 3, 76, 114
Yarnell, Allen, 156
Yates v. United States, 110
Ybarra, Michael, 97
You Can Trust the Communists, 200
Young Americans for
    Freedom, 201
Young Communist League, 134, 177,
    178, 179, 181
Youngdahl, Luther W., 108–109
Young, Nedrick, 304 n.27
Young People's Socialist League, 186
Young Socialist League, 186,
    188, 301 n.91
Youth for Christ, 117
Yugoslavia, 218

Zanuck, Darryl F., 83, 121
Zhdanov, Andrei, 256 n.11
Zionism, 118

About the Author

LARRY CEPLAIR is professor emeritus of history at Santa Monica College. His previous books include *The Marxist and the Movies: A Biography of Paul Jarrico* and, with Steven Englund, *The Inquisition in Hollywood: Politics in the Film Community*. He was the co-curator of the Academy of Motion Picture Arts and Sciences' exhibit "Reds and Blacklists in Hollywood" and served as the interviewer for the UCLA Oral History project on the motion picture blacklist.